CCNA
Third Edition

Michael Valentine
Andrew Whitaker

CCNA Exam Cram Third Edition

ISBN-13: 978-0-7897-3712-0
ISBN-10: 0-7897-3712-4
Library of Congress Cataloging-in-Publication Data

Valentine, Michael.
  CCNA exam cram : (exam 640-802) / Michael Valentine, Andrew Whitaker. -- 3rd ed.
    p. cm.
  ISBN 978-0-7897-3712-0 (pbk. w/cd)
  1. Electronic data processing personnel--Certification. 2. Computer networks--Examinations--Study guides. I. Whitaker, Andrew. II. Title.
  QA76.3.V356 2008
  004.6--dc22
                              2007043001
Printed in the United States of America
Second Printing: February 2008

Trademarks

All terms mentioned in this book that are known to be trademarks or service marks have been appropriately capitalized. Que Publishing cannot attest to the accuracy of this information. Use of a term in this book should not be regarded as affecting the validity of any trademark or service mark.

Warning and Disclaimer

Every effort has been made to make this book as complete and as accurate as possible, but no warranty or fitness is implied. The information provided is on an "as is" basis. The authors and the publisher shall have neither liability nor responsibility to any person or entity with respect to any loss or damages arising from the information contained in this book or from the use of the CD or programs accompanying it.

Bulk Sales

Que Publishing offers excellent discounts on this book when ordered in quantity for bulk purchases or special sales. For more information, please contact

U.S. Corporate and Government Sales
1-800-382-3419
corpsales@pearsontechgroup.com

For sales outside of the U.S., please contact

International Sales
international@pearsoned.com

Associate Publisher
David Dusthimer

Executive Editor
Brett Bartow

Senior Development Editor
Christopher Cleveland

Technical Editors
Brian D'Andrea
Tami Day-Orsatti

Managing Editor
Patrick Kanouse

Senior Project Editor
San Dee Phillips

Copy Editor
Barbara Hacha

Indexer
Tim Wright

Proofreader
Leslie Joseph

Publishing Coordinator
Cindy Teeters

Cover and Interior Designer
Gary Adair

Page Layout
TnT Design, Inc.

Safari BOOKS ONLINE This Book Is Safari Enabled

The Safari® Enabled icon on the cover of your favorite technology book means the book is available through Safari Bookshelf. When you buy this book, you get free access to the online edition for 45 days.

Safari Bookshelf is an electronic reference library that lets you easily search thousands of technical books, find code samples, download chapters, and access technical information whenever and wherever you need it.

To gain 45-day Safari Enabled access to this book:

▶ Go to http://www.quepublishing.com/safarienabled
▶ Complete the brief registration form
▶ Enter the coupon code **U2DX-BQYE-8EDB-UHE2-AMEI**

If you have difficulty registering on Safari Bookshelf or accessing the online edition, please email customer-service@safaribooksonline.com.

Contents at a Glance

Table of Contents

About the Author

Mike Valentine has been in the IT field for 12 years, focusing on network design and implementation. He is currently a Cisco trainer with Skyline Advanced Technology Services and specializes in Cisco Unified Communications instruction as well as CCNA and CCNP courses. His accessible, humorous, and effective teaching style has demystified Cisco for hundreds of students since he began teaching in 2002. Mike has a bachelor of arts degree from the University of British Columbia and currently holds the MCSE: Security, CCDA, CCNP, CCVP, CTP, Convergence+ and CEH certifications. In addition to the popular *Exam Cram 2: CCNA* book, Mike has contributed to and served as technical editor for the Cisco Press titles *CCNP ONT Official Exam Certification Guide* and *CCNA Flashcards* and is currently on the courseware development team for the new Cisco UCAD (Unified Communications Architecture and Design) course.

Andrew Whitaker (M.Sc., CISSP, CCVP, CCNP, CCSP, CCNA, CCDA, MCSE, MCTS, CNE, CEI, CEH, ECSA, Security+, A+, Network+, Convergence+, CTP) is the Director of Enterprise InfoSec and Networking for Training Camp, an international training company that helps certify thousands of IT professionals each year through its unique accelerated learning model. His expert teaching for Training Camp has garnered coverage by *The Wall Street Journal*, *The Philadelphia Inquirer*, *Certification Magazine*, and *Business Week* magazine. In addition to coauthoring *Exam Cram 2: CCNA*, Andrew coauthored the Cisco Press title *Penetration Testing and Network Defense* and has contributed articles on Cisco certification for CertificationZone. Andrew is currently working on authoring and technical editing other book projects.

Dedication

Mike Valentine: This one is for Rus Healy, a gentleman and a scholar.

Andrew Whitaker: Dedicated to Reagan and Makayla. Daddy loves you.

Acknowledgments

Mike Valentine: I'd like to thank my new friends at Skyline for making me feel welcome in the world of official Cisco training. Andy, Frank, Dave, and Toby have elevated my technical and professional expertise and given me great opportunities to learn and grow. It's my privilege to be a Skyliner.

As always, the good people at Pearson have done their best to direct the energies of an enthusiastic pair of irreverent writers. Brett, Vanessa, Chris, and all the people in the background, thank you for your wonderful work.

Steve Kalman's guidance has been invaluable; nothing could please me more than to have his sharp eye and careful critique on this book. Thanks, Steve.

Liana and Jaine, you bring purpose and joy to my life. Thank you for apple crisp and pirate princesses.

And finally, thank you to all my students. Remember everything I said.

Andrew Whitaker: Brett Bartow and Chris Cleveland, thanks for continuing to believe in my work.

Steve Kalman, Brian D'Andrea, and Tami Day-Orsatti, you have an amazing wealth of knowledge and attention to detail. I suppose I need to send you all a new supply of Wite-Out now.

Chris Porter, Steve Guadino, and Dave Minutella, don't worry—this was off the clock.

Jennifer, thanks for sharing me with Que.

The Starbucks on 192nd, thanks for letting me work for eight hours a day on a single cup of coffee.

Tell Us What You Think!

As the reader of this book, *you* are our most important critic and commentator. We value your opinion and want to know what we're doing right, what we could do better, what areas you'd like to see us publish in, and any other words of wisdom you're willing to pass our way.

As an associate publisher for Que Publishing, I welcome your comments. You can email or write me directly to let me know what you did or didn't like about this book—as well as what we can do to make our books better.

Please note that I cannot help you with technical problems related to the topic of this book. We do have a User Services group, however, where I will forward specific technical questions related to the book.

When you write, please be sure to include this book's title and author as well as your name, email address, and phone number. I will carefully review your comments and share them with the author and editors who worked on the book.

Email: feedback@quepublishing.com

Mail: Dave Dusthimer
             Associate Publisher
             Que Publishing
             800 East 96th Street
             Indianapolis, IN 46240 USA

Reader Services

Visit our website and register this book at www.informit.com/title/0789737124 for convenient access to any updates, downloads, or errata that might be available for this book.

Introduction

Welcome to *CCNA Exam Cram!* Whether this is your first or your fifteenth *Exam Cram* series book, you'll find information here that will help ensure your success as you pursue knowledge, experience, and certification. This introduction explains Cisco's certification programs in general and talks about how the *Exam Cram* series can help you prepare for The Cisco CCNA Exams, whether you choose the dual- or single-exam path. The materials in this book have been prepared with a very clear focus on testable concepts, configurations, and skills. As much extraneous material as possible, beyond what is needed for background comprehension, has been eliminated so that the book is a distillation of the necessary knowledge to take—and pass—the Cisco CCNA exam(s). The two sample tests with answer keys (Chapters 13–16) at the end of the book should give you a reasonably accurate assessment of your knowledge. We have also included challenge labs to give you the critical hands-on practice you will need to master the simulator questions on the CCNA exam(s). Read the book, understand the material, practice the labs, and you'll stand a very good chance of passing the test.

Exam Cram books help you understand and appreciate the subjects and materials you need to pass Cisco certification exams. *Exam Cram 2* books are aimed strictly at test preparation and review. They do not teach you everything you need to know about a topic. Instead, we present and dissect the topics and key points we've found that you're likely to encounter on a test. We've worked to bring together as much accurate information as possible about the latest CCNA exams.

Nevertheless, to completely prepare yourself for any Cisco test, we recommend that you begin by taking the Self-Assessment that is included in this book, immediately following this introduction. The Self-Assessment tool will help you evaluate your knowledge base against the requirements for a CCNA under both ideal and real circumstances.

Based on what you learn from the Self-Assessment, you might decide to begin your studies with some classroom training, some practice with the Cisco IOS, or some background reading. On the other hand, you might decide to pick up and read one of the many study guides available from Cisco or third-party vendors on certain topics, including the *CCNA Exam Prep* from Que Publishing. We also recommend that you supplement your study program with visits to www.examcram2.com to receive additional practice questions, get advice, and track the CCNA program.

We also strongly recommend that you practice configuring the Cisco devices that you'll be tested on because nothing beats hands-on experience and familiarity when it comes to understanding the questions you're likely to encounter on a certification test. Book learning is essential, but without a doubt, hands-on experience is the best teacher of all! This book includes a CD with a router and switch simulator and lab challenges that you can use to practice your skills.

Taking a Certification Exam

After you've prepared for your exam, you need to register with a testing center. The CCNA exam can be taken in either one or two steps: The single-exam option is the 640-801 exam, and costs $125. The two-exam option requires you to take both the 640-821 INTRO and 640-811 ICND exams, at a cost of $100 each. In the United States and Canada, tests are administered by Prometric and by VUE. Here's how you can contact them:

▶ **Prometric**—You can sign up for a test through the company's website, at www.prometric.com. Within the United States and Canada, you can register by phone at 800-755-3926. If you live outside this region, you should check the Prometric website for the appropriate phone number.

▶ **VUE**—You can sign up for a test or get the phone numbers for local testing centers through the Web at www.vue.com/ms.

To sign up for a test, you must possess a valid credit card or contact either Prometric or VUE for mailing instructions to send a check (in the United States). Only when payment is verified or your check has cleared can you actually register for the test.

To schedule an exam, you need to call the number or visit either of the web pages at least one day in advance. To cancel or reschedule an exam, you must call before 7 p.m. Pacific standard time the day before the scheduled test time (or you might be charged, even if you don't show up to take the test). When you want to schedule a test, you should have the following information ready:

▶ Your name, organization, and mailing address

▶ Your Cisco test ID

▶ The name and number of the exam you want to take

▶ A method of payment (As mentioned previously, a credit card is the most convenient method, but alternative means can be arranged in advance, if necessary.)

After you sign up for a test, you are told when and where the test is scheduled. You should try to arrive at least 15 minutes early. You must supply two forms of identification—one of which must be a photo ID—and sign a nondisclosure agreement to be admitted into the testing room.

All Cisco exams are completely closed book. In fact, you are not permitted to take anything with you into the testing area, but you are given a blank sheet of paper and a pen (or in some cases, an erasable plastic sheet and an erasable pen). We suggest that you immediately write down on that sheet of paper all the information you've memorized for the test. In *Exam Cram 2* books, this information appears on a tear-out sheet inside the front cover of each book. You are given some time to compose yourself, record this information, and take a sample orientation exam before you begin the real thing. We suggest that you take the orientation test before taking your first exam, but because all the certification exams are more or less identical in layout, behavior, and controls, you probably don't need to do this more than once.

When you complete a Cisco certification exam, the software tells you immediately whether you've passed or failed. If you need to retake an exam, you have to schedule a new test with Prometric or VUE and pay another $100 or $125.

TIP

> If you fail a Cisco test, you must wait five full days before you can take it again. For example, if you failed on Tuesday, you would have to wait until Monday to take it again.

Tracking Your Certification Status

As soon as you pass the Cisco CCNA single exam, or both the INTRO and ICND CCNA test, you are a CCNA. Cisco generates transcripts that indicate which exams you have passed. You can view a copy of your transcript at any time by going to the Cisco website and going to the certifications tracking tool. This tool enables you to print a copy of your current transcript and confirm your certification status.

After you pass the necessary set of exams, you are certified. Official certification is normally granted after three to six weeks, so you shouldn't expect to get your credentials overnight. The package for official certification that arrives includes

▶ A certificate that is suitable for framing, along with a wallet card.

▶ A license to use the applicable logo, which means that you can use the logo in advertisements, promotions, and documents, as well as on letterhead, business cards, and so on. Along with the license comes information on how to legally and appropriately use the logos.

Many people believe that the benefits of Cisco certification are among the most powerful in the industry. We're starting to see more job listings that request or require applicants to have CCNA, CCDA, CCNP, and other certifications, and many individuals who complete Cisco certification programs can qualify for increases in pay and/or responsibility. As an official recognition of hard work and broad knowledge, one of the Cisco credentials is a badge of honor in many IT organizations.

How to Prepare for an Exam

Preparing for the CCNA test requires that you obtain and study materials designed to provide comprehensive information about the product and its capabilities that will appear on the specific exam for which you are preparing. The following list of materials can help you study and prepare:

▶ The official Cisco study guides by Cisco Press.

▶ Practicing with real equipment or simulators.

▶ The CCNA Prep Center on Cisco's website, which features articles, sample questions, games and discussions to focus and clarify your studies.

▶ The exam-preparation advice, practice tests, questions of the day, and discussion groups on the www.examcram.com e-learning and certification destination website.

▶ *The CCNA Exam Cram*—This book gives you information about the material you need to know to pass the tests. Seriously, this is a great book.

▶ The *CCNA Exam Prep* book, also from Que publishing, goes into more detail on topics that are summarized in the Exam Cram.

Together, these two books make a perfect pair.

▶ **Classroom training**—Cisco training partners and third-party training companies (such as The Training Camp) offer classroom training for CCNA. These companies aim to help you prepare to pass the CCNA exam. Although such training can be expensive, most of the individuals lucky enough to partake find this training to be very worthwhile.

▶ **Other publications**—There's no shortage of materials available about CCNA. The "Need to Know More?" resource sections at the end of each chapter in this book give you an idea of where we think you should look for further discussion.

This set of required and recommended materials represents a good collection of sources and resources about the CCNA exam and related topics. We hope that you'll find that this book belongs in this company.

What This Book Will Not Do

This book will *not* teach you everything you need to know about networking with Cisco devices, or even about a given topic. Nor is this book an introduction to computer technology. If you're new to networking and looking for an initial preparation guide, check out www.quepublishing.com, where you will find a whole section dedicated to Cisco certifications and networking in general. This book will review what you need to know before you take the test, with the fundamental purpose dedicated to reviewing the information needed on the Cisco CCNA exam(s).

This book uses a variety of teaching and memorization techniques to analyze the exam-related topics and to provide you with ways to input, index, and retrieve everything you'll need to know in order to pass the test. Once again, it is *not* a comprehensive treatise on Cisco networking.

What This Book Is Designed To Do

This book is designed to be read as a pointer to the areas of knowledge you will be tested on. In other words, you might want to read the book one time, just to get an insight into how comprehensive your knowledge of networking with Cisco is. The book is also designed to be read shortly before you go for the actual test and to give you a distillation of the entire field of CCNA knowledge in as few pages as possible. We think you can use this book to get a sense of the underlying context of any topic in the chapters—or to skim read for Exam Alerts, bulleted points, summaries, and topic headings.

We've drawn on material from The Cisco listing of knowledge requirements, from other preparation guides, and from the exams themselves. We've also drawn from a battery of third-party test-preparation tools and technical websites, as well as from our own experience with Cisco equipment and the exam. Our aim is to walk you through the knowledge you will need—looking over your shoulder, so to speak—and point out those things that are important for the exam (Exam Alerts, practice questions, and so on).

The CCNA exam(s) make a basic assumption that you already have a strong background of experience with the general networking and its terminology. On the other hand, because the CCNA is an introductory-level test, we've tried to demystify the jargon, acronyms, terms, and concepts.

About This Book

If you're preparing for the CCNA exam for the first time, we've structured the topics in this book to build upon one another. Therefore, the topics covered in later chapters might refer to previous discussions in earlier chapters.

We suggest that you read this book from front to back. You won't be wasting your time because nothing we've written is a guess about an unknown exam. We've had to explain certain underlying information on such a regular basis those explanations are included here.

After you've read the book, you can brush up on a certain area by using the Index or the Table of Contents to go straight to the topics and questions you want to reexamine. We've tried to use the headings and subheadings to provide outline information about each given topic. After you've been certified, we think you'll find this book useful as a tightly focused reference and an essential foundation of CCNA knowledge.

Chapter Formats

Each *Exam Cram* chapter follows a regular structure, along with graphical cues about especially important or useful material. The structure of a typical chapter is as follows:

- ▶ **Opening hotlists**—Each chapter begins with lists of the terms you'll need to understand and the concepts you'll need to master before you can be fully conversant with the chapter's subject matter. We follow the hotlists with a few introductory paragraphs, setting the stage for the rest of the chapter.

- ▶ **Topical coverage**—After the opening hotlists, each chapter covers the topics related to the chapter's subject.

- ▶ **Alerts**—Throughout the topical coverage section, we highlight material most likely to appear on the exam by using a special Exam Alert layout that looks like this:

EXAM ALERT

This is what an Exam Alert looks like. An Exam Alert stresses concepts, terms, software, or activities that will most likely appear in one or more certification exam question. For that reason, we think any information found offset in Exam Alert format is worthy of unusual attentiveness on your part.

Even if material isn't flagged as an Exam Alert, *all* the content in this book is associated in some way with test-related material. What appears in the chapter content is critical knowledge.

▶ **Notes**—This book is an overall examination of basic Cisco networking. As such, we'll dip into many aspects of .NET application development. Where a body of knowledge is deeper than the scope of the book, we use notes to indicate areas of concern or specialty training, or refer you to other resources.

NOTE

Cramming for an exam will get you through a test, but it won't make you a competent IT professional. Although you can memorize just the facts you need in order to become certified, your daily work in the field will rapidly put you in water over your head if you don't know the underlying principles of networking with Cisco gear.

▶ **Tips**—We provide tips that will help you to build a better foundation of knowledge or to focus your attention on an important concept that will reappear later in the book. Tips provide a helpful way to remind you of the context surrounding a particular area of a topic under discussion.

▶ **Practice questions**—This section presents a short list of test questions related to the specific chapter topic. Each question has a following explanation of both correct and incorrect answers. The practice questions highlight the areas we found to be most important on the exam.

The bulk of the book follows this chapter structure, but there are a few other elements that we would like to point out:

▶ **Practice Exams**—The Practice exams are very close approximations of the types of questions you are likely to see on the current CCNA exam(s). The Answer Key for each Practice Exam will help you determine which areas you have mastered and which areas you need to study further.

▶ **Answer keys**—These provide the answers to the sample tests, complete with explanations of both the correct responses and the incorrect responses.

▶ **Glossary**—This is an extensive glossary of important terms used in this book.

▶ **The Cram Sheet**—This appears as a tearaway sheet, inside the front cover of this *Exam Cram* book. It is a valuable tool that represents a collection of the most difficult-to-remember facts and numbers we think you should memorize before taking the test. Remember, you can dump this information out of your head onto a piece of paper as soon as you enter the testing room.

These are usually facts that we've found require brute-force memorization. You only need to remember this information long enough to write it down when you walk into the test room. Be advised that you will be asked to surrender all personal belongings before you enter the exam room itself.

You might want to look at the Cram Sheet in your car or in the lobby of the testing center just before you walk into the testing center. The Cram Sheet is divided under headings, so you can review the appropriate parts just before each test.

▶ **The CD**—The CD features an innovative practice test engine powered by MeasureUp, including a full practice exam and two router simulations, giving you the opportunity to assess your readiness for the exam. Cisco simulations validate a person's hands-on skills in addition to knowledge. MeasureUp's Cisco simulations model real-life networking scenarios by requiring the user to perform tasks on simulated Cisco networking devices, measuring troubleshooting and problem-solving skills to address realistic networking problems.

Contacting the Authors

We've tried to create a real-world tool that you can use to prepare for and pass the CCNA certification exams. We're interested in any feedback you would care to share about the book, especially if you have ideas about how we can improve it for future test takers. We'll consider everything you say carefully and will respond to all reasonable suggestions and comments. You can reach us via email at mvalentine@trainingcamp.com and awhitaker@trainingcamp.com.

Let us know if you found this book to be helpful in your preparation efforts. We'd also like to know how you felt about your chances of passing the exam *before* you read the book and then *after* you read the book. Of course, we'd love to hear that you passed the exam—and even if you just want to share your triumph, we'd be happy to hear from you.

Thanks for choosing us as your personal trainers, and enjoy the book. We would wish you luck on the exam, but we know that if you read through all the chapters and work with the product, you won't need luck—you'll pass the test on the strength of real knowledge!

Self-Assessment

This section helps you to determine your readiness for the Cisco Certified Network Associate certification exam. You will be invited to assess your own skills, motivations, education, and experience and see how you compare against the thousands of CCNA candidates we have met.

> **TIP**
>
> You can also pre-assess your CCNA readiness by using the accompanying CD.

CCNA in the Real World

The Cisco Certified Network Associate remains one of the most popular certifications in the IT industry. Although Cisco does not publish certification statistics for CCNA, it is safe to say that thousands of new CCNAs are minted each year from all over the world. In the face of a backlash against so-called "paper-only" certification holders, Cisco has worked hard to maintain the credibility of its certifications by making them difficult to achieve, as well as ensuring that the exams test not only their own products and services, but also general networking knowledge. In the past few years, Cisco has added router and switch simulators to computer-based tests to test the applied knowledge of candidates, and we can expect this trend to continue. A Cisco certification is still the gold standard for networking professionals.

A candidate who has passed the CCNA has demonstrated three significant capabilities:

▶ **A mastery of technical knowledge**—The successful CCNA candidate knows the technical material and has an elevated level of retention and accuracy. The CCNA exam has a pass mark of 849 out of 1,000. Very little room for technical error exists. Successful candidates know their stuff.

▶ **A demonstrated ability to apply the technical knowledge**—The addition of simulator questions has greatly reduced the possibility that a candidate can simply memorize all the information and pass the exam. A CCNA is supposed to be able to apply basic router and switch configurations; the simulator questions help prove that the candidate can do so.

▶ **The ability to perform under pressure**—The CCNA exam(s) require that you proceed at a fairly rapid pace, spending about one minute per question on average. Many candidates find that they have little time left when they finish, and indeed many run out of time altogether—and some fail as a result. Add to this the stress of being in an exam environment, the potential of having an employer's performance expectations, personal expectations, and possibly financial or career implications pressuring you as well, and the exam turns into a pressure cooker. All of this is intimidating—and unfortunate for the unprepared— so be prepared.

Imagine yourself as an employer looking for a junior networking professional. You want someone who knows their stuff, who can reliably do the actual work of setting up and configuring equipment, and who can do all that under the pressures of time, screaming bosses and customers, and critical deadlines. Enter the successful CCNA candidate.

The Ideal CCNA Candidate

Other than a photographic memory, typing speed that would make Mavis Beacon jealous, and nerves of steel, what makes for the "ideal" CCNA candidate? A combination of skills and experience is the short answer. The successful candidates we have seen—and we have seen thousands from classes that we have taught—had a good mix of the following traits:

▶ **Motivation**—Why are you taking the CCNA? Here are some of the most common answers to this question that we have seen:

  ▶ Because I want to further my career and get a promotion.

  ▶ To expand my knowledge; I'm interested in it.

  ▶ My job is changing, and the company needs me to get the certification.

  ▶ I am unemployed and/or starting a new career.

  ▶ The company needs more Cisco-certified people to gain a certain partner status as a reseller.

  ▶ We're just burning the training budget for this year.

  ▶ I've heard that the computer industry is a good field and that a CCNA guarantees you $85,000 a year.

So what motivates you? Who is paying for the training and exams? What are the implications if you fail? Successful candidates are highly motivated. If you don't care, your chances of passing drop tremendously.

► **An interest in learning and an ability to learn**—Passing a CCNA exam requires taking on board a great deal of new information, much of it obscure and without a referential pattern to make it easier to recall. Candidates who have acquired the skills to do this—and rest assured, these are skills that can be learned—will do better than those who have trouble retaining information. Candidates who simply enjoy learning will find it easier and will do better as a result.

If you have trouble retaining and recalling information quickly and accurately, you will find CCNA certification a difficult thing to achieve. This book is not aimed at teaching you these skills; other books are. In the absence of the ability to learn and retain quickly, patience and persistence are a good substitute. If it takes you a year to pass, you have still passed.

► **A decent background in IP networking**—"Decent" is intentionally vague. We have seen candidates with little experience succeed and candidates with extensive experience fail. Experience is not a guarantee, but it absolutely helps. Many CCNA questions test the basics of networking; many others assume that you know the basics and incorporate the requirement of that knowledge into a more advanced question—the old "question-within-a-question" trick. As a guideline, if you have been involved with business-class networks for about a year, you will probably have absorbed enough knowledge to give you an advantage when it comes to the basics. After a certain point, experience can be a weakness: In the immortal words of Han Solo, "Don't get cocky." If you think that CCNA will be easy because you have 10 years of experience, you are in for a rude awakening.

Put Yourself to the Test

Now is the time to take a close look at your education, experience, motivation, and abilities. It's worth being honest with yourself; being aware of your weaknesses is as important as being aware of your strengths. Maybe you know someone who can help you with an objective assessment—a friend, a teacher, or an HR person perhaps. Above all, realize that the following questions and comments simply summarize our experience with CCNA candidates. That experience is pretty solid; we have taught CCNA to more than a thousand people. By the same token, though, there is no magic formula; every person is a different story. Your best plan is to be as prepared as you can be in all respects. Now, time to look inward...

Educational Background

Although in theory anyone can attempt the CCNA exam, in reality some are better prepared than others. Educational background forms a big part of this preparation. These questions will help to identify education and training that will be of benefit:

1. Have you ever taken any computer science courses at a college level?

   Most college-level IT courses include an element of networking theory. Also, if you are taking this kind of course, you are probably already interested in this topic and will find it easier to master the basics and pick up the advanced stuff. If you have never taken an IT course at this level, you have a steeper learning curve and might be at a disadvantage.

2. Did you attend college and major in a computer-related field?

   If so, you should have most of the basics covered—unless you studied programming; in which case, you might not have covered much in the way of networking. Some colleges actually offer the CCNA as part of the curriculum. Doing a college major in IT is not a prerequisite by any means, but it might be helpful.

3. Have you ever held an IT certification?

   If you have been certified before, you have some idea of what is coming in terms of the depth of knowledge required and the examination process; it also implies at least some involvement in computers and networking.

4. Which certification(s) have you held?

   A previous CCNA will definitely be an asset—but not a guarantee. The CCNA has changed dramatically in the past three years. Previous certification in general networking (perhaps a Net+), or an MCSE, will cover the basics, but not the Cisco-specific information. On the flip side, a certification in Visual Basic or Oracle might not be very helpful for CCNA.

5. Do you currently hold any IT certifications?

   Current information is more relevant—especially in the IT world. Some certifications are more relevant than others, of course, as noted previously.

6. Which certification(s) do you currently hold?

   You might hold other Cisco specialization certs, or current certs from Microsoft, CompTia, or Novell. Again, anything that has tested your networking knowledge will be an asset.

7. Have you ever taken any IT training courses in networking?

   Many people take training courses but do not certify. Any exposure and knowledge gained from these courses will be useful.

8. How much self-study have you done?

   Although it is difficult to do pure self-study and pass the new CCNA, the more you study, the better the chances are that you will retain information. In our experience, it is always more productive to get some training— whether online, with a mentor/tutor, or from a training company—but a significant amount of self-study is always required regardless. The fact that you are holding this book is a very good sign. Read all of it!

9. How long have you been studying for your CCNA?

   This is a tricky equation. The longer you study, the more you are likely to know—but the more you are likely to forget, as well.

10. Is there a formal or informal training plan for you at your workplace?

    Work experience is a great way to gain the knowledge and skills you need for the exam. A training plan can be a good motivator because you might have someone coaching and encouraging you and also because there may be a reward—perhaps a promotion or raise—for completing the program.

Hands-on Experience

It is the rare individual who really understands networks but has never built, broken, and then rebuilt one. For the CCNA exam, a certain amount of hands-on experience is a must. The new simulator questions require you to actually type in router configurations. Ask yourself the following:

1. Does your job allow you to work with Cisco routers and switches on a regular basis?

2. Is there a lab where you can practice? Perhaps at home with borrowed or purchased gear?

3. How long have you been working with Cisco equipment?

4. Are you completely fluent in subnetting?

At a minimum, you should get a simulator that includes lab exercises for you to practice key skills. If you have access to a lab and equipment you can play with, as you become more advanced, you can build more complicated and realistic test networks.

The major skill areas you need hands-on experience in are

▶ Basic configuration: IP addresses, passwords

▶ Subnetting

▶ Dynamic routing protocol configuration

▶ NAT/PAT (network/port address translation)

▶ Basic WAN protocols and configuration

▶ Switching, VLANs, VLAN Trunking Protocol, Trunking

▶ IP Access Lists

As you think about those areas, picture yourself in front of a Cisco router and assess your level of confidence in being able to quickly and correctly configure it. You should feel no intimidation or uncertainty in being able to tackle these kinds of configurations. Subnetting in particular is heavily emphasized and is one of the main areas where people have difficulty. You must be totally, unequivocally confident with subnetting or you will face a serious challenge on your exam.

Testing Your Exam Readiness

The CCNA exam will demand a high degree of technical accuracy, applied skill, and the ability to perform quickly under pressure. You can give yourself experience in this environment by practicing on an exam simulator until you are comfortable. You must become technically accurate to about 90–95%, have no difficulty with the simulator tasks, and be able to complete the exam in the appropriate time frame. This can be achieved by repetition, but be careful that you do not simply memorize all the questions in the test pool!

Assessing Your Readiness for the CCNA Exam

There are three "pillars" of success on the CCNA exam: technical excellence, applied skills, and the ability to perform under pressure. Technical excellence is achieved with study, training, and self-testing. Applied skills are learned through practice labs and exams, work experience, and hands-on training and experience. The ability to perform under pressure is gained from situational training such as exam simulators and challenge labs, perhaps with a trainer or mentor. The goal is to increase your confidence level so that you feel as if you *own* the material and want to be challenged to a duel by the exam.

With a combination of educational and work experience, CCNA-specific training, self-study and hands-on practice, you will put yourself in the best position to approach the exam with a high degree of confidence—and pass. Good luck; study hard.

CHAPTER ONE

Networking Fundamentals

Terms You'll Need to Understand:

✓ Network

✓ LAN

✓ WAN

✓ Mesh

✓ Point-to-point topology

✓ Star topology

✓ Ring topology

✓ Bus topology

Techniques You'll Need to Master:

✓ Identifying network technologies

✓ Understanding Ethernet

Introduction

A qualified CCNA is expected to have a broad understanding of different network technologies and a more detailed knowledge of a few specific ones. This chapter introduces the basics of networking and points out some of the concepts that are tested on the CCNA exam(s).

Components and Terms

A *network* is a set of devices, software, and cables that enables the exchange of information between them. *Host devices* are computers, servers, laptops, Personal Digital Assistants (PDAs), or anything a person uses to access the network. *Network devices* are hubs, repeaters, bridges, switches, routers, and firewalls (to name a few). Cables can be copper, fiberoptic, or even wireless radio (which isn't really a cable, but serves the same purpose). The applications used on a network include those that actually enable network connectivity, such as the Transmission Control Protocol/Internet Protocol (TCP/IP) protocol, those that test network links, such as the Internet Control Message Protocol (ICMP), and end-user applications, such as email and File Transfer Protocol (FTP). There are thousands of networkable applications; we are concerned with a small number of them.

Topologies

A topology describes the layout of a network. You need to know several topologies for the exam. These are

> ➤ *Point-to-Point*—A point-to-point topology involves two hosts or devices that are directly connected to each other and to nothing else; anything sent by one can be received only by the other. Serial communication is usually point-to-point, but not always.

> ➤ *Star*—A star topology is one in which one host or device has multiple connections to other hosts; this is sometimes called hub-and-spoke as well. In a star topology, if a host wants to send to another host, it must send traffic through the hub or central device. Ethernet, if using a hub or a switch and Twisted Pair cabling, is star-wired.

> ➤ *Ring*—A ring topology is created when one device is connected to the next one sequentially, with the last device being connected to the first. The actual devices don't necessarily form a circle, but the data moves in a logical circle. FDDI and Token Ring are examples of ring topologies.

> ➤ *Bus*—A bus topology uses a single coaxial cable, to which hosts are attached at intervals. The term bus comes from an electrical bus, which is a point from which electrical power can be drawn for multiple connections. Ethernet that uses coaxial cable creates a bus topology.

> ➤ *Mesh*—A *full mesh* is a topology with multiple point-to-point connections that connect each location to the others. The advantage is that you can send data directly from any location to any other location instead of having to send it through a central point. There are more options for sending if one of the connections fails. The disadvantages are that it is expensive and complex to implement a full mesh. You can compromise and build a *partial mesh*, which is when only some locations are connected to the other locations.

LAN Technologies

LAN stands for local area network. LANs are short-range, high-speed networks typically found in schools, offices, and, more recently, homes. Over the years, there have been many types of LANs. Currently, Ethernet is king, and other than wireless technologies, it is the only LAN technology you need to know for the CCNA exam.

Ethernet

Ethernet is the most common LAN technology in use today. Ethernet is a family of implementations, which have evolved into faster and more reliable solutions all based on a common technology.

Ethernet was pioneered by Digital Equipment Corporation, Intel, and Xerox and first published in 1980. The IEEE modified it and gave it the specification 802.3. The way Ethernet works is closely linked to its original connection type: A coaxial cable was used to join all the hosts together. This formed a *segment*. On a single segment, only one host could use the cable at a time; because the wire was coaxial, with one positive conductor and one negative conductor, it created a single electrical circuit. This single circuit could be energized by only one host at a time, or a conflict would result as two hosts tried to talk at once and nothing got through. Much the same thing happens when you and a friend try to send at the same time using walkie-talkies; all that is heard is noise. This conflict is called a *collision*.

CSMA/CD (Carrier Sense Multiple Access with Collision Detection) is the method Ethernet uses to deal with collisions. When a host wants to transmit, it first listens to the wire to see if anyone else is transmitting at that moment. If it is clear, it can transmit; if not, it will wait for the host that is transmitting to stop. Sometimes, two hosts decide at the same instant that the wire is clear, and collide with each other. When this happens, the hosts that were involved with the collision send a special *jam signal* that advises everyone on that segment of the collision. Then all the hosts wait for a random period of time before they check the wire and try transmitting again. This wait time is tiny—a few millionths of a second—and is determined by the backoff algorithm. (The backoff algorithm is the mathematical equation a host runs to come up with the random number.) The theory is that if each host waits a different amount of time, the wire should be clear for all of them when they decide to transmit again.

Any Ethernet segment that uses coaxial cable (10-BASE 2, 10-BASE 5) or a hub with twisted-pair cabling is a collision environment.

EXAM ALERT

When a collision occurs
1. A Jam Signal is sent.
2. All hosts briefly stop transmitting.
3. All hosts run the backoff algorithm, which decides the random time they will wait before attempting to transmit again.

Collisions have the effect of clogging up a network because they prevent data from being sent. The more hosts you have sharing a wire, and the more data they have to send, the worse it gets. A group of devices that are affected by one another's collisions is called a *collision domain*. As networks grew, it became necessary to break up collision domains so that there were fewer collisions in each one. Devices called *bridges* and *switches* did this; these devices are covered in Chapter 6, "Catalyst Switch Operations and Configuration."

It is possible to eliminate collisions altogether if we can provide separate send and receive circuits; this is more like a telephone (which allows us to speak and hear at the same time) than a walkie-talkie. This requires four conductors—a positive and negative pair for each circuit. The use of twisted-pair cabling (not coax), which has at least four conductors (and more likely eight) allows us to create a full duplex connection, with simultaneous send and receive circuits. Full-duplex connections eliminate collisions because the host can now send and receive simultaneously.

Modern Ethernet is fast, reliable, and collision free if you set it up right. Speeds of up to 10 gigabits per second are possible with the correct cabling.

Table 1.1 summarizes some of the different Ethernet specifications, characteristics, and cable types. This is not all of them, just an idea of how far Ethernet has come.

TABLE 1.1   Comparing Ethernet Implementations

IEEE	Cabling	Topology	Speed/Duplex/Media	Maximum Range
802.3	10-BASE 5	Bus	10Mbs Half duplex Thicknet	500m
802.3	10-BASE 2	Bus	10Mbs Half duplex Thinnet	185m
802.3	10/100-BASE T	Star	10/100Mbs Half-duplex UTP	100m
802.3u	100-BASE T	Star	100Mbs Half/Full duplex UTP	100m
802.3u	100-BASE FX	Star	100Mbs Full duplex Multimode Fiber Optic	400m
802.3ab	1000-BASE T	Star	1000Mbs Full duplex UTP	100m
802.3z	1000-BASE ZX	Star	1000Mbs Full duplex Single-Mode Fiber Optic	100km

EXAM ALERT

You should be familiar with the contents of Table 1.1.

WAN Technologies

A wide area network (WAN) serves to interconnect two or more LANs. WAN technology is designed to extend network connectivity to much greater distances than any LAN technology is capable of. Most companies can't afford to build their own WAN, so it is usual to buy WAN service from a service provider. Service providers are in the business of building and selling WAN connectivity; they invest in the equipment, cabling, and training to build transcontinental networks for other businesses to rent. For the CCNA exam, you need to be familiar with four types of WAN connections and the protocols associated with them. WAN connectivity and configuration is covered in detail in Chapter 10, "Introduction to WANs." The four WAN connection types are outlined in the following sections.

Dedicated Leased Line Connections

A leased line refers to a connection that is installed and provisioned for the exclusive use of the customer. Essentially, when you order a leased line, you get your very own piece of wire from your location to the service provider's network. This is good because no other customer can affect your line, as can be the case with other WAN services. You have a lot of control over this circuit to do things such as Quality of Service and other traffic management. The downside is that a leased line is expensive and gets a lot more expensive if you need to connect offices that are far apart.

A leased line is typically a point-to-point connection from the head office to a branch office, so if you need to connect to multiple locations, you need multiple leased lines. Multiple leased lines get even more expensive. Leased-line circuits typically run the Point-to-Point Protocol (PPP), High-Level Data-Link Control Protocol (HDLC), or possibly Serial Line Internet Protocol (SLIP). (These protocols are covered in detail in Chapter 10.)

Circuit-Switched Connections

A circuit-switched WAN uses the phone company as the service provider, either with analog dial-up or digital ISDN connections. With circuit-switching, if you need to connect to the remote LAN, a call is dialed and a circuit is established; the data is sent across the circuit, and the circuit is taken down when it is no longer needed. Circuit-switched WANs usually use PPP, HDLC, or SLIP, and they tend to be really slow—anywhere from 19.2K for analog dialup to 128K for ISDN using a Basic Rate Interface (BRI). They can also get expensive because most contracts specify a pay-per-usage billing.

Packet-Switched Connections

Packet-switched WAN services allow you to connect to the provider's network in much the same way as a PC connects to a hub: When connected, your traffic is affected by other customers' and theirs by you. This can be an issue sometimes, but it can be managed. The advantage of this shared-bandwidth technology is that with a single physical connection from your router's serial port (typically), you can establish virtual connections to many other locations around the world. So if you have a lot of branch offices and they are far away from the head office, a packet-switched solution is a good idea. Packet-switched circuits usually use Frame Relay or possibly X.25.

Cell-Switched Connections

Cell switching is similar to packet switching; the difference is that with packet-switched networks, the size of the units of data being sent (called *frames*) is variable. Cell-switched units (cells) are of a constant size. This makes dealing with heavy traffic loads easier and more efficient. Cell-switched solutions such as Asynchronous Transfer Mode (ATM) tend to be big, fast, and robust.

Wireless Networks

There has been a boom recently in the deployment of wireless networks for both LAN and WAN applications. The IEEE 802.11 Wireless Fidelity standard, affectionately known as Wi-Fi, specifies a growing set of standards for short-range, high-speed wireless systems that are good for everything from mobile device connectivity to home media center systems. The advantages are the elimination of cables and the freedom of movement; the disadvantages are in range, reliability, and security. Wireless is a good WAN choice for moderate distances (less than 10 miles, for example) with line-of-sight between them—for example, between buildings in a campus. Special antennas are used to make the wireless signal directional and increase the range, often to more than 20 kilometers.

> **NOTE**
>
> Wireless networking will be covered in more detail in Chapter 8, "Wireless LANs."

Other Network Technologies

The CCNA exam is chiefly concerned with the previous LAN/WAN systems, but it is interesting to note some of the other directions that networks are headed as well. Following are other types of networks:

➤ A **MAN**, or metropolitan area network, uses fiber-optic connections to dramatically extend the reach of high-speed LAN technologies. This service is typically found only in urban business centers where large corporations need high bandwidth, hence the metro name.

➤ A **SAN** is a storage area network. This is a very high-speed, medium-range system that allows a server (or cluster of servers) to access an external disk storage array as if it were a locally connected hard drive. This opens up huge possibilities for fault-tolerant and centrally-managed data systems, but it's expensive.

➤ **Content Networks** are developed in response to the huge amount—as well as the kind—of information available on the Internet. Content networks deal with making access to the information faster, as well as logging and controlling access to certain kinds of material.

However, these specialized network types are beyond the scope of CCNA.

Exam Prep Questions

1. Your boss asks you to explain what happens when a collision occurs on an Ethernet segment. Which of the following are accurate? Choose 3.

   ○ **A.** Every device stops transmitting for a short time.

   ○ **B.** When it is safe to transmit again, the devices that collided get priority access to the wire.

   ○ **C.** The collision starts a random backoff algorithm.

   ○ **D.** A jam signal is sent to alert all devices of the collision.

   ○ **E.** Only the devices involved in the collision stop transmitting briefly to clear the wire.

2. How is equal access to the wire managed in a collision-oriented environment such as Ethernet?

   ○ **A.** The hosts are given equal access based on the circulation of a token; hosts can only transmit when they hold the token.

   ○ **B.** Hosts are given prioritized access to the wire based on their MAC address.

   ○ **C.** Hosts are given equal access to the wire by being allowed to transmit at specified time intervals.

   ○ **D.** Hosts signal their desire to transmit by sending a contention alert.

   ○ **E.** Hosts check the wire for activity before attempting to send; if a collision happens, they wait a random time period before attempting to send again.

3. Which of the following are commonly used WAN protocols? Choose 3.

   ○ **A.** WEP

   ○ **B.** WING

   ○ **C.** Frame Relay

   ○ **D.** HDLC

   ○ **E.** AAA

   ○ **F.** PPP

4. Which of the following are IEEE specifications for Gigabit Ethernet? Choose 2.

   ○ **A.** 802.1d

   ○ **B.** 802.11

   ○ **C.** 802.3z

   ○ **D.** 802.1q

   ○ **E.** 802.3ab

5. Which technology is cell-switched?

   ○ **A.** Token Ring

   ○ **B.** FDDI

   ○ **C.** Ethernet

   ○ **D.** Frame Relay

   ○ **E.** ATM

   ○ **F.** PPP

6. Which devices were designed to segment collision domains? Choose 2.

   ○ **A.** Hubs

   ○ **B.** Repeaters

   ○ **C.** MAU

   ○ **D.** Bridge

   ○ **E.** Switch

7. You have just acquired some new office space in a building across the street from your current space, about 350 meters away. You want to arrange for high-speed (10Mbs) network connectivity between them; which of the following choices is a valid connection option?

   ○ **A.** Analog dial-up

   ○ **B.** ISDN BRI

   ○ **C.** Ethernet using 100-BASE TX cabling

   ○ **D.** 802.11 Wireless using specialized antennas

8. Which WAN technology is the best choice if you have many remote offices that are in different states, you need always-on connectivity, and you don't have money to burn?

    ○ **A.** Circuit-switched

    ○ **B.** Leased line

    ○ **C.** Packet switched

    ○ **D.** Wireless

Answers to Exam Prep Questions

1. Answers A, C, and D are the correct answers. B is incorrect because there is no method to prioritize access to the wire in Ethernet. Answer E is incorrect because all devices stop transmitting in the event of a collision.

2. Answer is E the correct answer. CSMA/CD is the technology that enables hosts to send if the wire is available and to wait a random time to try again if a collision happens. Answer A is incorrect because it describes Token Ring, not Ethernet. Answers B, C, and D are incorrect because they are fictitious.

3. Answers C, D, and F are correct. The big three WAN protocols are PPP, Frame Relay, and HDLC. There are others, but CCNA does not cover them. Answer A is incorrect because WEP is Wired Equivalent Privacy, a security scheme for wireless networks. Answer B is incorrect because it is fictional. Answer E is incorrect because AAA stands for Authentication, Authorization, and Accounting, a scheme to manage access and activities on networked devices.

4. Answers C and E are correct. 802.3z specifies 1Gb on fiber, and 802.3ab specifies 1Gb on copper. Answers A, B, and D are incorrect; those are the specs for STP, Wi-Fi, and Inter-switch VLAN tagging, respectively.

5. Answer E is correct. ATM is a cell-switched technology. Answers A, B, C, D, and F are incorrect because they use variable-sized frames, not cells.

6. Answers D and E are correct. Bridges and switches segment collision domains. Answers A and B are incorrect because hubs and repeaters have the opposite effect: They make collision domains bigger and more of a problem.

7. Answer D is correct. 802.11 Wireless using specialized antennas is a good choice for this application. Answers A and B are incorrect because analog and ISDN BRI do not provide the required bandwidth. Answer C is incorrect because 100-BASE TX is copper cabling, which has a maximum range of 100 meters. (You might be able to go with Ethernet over fiber-optic cabling, but it is expensive—and it is not one of the offered choices here anyway.)

8. Answer C is the correct answer. Packet-switched networks are a good choice in this context. Answer A is incorrect; circuit-switched connections are a poor choice because they are not usually always on, and they get expensive the longer they are connected. Answer B is incorrect because leased lines have always-on connectivity, but at a prohibitive cost. Answer D is incorrect; wireless does not have the range to cover interstate distances.

CHAPTER TWO

Network Models

Terms You'll Need to Understand

✓ Access

✓ Distribution

✓ Core layer

✓ Application layer

✓ Presentation layer

✓ Session layer

✓ Transport layer

✓ Network layer

✓ Data link layer

✓ Physical layer

✓ Connection-oriented transmission

✓ Connectionless transmission

Concepts and Techniques You'll Need to Master

✓ Associating network processes to OSI model layers

✓ Associating applications and protocols to their OSI layer

✓ Understanding the encapsulation and decapsulation process

✓ Understanding interhost communication

✓ Identifying protocols and their port numbers

Introduction

Any complex operation requires a certain degree of structure in order to be understood. When dealing with millions of individuals all designing and building programs, protocols, and equipment that is intended to network together, the use of a theoretical model as a basis for understanding and interoperability is critical. This chapter reviews the Open Standards Interconnect (OSI) model and compares it to the TCP/IP model. The Cisco three-layer hierarchical model is also mentioned. All of these models are tested, and a strong understanding of the OSI model is necessary for success on the exam as well as useful in the real world.

Cisco Hierarchical Model

Cisco has created a reference model for the functions its equipment performs. The *three-layer hierarchical model* describes the major functional roles in any network and provides a basis for understanding and troubleshooting scalable networks. Figure 2.1 shows a representation of the three-layer model with switches and routers in their typical layers. The following sections describe each layer in more detail.

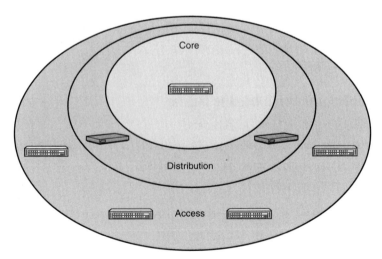

FIGURE 2.1 The three-layer hierarchical model.

Access Layer

The access layer is the point that connects end users to the network. This can be achieved by a hub or switch to which PCs are connected, a wireless access point, a remote office connection, a dial-up service, or a VPN tunnel from the Internet into the corporate network.

Distribution Layer

The distribution layer provides routing, packet filtering, WAN access, and QoS (Quality of Service). The access layer devices (usually switches) connect to a router or Layer 3 switch so that traffic can be routed to another network. Packet filtering refers to the use of access control lists to identify certain types of traffic and control where it might go—or block it altogether. (We look at ACLs in detail in Chapter 13, "IP Access Lists.")

Traditional WAN access usually involves a specialized interface—perhaps a serial port or ISDN Primary Rate Interface controller. These specialized functions are found on Distribution layer devices such as routers. If our network needs to use QoS features to make it run well, these features are typically first implemented at the distribution layer.

If our network includes different LAN technologies (Token Ring, Fiber-Distributed Data Interchange, and Ethernet, for example), the translation between these different media types is usually done by a distribution layer device. Because these devices are typically routers and Layer 3 switches, this is also where broadcast domain segmentation happens.

Core Layer

The Core layer is all about speed. Here, we typically find big, fast switches that move the data from the distribution layer to centralized resources such as mail and database servers, or to other distribution layer devices, as quickly as possible. The core does not usually do any routing or packet filtering, but it might do QoS if that is an important part of the network (if using Voice over IP [VoIP], for example).

Advantages of the Three-Layer Model

The exam will focus on the benefits of the Cisco model as well as its particulars. Keep the following points in mind as advantages of the Cisco layered approach to networks:

▸ Scalability—If we want to add users, it is easy to put an additional access layer device in place, without having to replace all the distribution and core devices at the same time. It is easier to add extended functionality to one layer at a time as needed instead of all at once.

▸ Cost Savings—An access layer device is much cheaper than a distribution or core device; also, by upgrading only one layer, we do not have to upgrade all three layers at once, incurring unnecessary costs.

▸ Easier Troubleshooting—If a component at one layer fails, it will not affect the entire system. It is also easier to find the problem if the failed device affects only one layer.

OSI Model

The International Standards Organization (ISO) defined a seven-layer model to standardize networking processes. The *Open Systems Interconnection (OSI)* model facilitates the understanding of the complexities of networking by defining what happens at each step of the process.

You should be clear that the OSI model does not impose rules on network equipment manufacturers or protocol developers; rather, it sets guidelines for functions so that inter-vendor operability is possible and predictable.

Each of the seven layers in the model communicates with the layers above and below, using standardized coding at the beginning of the message that can be interpreted by another device regardless of who made it. So if a vendor decides that they want to build a network device, they have the option of building a completely unique, proprietary system and trying to convince people to buy it; or, they can build a device that works with other devices according to the OSI model.

The seven different layers break up the process of networking, making it easier to understand and to troubleshoot problems. It is possible to test the functionality of each layer in sequence, to determine where the problem is and where to begin repairs.

The seven layers, in order, are as follows:

7. Application

6. Presentation

5. Session

4. Transport

3. Network

2. Data link

1. Physical

> **EXAM ALERT**
>
> You must know the names of the layers, in order. Start memorizing! You could use a mnemonic; there are several, some of them unprintable, but this one works pretty well: "All People Seem To Need Data Processing."
>
> I don't know if Dave Minutella made that one up, but I'll give him the credit because he taught it to me…

Let's examine what happens at each layer as we send data to another computer.

Layer 7: The Application Layer

If you are using any program or utility that can store, send, or retrieve data over a network, it is a Layer 7 application. Layer 7 is sometimes called the user interface layer; for example, when you launch a web browser and type in an address, you are working with a network-aware application and instructing it what to do on the network—that is, go and retrieve this web page. The same thing happens when you save a document to a file server or start a Telnet connection—you create some data that is to be sent over the network to another computer. Some applications or protocols are "hidden" from the user; for example, when you send and receive email, you might use Microsoft Outlook or Eudora or any other mail program you care to name, but the protocols that send and receive your mail are almost always going to be SMTP and POP3.

The application layer protocols (and deciphered acronyms) that you should know are as follows:

► **HTTP** (Hypertext Transfer Protocol)—Browses web pages.

► **FTP** (File Transfer Protocol)—Reliably sends/retrieves all file types.

► **SMTP** (Simple Mail Transfer Protocol)—Sends email.

- ▸ **POP3** (Post Office Protocol v.3)—Retrieves email.

- ▸ **NTP** (Network Time Protocol)—Synchronizes networked device clocks.

- ▸ **SNMP** (Simple Network Management Protocol)—Communicates status and allows control of networked devices.

- ▸ **TFTP** (Trivial File Transfer Protocol)—Simple, lightweight file transfer.

- ▸ **DNS** (Domain Naming System)—Translates a website name (easy for people) to an IP address (easy for computers).

- ▸ **DHCP** (Dynamic Host Configuration Protocol)—Assigns IP, mask, and DNS server (plus a bunch of other stuff) to hosts.

- ▸ **Telnet**—Provides a remote terminal connection to manage devices to which you are not close enough to use a console cable.

EXAM ALERT

You should be ready to name any of the application layer protocols, as well as recognize them either by name or acronym. This gets easier the more experience you have, as they are constantly mentioned in the context of everyday networking.

Layer 6: The Presentation Layer

The presentation layer is responsible for formatting data so that application-layer protocols (and then the users) can recognize and work with it. If you think about file extensions—such as .doc, .jpg, .txt, .avi, and so on—you realize that each of these file types is formatted for use by a particular type of application. The presentation layer does this formatting, taking the application layer data and marking it with the formatting codes so that it can be viewed reliably when accessed later. The presentation layer can also do some types of encryption, but that is not as common as it used to be since there are better ways to encrypt that are easier on CPU and RAM resources.

Layer 5: The Session Layer

The session layer deals with initiating and terminating network connections. It provides instructions to connect, authenticate (optionally), and disconnect from a network resource. Common examples are the login part of a Telnet or SQL session (not the actual data movement) and Remote Procedure Call (RPC) functions. The actual movement of the data is handled by the lower layers.

Layer 4: The Transport Layer

The transport layer is possibly the most important layer for exam study purposes. A lot is going on here, and it is heavily tested.

The transport layer deals with exactly how two hosts are going to send data. The two main methods are called *connection-oriented* and *connectionless*. Connection-oriented transmission is said to be reliable, and connectionless is *unreliable*. Every network protocol stack will have a protocol that handles each style; in the TCP/IP stack, reliable transmission is done by *TCP*, and unreliable by *UDP*. Now, don't get too wrapped up in the term "unreliable"; this doesn't mean that the data isn't going to get there; it only means that it isn't *guaranteed* to get there.

Think of your options when you are sending a letter: you can pop it in an envelope, throw a stamp on it and put it in the mailbox, and chances are good that it will get where it's supposed to go—but there is no guarantee, and stuff does go missing once in a while. On the other hand, it's cheap.

Your other choice is to use a courier—FedEx's motto used to be, "When it absolutely, positively has to be there overnight." For this level of service, you have to buy a fancy envelope and put a bunch of extra labels on it to track where it is going and where it has been. But, you get a receipt when it is delivered, you are guaranteed delivery, and you can keep track of whether your shipment got to its destination. All of this costs you more—but it is reliable!

This analogy works perfectly when describing the difference between UDP and TCP: UDP is the post office, and TCP is FedEx. Let's look at this more closely, starting with TCP.

Reliable Communication with TCP

The key to reliable communication using TCP is the use of sequence and acknowledgment numbers. These numbers are attached to the various segments of information that are sent between two hosts to identify what order they should be assembled in to re-create the original data, and to keep track of whether any segments went missing along the way. When a host sends a segment of data, it is labeled with a *sequence number* that identifies that segment and where it belongs in the series of segments being sent. When the receiving host gets that segment, it sends an acknowledgment back to the sender with an *acknowledgment number*; the value of this number is the sequence number of the last segment it received, plus one. In effect, the receiver is saying, "I got your last one, now I am ready for the next one."

The first step in establishing a reliable connection between hosts is the *three-way handshake*. This initial signaling allows hosts to exchange their starting sequence numbers and to test that they have reliable communication between them. Figure 2.2 illustrates the three-way handshake in TCP communication.

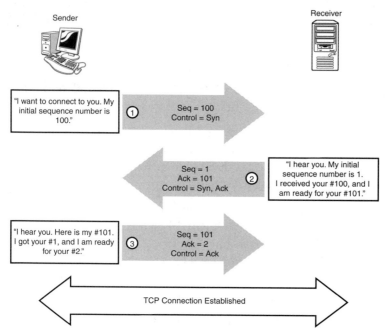

FIGURE 2.2   The TCP three-way handshake.

From this point, the sender continues to send segments of data. A system known as *PAR (Positive acknowledgment and Retransmission)* makes sure that all the segments get where they are going. Following are the three main elements of PAR:

1. The sender starts a timer when it sends a segment, and will re-transmit that segment if the timer expires before an acknowledgment is received for that segment.

2. The sender keeps a record of all segments sent and expects an acknowledgment of each one.

3. The receiving device acknowledges the receipt of a segment by sending a segment back to the sender indicating the next sequence number it expects.

If any of the segments of data should go missing—perhaps due to interference, collisions, or a link failure—the sender will not receive an acknowledgment of it and will retransmit it. The sequence number enables the receiver to put all the segments back in the correct order.

The TCP Sliding Window

Sometimes a receiver can get very busy—imagine a web server that is getting millions of hits an hour. If it receives more segments than it can handle, it might be forced to drop (discard) some; this is not desirable because the senders would then have to retransmit them; this wastes time and bandwidth and increases delay.

The receiver has a method to tell the sender(s) to slow down the transmission rate. It's called the *sliding window*. The window size indicates how many segments can be sent before an acknowledgment will be sent. If it is not busy, the receiver can handle a large number of segments and send a single acknowledgment. If it gets very busy, it can make the window size very small, allowing the sender(s) to send only a few segments before an acknowledgment is sent.

The window size of the sender and receiver is included in the segment header and can change during the lifetime of the conversation. Figure 2.3 shows how the sliding window feature of TCP operates.

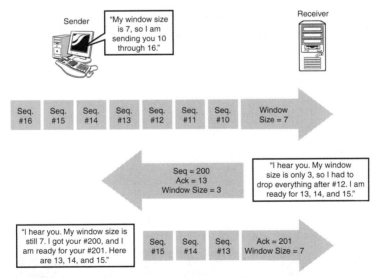

FIGURE 2.3 The TCP sliding window controls how much data is sent before an acknowledgment is needed.

Port Numbers

Imagine a server that performs a number of functions—for example email, web pages, FTP, and DNS. The server has a single IP address, but can perform all these different functions for all the hosts that want to connect to it. The transport layer (layer 4) uses port numbers to distinguish between different types of traffic that might be headed for the same IP address.

Port numbers are divided into ranges by the IANA. Following are the current port ranges:

0–1023	Well-Known—For common TCP/IP functions and applications
1024–49151	Registered—For applications built by companies
49152–65535	Dynamic/Private—For dynamic connections or unregistered applications

Port numbers are used by both TCP and UDP protocols. Table 2.1 lists some of the common port numbers you should know for the CCNA exam:

TABLE 2.1 Common TCP and UDP Port Numbers

TCP		UDP	
FTP	20, 21	DNS	53
Telnet	23	DHCP	67, 68
SMTP	25	TFTP	69
DNS	53	NTP	123
HTTP	80	SNMP	161
POP	110		
NNTP	119		
HTTPS	443		

When a host sends a segment, it specifies the *destination port* that matches the service it wants to connect to. It also includes a *source port* (a random port number from the dynamic range) that acts as a return address for that connection. In this way, a single host can have multiple—possibly hundreds—of connections with the same server, and the server can track each of them because of the different source port numbers for each connection. When the server sends its replies back to the host, the host source ports become the server's destination ports. This system enables the transport layer to *multiplex* connections—meaning, support multiple connections between the same two hosts.

To understand this better, let's say that Host A wants to start a Telnet session to Server Z. A will send a segment to Z's IP address, with the destination port of 23 and a random source port number (generated by the host operating system) from the dynamic range—let's choose 55440.

When Server Z receives the segment, it looks at the destination port of 23 and realizes that this segment is intended for its Telnet application, so it sends the data (which, in this case, is a request to start a Telnet session) to its Telnet application. When the Telnet application answers, the server sends a reply back to the host. The destination port of this reply is the original source port of the host, and the source port is the original segment, it specifies the *destination port* that destination port of the host. Figure 2.4 shows this exchange in action.

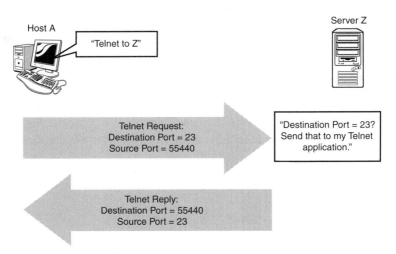

FIGURE 2.4 Source and destination ports in action.

Using TCP means that we have to include a lot of information with each segment: the sequence number, the acknowledgment number, the source and destination ports, and the window size. All this information is contained in the layer

4 header. A *header* is a label attached to the beginning of the data being sent that contains all the control information; once the header is attached, the data is called a *segment*. Figure 2.5 shows the fields in a TCP header.

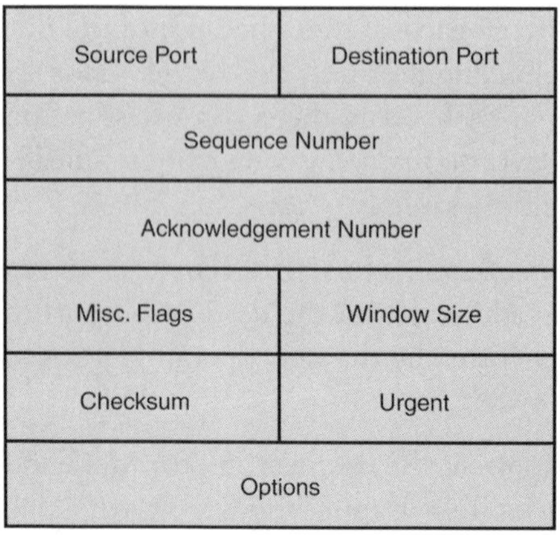

Source Port	Destination Port
Sequence Number	
Acknowledgement Number	
Misc. Flags	Window Size
Checksum	Urgent
Options	

FIGURE 2.5   The TCP header.

Unreliable Communication with UDP

When you look at all the control information that TCP needs to work, and factor in the need to do the three-way handshake before any data is sent, you begin to realize that TCP is a pretty high-overhead operation. For every unit of data being sent, a ton of control information needs to be sent along with it. For some types of communication, we don't need all that control—sometimes, just dropping a postcard in the mail is fine. That is where UDP comes in.

UDP does not use any of the control and reliability features we just discussed in TCP. In fact, if you look at Figure 2.6, which shows what the UDP header looks like, you can see that the only elements in common are the port numbers and the checksum.

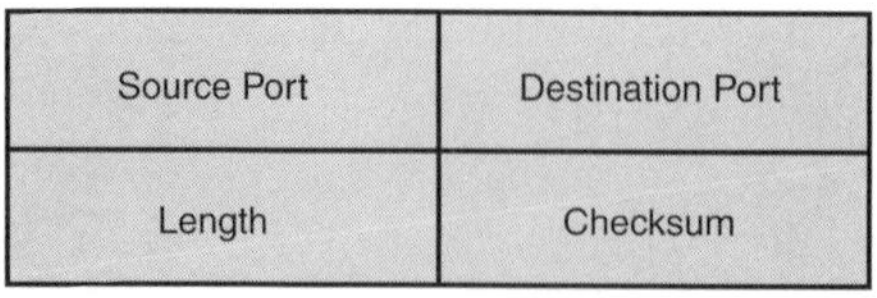

Source Port	Destination Port
Length	Checksum

FIGURE 2.6   The UDP header is a lightweight.

There is no sequencing, no acknowledgments, no window size—and no three-way handshake, either. So you can see that *much* less control information is sent with each segment. With UDP, there is no PAR. You ask for something, and then you get it. If it doesn't work, you have to ask all over again. Most applications, such as a TFTP server for example, will handle any errors and retransmissions—which means that the application itself (up at Layer 7) is doing the reliability, *not* Layer 4.

The typical UDP connection goes something like this:

Host A: "Hey Server Z, what's the IP address of www.google.com?"

Server Z: "www.google.com is 66.102.7.147."

Or perhaps:

Host B: "Hey Server Z, send me that file using TFTP."

Server Z: "Here's the file."

UDP is good when reliability is not needed—for DNS lookups or TFTP transfers, for example—or when the overhead of TCP would cause more problems than it solves—for example, when doing VoIP. TCP signaling would introduce so much delay that it would degrade the voice quality—plus, by the time any missing voice segment was retransmitted, it would be too late to use it! VoIP uses UDP because it is faster than TCP, and reliability is less important than minimizing delay.

> **EXAM ALERT**
>
> You must be able to identify a TCP header on sight, when compared to a UDP header. Be ready for a twist on the wording such as, "Which provides reliable connections?" So not only do you need to know which header is TCP and which is UDP, but also which one is reliable!

Layer 3: The Network Layer

The network layer deals with logical addressing—in our CCNA world, that means IP addresses, but it could also mean IPX, AppleTalk, SNA, and a bunch of others. A logical address is one that is assigned to an interface in software—as opposed to one that is burned onto an interface at the factory (as is the case with MAC addresses, as you will see in a minute).

For two IP hosts to communicate, they must be in the same network (Chapter 3, "Concepts in IP Addressing," elaborates on this). If they are in different networks, we need a router to connect the two networks. Finding the way between networks, potentially through hundreds of routers, is called *path determination*. This is the second function of the network layer. Path determination means routing, and routers are a Layer 3 device (so are Layer 3 switches, oddly enough).

The last function of the network layer is to communicate with the layer above (transport) and the layer below (data link). This is achieved by attaching a header to the beginning of the segment that Layer 4 built. The addition of this header makes the segment into a *packet* (sometimes called a datagram, but we like packet better). The packet header has a field that indicates the type of segment it is carrying—TCP or UDP, for example—so that the packet can be sent to the correct function at Layer 4. Communicating with Layer 2 in this case means that an IP packet can be sent to Layer 2 to become an Ethernet frame, Frame Relay, Point-to-Point Protocol, or almost any other Layer 2 technology. We'll elaborate on this a little later.

One of the big advantages of a logical addressing scheme is that we can make it *hierarchical*. Hierarchical means "organized into a formal or ranked order." Because all the networks are numbered, and we have control over where those networks are set up, it's easy for us to build a really big system: Big networks are broken into smaller and smaller pieces, with the routers closer to the core knowing the big picture and no details, and the routers at the edge knowing their little set of detailed information but nothing about anyone else's. This makes it easier to organize and find all the millions of different networks, using routers. It's roughly equivalent to a postal address. For example, look at the following address:

24 Sussex Drive

Ottawa, Ontario

Canada K1N 9E6

You could probably find it, eventually, because you would know to get to Canada first, and then to the province of Ontario, and then the city of Ottawa (beautiful place). Grab yourself a map, and soon you'll be standing in front of that address—which happens to be the Prime Minister's house, so don't be surprised if the Mounties are curious about you being there.

The alternative to a nicely organized hierarchical system like that is a *flat* topology. In a flat system, there is no efficient way to determine where a single address is, because they are not organized. Imagine if the address were this instead:

30000000

Okay, where is it? We have no idea. Unless we can ask everyone at once if it's their address, we don't really stand a chance of finding it. Flat networks (Layer 2) work as long as there are not very many addresses; hierarchical is scalable. Layer 3 is hierarchical, logical addressing that allows us to perform path determination.

You should be familiar with the protocols that exist at Layer 3 as well. Table 2.2 lists the ones you need to know, along with a very brief description.

Table 2.2   Layer 3 Protocols

Protocol	Description
IP	IP is the "mother protocol" of TCP/IP, featuring routable 32-bit addressing.
IPX	The equivalent of IP in Novell Netware.
ICMP	Internet Connection Management Protocol. Incorporates Ping and Traceroute, which are layer 3 link testing utilities.
OSPF, IGRP, EIGRP, RIP, ISIS	Dynamic routing protocols that learn about remote networks and the best paths to them from other routers running the same protocol.
ARP, RARP	Address Resolution Protocol (and Reverse ARP). ARP learns what MAC address is associated with a given IP address. Reverse ARP learns an IP address given a MAC address.

EXAM ALERT

You should be familiar with Table 2.2.

Remember that Layer 3 is about logical, hierarchical addressing and path determination using that hierarchy—which means routing.

Layer 2: The Data Link Layer

The data link layer is responsible for taking the Layer 3 packet (regardless of which protocol created it—IP, IPX, and so on) and preparing a frame for the packet to be transmitted on the media. There are, of course, many different layer 2 frame types; in CCNA, we are interested in only the following:

- Ethernet
- Frame Relay
- Point-to-Point Protocol (PPP)
- High-Level Data Link Control protocol (HDLC)
- Cisco Discovery Protocol (CDP)

The type of frame created depends on the type of network service in use; if it is an Ethernet interface, obviously it will be creating Ethernet frames. A router serial port can create several different frame types, including PPP, HDLC, and Frame Relay.

The data link layer uses flat addressing—not hierarchical as in Layer 3. In Ethernet, the addresses in question are MAC addresses. MAC stands for Media

Access Control. A MAC address is a number assigned by the manufacturer of a NIC, burned in at the factory. For this reason, it is sometimes called a hardware or physical address, again as opposed to the logical addressing at Layer 3. A valid MAC address will consist of 12 hexadecimal characters. The first six characters are called the *OUI (Organizationally Unique Identifier)*, and identify the company that made the card. The last six characters are the card serial number. Following are some valid MAC addresses as examples:

00-0F-1F-AE-EE-F0

00-00-0C-01-AA-CD

A MAC address must be unique within a broadcast domain. This is because one of the functions of Ethernet is that a host will broadcast an ARP request to find out the MAC address of a particular IP; if there are two identical MACs in that broadcast domain, there will be serious confusion.

In other Layer 2 network types, the addresses are not MACs but serve an equivalent purpose. Frame Relay, for example uses DLCIs (Data Link Connection Identifiers). A dial-up link using regular analog phone or digital ISDN will use the phone number as the Layer 2 address of the IP you are trying to reach. Remember that you must always resolve an IP address down to some type of Layer 2 address, and there will always be a mechanism to do so.

> **EXAM ALERT**
>
> You must be able to recognize a valid MAC address: 12 valid hex characters.
>
> The first six characters are the OUI or vendor code. All MAC addresses are assigned by the NIC manufacturer and "burned in" at the factory.
>
> MAC addresses are also called hardware or physical addresses.

Layer 2 devices include switches and bridges. These devices read MAC addresses in frames and forward them to the appropriate link. (We'll go into more detail on switching technology in Chapter 6, "Basic Catalyst Switch Operations and Configuration.")

Layer 1: The Physical Layer

The last piece of the OSI puzzle is the actual connection between devices. At some point, you have to transmit your signal onto a wire, an optical fiber, or a wireless medium. The physical layer defines the mechanical, procedural, and electrical standards for accessing the media so that you can transmit your Layer 2 frames.

All signaling at Layer 1 is digital, which means that we are sending binary bits onto the wire. This can mean energizing a copper cable with electricity, where "electricity on" indicates a binary 1 and "electricity off" indicates a binary 0; or, it can mean blinking a laser down an optical fiber where on = 1 and off = 0. Wireless systems do much the same thing.

By defining standards for the physical layer, we can be assured that if we buy an RJ-45 patch cord (for example), it will fit into and work properly in any interface designed to use it.

Sending Data Between Hosts

You also need to understand the flow of information between two networked hosts. The OSI model describes the framework for this flow. As we move down the layers from application to physical, the data is *encapsulated*, which means that headers and trailers are added by each layer. The following section describes the process of creating a piece of data on one host and sending it to another host:

- ▶ At Layer 7, the user generates some *data*, perhaps an email message or a Word document. This data is passed down to Layer 6.

- ▶ At Layer 6, the *data* is formatted so that the same application on the other host can recognize and use it. The data is passed down to Layer 5.

- ▶ At Layer 5, the request to initiate a session for the transfer of the *data* is started. The data is passed down to Layer 4.

- ▶ At Layer 4, the data is encapsulated as either a TCP or UDP *segment*. The choice depends on what application generated the data. Source and destination port numbers are added, as are sequence and acknowledgment numbers and window size. The segment is passed down to Layer 3.

- ▶ At Layer 3, the segment is encapsulated with a Layer 3 header and becomes a *packet*. The packet header contains source and destination IP addresses and a label indicating what Layer 4 protocol it is carrying. The packet is passed down to Layer 2.

- ▶ At Layer 2, a header with source and destination MAC addresses is added. This encapsulation creates the *frame*. The trailer at this layer contains an error-checking calculation called the FCS (Frame Check Sequence). The frame header also contains a label indicating which Layer 3 protocol it is carrying (IP, IPX, and so on). The frame is sent to the interface for transmission onto the media (Layer 1).

- ▶ At Layer 1, the binary string that represents the frame is transmitted onto the media, whether electrically, optically, or by radio. *Bits* are transmitted across the media to the network interface of the other host.

- ▶ When received by the other host, the Layer 1 bits are sent up to Layer 2.

- ▶ At Layer 2, the destination MAC is examined to make sure that the frame was intended for this host. The FCS is calculated to check the frame for errors. If there are errors, the frame is discarded. If there are none, the frame is *decapsulated* and the packet is sent to the correct Layer 3 protocol based on the protocol ID in the header.

▶ At Layer 3, the destination IP address is checked to see if it is intended for this host. The packet header is checked to see which Layer 4 protocol to send it to. The packet is decapsulated, and the segment is sent up to Layer 4.

▶ At Layer 4, the destination port in the segment header is checked and the segment is decapsulated. The data is sent to the correct upper layer application. Depending on the application, it might go directly to Layer 7 or through 5 and 6.

This process of encapsulation, transmission, and decapsulation makes data flow in an organized and manageable fashion down the OSI stack on the sender, across the transmission media, and up the OSI stack on the receiving host. It is important to understand that layer 3 on the sender is communicating with layer 3 on the receiver as well by way of the information in the headers.

EXAM ALERT

You must be totally comfortable with visualizing how this process works. You must remember the names of the encapsulations at each layer, in order, backward and forward. These are generically called PDUs (Protocol Data Units):

Layer	PDU
Application	Data
Presentation	Data
Session	Data
Transport	Segment
Network	Packet
Data Link	Frame
Physical	Bits

Try a mnemonic: "Did Sally Pack for Bermuda?"

TCP/IP Model

Although the TCP/IP protocol can be fit into the OSI model, it actually uses its own model, which is slightly different. Remember that the OSI model is intended to be a standardized framework, and TCP/IP was originated as a proprietary Department of Defense protocol. It stands to reason that there will be some variances from the official OSI stack. The following section describes these differences.

The TCP/IP model has only four layers:

▶ Application

▶ Transport

▶ Internet

▶ Network interface

OSI Layers 5, 6, and 7 have been amalgamated into a single layer called the application layer. The Application layer features all the same protocols as found in OSI Layer 7: Telnet, FTP, TFTP, SMTP, SNMP, and so on. The transport layer is equivalent to OSI Layer 4. TCP and UDP are located here.

The Internet layer corresponds to OSI Layer 3. IP, ARP, and ICMP are the primary protocols here.

Layer 1 and 2 are fused into the network interface layer. This is confusing because it is illogical to have a protocol software stack define a physical interface; just remember that the TCP/IP model is a logical framework, and the fact that physical standards are included is necessary because it must connect to the media at some point. The TCP/IP model uses the same definitions for Network Interface standards as the OSI model does for data link and physical layers.

Figure 2.7 directly compares and contrasts the OSI model with the TCP/IP model.

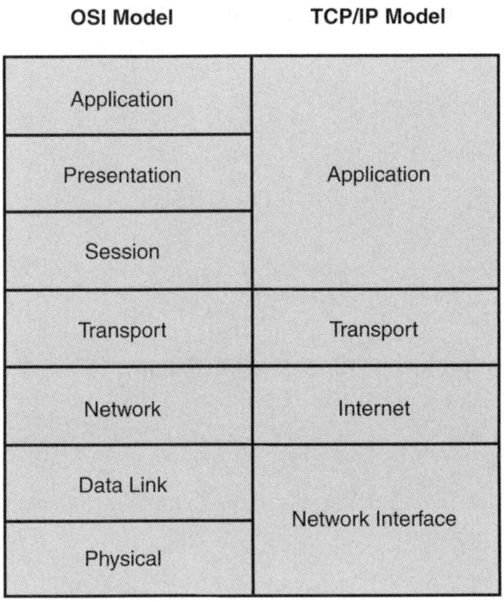

OSI Model	TCP/IP Model
Application	Application
Presentation	
Session	
Transport	Transport
Network	Internet
Data Link	Network Interface
Physical	

FIGURE 2.7 OSI and TCP/IP models compared.

EXAM ALERT

A great deal of overlap exists between the OSI and TCP/IP models, but you must be clear on the differences and watch for what the exam question is asking about; Cisco is fond of trying to trick you into answering with an OSI answer when it is, in fact, a TCP/IP model question.

Exam Prep Questions

1. Which protocol will allow you to test connectivity through Layer 7?

   - ○ **A.** ICMP
   - ○ **B.** ARP
   - ○ **C.** RIP
   - ○ **D.** Telnet

2. Which answer correctly lists the OSI PDUs in order?

   - ○ **A.** Data, Packet, Frame, Segment, Bit
   - ○ **B.** Bit, Data, Packet, Segment, Frame
   - ○ **C.** Data, Segment, Packet, Frame, Bit
   - ○ **D.** Bit, Frame, Segment, Packet, Data

3. Which transport layer protocol provides connection-oriented, reliable transport?

   - ○ **A.** TFTP
   - ○ **B.** UDP
   - ○ **C.** Ethernet
   - ○ **D.** TCP
   - ○ **E.** Secure Shell

4. Which of the following are application layer protocols? Choose all that apply.

   - ○ **A.** Ethernet
   - ○ **B.** CDP
   - ○ **C.** FTP
   - ○ **D.** TFTP
   - ○ **E.** Telnet
   - ○ **F.** ARP
   - ○ **G.** ICMP
   - ○ **H.** ATM

5. Match the protocol with its port number:

FTP	80
Telnet	69
TFTP	20, 21
DNS	123
SNMP	25
SMTP	110
NTP	161
POP3	53
HTTP	23

6. Which protocols use TCP? Choose all that apply.

- ○ **A.** DNS
- ○ **B.** SNMP
- ○ **C.** SMTP
- ○ **D.** FTP
- ○ **E.** TFTP
- ○ **F.** POP3

7. Which port numbers are used by well-known protocols that use connectionless transport?

- ○ **A.** 25
- ○ **B.** 53
- ○ **C.** 20
- ○ **D.** 69
- ○ **E.** 161
- ○ **F.** 110

8. Which are elements of PAR? Choose all that apply.

   ○ **A.** Devices that collide must wait to retransmit.

   ○ **B.** The source device starts a timer for each segment and will retransmit that segment if an acknowledgment is not received before the timer expires.

   ○ **C.** Devices will broadcast for the hardware address of the receiver.

   ○ **D.** Source devices keep a record of all segments sent and expect an acknowledgment for each one.

   ○ **E.** The receiving device will drop frames that it cannot buffer.

   ○ **F.** The receiving device will acknowledge receipt of a segment by sending an acknowledgment indicating the next segment it expects.

9. Which layer of the TCP/IP model is responsible for interhost data movement, using either connection-oriented or connectionless protocols?

   ○ **A.** Network

   ○ **B.** Internet

   ○ **C.** Transport

   ○ **D.** Network interface

   ○ **E.** Application

10. Which of the following depicts a TCP header?

    ○ A.

    ○ B.

Answers to Exam Prep Questions

1. Answer D is the correct answer; Telnet is the only Layer 7 protocol listed. All the others only operate at Layer 3, so they do not test above Layer 3.

2. Answer C is the correct answer. "Did Sally Pack for Bermuda?"

3. Answer D is the correct answer. TCP is a transport-layer protocol that uses sequencing, acknowledgments, and retransmission for reliability. Answers A, C, and E are incorrect because TFTP, Ethernet, and Secure Shell are not transport-layer protocols; Answer B is incorrect because UDP does not provide reliability.

4. Answers C, D, and E are correct. Answers A, B, and H are Layer 2 protocols; Answers F and G are Layer 3 protocols.

5. Answer:

FTP	20, 21
Telnet	23
TFTP	69
DNS	53
SNMP	161
SMTP	25
NTP	123
POP3	110
HTTP	80

6. Answers A, C, D, and F are correct. DNS uses both TCP and UDP; B and E use UDP only.

7. Answers B, D, and E are correct. These ports are used by DNS, TFTP, and SNMP—all of which use unreliable/connectionless UDP transport.

8. Answers B, D, and F are correct; PAR provides reliability by using these three functions. Answer A describes CSMA/CD; Answer C describes ARP; Answer E is a basic hardware function that has nothing to do with the process of PAR although PAR might react to the lost frames by retransmitting them.

9. Answer C is correct; connectionless and connection-oriented protocols are found at Layer 4 (transport). Answer A is incorrect because it is an OSI layer name; Answers B, D, and E are incorrect because those layers do not use connection-oriented or connectionless protocols.

10. Answer A is correct. It depicts a TCP header.

CHAPTER THREE

Concepts in IP Addressing

Terms You'll Need to Understand:

- ✓ Binary
- ✓ Hexadecimal
- ✓ Decimal
- ✓ Octet
- ✓ IP address
- ✓ Subnet Mask
- ✓ Subnet
- ✓ Host
- ✓ Increment

Techniques You'll Need to Master:

- ✓ Identifying Address Class and Default Mask
- ✓ Determining Host Requirements
- ✓ Determining Subnet Requirements
- ✓ Determining the Increment

Introduction

The CCNA exam(s) require a perfect fluency in subnetting. Success requires speed and accuracy in answering the many questions you will see on this topic. The key to this level of fluency is practice—you must work at your skills until they become second nature.

The following sections discuss binary and hexadecimal numbering systems as compared with the more familiar decimal system. An understanding of binary, in particular, is crucial to success on the test as it is fundamental to computer systems in general, and to topics such as subnetting, access lists, routing, and route summarization.

Binary

Binary is the *language* of digital electronic communication. Binary is another name for Base2 numbering. Our usual numbering system is Base10, in which a single character or column can represent one of 10 values: 0, 1, 2, 3, 4, 5, 6, 7, 8, or 9. The first column indicates how many ones there are in a given value. To represent a value greater than 9, we need another column, which represents how many "tens" there are; if the value we want to represent is greater than 99, we use another column for the "hundreds," and so on. You might notice that each additional column is ten times greater than the preceding one: ones, tens, hundreds, thousands, and so forth—all "Powers of 10": 10^1, 10^2, 10^3, and so on. Base10 is easy because most of us have 10 fingers and have known how to count from an early age.

In binary, or Base2, a single character or column can represent one of only two values: 0 or 1. The next column represents how many "twos" there are; the next column how many "fours," and so on. You'll notice here that the value of each additional column is two times greater than the previous—all "Powers of 2": 2^1, 2^2, 2^3, and so on. This is not a coincidence.

Given that a Base2 or binary column can have only two possible values (0 or 1), this makes it easy to represent a binary value as an electrical value: either off (0) or on (1). Computers use binary because it is easily represented as electrical signals in memory or digital values on storage media. The whole system works because computers are quick at computing arithmetic, and as you'll learn, pretty much all computer operations are really just fast binary math.

Let's take a look at some Base10 (or decimal) to binary conversions. Take the decimal number 176. Those three digits tell us that we have one 100, plus seven 10s, plus six 1s. Table 3.1 illustrates how decimal numbers represent this distribution of values.

TABLE 3.1 Decimal Values

100,000s	10,000s	1000s	100s	10s	1s
0	0	0	1	7	6

Notice that we have some zeroes in the high-value columns; we can drop those from the beginning if we want to. You will not have to analyze decimal numbers in this way on the exam; we are simply demonstrating how Base10 works so it can be compared to Base2 and Base16 in the same way.

In binary, the columns have different values—the powers of 2. Table 3.2 lists the values of the lowest eight bits in binary.

TABLE 3.2 Binary Values

128	64	32	16	8	4	2	1

> **NOTE**
>
> The biggest values in a binary string (the ones at the left) are often called the "high-order" bits because they have the highest value. Similarly, the lowest-value bits at the right are referred to as the "low-order" bits.

> **TIP**
>
> You must know the value of each binary bit position! If you have difficulty memorizing them, try starting at 1 and keep doubling as you go to the left.

To represent the decimal number 176 in binary, we need to figure out which columns (or bit positions) are "on" and which are "off." Now, because this is arithmetic, there are a few different ways to do this.

Start with the decimal number you want to convert:

176

Next, look at the values of each binary bit position and decide if you can subtract the highest column value and end up with a value of 0 or more. Ask yourself: "Can I subtract 128 from 176?" In this case, 176-128 = 48.

Yes, you can subtract 128 from 176 and get a positive value, 48. Because we "used" the 128 column, we put a 1 in that column, as shown in Table 3.3.

TABLE 3.3   Building a Binary String, Part 1

128	64	32	16	8	4	2	1
1							

Now, we try to subtract the next highest column value from the remainder. We get 176 – 128 = 48. We take the 48 and subtract 64 from it.

Notice that you can't do this without getting a negative number; this is not allowed, so we can't use the 64 column. Therefore, we put a 0 in that column, as shown in Table 3.4.

TABLE 3.4   Building a Binary String, Part 2

128	64	32	16	8	4	2	1
1	0						

Move along and do the math for the rest of the columns: 48 – 32 = 16. We then subtract 16 from 16 and get 0.

Note that when you get to 0, you are finished—you need to only fill the remaining bit positions with 0s to complete the 8-bit string. So, we used only the 128 column, the 32 column, and the 16 column. Table 3.5 is what we end up with.

TABLE 3.5   Completed Binary Conversion

128	64	32	16	8	4	2	1
1	0	1	1	0	0	0	0

176 decimal = 10110000 binary.

If you add up 128+32+16, you get 176. That is how you convert from binary to decimal: Simply add up the column values where there is a 1.

EXAM ALERT

You will see several questions on converting from decimal to binary and back, so prepare accordingly.

Hexadecimal

The CCNA exam(s) will ask you a few questions on the conversion of binary to hexadecimal and back, so you need to understand how it works. An understanding of hex is also a useful skill for other areas of networking and computer science.

Binary is Base2; Decimal is Base10; Hexadecimal is Base16. Each column in hex can represent 16 possible values, from 0 through 15. In order to represent a value of 10 through 15 with a single character, hex uses the letters A through F. It is important to understand that the values of 0 through 15 are the possible values of a 4-bit binary number, as shown in Table 3.6.

TABLE 3.6 Decimal, Binary, and Hex Values Compared

Decimal	Binary	Hex
0	0000	0
1	0001	1
2	0010	2
3	0011	3
4	0100	4
5	0101	5
6	0110	6
7	0111	7
8	1000	8
9	1001	9
10	1010	A
11	1011	B
12	1100	C
13	1101	D
14	1110	E
15	1111	F

EXAM ALERT

You should be able to reproduce Table 3.6 as a quick reference for the exam.

Conversion Between Binary, Hex, and Decimal

The following sections provide an introduction to converting between binary, hex, and decimal. Again, there is more than one mathematical approach to finding the correct answer, but the method shown is simple and reliable.

Decimal to Hexadecimal Conversions

The easiest way to get from decimal to hexadecimal and back is to go through binary. Take the example we used earlier in which we converted 176 decimal to binary:

176 = 10110000

Given that a single hex character represents 4 binary bits, all we need to do is to break the 8-bit string 10110000 into two 4-bit strings like this:

1011   0000

Now, simply match the 4-bit strings to their hex equivalent:

1011 = B

0000 = 0

The answer is simply 10110000 = 0xB0.

The "0x" in front of the answer is an expression that means "the following is in hex." This is needed because if the hex value was 27, we could not distinguish it from 27 decimal.

Hexadecimal to Decimal Conversions

The reverse of the procedure is easier than it seems, too. Given a hex value of 0xC4, all we need to do is to first convert to binary, and then to decimal.

To convert to binary, take the two hex characters and find their binary value:

C = 1100

0100 = 4

Now, make the two 4-bit strings into one 8–bit string:

11000100

Finally, add the bit values of the columns where you have a 1:

128 + 64 + 4 = 196

> **EXAM ALERT**
>
> It is critical to polish your skills in binary. You must be confident and quick in conversions, and the better your understanding of binary, the easier subnetting and other advanced IP topics will be for you. Practice, practice, practice!

IP Address Components

CCNA candidates need to be fluent in their understanding of IP addressing concepts. The following sections detail how IP addresses are organized and analyzed, with a view to answering subnetting questions.

Address Class

Early in the development of IP, the IANA (Internet Assigned Numbers Authority) designated five classes of IP address: A, B, C, D, and E. These classes were identified based on the pattern of high-order bits (the high-value bits at the beginning of the first octet). The result is that certain ranges of networks are grouped into classes in a pattern based on the binary values of those high-order bits, as detailed in Table 3.7:

TABLE 3.7   Address Class and Range

Class	High-Order Bits	1st Octet Range
A	0	1–126
B	10	128–191
C	110	192–223
D	1110	224–239
E	11110	240–255

You might notice that 127 is missing. This is because at some point the address 127.0.0.1 was reserved for the loopback (sometimes called "localhost") IP—this is the IP of the TCP/IP protocol itself on every host machine.

EXAM ALERT

You absolutely must be able to identify the class of an address just by looking at what number is in the first octet. This is critical to answering subnetting questions.

Default Subnet Mask

Each class of address is associated with a default subnet mask, as shown in Table 3.8. An address using its default mask defines a single IP broadcast domain—all the hosts using that same network number and mask can receive each other's broadcasts and communicate via IP.

TABLE 3.8   Address Class and Default Masks

Class	Default Mask
A	255.0.0.0
B	255.255.0.0
C	255.255.255.0

One of the rules that Cisco devices follow is that a subnet mask must be a contiguous string of 1s followed by a contiguous string of 0s. There are no exceptions to this rule: A valid mask is always a string of 1s, followed by 0s to fill up the rest of the 32 bits. (There is no such rule in the real world, but we will stick to the Cisco rules here—it's a Cisco exam, after all.)

Therefore, the only possible valid values in any given octet of a subnet mask are 0, 128, 192, 224, 240, 248, 252, 254, and 255. Any other value is invalid.

EXAM ALERT

You should practice associating the correct default subnet mask with any given IP address; this is another critical skill in subnetting.

The Network Field

Every IP address is composed of a network component and a host component. The subnet mask has a single purpose: to identify which part of an IP address is the network component and which part is the host component. Look at a 32-bit IP address expressed in binary, with the subnet mask written right below it. Figure 3.1 shows an example.

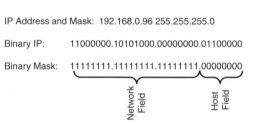

IP Address and Mask: 192.168.0.96 255.255.255.0

Binary IP: 11000000.10101000.00000000.01100000

Binary Mask: 11111111.11111111.11111111.00000000

Network Field   Host Field

Figure 3.1   IP address and mask in binary, showing network and host fields.

Anywhere you see a binary 1 in the subnet mask, it means "the matching bit in the IP address is part of the network component." In this example, the network part of the address is 192.168.0.X, and the last octet (X) will be the host component.

Because there are 24 bits in a row in the mask, we can also use a shortcut for the mask notation of /24. These examples show how a dotted decimal mask can be expressed in slash notation:

192.168.1.66 255.255.255.0 = 192.168.1.66 /24

172.16.0.12 255.255.0.0 = 172.16.0.12 /16

10.1.1.1 255.0.0.0 = 10.1.1.1 /8

This slash notation is sometimes called CIDR (Classless Inter-Domain Routing) notation. For some reason, it's a concept that confuses students, but honestly it's the easiest concept of all: The slash notation is simply the number of 1s in a row in the subnet mask. The real reason to use CIDR notation is simply that it is easier to say and especially to type—and it appears interchangeably with dotted decimal throughout the exam. CIDA notation also appears in the output of various IOS commands.

Every IP address has a host component and a network component, and the 1s in the mask tell us which bits in the address identify the network component.

The Host Field

If the 1s in the mask identify the network component of an address, the 0s at the end of the mask identify the host component. In the preceding example, the entire last octet is available for the host IP number.

The number of 0s at the end of the mask mathematically define how many hosts can be on any given network or subnet. The 1s in the mask always identify the network component, and the 0s at the end of the mask always identify the host component of any IP address.

Non-Default Masks

At this point, you should be able to recognize what class an address belongs to, and what its default mask is supposed to be. Here's the big secret: If a mask is longer than it is supposed to be, that network has been subnetted. So it is clearly another critical skill that you be able to spot those non-default masks.

The Subnet Field

Because we have extended the subnet mask past the default boundary into the bits that were previously host bits, we identify the bits we "stole" from the host part as the subnet field. The subnet field is relevant because those bits mathematically define how many subnets we create. Figure 3.2 uses the same IP address from our previous example, but now we have applied a subnetted mask that is longer than the default. Note that this creates the subnet field.

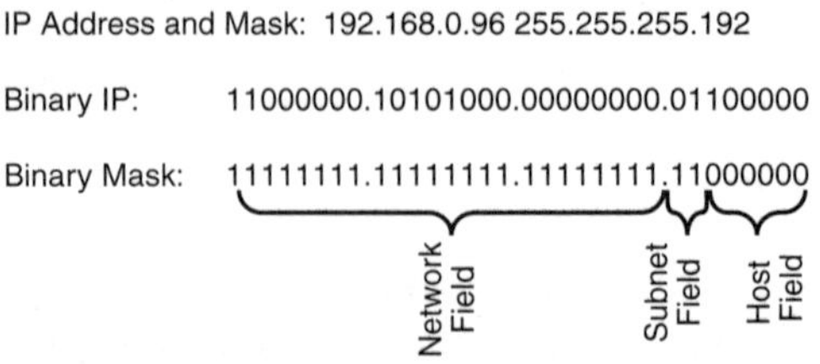

IP Address and Mask: 192.168.0.96 255.255.255.192

Binary IP: 11000000.10101000.00000000.01100000

Binary Mask: 11111111.11111111.11111111.11000000

Network Field   Subnet Field   Host Field

FIGURE 3.2   IP address and non-default mask in binary illustrating the subnet field.

Figure 3.2 identifies the two extra bits past the default boundary as the subnet field—they used to be in the host field, but we subnetted and stole them to become the subnet field.

Subnetting

Subnetting is not as difficult as it initially seems. Because we are dealing with arithmetic, there is definitely more than one way to do this, but the method shown here has worked well. The following sections work through the process of subnetting. Then, we work on some shortcuts to show how you can subnet quickly because CCNA exam candidates often find that they are pressed for time on the exam.

Address Class and Default Mask

Subnetting happens when we extend the subnet mask past the default boundary for the address we are working with. So it's obvious that we first need to be sure of what the default mask is supposed to be for any given address. Previously, we looked at the IANA designations for IP address classes and the number ranges in the first octet that identify those classes. If you didn't pick up on this before, you should memorize those immediately.

When faced with a subnetting question, the first thing to do is decide what class the address belongs to. Here are some examples:

192.168.1.66

The first octet is between 192 and 223: Class C

Default mask for Class C: 255.255.255.0

188.21.21.3

The first octet is between 128 and 191: Class B

Default mask for Class B: 255.255.0.0

24.64.208.5

The first octet is between 1 and 126: Class A

Default mask for Class A: 255.0.0.0

It's important to grasp that if an address uses the correct default mask for its class, it is not subnetted. This means that regardless of how many hosts the 0s at the end of the mask create, all those hosts are on the same network, all in the same broadcast domain. This has some implications for *classful networks* (ones that use the default mask for the address). Take a Class A for example: A Class A network can have 16,777,214 hosts on it. Almost 17 million PCs on one network would never work—there would be so much traffic from broadcasts alone, never mind regular data traffic, that nothing could get through and the network would collapse under its own size. Even a Class B network has 65,534 possible host IPs. This is still too many. So, either we waste a lot of addresses by not using the whole classful A or B network, or we subnet to make the networks smaller.

This is actually one of the most common reasons we subnet: The default or classful networks are too big, causing issues such as excessive broadcast traffic and wasted IP address space. Subnetting creates multiple smaller subnetworks out of one larger classful network, which allows us to make IP networks the "right" size—big or small—for any given situation.

The Increment

By definition, the process of subnetting creates several smaller classless subnets out of one larger classful one. The spacing between these subnets, or how many IP addresses apart they are, is called the *Increment*. Because we are working with binary numbers, a pattern emerges in which the Increment is always one of those powers of 2 again—another good reason to memorize those numbers.

The Increment is really easy to figure out. It is simply the value of the last bit in the subnet mask. Let's look at some examples. Figure 3.3 shows an IP address and subnet mask in binary.

IP Address and Mask: 192.168.21.1 255.255.255.0

Binary IP: 11000000.10101000.00010101.00000001

Binary Mask: 11111111.11111111.11111111.11000000

FIGURE 3.3 IP address and mask in binary.

Note that this is a Class C address, and it uses the correct default mask—so it is not subnetted. This means that there is only one network, so there isn't really an increment to worry about here. It's sufficient at this point to recognize that an address that uses its default mask creates one network (no subnets), so there is no spacing between subnets to consider.

Let's take the same address and subnet it by extending the mask past the default boundary, as shown in Figure 3.4.

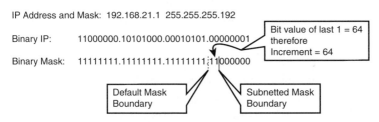

IP Address and Mask: 192.168.21.1 255.255.255.192

Binary IP: 11000000.10101000.00010101.00000001

Binary Mask: 11111111.11111111.11111111.11000000

Bit value of last 1 = 64 therefore Increment = 64

Default Mask Boundary

Subnetted Mask Boundary

FIGURE 3.4 IP address and subnetted mask.

The very last bit in the subnet mask in the figure is in the bit position worth 64—so the Increment in this case is 64, which means that the subnets we made are evenly spaced at 64 IP addresses apart.

Think about this for a second. We are doing the subnetting in the fourth octet—that is where the mask changes from 1s to 0s. (The octet where this happens is sometimes referred to as the "Interesting" octet.) The lowest possible value in that fourth octet is 0. If the subnets are 64 IP addresses apart, this means that the first subnet starts at 0, the next one starts at 64, the third at 128, and the fourth at 192—all multiples of the Increment. Note that if we add another 64 to that last 192, we get 256—and that is larger than 255, the largest value that is possible in one octet. So this means we only have room for four subnets. Figure 3.5 illustrates this pattern more clearly:

.0	.64	.128	.192
.1	.65	.129	.193
.	.	.	.
.	.	.	.
.	.	.	.
.62	.126	.190	.254
.63	.127	.191	.255

FIGURE 3.5 Subnets created with Increment of 64.

The multiples of the Increment—0, 64, 128, and 192—are the starting address-es of the subnets we created. The subnets are all 64 addresses long, so we have room to make four subnets before we run out of addresses in the fourth octet.

Figure 3.6 shows our IP and subnet mask—note that the value of the last bit in the mask is 16—and the subnets created with that Increment of 16.

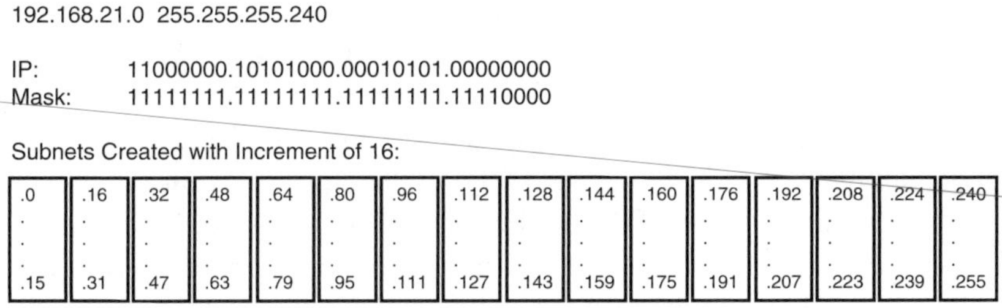

192.168.21.0 255.255.255.240

```
IP:     11000000.10101000.00010101.00000000
Mask:   11111111.11111111.11111111.11110000
```

Subnets Created with Increment of 16:

.0	.16	.32	.48	.64	.80	.96	.112	.128	.144	.160	.176	.192	.208	.224	.240
.	.	.	.	.	.	.	.	.	.	.	.	.	.	.	.
.15	.31	.47	.63	.79	.95	.111	.127	.143	.159	.175	.191	.207	.223	.239	.255

FIGURE 3.6 IP address and subnet mask with Increment of 16.

First of all, you should notice that we are subnetting again—the mask extends past the default boundary. The last 1 in the mask is in the bit position worth 16, so our Increment is 16. The multiples of 16 are 0, 16, 32, 48, 64, 80, 96, 112, 128, 144, 160, 176, 192, 208, 224, and 240. Again, we can't make another sub-net because 240 + 16 = 256. Be careful not to start doubling as we did with the binary values; here we are just adding the Increment value each time. It's easy to get confused!

The Increment is really the key to subnetting; if you can determine the Increment, you can see how big your subnets are and how many you have cre-ated. Remember, the easy way to find the Increment is to just determine the bit value of the last 1 in the mask.

Number of Hosts

The number of 0s at the end of the mask always defines the number of hosts on any network or subnet. There is a simple mathematical formula that defines how many IP addresses are available to be assigned to hosts.

> **NOTE**
>
> *Hosts* is another word for computers, router interfaces, printers, or any other network component that can be assigned an IP address.

Now, no one expects you to be a big fan of algebra, but you need to see and understand the formula.

The number of binary bits you have to use determines the maximum number of different values you can express using those bits. If you have three bits, you can make eight different values—0 through 7, or 000 through 111 in binary. Three bits, and $2^3=8$—this is not a coincidence. The binary values you learned earlier— 1, 2, 4, 8, 16, 32, 64, 128—are all powers of 2 and define the maximum number of different values you can create if the mask ends in that bit position. So it should come as no surprise that the formula for the number of hosts on any network or subnet is 2^H-2, where H is the number of 0s at the end of the mask.

But why do we subtract 2 in the formula? It's pretty straightforward: Every network or subnet has two reserved addresses that cannot be assigned to a host. The rule is that no host can have the IP address in which all the host bits are set to 0, and no host can have the IP address in which all the host bits are set to 1. These addresses are called the Network ID and the Broadcast ID, respectively. They are the first and last IPs in any network or subnet. We lose those two IP addresses from the group of values that could be assigned to hosts.

Think of a network or subnet as a street with houses on it. Each house has a unique address, and the street has a name. The Network ID is like the street name, and all the houses are hosts on a subnet that is known by its Network ID street name. If two hosts have identical network and subnet fields in their addresses, they are on the same network, and can ping each other and exchange data and all that good stuff. If the network and subnet fields are different, even by one bit, they are on different networks and can't communicate until we put a router between them. The routers act like street intersections; you must get to the right intersection (router) before you can get on to the street you want... but we'll save that for later.

In a network where there are no routers, devices running TCP/IP make a decision about whether a particular IP address is on the network by performing a logical AND operation. The AND is a Boolean function that works like this:

1 AND 1 = 1

1 AND 0 = 0

0 AND 0 = 0

This operation applies to IP networking like this: A host does a logical AND between its own IP and its mask. This determines its Network ID. The host can then do an AND between another IP address and its own mask to determine if that second address is on the same network or some other one.

Let's take the IP address and mask of an imaginary host and display them in binary, as shown in Figure 3.7. The AND operation takes each bit in the address and ANDs it with the corresponding bit in the mask below it; the result is the NetID of the host.

IP Address and Mask: 192.16.20.12 255.255.255.0

Binary IP: 11000000.00010000.00010100.00001100

Binary Mask: 11111111.11111111.11111111.00000000

AND Result: 11000000.00010000.00010100.00000000

           NetID = 192.16.20.0

FIGURE 3.7 The AND operation determines the NetID.

Now the host knows its own NetID and can compare any other host's address to that to see if the other host has the same NetID. If the two NetIDs are different, traffic has to be sent through a router to get to the other network—and if there is no router, the two hosts can't communicate.

EXAM ALERT

Being able to do the AND operation is a useful skill; a lot of test questions center around the NetID, and being able to find it quickly is a big help.

The Broadcast ID

The *Broadcast ID* is the address of everybody on that network or subnet. Sometimes called a directed broadcast, it is the common address of all hosts on that Network ID. This should not be confused with a full IP broadcast to the address of 255.255.255.255, which hits every IP host that can hear it; the Broadcast ID hits only hosts on a common subnet.

Let's take the previous example of an Increment of 64 and expand on the detail, as shown in Figure 3.8:

Subnets Created with Increment of 64 – NetID and Broadcast ID shown:

.0 N	.64 N	.128 N	.192 N
.1	.65	.129	.193
.	.	.	.
.	.	.	.
.	.	.	.
.62	.126	.190	.254
.63 B	.127 B	.191 B	.255 B

FIGURE 3.8   Subnets from Increment of 64 with NetID and Broadcast ID shown.

Note that all the multiples of the Increment—the numbers that mark the start of each subnet—have been identified by an "N" for Network ID, and the last IP in every subnet is marked with a "B" for Broadcast ID. This leaves us with 62 IPs left over in each subnet, and any of these (but only these) can be assigned to a host.

This leaves us with a range of IP addresses within every network or subnet that can be assigned to hosts. There is an unofficial convention that the gateway or router for a subnet is assigned the first or the last IP address available, but that is entirely arbitrary.

EXAM ALERT

You need to know exactly what the first and last IP addresses are in any subnet; a lot of questions ask for them, and it's fundamental to understanding what is happening when you subnet.

The first valid IP address is defined as

NetID + 1

In Figure 3.8, the first valid host IPs in each subnet are .1, .65, .129, and .193.

The last valid host is defined as

BroadcastID − 1

In Figure 3.8, the last valid host IPs in each subnet are .62, .126, .190, and .254.

See how the subnetted mask in the previous example has shortened the number of 0s at the end of the mask as compared to the default of 8? We now have only six 0s in the host part, so our formula would be

$$2^6 - 2 = 62$$

Here's something interesting: It doesn't matter what IP address you use with this mask; that mask will always give you 62 hosts on each subnet. You can pick a Class A address, say 22.1.1.0, and that mask would still make 62 hosts per subnet. The number of 0s at the end of the mask always drives how many hosts are on each subnet, regardless of the address.

So, what happened to all the other host IPs we started with? Remember that subnetting takes a classful A, B, or C network and splits it into several equal-sized pieces. It's just like cutting a pie into pieces; the original amount of pie is still there, but each piece is now separate and smaller.

Remember that the number of 0s at the end at the mask always defines how many hosts are on each subnet, regardless of the address in use.

Number of Subnets

Following on with the pie analogy, we know that we slice a classful network into pieces—but how many pieces? There is a simple mathematical relationship to this as well, but it is slightly more complex because of an old rule that we sometimes have to deal with.

The basic formula for the number of subnets is similar to the hosts formula. It is simply 2^S, where S is the number of bits in the subnet field—that means the number of 1s in the mask past the default boundary for that address. If you look at Figure 3.9, you can see how this works.

The default boundary for that Class C address should be at the 24th bit, where the third octet ends and the fourth begins. The subnetted mask extends that by 2 bits into the fourth octet. So, we have stolen 2 bits, and our formula would look like this:

# of subnets = 2^s

$S = 2$

$2^2 = 4$

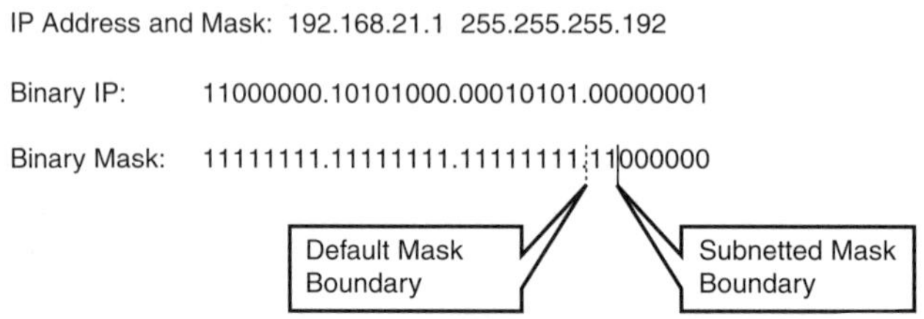

IP Address and Mask: 192.168.21.1 255.255.255.192

Binary IP: 11000000.10101000.00010101.00000001

Binary Mask: 11111111.11111111.11111111.11000000

Default Mask Boundary   Subnetted Mask Boundary

FIGURE 3.9   Subnetted Class C with Increment of 64.

We made four subnets, as you saw earlier. To figure out how many bits we stole, we first must know where the default boundary is so that we know where to start counting. This is where knowing the address classes and the correct default masks is critical; if you can't figure this out, you will not be able to answer most subnetting questions correctly, and that would be bad.

Now here's where things get tricky. A rule that some older systems use says that the first and last subnets created are invalid and unusable. The rule is known as the Subnet Zero Rule, and obviously if it is in effect, we lose two subnets from the total we create. These two subnets will be referred to from now on as the *zero subnets*. Newer systems do not use the Zero Subnets Rule, including newer Cisco devices. This is confusing and makes things more difficult—but difficult is not something Cisco shies away from on its certification exams. So if you want your CCNA, pay attention to the question and don't complain about how hard it is.

EXAM ALERT

Cisco tests might be difficult and tricky, but they are fair—they will not withhold information you need to answer the question. The test question will always tell you whether somehow the Zero Subnets Rule is in effect; yes, both types of questions are asked.

The Cisco IOS supports the use of the Zero Subnets. The command "ip subnet zero" turns on the ability to use them, so that might be how the question is telling you whether they are in effect. Once you pass your CCNA, you will not likely have to worry about the Zero Subnets Rule again, unless you lose your mind and decide to become a Cisco trainer.

TIP

After you determine whether the zero subnets are available, use the following to get the calculation for the number of subnets right:

Zero subnets not available?   Subtract 2 subnets: formula is 2S-2

Zero subnets available?   Keep all subnets: formula is 2S

Working with Subnetting Questions

EXAM ALERT

The approach you need to take to any subnetting question is very simple. After you become fluent in subnetting, you can take some shortcuts; but to build a solid understanding, you need to be methodical.

Every subnetting question you ever see will be about one of three things:

▶ **Number of hosts**

▶ **Number of subnets**

▶ **The Increment**

Your task will be to simply figure out what the question is asking for and solve it without getting confused or distracted.

Determining Host Requirements

There are only two scenarios when determining the host requirements: Either you are given a mask and asked how many hosts per subnet this creates, or you are given a requirement for a certain number of hosts and asked to provide the appropriate mask. Either way, the number of 0s at the end of the mask drives how many hosts per subnet there will be; the address to which that mask is applied is irrelevant. Your task is to put the correct number of 0s at the end of the mask such that 2H-2 is greater than or equal to the desired number of hosts, or to determine what the value of 2H-2 actually is. From there, you must choose the correct expression of the mask, either in dotted decimal or CIDR notation.

Determining Subnet Requirements

The scenarios for determining subnet requirements are quite similar to the host questions; either you are told how many subnets you need and asked to provide the appropriate mask, or you are given a mask and asked how many subnets it creates. Note that in both cases (unlike hosts questions), you must know the IP address or at least the class of address you are working with. Creating subnets happens by extending the default mask, so you must know where the mask should end by default—and for that you need to know the class of address. Once you know where to start, simply extend the mask by the correct number of subnet bits such that 2S-2 (or possibly just 2S) gives you the correct number of subnets.

> **EXAM ALERT**
>
> Remember that the zero subnets rule might come into play here; although the majority of questions say that the zero subnets are not valid and therefore the formula should be 2S-2, some questions—and probably more as time goes on—will clearly state that zero subnets are available. Read the question!

Determining Increment-based Requirements

Increment questions are the most challenging and complex subnetting questions, often requiring you to do a lot of legwork before you can get to the answer.

Increment questions often give you two or more IP addresses and masks, and ask you things such as, "Why can't Host A ping Host B?" The answer could be that A and B are on different subnets; to determine this, you need to understand where those subnets begin and end, and that depends on the Increment. Another popular question gives you several IP addresses and masks that are applied to PCs, servers, and routers. The system, as it is described, is not working, and you need to determine what device has been incorrectly configured—perhaps two IPs in different subnets, perhaps a host that is using a NetID or BroadcastID as its address.

The key is to first determine what the Increment is or should be; then, carefully plot out the multiples of the Increment—the Network IDs of all the subnets. Then you can add the Broadcast IDs, which are all one less than the next Network ID. Now you have a framework into which you can literally draw the host IP ranges, without risk of "losing the picture" if you do this all in your head.

All of these skills take practice. Everyone goes through the same process in learning subnetting: For quite a while, you will have no idea what is going on—then suddenly, the light goes on and you "get it." Rest assured that you will get it. It takes longer for some than others, and you do need practice or you will lose the skill.

The Subnetting Chart

So now you should understand concepts and mechanics of subnetting. You can do it and get the right answer almost all of the time, but it takes you a while. This is good—congratulations! If you are not at that point yet, you should practice more before you look at this next section.

What follows is one of many variations of a subnetting chart. This is a good one because it is easy to use under pressure when your brain will behave unpredictably.

> **CAUTION**
>
> You must be able to re-create this chart exactly and correctly before you start your exam. If you make a simple mistake in creating your chart, you could easily get all of your subnetting questions wrong, and that would probably cause you to fail.

The chart represents the last two octets of a subnet mask, and what effect a 1 or a 0 in the different bit positions will have. It lists the Increment, CIDR notation, the mask in decimal, the number of hosts created, and the number of subnets formed from a Class B and C address. Figure 3.10 shows a completed version.

Increment	128	64	32	16	8	4	2	1	128	64	32	16	8	4	2	1
CIDR:	/17	/18	/19	/20	/21	/22	/23	/24	/25	/26	/27	/28	/29	/30	/31	/32
Mask:	128	192	224	240	248	252	254	255	128	192	224	240	248	252	254	255
Hosts:	32,766	16,382	8190	4094	2046	1022	510	254	126	62	30	14	6	2	-	-
B Subnets:	0	2	6	14	30	62	126	254	510	1024	2046	4094	8190	16,382	-	-
C Subnets:	1	1	1	1	1	1	1	1	0	2	6	14	30	62	-	-

FIGURE 3.10 The subnetting chart.

Following are steps to recreate the chart:

1. The first row is simply the binary bit position values—the powers of 2. Start at the right with 1 and keep doubling the value as you go left: 1, 2, 4, 8, 16, 32, 64, 128. Repeat for the third octet.

2. The second row is the CIDR notation—the number of 1s in a row in the mask. Our chart starts at the 17th bit, so number the second row starting at 17, through 32.

3. The third row is the mask in binary. Add consecutive bit values together from left to right to get the valid mask values of 128, 192, 224, 240, 248, 252, 254, and 255. Or you can just memorize them.

4. The fourth row is the number of hosts created. Starting at the right side of the fourth octet, subtract 2 from the increment line (the first line) and enter that value. Do this for the whole fourth octet. When you get to the third octet (the left half of the chart), you will have to change your approach: The value will keep increasing in the same pattern, but subtracting 2 from the top row won't work anymore because the top row resets for the third octet. The simplest approach is to double the last value and add 2. For example, (126x2)+2=254; (254x2)+2=510; and so on.

5. The fifth row is the number of subnets created from a Class B address. Starting at the left side of the chart (the third octet), repeat the values from the fourth line, but in reverse order. Remember to start with a single 0 instead of two.

CAUTION

> Remember that the Subnet Zero Rule will change your answers and how you use your chart. If the Zero Subnets are allowed, add 2 to the values in lines 5 and 6 of your chart in the appropriate octet.

6. The sixth row of the chart is the number of subnets created from a Class C address. Remember, with a Class C, we do not make any subnets (that is, we have only one network) in the third octet, so we have all 1s there. For the fourth octet, the numbers are the same as in Row 5; just start them in the fourth octet instead. The same caution and tactic about the Zero Subnets applies.

Provided you have built it correctly, your chart is a huge help in answering subnetting questions quickly and accurately. All you need to do is determine what the question is asking for, and then look up that value on your chart. All of the answers you need will be in the same column. Practice building and using the chart until it becomes something you can do without thinking. You will need your brain for other more complicated problems.

Exam Prep Questions

1. Which of the following are alternate representations of the decimal number 227? Choose 2.

   ○ **A.** 0x227

   ○ **B.** 11100011

   ○ **C.** 0x143

   ○ **D.** 0xE3

   ○ **E.** 11100110

2. Which of the following are alternate representations of 0xB8? Choose two.

   ○ **A.** 10110100

   ○ **B.** 10111111

   ○ **C.** 10111000

   ○ **D.** 184

   ○ **E.** 0x184

3. You have been asked to create a subnet that supports 16 hosts. What subnet mask should you use?

   ○ **A.** 255.255.255.252

   ○ **B.** 255.255.255.248

   ○ **C.** 255.255.255.240

   ○ **D.** 255.255.255.224

4. Given the mask 255.255.254.0, how many hosts per subnet does this create?

   ○ **A.** 254

   ○ **B.** 256

   ○ **C.** 512

   ○ **D.** 510

   ○ **E.** 2

5. You are a senior network engineer at True North Technologies. Your boss, Mr. Martin, asks you to create a subnet with room for 12 IPs for some new managers. Mr. Martin promises that there will never be more than 12 managers, and he asks you to make sure that you conserve IP address space by providing the minimum number of possible host IPs on the subnet. What subnet mask will best meet these requirements?

○ **A.** 255.255.255.12

○ **B.** 255.255.255.0

○ **C.** 255.255.240.0

○ **D.** 255.255.255.240

○ **E.** 255.255.255.224

6. Your boss Duncan does not seem to be able to grasp subnetting. He comes out of a management meeting and quietly asks you to help him with a subnetting issue. He needs to divide the Class B address space the company uses into six subnets for the various buildings in the plant, while keeping the subnets as large as possible to allow for future growth. Because the company has not upgraded their Cisco equipment since it was purchased several years ago, none of the routers supports the "ip subnet zero" command. What is the best subnet mask to use in this scenario?

○ **A.** 255.255.0.0

○ **B.** 255.255.248.0

○ **C.** 255.255.224.0

○ **D.** 255.255.240.0

○ **E.** 255.255.255.224

7. You have purchased several brand-new Cisco routers for your company. Your current address space is 172.16.0.0 /22. Because these new routers support the "ip subnet zero" command, you realize you are about to gain back two subnets that you could not use with the old gear. How many subnets total will be available to you once the upgrades are complete?

○ **A.** 4

○ **B.** 2

○ **C.** 32

○ **D.** 62

○ **E.** 64

8. Which of the following are true about the following address and mask pair: 10.8.8.0 /24? Choose all that apply.

   ○ **A.** This is a Class B address.

   ○ **B.** This is a Class A address.

   ○ **C.** This is a Class C address.

   ○ **D.** 16 bits were stolen from the host field.

   ○ **E.** 24 bits were stolen from the host field.

   ○ **F.** The default mask for this address is 255.0.0.0.

   ○ **G.** The mask can also be written as 255.255.255.0.

   ○ **H.** The mask creates 65,536 subnets total from the default address space.

   ○ **I.** Each subnet supports 256 valid host IPs.

   ○ **J.** Each subnet supports 254 valid host IPs.

9. Indy and Greg have configured their own Windows XP PCs and connected them with crossover cables. They can't seem to share their downloaded MP3 files, however. Given their configurations, what could be the problem?

Indy's configuration:

IP: 192.168.0.65

Mask: 255.255.255.192

Greg's configuration:

IP: 192.168.0.62

Mask: 255.255.255.192

   ○ **A.** Indy is using a Broadcast ID for his IP.

   ○ **B.** Greg is using an invalid mask.

   ○ **C.** Indy's IP is in one of the Zero Subnets.

   ○ **D.** Greg and Indy are using IPs in different subnets.

10. You are given an old router to practice for your CCNA. Your boss Dave has spent a lot of time teaching you subnetting. Now he challenges you to apply your knowledge. He hands you a note that says:

"Given the subnetted address space of 192.168.1.0 /29, give the E0 interface the first valid IP in the eighth subnet. Give the S0 interface the last valid IP in the twelfth subnet. The Zero Subnets are available. You have 10 minutes. Go."

Which two of the following are the correct IP and Mask configurations? Choose 2.

- ○ **A.** E0: 192.168.1.1   255.255.255.0
- ○ **B.** E0: 192.168.1.56   255.255.255.248
- ○ **C.** E0: 192.168.1.57   255.255.255.248
- ○ **D.** S0: 192.168.1.254   255.255.255.0
- ○ **E.** S0: 192.168.1.95   255.255.255.248
- ○ **F.** S0: 192.168.1.94   255.255.255.248

11. The following questions are part of a Subnetting SuperChallenge. This monster question will stretch your subnetting skills, especially if you give yourself a time limit. Start with 10 minutes and see if you can get down to 5.

    The Vancouver Sailing Company has four locations: a head office and three branch offices. Each of the branches is connected to the head office by a point-to-point T1 circuit. The branches have one or more LANs connected to their routers. The routers are called Main, Jib, Genoa, and Spinnaker. The company has been assigned the 172.16.0.0/20 address space to work within.

    Your task will be to choose the correct IP address and mask for each interface, based on the information provided. Remember that no IP address may overlap with any address in another subnet, and that the required number of hosts for each subnet will affect your decision as to which address to use.

    Here are the known IP configurations for the routers:

    Main:

    S0/0:172.16.0.1 /30

    S0/1:172.16.0.5 /30

    S0/2:172.16.0.9 /30

    Fa1/0:172.16.4.1 /23

    Fa1/1:172.16.6.1 /23

    Jib:

    S0/0: Connects to Main S0/0.

    Fa1/0: 172.16.8.33/27.

    Fa1/1: 30 hosts needed.

    Genoa:

    S0/0: Connects to Main S0/1.

    Fa1/0: 172.16.8.129/26.

Fa1/1: 100 hosts needed.

Fa2/0: 100 hosts needed.

Fa2/1: 172.16.13.0/24.

Spinnaker:

S0/0: connects to Main S0/2.

Fa1/0: 500 Hosts needed.

Choose the correct IP and mask assignments for each router:

- ❍ **A.** Jib Fa1/1: 172.16.8.62/27
- ❍ **B.** Jib Fa1/1: 172. 16.8.64/27
- ❍ **C.** Jib Fa1/1: 172.16.8.65/28
- ❍ **D.** Jib Fa1/0: 172.16.8.65/27
- ❍ **E.** Jib Fa1/1: 172.16.8.65/27
- ❍ **F.** Genoa S0/0: 172.16.0.2/30
- ❍ **G.** Genoa S0/0:172.16.0.6/30
- ❍ **H.** Genoa Fa1/1:172.16.12.1/26
- ❍ **I.** Genoa Fa1/1:172.16.12.1/25
- ❍ **J.** Genoa Fa2/0:172.16.12.129/24
- ❍ **K.** Genoa Fa2/0:172.16.12.129/25
- ❍ **L.** Genoa Fa2/1:172.16.12.193/25
- ❍ **M.** Genoa Fa2/1:172.16.13.1/25
- ❍ **N.** Genoa Fa0/2:172.16.13.1/24
- ❍ **O.** Spinnaker S0/0: 172.16.0.10/30
- ❍ **P.** Spinnaker S0/0: 172.16.0.12/30
- ❍ **Q.** Spinnaker Fa1/0: 172.16.13.0/23
- ❍ **R.** Spinnaker Fa1/0: 172.16.14.0/23
- ❍ **S.** Spinnaker Fa1/0: 172.16.14.1/23

Answers to Exam Prep Questions

1. Answers B and D are correct. Answer A in decimal would be 551. Answer C in decimal would be 323. Answer E in decimal is 230.

2. Answers C and D are correct. Answer A in hex is 0xB4. Answer B in hex is 0xBF. Answer E is simply an attempt to trick you—the correct decimal answer is incorrectly expressed as a hex value.

3. Answer D is correct. A will only support 2 hosts; B only 6, and C only 14. Watch out for the minus 2 in the host calculation! Answer C creates 16 hosts on the subnet, but we lose 2—one for the Net ID and one for the Broadcast ID.

4. Answer D is correct. The mask 255.255.254.0 gives us nine 0s at the end of the mask; 2^9-2 = 510. Answer A is checking to see if you missed the 254 in the third octet because you are used to seeing 255. Answer B does the same thing plus tries to catch you on not subtracting 2 from the host calculation. Answer C tries to catch you on not subtracting 2, and Answer E is the Increment of the given mask that you might pick if you were really off track.

5. The correct answer is D. Disregarding for the moment the possibility that Mr. Martin might be wrong, let's look at the requirements. He says make room for 12 managers, and make the subnets as small as possible while doing so. You need to find the mask that has sufficient host IP space without making it bigger than necessary. Answer A is invalid; 12 is not a valid mask value. Remember, a mask is a continuous string of 1s followed by a continuous string of 0s. In answer B, the mask is valid, but it is not correct. This mask has eight 0s at the end, which, when we apply the formula 28 -2 gives us 254 hosts. That makes more than enough room for the 12 managers, but does not meet the "as small as possible" requirement. Answer C has the correct mask value in the wrong octet. That mask gives us eight 0s in the fourth octet, plus another four in the third octet; that would give us 4094 hosts on the subnet. Answer E gives us 30 hosts per subnet, but that only meets half the requirement. This mask does not provide the minimum number of hosts.

6. The correct answer is C. The default mask for a Class B is 255.255.0.0. Answer C extends that mask by three bits, creating eight subnets (2^3=8). The Zero Subnets are lost because the routers cannot use them, so we are left with six subnets. Answer A is incorrect because it is the default mask for a Class B and not subnetted at all. Answers B and D are incorrect because although they create sufficient subnets, they do not maximize the number of hosts per subnet and so are not the best answer. Answer E uses the correct mask in the wrong octet.

7. Answer E is correct. With "ip subnet zero" enabled, all 64 subnets created by the mask in use become available. Answers A, B, and C are not even close and are simply distracters. Answer D wants to catch you by subtracting the zero subnets.

8. The correct answers are B, D, F, G, H, and J. Answers A and C are incorrect because this is a Class A address. Answer E is incorrect because only 16 bits were stolen. Answer I is incorrect because it does not subtract the two IPs for the NetID and Broadcast ID.

9. Answer D is correct. With that mask, the Increment is 64. Greg is in the first subnet, and Indy is in the second. Without a router between them, their PCs will not be able to communicate above layer 2. Answer A is incorrect; the Broadcast ID for Indy would be .63. Answer B is incorrect; nothing is wrong with the mask. Answer C is incorrect; the Zero Subnets are the first and last created, and Indy is in the second subnet. The question does not mention the Zero Subnets, and in any case Windows XP fully supports them.

10. The correct answers are C and F. This is an Increment question. The Increment here is 8, so you should start by jotting down the multiples of 8 (those are all the NetIDs), and then noting what 1 less than each of the NetIDs is (those are the Broadcast IDs). From there, it is easy to find what the first and last IPs in each subnet are. (Remember that Dave says we can use the Zero Subnets.) Answers A and D are incorrect because they do not use the subnetted address space Dave requested. Answer B is incorrect because it is a NetID. Answer E is incorrect because it is a Broadcast ID.

11. SuperChallenge answers:

    A. Incorrect (same subnet as Fa1/0)

    B. Incorrect (Network ID)

    C. Incorrect (Not enough Hosts)

    D. Incorrect (Fa1/0 IP already assigned)

    E. Correct

    F. Incorrect (Wrong subnet—not on the same network as the connected interface on Main)

    G. Correct

    H. Incorrect (Not enough hosts)

    I. Correct

    J. Incorrect (Overlaps with Fa1/1)

    K. Correct

    L. Incorrect (Overlaps with Fa2/0)

    M. Incorrect (Not enough hosts)

    N. Incorrect (There is no Fa0/2 interface on Genoa)

    O. Correct

    P. Incorrect (Network ID)

    Q. Incorrect (Overlaps with Genoa)

    R. Incorrect (Network ID)

    S. Correct

CHAPTER FOUR

Working with Cisco Equipment

Terms You'll Need to Understand

✓ Interface
✓ Line
✓ User EXEC
✓ Privileged EXEC
✓ Configuration Register
✓ ROM
✓ RAM
✓ NVRAM
✓ FLASH

Techniques You'll Need to Master

✓ Navigating the Cisco IOS Command Line Interface
✓ Assigning IP Addresses
✓ Configuring Clock Rate, Bandwidth, Speed, and Duplex
✓ Enabling an Interface
✓ Troubleshooting Connectivity

Introduction

This chapter introduces you to Cisco equipment. We examine how to connect to it and make initial configurations, as well as how to connect it to other devices to build a network. We review the different types of network connections available, with particular emphasis on those that are tested in the CCNA exams. We also look at where a Cisco device stores the various files it needs to operate, the files needed for the boot process, and the backup and restoration of system files.

Products

The CCNA exam does not test you about product-specific knowledge. That is to say, you are not expected to know what feature cards are available for a 6500 series switch, but you do need to understand the differences between a router and a switch, and you need to understand how their configuration requirements vary.

For our purposes, we use a Catalyst 2960 or 3560 switch and a 1600, 1700, or 2600 series router as example devices. Most of the commands you learn in this chapter also apply to more advanced models.

External Connections

Cisco devices make connections to other devices, and collectively they all create a network. At some point, making a connection means plugging in a cable—even with a wireless system. This section examines some of the various connections found on Cisco routers and switches.

Console

When you first obtain a new Cisco device, it won't be configured. That is to say, it will not do any of the customized functions you might need; it does not have any IP addresses, and it is generally not going to do what you paid for. However, if you buy a 2960 switch, turn on the power, and plug PCs in to it, it will work to connect those PCs with no further configuration, but you are missing out on all the cool stuff and advanced features. Your new router, on the other hand, will not be capable of doing much for you at all, even if you plug devices into the interfaces. Routers need basic configuration to function on a network, or they simply consume power and blink at you.

The console port is used for *local management* connections. This means that you must be able to physically reach the console port with a cable that is typically about six feet long. The console port looks exactly like an Ethernet port. It uses the same connector, but it has different wiring and is often (but not always) identified with a pale blue label that says "CONSOLE." If the device is not configured at all—meaning, if it is new or has had a previous configuration erased—the console port is the only way to connect to it and apply configurations. Figure 4.1 shows what a console port looks like.

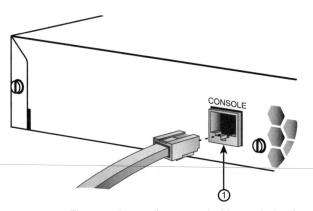

FIGURE 4.1 The console port (image used with permission from Cisco Systems, Inc.).

Connecting to the console port is done with a special *rollover* cable; a rollover cable has pins 1 through 8 wired to the opposite number, as shown in Figure 4.2.

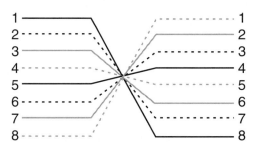

FIGURE 4.2 Rollover cable pinouts.

One end of the rollover cable has the RJ-45 connector to connect to the console port; the other has either a molded-in 9-pin serial connector, or another RJ-45 and adapters for 9-pin or 15-pin serial connections. Because many new laptops do not have the EIA/TIA 9- or 15-pin serial connections and feature USB ports only, you might need to buy yourself a USB to serial adapter. The serial connection on the rollover cable attaches to your workstation's COM port.

Now that you are plugged in, you need to configure a terminal application to communicate with the Cisco device over the rollover cable. You can use Hyperterminal, Procomm, TeraTerm, SecureCRT, or any of a number of others that support character-based terminal emulation. The settings for your terminal session are as follows:

Baud Rate: 9600
Data Bits: 8
Parity: None
Stop Bits: 1
Flow Control: None

Your COM port for this connection will vary.

Aux Port

The AUX port is really just another console port that is intended for use with a modem, so you can remotely connect and administer the device by phoning it. This is a great idea as long as the modem is connected, powered up, and plugged in to the phone system; however, doing so can create some security issues, so make sure that you get advice on addressing those before setting this up. Note that not all routers will have an AUX port.

Ethernet Port

An Ethernet port (which might be a FastEthernet or even a GigabitEthernet port, depending on your router model) is intended to connect to the LAN. Some routers have more than one Ethernet or FastEthernet port; it really depends on what you need and of course what you purchase. The Ethernet port usually connects to the LAN switch with a *straight-through cable.*

A straight-through cable has pin 1 connected to pin 1, 2 to 2, 3 to 3, and so on. It is used to connect routers and hosts to switches or hubs.

If you have two or more Ethernet ports, you can connect the others to a high-speed Internet connection such as a cable modem or DSL, or to another, separate LAN.

A crossover cable is used to connect two devices that each use the same pins for the transmit and receive functions; this means that if we use a straight-through cable to connect them, the Layer 1 circuit will not come up, and the connection will not work. For example, suppose I want to connect my router's FastEthernet0/1 interface to another router's FastEthernet0/1 interface. If I use a straight-through cable, the link will not work. Instead, I will use a crossover cable, which changes the pinouts of the transmit and receive pairs so that they line up, respectively, with the receive and transmit pairs on the other device. When I attach the crossover cable, the link lights should come on, and Layers 1 and 2 should change to up.

A crossover cable should be used between two routers, two switches, a switch and a hub, a PC's NIC direct to another PC's NIC—in general, two "like" devices will be connected by a crossover cable. Here's a tricky one, though: To connect a PC's NIC directly to your router's Ethernet interface, you need a crossover cable— even though those two devices are not "like." In the real world, some devices sense when a connection needs to be crossed over, and will automatically "rewire" the port to the correct pinouts. This autosensing function is unfortunately not a factor for the CCNA exams, so you will need to know how to correctly set up your connections the old-fashioned way.

Figure 4.3 shows the straight-through and crossover pinouts, as well as examples of where each type of cable is used.

EXAM ALERT

You must understand how to use rollover, straight-through, and crossover cables, and you must know how to identify them from a diagram of their pinouts.

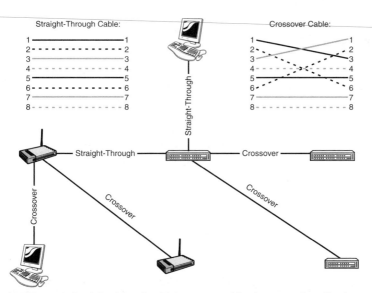

FIGURE 4.3 Straight-through and crossover cable pinouts and applications.

Serial Port

A Cisco serial port is a proprietary design, a 60-pin D-sub. This connector can be configured for almost any kind of serial communication. You need a cable that has the Cisco connector on one end and the appropriate type of connector for the service you want to connect to on the other.

Serial ports are almost always used for WAN connections and use one of several Layer 2 protocols including Frame Relay, PPP, and HDLC. Serial ports can also connect to an ISDN Primary Rate Interface (PRI) service or regular analog telephone service. (For a telephone service, you need a special hardware type called an asynchronous serial port and a modem.)

HDLC is the default encapsulation on a Cisco serial port, and the HDLC protocol here is a Cisco proprietary version of the standardized ISO HDLC that can run multiple Layer 3 protocols, which the ISO version can't do.

You might have one or more serial ports depending on what you need and what you buy.

> **EXAM ALERT**
>
> You will need to know the three WAN encapsulations for a serial port: HDLC, PPP, and Frame Relay. These will be discussed in more detail later.
> Know that Cisco's HDLC is the default encapsulation for serial ports.

Other Connections

Your router may use a T1 controller card to connect to a T1 WAN service. The controller will probably have a label that reads "T1 CSU/DSU," with a plug that looks like the RJ-45 connector but is actually an RJ-48.

You can also buy ports for High-Speed Serial communication (perhaps ATM) or even different fiber-optic connections. What you purchase will depend on the services you need to connect to, the model of router you buy, and of course how much money you want to spend.

Although the "Other Connections" listed here are by no means an exhaustive list of your options, they are the most commonly used. These connection types are not tested, but are included here for your interest.

Connecting and Configuring Cisco Devices

Now that we have examined what our connection options are, we will look at how Cisco devices operate, including the boot sequence, operating system and configuration file location, and basic command-line functions.

Device Memory Locations

A Cisco device has four memory types. Each is used for a specific purpose:

▶ *ROM*, or read-only memory, holds the POST, bootstrap, ROMMON, and RXBoot microcode. The *POST* (*power-on self test*) is a basic inventory and test of the hardware in the device. The *bootstrap* is responsible for finding an operating system to load. *ROMMON* is a minimal command set that can be used to connect to a TFTP server and restore a missing or corrupted IOS image. *RXBOOT* is a mini-IOS that has a much more familiar command set than ROMMON and more features, so it is easier to use for IOS restoration from TFTP.

▶ *Flash* memory normally stores the IOS image file. Because flash is simply a file storage area, assuming that you have enough space, you could store other files here as well, perhaps another IOS version or backups of a configuration. Flash can be either SIMM cards on the motherboard or PCMCIA cards either externally accessible or inside the case of the router on the motherboard.

▶ *NVRAM* is Non-Volatile RAM; this means that it will not lose the data stored in it when the power is turned off or fails. The startup-configuration file is stored here.

▶ *RAM* is similar to RAM on a PC; this very fast memory is where all dynamically learned information is stored, such as routing tables, ARP cache, and buffers.

IOS Startup Process

When you turn on the power, you will see information scrolling down your terminal screen almost immediately. It is a good idea to watch this information, because important messages can be seen here if failures occur during boot.

The IOS startup process is actually more complex than it appears. The basic steps are as follows:

1. Run the POST.

2. Find the IOS.

3. Load the IOS to RAM.

4. Find the configuration.

5. Load the configuration to RAM.

EXAM ALERT

Know the basic steps in the boot process.

Let's look at the process in more detail. The default behavior for a router or switch is as follows:

1. The POST runs.

2. Assuming that there are no critical errors with the POST run, the boot-strap checks the startup-config file in NVRAM for boot system commands. These commands might have been entered by the router admin to override the default behavior, perhaps to load a different IOS for test purposes.

3. Assuming that there are no boot system commands, the router loads the first valid IOS image it finds in the flash memory.

4. If there is no usable IOS in flash, the router will begin broadcasting for a TFTP server in the hopes of finding an IOS it can download and use. Cisco has programmed several preconfigured filenames if you want to set up such a system.

5. If no TFTP server can be contacted, or if no valid IOS is found on one, the router will load the RXBOOT mini-IOS. This IOS has a familiar command set, and some of the features of a full IOS. The main purpose of RXBOOT is to allow you to manually connect to a TFTP server to download a valid IOS to flash. The command prompt for RXBOOT looks like this:

```
Router(boot)>
```

6. In the unlikely event that RXBOOT fails, the router will load the ROM Monitor (ROMMON). ROMMON can also connect to a TFTP server, but if your router has dropped into ROMMON all by itself, chances are that you have a pretty serious problem. ROMMON command prompts vary with hardware type.

7. After an IOS is loaded (except for ROMMON), the router looks for the startup-config file in NVRAM. If it is found, it is copied to RAM and renamed running-config.

8. If there is no startup-config file in NVRAM, the router will broadcast for a TFTP server to see if there is a configuration file available for it.

9. If that fails, the router will launch Setup mode.

Note that on most devices, the IOS image is decompressed and copied to RAM to run from there; similarly, the startup-config file is copied from NVRAM and renamed running-config as it is copied into RAM.

Setup Mode

Cisco devices include a feature called Setup mode to help you make a basic initial configuration. Setup mode will run only if there is no configuration file in NVRAM—either because the router is brand-new, or because it has been erased. Setup mode will ask you a series of questions and apply the configuration to the device based on your answers. You can abort Setup mode by typing CTRL+C or by saying "**no**" either when asked if you want to enter the initial configuration dialog or when asked if you want to save the configuration at the end of the interview.

Configuration Register

The configuration register is a four-character hexadecimal value that can be changed to manipulate how the router behaves at bootup. The default value is 0x2102.

> **NOTE**
>
> The characters "0x" indicate that the characters that follow are in hexadecimal. This makes it clear whether the value is "two thousand one hundred and two" or, as in this case, "two one zero two hexadecimal".

The fourth character in the configuration register is known as the boot field. Changing the value for this character will have the following effects:

- ▶ 0x210**0** = Always boot to ROMMON. There are very few good reasons to do this, except possibly for training or a practical joke.

- ▶ 0x210**1** = Always boot to RXBOOT. Again, there are not many reasons to force this.

- ▶ 0x210**2** through 0x210**F** = Load the first valid IOS in flash; values of 2 through F for the fourth character specify other IOS image files in flash.

Password Recovery

The third character in the configuration register can modify how the router loads the configuration file. The setting of 0x2142 causes the router to ignore the start-up-config file in NVRAM (which is where the password is stored) and proceed without a configuration—as if the router were brand new or had its configuration erased.

This is a useful setting for those times when you do not know the password to enable the router and configure it. Perhaps you forgot the password (we hope not); maybe you bought a used router, or maybe a student configured a password in a previous lab. Perhaps the previous admin quit, got fired, or was hit by a bus. In any event, we need the password to log in and make changes, so we need to bypass the existing password and change it to something we know. This process is called Password Recovery.

Password Recovery

The Password Recovery process is simple and takes about five minutes depending on how fast your router boots:

1. Connect to the console port, start your terminal application, and power cycle the router. When you see the boot process beginning, hit the Break sequence. (This is usually Ctrl+Break, but it might differ for different terminal applications.) Doing this interrupts the boot process and drops the router into ROMMON.

2. At the ROMMON prompt, enter the command **confreg 0x2142** to set the configuration register to 0x2142.

3. Restart the router by power cycling it or by issuing the command **reset**.

4. When the router reloads, the configuration register setting of 0x2142 instructs the router to ignore the startup-config file in NVRAM. You will be asked if you want to go through Setup mode because the router thinks it has no startup-configuration file. Exit from Setup mode.

5. Press Return and enable command **enable** to go into privileged EXEC command mode. No password is required because the startup config file was not loaded.

6. Load the configuration manually by entering **copy startup-config running-config**.

7. Go into the Global Configuration mode using the command **configure terminal** and change the password with the command **enable password** password or **enable secret password**.

8. Save the new password by entering **copy running-config startup-config**.

9. Go to the global config prompt, and change the configuration register back to the default setting with the command **config-register 0x2102**. Exit back to the privileged exec prompt.

10. Reboot the router using the **reload** command. You will be asked to save your changes; you can do so if you have made additional configuration changes.

That's all there is to it. Don't tell anyone how easy this is.

Command Line Modes

Access to a router or switch command line is referred to as an *EXEC session*. There are two levels of access: *user EXEC* and *privileged EXEC*. In user exec mode, you have limited access to information and diagnostic commands, and you are not able to make configuration changes to the router. Privileged EXEC mode gives you the complete command set and full authority to change or erase the configuration.

When you connect to a router using the console port, you see a message like this:

```
Router Con0 is now available.

Press RETURN to get started!
```

Pressing Return takes you to the User Exec Prompt, which looks like this:

```
Router>
```

To go to Privileged EXEC mode, you must enter the command **enable**. The prompt will change from > to #, as shown:

```
Router>enable
Router#
```

From this point, you can enter commands to view the status and settings of the router, make some kinds of changes, and erase, back up, or restore the IOS and configuration files.

To make most kinds of changes, however, you must enter the Global Configuration mode. This is done by entering the command configure terminal from the Privileged EXEC mode:

```
Router#configure terminal
Router(config)#
```

Notice that the command prompt changes to Router(config)#. From this prompt, you can make changes to functions that affect the whole router, or you can enter a more specific configuration mode to work with specialized functions. Some of the possible modes are listed and explained in the following:

```
Router(config)#interface serial 0
Router(config-if)#
```

This is the *Interface configuration mode*. Here you can set IP addresses and subnet masks, change speed, duplex, clock rate and bandwidth, or change the Layer 2 encapsulation of the interface. Changes made here affect only the interface you specified in the interface command.

```
Router(config)#line console 0
Router(config-line)#
```

Line Configuration mode allows you to set up line parameters. Lines include the console, AUX, TTY, and VTY connections. The console and aux lines are the local administration connections. TTY lines are synchronous serial connections, usually for analog dialup access with modems. The VTY lines are virtual connections for Telnet access to the router to perform remote administration over an IP network.

```
Router(config)#router rip
Router(config-router)#
```

The *Router configuration mode* is where you set up dynamic routing protocols such as RIP, IGRP, EIGRP, and OSPF. Chapter 14, "Routing," covers this material in detail.

It is important to understand—and get used to navigating between—the different configuration modes. Some commands work only at a specific configuration mode, and getting used to the IOS quirks is a big part of being prepared for the CCNA exam and being a capable Cisco admin.

Command Shortcuts

Take a look at this command. It backs up the current configuration and saves it so that the router will use it next time it boots up:

```
Router#copy running-config startup-config
```

That's a big hunk of typing. More typing means more time and more errors, so to save time, we can use truncation. As long as the truncation provides enough information for the IOS to figure out what command you are trying to enter, you can reduce the amount of typing you have to do, saving yourself time:

```
Router#copy run start
```

Or even smaller

```
Router#cop ru st
```

That's a big savings in typing effort.

As you get used to working with the IOS, you will develop your own shortcuts.

The IOS will tell you when you make a mistake, too. There are three error messages:

▶ Incomplete Command—The IOS needs more command keywords to complete the command. It advises you of the error, and retypes what you entered so that you can complete it. The error looks like this:

```
Router#copy running-config
% Incomplete Command
Router#copy running-config
```

▶ Ambiguous Command—The IOS is not sure what command you mean because you truncated too much:

```
Router#co ru st
%Ambiguous command
```

▶ Invalid Input—You made a typo or entered a command at the wrong prompt. Notice that the IOS will also show you exactly where the problem happens with a little pointer:

```
Router#cpy run start
          ^
%Invalid input detected at '^' marker
```

Context-Sensitive Help

The IOS has a complete listing of all the commands available. If you get stuck, you can use the question mark ? to access this help. You can use it in different ways:

On its own, to see a list of all the available command words at a particular prompt

```
Router(config-if)#?
Interface configuration commands:
access-expression    Build a bridge boolean access expression
arp                  Set arp type (arpa, probe, snap) or timeout
backup               Modify dial-backup parameters
bandwidth            Set bandwidth informational parameter
bridge-group         Transparent bridging interface parameters
carrier-delay        Specify delay for interface transitions
cdp                  CDP interface subcommands
cmns                 OSI CMNS
custom-queue-list    Assign a custom queue list to an interface
default              Set a command to its defaults
delay                Specify interface throughput delay
description          Interface specific description
exit                 Exit from interface configuration mode
fair-queue           Enable Fair Queuing on an Interface
help                 Description of the interactive help system
hold-queue           Set hold queue depth
ip                   Interface Internet Protocol config commands
ipx                  Novell/IPX interface subcommands
keepalive            Enable keepalive
llc2                 LLC2 Interface Subcommands
load-interval        Specify interval for load calculation for an interface
—More—
```

After a command word, to see the next possible command words

```
Router# copy ?
  running-config
  startup-config
  tftp:
  flash:
```

Don't be afraid to use the help, especially when you are learning. The help commands also function (with limited capabilities) in the router simulator questions on the CCNA exam.

Basic Switch Configuration

A Cisco switch will function perfectly well right out of the box with no configuration required; however, it's a good idea to do a few basic configurations to personalize, secure, and optimize the device.

Setting the Hostname

The default hostname is "Switch," which not only lacks imagination, but also is confusing if you have a lot of them. Changing the hostname is simple:

```
Switch(config)#hostname My2960
My2960(config)#
```

Notice that the hostname instantly changed!

Setting a Management IP Address

If you want to Telnet to your switch to manage it remotely, have it participate in an SNMP system, or use the integrated HTTP server for monitoring, your switch needs an IP address and gateway address. This IP address is applied to the VLAN1 interface and the default gateway is a global command on a switch—unlike a router, a switch has no physical ports that can be assigned IP addresses, so the virtual interface of VLAN1 (the management VLAN) gets the addresses:

```
My2960(config)#interface vlan1
My2960(config-if)#ip address 192.168.1.2 255.255.255.0
My2960(config-if)#exit
My2960(config)#ip default-gateway 192.168.1.1
```

> **NOTE**
>
> A default gateway is an IP address of a router that can connect you to another network. A switch needs a default gateway if it is going to communicate with any device on any IP network other than the one its VLAN1 IP address is in. This is most commonly needed for remote management of the switch using Telnet or SSH, for the switch to participate in SNMP, or any other IP operation that crosses to another network or subnet.

Setting Speed and Duplex on Ethernet Ports

Although the Ethernet interfaces will auto-detect the duplex and speed setting on a 2960, it is usually a good idea to hard-code them when you are sure of what you are connecting to (such as a server, a switch, or router):

```
My2960(config)#interface f0/24
My2960(config-if)#speed 100
My2960(config-if)#duplex full
```

Basic Router Configuration

Routers need a little more configuration than switches to function properly; every interface that you want to use needs an IP address and mask, as well as to be enabled. You will probably need to add static routes or perhaps run a dynamic routing protocol. You need to configure your serial port for connectivity as well.

Serial Port Configuration

As we mentioned before, a Cisco serial port can run several different Layer2 encapsulations—meaning, it can connect to different types of networks. You must be sure that the encapsulation type matches that of the device you are connecting to. In CCNA, we are interested only in three serial encapsulations: HDLC, PPP, and Frame Relay. The command to change the encapsulation is executed at the interface configuration prompt:

```
Router(config)#interface serial 0
Router(config-if)#encapsulation [hdlc ¦ frame-relay ¦ ppp]
```

You might also need to set up the serial speed by configuring a clock rate. Usually this is supplied by the service provider's device (the DCE—Data Communication Equipment), but in training labs we will hook a router directly to another router with a special back-to-back cable. In this situation, one of the devices must emulate the DCE, and the DCE sets the clock. Only one device needs the clock rate set.

You can also configure a bandwidth statement on the interface. This one is a little tricky; it looks like we are setting the bandwidth (as in bits per second) of the interface, but we really aren't—the clock rate sets the physical data rate. What we are doing with the bandwidth command is reporting to the routing protocols about the capacity of the interface (more on this in Chapter 9). It might have an actual clock rate of 64000 (64K), but we could lie and set the bandwidth to 56K for the purposes of routing information:

```
Router(config-if)#clock rate 64000
Router(config-if)#bandwidth 56
```

> **NOTE**
>
> Be aware of the syntax for clock rate and bandwidth: Clock rate is in bps, and bandwidth is in kbps. I remember it this way: clock rate is a longer command and needs a longer number (64000), and bandwidth, truncated as band so it's short, needs a shorter number (64).

Enabling Interfaces

By default, every interface on a router (whether it is brand new or has had its configuration erased) is in a *shutdown* state. This is also known as *administratively down*; although the interface might have been perfectly configured with an IP and mask, encapsulation, and whatever else is needed, the interface is effectively *off*—even Layer 1 is down. A shutdown interface doesn't send or receive any data at all, and it causes the other end of a serial link to think it is dead altogether. So when you first configure a new router or one that has had its configuration erased, remember to issue the no shutdown command at each interface, or none of the interfaces will work!

```
Router(config-if)#no shutdown
```

> **EXAM ALERT**
>
> Understand that all interfaces are shut down by default until the 'no shut' command is issued.

On a router, every interface is a gateway to another network. For this reason, we do not need to supply a default gateway. However, every interface you intend to use will need an IP address and mask. The commands to set an IP are exactly the same as on a switch. Don't forget the no shutdown (no shut for short):

```
Router(config)#interface s0
Router(config-if)#ip address 10.0.0.1 255.0.0.0
Router(config-if)#no shut
Router(config-if)#interface e0
Router(config-if)#ip address 172.16.0.1 255.255.0.0
Router(config-if)#no shut
```

Securing Routers and Switches

In CCNA land, security is an increasing concern. CCNA will not make you a security expert, but you will learn the very basics of good networking security and a little about how to apply them.

Initially, your router or switch will have no passwords at all; pressing Enter will grant you first User EXEC, then Privileged EXEC access by using the **enable** command. The Telnet lines are secured by default—they will refuse connections until they are configured with a password.

The minimum security configuration would be to require a password to log in to your devices. Passwords can be applied to the console port, to the VTY lines (controlling Telnet/SSH access), and to the Privileged EXEC prompt.

The following commands illustrate how to apply basic password security to your router or switch, for the console port (User EXEC), VTY lines (for remote User EXEC administration using Telnet), and the Privileged EXEC prompt. Lines that begin with an exclamation point are informational remarks and do not configure the device:

```
Router(config)#line con 0
!    The console port is always con 0
Router(config-line)#login
!    Requires a password to access User Exec over the console port
Router(config-line)#password ExamCram2
!    Specifies the password - Note: passwords are case-sensitive.
Router(config)#line vty 0 4
!    There are 5 VTY lines, numbered 0 through 4
Router(config-line)#login
Router(config-line)#password 23StanleyCups
!
Router(config)#enable password cisco
!    sets the Privileged Exec password to 'cisco'
```

NOTE

A word about VTY lines: A VTY line is used by both Telnet and SSH connections. The "V" in VTY stands for Virtual, because there is no associated hardware as there would be with the Console port or asynchronous serial (TTY) ports for modems. For our purposes, there are five VTY lines, numbered 0, 1, 2, 3 and 4. The command **line vty 0 4** shown previously allows you to configure all of them at once by specifying the range of "0 [through] 4". Some newer switches and routers will show 16 lines, numbered 0 through 15; it's unlikely that this feature will be a factor on your test, however.

Why have so many VTY lines, when only one is used by a Telnet session? For that same reason, actually: One Telnet/SSH session uses one VTY line. If you Telnet in, then Telnet out to some other device, you use 2 VTY lines. It's common to Telnet to multiple devices concurrently when you are working on a network; it's also possible that multiple admins could be working on or from the same device at the same time, each admin needing at least one VTY line.

By the way, there is no easy way to determine or predict which VTY line you are going to connect to. They are used in a round-robin fashion, so setting a different password for each one is probably more of a hassle than a security benefit; you can't be sure which line you just connected to and therefore which password to enter!

These passwords will all appear in your configuration file in plain text; anyone with access to that file could read them. To encrypt your Privileged EXEC password with an MD5 hash, use the **enable secret** command:

```
Router(config)#enable secret squirrel42
```

You can also apply encryption to the other passwords for the console, Privileged EXEC VTY and TTY lines (but *not* the **enable secret** password [this Privileged EXEC password is already encrypted]) using the **service password-encryption** command:

```
Router(config)#service password-encryption
```

EXAM ALERT

Know the password configuration commands cold.

Configuring SSH Access to Your Router

Telnet is a simple and effective way to remotely administer your router or switch, but it has one significant disadvantage: it is completely unencrypted, which means that everything you send across the network via Telnet could be read easily if intercepted. That's not a good thing.

Secure Shell, or SSH, is a good alternative. It is slightly more complicated (but not difficult) to set up and provides a secured remote command-line interface using public key exchange and decent encryption. Cisco recommends (and we do, too!) that SSH always be used instead of Telnet for security reasons. Your IOS version must include support for DES or 3DES crypto features, or this will not work.

The following are the basic steps to set up a router for SSH support:

1. Define a username and password. SSH can't use the line password we created for Telnet access, so we must create a username/password pair for SSH to use. You might choose to make more than one, for different admins.

   ```
   Router(config)#username Admin007 password ExamCram2
   ```

2. Configure the router to use the username/password. (We could use AAA instead of the command shown, but that is quite a large topic that we don't need to get into here).

   ```
   Router(config-line)#login local
   ```

3. Set the router's domain name. This does not necessarily have to be the actual domain name of the company, but it makes sense if it is the domain that the router actually operates in. If there is not a defined domain in use, make one up. I used ExamCramLab.local in this example.

   ```
   Router(config)#ip domain-name ExamCramLab.local
   ```

4. Create the public key. Simply put, this command creates the public key that will be used to allow secure connections from users supplying the correct credentials. This is the command that will fail if your IOS doesn't support the right crypto features.

   ```
   Router(config)#crypto key generate rsa
   ```

5. (Optional) Restrict VTY line connections to SSH only, instead of both Telnet and SSH. It makes sense to do this, although it is not strictly required for SSH to work.

```
Router(config)#line vty 0 4
Router(config-line)#transport input ssh
```

There's one other catch to using SSH instead of Telnet: You must have an SSH client application. Windows XP and Vista include a command-line SSH capability; I prefer to use terminal applications such as SecureCRT because they are feature rich and easier to use, in my opinion.

To connect to your router using SSH, launch your SSH client of choice, give it the IP address of the device you want to SSH to, and when prompted, supply the username and password you configured.

TIP

If you have access to the Web, you can find tons of good references about SSH configuration on cisco.com. If you don't have access to the Web, you need to get it!

EXAM ALERT

SSH is an important component of network security. You may be asked to identify why SSH is preferred over Telnet and what the required steps are to configure it. Although we have not seen it yet, we think it would be a great simulator question topic. You should know how to configure it.

Table 4.1 lists some useful commands to find out information about your router or switch.

Table 4.1 Commands to Retrieve Basic Information

Command	Description
show flash	Lists what files (IOS images, typically) are stored in flash, as well as how much flash memory is used, available, and the total amount.
show interface	Shows diagnostic information about all interfaces, including whether they are shut down.
show version	Lists the version of IOS image in use, the actual IOS filename, and the current value of the configuration register.
show running-config	Shows the current configuration in RAM.
show startup-config	Shows the configuration that will be loaded the next time the router boots.

Exam Prep Questions

1. Bob types in an excellent initial configuration on his new router, but when he tries to ping the interfaces, they don't answer. What could be wrong?

   ○ **A.** Bob changed the configuration register to suppress pings.

   ○ **B.** Bob needs a new router; this one is clearly defective.

   ○ **C.** The router does not support the IP protocol by default.

   ○ **D.** Bob neglected to issue the `no shut` command at each interface.

2. For which of the following connections will you need a crossover cable?

   ○ **A.** PC's NIC direct to Router's Fa0/1

   ○ **B.** PC's COM port to Router's Console port

   ○ **C.** PC to Switch

   ○ **D.** Router to Switch

   ○ **E.** Hub to Router

   ○ **F.** Hub to Switch

3. Which two actions will get you out of Setup mode?

   ○ **A.** Typing `abort setup`

   ○ **B.** Answering 'no' when asked if you want to keep the configuration at the end of Setup mode

   ○ **C.** Waiting until it times out

   ○ **D.** Pressing `ctrl+c`

4. What command lists the IOS images stored in flash?

   ○ **A.** `show ios`

   ○ **B.** `list flash`

   ○ **C.** `show flash`

   ○ **D.** `show version`

5. Jaine sets her configuration register to 0x2142. What is she up to?

    ○ **A.** Changing which IOS image in flash to boot from

    ○ **B.** Forcing the router to boot from RXBOOT

    ○ **C.** Forcing the router to boot from ROMMON

    ○ **D.** Performing a password recovery

6. Which of the following correctly summarizes the boot sequence?

    ○ **A.** Find IOS, Load IOS, POST, Find config, Load config

    ○ **B.** Post, Find IOS, Load IOS, Find config, Load config

    ○ **C.** POST, Find config, Load config, Find IOS, Load IOS

    ○ **D.** ROMMON, RXBOOT, Load IOS, Load config

7. Which of the following applies an encrypted password of `cisco` to the Privileged Exec prompt?

    ○ **A.** `enable password cisco`

    ○ **B.** `enable password cisco encrypted`

    ○ **C.** `enable cisco secret`

    ○ **D.** `enable secret cisco`

8. What commands apply a password of "Vienna" to the first five Telnet connections on a router?

    ○ **A.**
```
line vty 5
login
password Vienna
```

    ○ **B.**
```
line vty 0 4
login
password vienna
```

    ○ **C.**
```
interface vty 0 4
login
password Vienna
```

    ○ **D.**
```
line vty 0 4
login
password Vienna
```

9. Match the entries in the list on the left with the descriptions on the right:

   ROM   Stores compressed IOS images

   RAM   Stores startup-config file

   FLASH   Stores running config and decompressed IOS

   NVRAM   Stores mini-IOS and ROMMON images

10. What command must be entered on the DCE device to enable serial communication at a speed of 64 kilobits per second?

   ○ **A.** Router(config)#`clock rate 64000`

   ○ **B.** Router(config-if)#`interface-type dce`

   ○ **C.** Router(config-if)#`bandwidth 64`

   ○ **D.** Router(config-if)#`clock rate 64000`

Answers to Exam Prep Questions

1. Answer D is correct. Until you issue the `no shut` command at each interface, the interfaces will effectively be switched off. A is incorrect; you can't use the config register to suppress ping. B may be true, but it is unlikely, so it is not the best choice. C is incorrect because it is false; every IOS supports only IP until you upgrade to one that supports other network protocols as well.

2. Answers A and F are correct. Answer B requires a rollover. Answers C, D, and E require a straight-through.

3. Answers B and D are correct. Answer A is not a valid command. Answer C is incorrect because Setup mode does not time out.

4. Answer C is correct. Answers A and B, show ios and list flash, are not valid commands; Answer D, the show version command, is incorrect because it lists only the file in use, not all the images in flash.

5. Answer D is correct. 0x2142 is one of the steps in password recovery. Answers A, B, and C (changing which IOS image in flash to boot from, forcing the router to boot from RXBOOT, and forcing the router to boot from ROMMON) are controlled by the config register, but use values other than 0x2142.

6. Answer B is correct. Answers A, C, and D are either out of order or incorrect (D).

7. Answer D is correct. The enable secret cisco applies to an encrypted password cisco. Answer A is incorrect; it is a valid syntax but does not encrypt the password. Answers B and C are not valid syntax.

8. Answer D is correct both in syntax and exact password match. Answer A is incorrect; we must specify a range for the vty lines, 0 through 4. Answer B is incorrect, although it is close to correct; however, the password does not match because it is not capitalized. Answer C is incorrect because it uses interface instead of line.

9. ROM $\rightarrow$ Stores mini-IOS and ROMMON images

RAM $\rightarrow$ Stores running config and decompressed IOS

FLASH $\rightarrow$ Stores compressed IOS

NVRAM $\rightarrow$ Stores startup-config file

10. Answer D is correct. Answer A is incorrect because it is executed at the wrong command prompt. Answer B is incorrect because it is invalid syntax, and Answer C is incorrect because it sets the bandwidth for routing metrics, not the required DCE clock speed.

CHAPTER FIVE

Managing Your Router

Terms You'll Need to Understand

✓ CDP (Cisco Discover Protocol)

✓ ICMP (Internet Control Message Protocol)

✓ Telnet

✓ Secure Shell (SSH)

Concepts and Techniques You'll Need to Master

✓ Using Telnet

✓ Using Secure Shell (SSH)

✓ IOS Naming Conventions

✓ Backing Up and Restoring Your IOS

✓ Backing Up and Restoring Your Configuration

Introduction

This chapter deals with managing your Cisco router. It covers IOS naming conventions, backing up and restoring your IOS and configuration, and using the Cisco Discovery Protocol, Telnet, and ICMP.

IOS Naming Conventions

An IOS filename is broken down into four parts:

- ▶ Platform
- ▶ Feature set
- ▶ Run location and compression
- ▶ Version

For example, if our IOS name was C2500-D-L.120-9.bin, we could break it down as follows:

- ▶ Platform: C2500
- ▶ Feature Set: D
- ▶ Run Location: L
- ▶ IOS Version: 12.0(9)

The feature set identifies the feature contents on the router. Common feature sets include "j" for enterprise, "d" for desktop, and "s" for plus features such as Network Address Translation (NAT), InterSwitch Link (ISL), and Virtual Private Dial-up Networks (VPDN). Although the number of feature sets is too many to list here, Table 5.1 lists the more common ones found on a 2500 platform.

TABLE 5.1   Feature Sets

Feature Set	Description
I	IP
IS	IP PLUS
J	Enterprise
JS	Enterprise Plus
JK8S	Enterprise Plus with IPSec
D	Desktop

The run location indicates both its execution area and, when applicable, the compression identifiers. Table 5.2 illustrates the common run locations.

TABLE 5.2 Memory Locations

Code	Location
F	Image runs in flash
M	Image runs in Random Access Memory (RAM)
R	Image runs in Read Only Memory (ROM)
L	Image will be relocated at runtime

The compression identifiers indicate what type of compression is used on the image. Common compression identifiers are shown in Table 5.3.

TABLE 5.3 Compression Identifiers

Code	Compression
Z	Image is Zip compressed
X	Image is Mzip compressed
W	Image is Stac compressed

For example, image c7200-js-mz is an IOS for the 7200 series router, with enterprise plus software, executed in RAM, and is Mzip compressed.

You can view the IOS files you have stored in flash memory by executing the command **show flash**. This command can be executed from either user EXEC or privileged EXEC mode. Following is the output of the show flash command on a 1604 router:

```
Router>show flash
PCMCIA flash directory:
File  Length   Name/status
  1   6611048  /c1600-nosy-l.120-25.bin
[6611112 bytes used, 1777496 available, 8388608 total]
8192K bytes of processor board PCMCIA flash (Read ONLY)
```

In this instance, there is only one IOS in flash. Taking the filename, c1600-nosy-l.120-25.bin, you can see that the platform is a 1600 series router with a feature set of 'nosy' (the 1600 designation for IP/IPX/FW Plus) and is relocated at run-time but not compressed. The IOS version is 12.0(25).

Although the **show flash** command will show you all IOS files that you have in flash, it will not show you the IOS that you are currently using if you have more than one IOS. To view the IOS that you are currently using on your router, execute the command **show version**. Like the **show flash** command, the **show version** command may be executed from user EXEC or privileged EXEC. Following is the output of the show version command with the relevant portions in bold text.

```
Router>show version
Cisco Internetwork Operating System Software
IOS (tm) 1600 Software (C1600-NOSY-L), Version 12.0(25), RELEASE SOFTWARE (fc1)
Copyright (c) 1986-2002 by cisco Systems, Inc.
Compiled Tue 31-Dec-02 12:29 by srani
Image text-base: 0x080357F8, data-base: 0x02005000

ROM: System Bootstrap, Version 11.1(10)AA, EARLY DEPLOYMENT RELEASE SOFTWARE
(fc1)
ROM: 1600 Software (C1600-BOOT-R), Version 11.1(10)AA, EARLY DEPLOYMENT RELEASE
SOFTWARE (fc1)

Router uptime is 6 minutes
System restarted by power-on
System image file is "flash:/c1600-nosy-l.120-25.bin"
<output omitted for brevity>
```

EXAM ALERT

Know the difference between the **show flash** and the **show version** commands. **show flash** will show all IOS files that you have in flash memory, whereas the **show version** command will show you which IOS file you are currently using.

Back Up and Restore IOS

At some point in your career, you will need to back up, restore, or upgrade your IOS. You can use TFTP, FTP, or RCP to transfer an IOS image to or from a server. TFTP is the most common so that is covered here. (It is also covered in the CCNA exam.)

TFTP is the trivial file transfer protocol. Unlike FTP, there are no means of authenticating with a username or password or navigating directories. To back up your IOS, you will use the **copy** command from within privileged EXEC mode. The syntax of this command is **copy** *<from>* *<to>*. Thus, if you want to copy an IOS from your IOS to a TFTP server, the syntax would be **copy tftp** `flash`. After executing this command, you will be prompted with a number of questions asking for such things as the IOS filename and IP address of the TFTP server. Following is the output of this command. The TFTP server in this example is located at the IP address 172.16.0.254.

```
Router#copy flash tftp

PCMCIA flash directory:
File  Length   Name/status
5148040  /c1600-sy56i-mz.121-20.bin
[5148104 bytes used, 3240504 available, 8388608 total]
Address or name of remote host [255.255.255.255]? 172.16.0.254
Source file name?/c1600-sy56i-mz.121-20.bin
Destination file name [c1600-sy56i-mz.121-20.bin]?
Verifying checksum for 'c1600-sy56i-mz.121-20.bin' (file # 1)...  OK
Copy 'c1600-sy56i-mz.121-20.bin' from Flash to server
as 'c1600-sy56i-mz.121-20.bin'? [yes/no]y
!!!!!!!!!!!!!!!!!!!!!!!!!!!!!!!!!!!!!!!!!!!!!!!!!!!!!!!!!!!!!!!!!!!!!!
!!!!!!!!!!!!!!!!!!!!!!!!!!!!!!!!!!!!!!!!!!!!!!!!!!!!!!!!!!!!!!!!!!!!!!
!!!!!!!!!!!!!!!!!!!!!!!!!!!!!!!!!!!!!!!!!!!!!!!!!!!!!!!!!!!!!!!!!!!!!!
!!!!!!!!!!!!!!!!!!!!!!!!!!!!!!!!!!!!!!!!!!!!!!!!!!!!!!!!!!!!!!!!!!!!!!
!!!!!!!!!!!!!!!!!!!!!!!!!!!!!!!!!!!!!!!!!!!!!!!!!!!!!!!!!!!!!!!!!!!!!!
!!!!!!!!!!!!!!!!!!!!!!!!!!!!!!!!!!!!!!!!!!!!!!!!!!!!!!!!!!!!!!!!!!!!!!
!!!!!!!!!!!!!!!!!!!!!!!!!!!!!!!!!!!!!!!!!!!!!!!!!!!!!!!!!!!!!!!!!!!!!!
!!!!!!!!!!!!!!!!!!!!!!!!!!!!!!!!!!!!!!!!!!!!!!!!!!!!!!!!!!!!!!!!!!!!!!
!!!!!!!!!!!!!!!!!!!!!!!!!!!!!!!!!!!!!!!!!!!!!!!!!!!!!!!!!!!!!!!!!!!!!!
!!!!!!!!!!!!!!!!!!!!!!!!!!!!!!!!!!!!!!!!!!!!!!!!!!!!!!!!!!!!!!!!!!!!!!
Upload to server done

Flash device copy took 00:01:24 [hh:mm:ss]
```

To restore or upgrade your IOS from a TFTP server to a router, the syntax would be **copy tftp flash**.

Remember the following troubleshooting steps if you are having difficulties using TFTP:

- ▶ Verify that the TFTP server is running.

- ▶ Verify cable configurations. You should use a crossover cable between a router and a server or, if you have a switch, use a straight-through cable from the router to the switch and from the switch to the server.

- ▶ Verify that your router is on the same subnet as your TFTP server or has a means to route to it somehow (static route or routing protocol).

Backup and Restore Configurations

Backing up and restoring your configuration is no different than it was for your IOS. To save your configuration, you will copy your running-config in RAM to your startup-config in NVRAM by executing the privileged EXEC command copy running-config startup-config. If you want to copy your startup-config file to a TFTP server, you would type copy startup-config tftp. If you want to restore your configuration from a TFTP server, you would execute the command copy tftp running-config. (You can also elect to copy it to your startup-config.) Finally, the copy tftp running-config command will merge a configuration file on a TFTP server with your current configuration.

> **TIP**
>
> If you are using a Linux TFTP server, make sure that you first use the touch command to create a zero-byte file with the name of the IOS image; otherwise, the file will not copy to the TFTP server. Consult the Linux documentation for more information.

Troubleshooting and Remote Management

Having the ability to remotely manage your router is crucial to any network engineer. If you have a wide area network that spans across the world, you do not want to have to fly out to a location every time you have a problem with a router. Four protocols you can use to help you in troubleshooting and remotely manage your routers are

- ▶ Telnet
- ▶ Secure Shell (SSH)
- ▶ CDP
- ▶ ICMP

Telnet

Telnet operates at the application layer of the OSI model and is used to remotely connect into a router. Configuring Telnet authentication is covered in Chapter 4, "Working with Cisco Equipment." As a review, however, the commands to configure a router to allow Telnet access are as follows (the password 'cisco' is used in this example):

```
Router(config)#enable secret cisco
Router(config)#line vty 0 4
Router(config-line)#login
Router(config-line)#password cisco
```

You must have an enable password for Telnet access to work. If you do not, you will get the following output when you attempt to access privileged EXEC mode:

```
Router#telnet 192.168.1.1
Trying 192.168.1.1 ... Open
User Access Verification
Password:
Router>en
% No password set
Router>
```

To close out an active Telnet session, type **exit**.

It is also possible to suspend a Telnet session and resume it later. This is helpful as it keeps you from having to remember the IP address of a router. Instead, you can suspend your Telnet session and resume it later based on its session number, not IP address.

To suspend a Telnet session, press Ctrl+Shift+6, x. (Hold down the Ctrl, Shift, and 6 buttons at the same time. Release them, and then press x.)

To see what sessions you have suspended, execute the show sessions command from user EXEC or privileged EXEC mode. In the output that follows, there are two Telnet sessions that have been suspended:

```
Router#show sessions
Conn Host              Address          Byte  Idle Conn Name
   1 192.168.1.1       192.168.1.1         0     0 192.168.1.1
*  2 172.16.0.1        172.16.0.1          0     0 172.16.0.1
```

Entries that have an asterisk (*) next to them indicate the last session you were using. There are four methods of resuming a session:

> ➤ **Enter** key   Pressing the Enter key will take you to the last session you were currently using (as shown by the asterisk in the **show sessions** command).

> ➤ **Resume**   Typing **resume** without specifying a session number will allow you to resume the last session you were using. This is the same as pressing the Enter key.

> ➤ **Resume #**   Typing resume followed by the session number will resume Telnet for that session. For example, typing **resume 1** would resume Telnet for the 192.168.1.1 router.

> ➤ **Resume** [*IP address | hostname*]   Instead of giving a Telnet session number, you can also give the IP address or, if you have DNS lookups enabled with a DNS server, you can type in the hostname of the remote router.

> **EXAM ALERT**
>
> Know the commands you use to resume and close a Telnet session (Ctrl+Shift+6, x; show sessions; resume; disconnect). Also, remember that the **exit** command will close an *active* session, whereas the **disconnect** command will close a *suspended* session.

Secure Shell (SSH)

In addition to Telnet, you can also use *Secure Shell (SSH)* to remotely manage your routers. Configuring your router for SSH is covered in Chapter 4. Now you will learn how to use your router as an SSH client to connect into other routers.

SSH is preferred by many engineers because it secures your communication to your router when remotely managing it. This is done by encrypting the communication with algorithms such as Triple Data Encryption Standard (3DES) and Advanced Encryption Standard (AES), as well as by securing the authentication to the router through password hashing algorithms such as Message Digest 5 (MD5) and Secure Hash Algorithm 1 (SHA-1). Encrypting communication and hashing the password prevents malicious hackers from eavesdropping on you when you are configuring your router.

Starting an encrypted SSH session with a router is done with the **ssh** command. This command can be entered from either user EXEC or privileged EXEC mode. It has several options as outlined in Table 5.4.

TABLE 5.4 SSH Options

Command Option	Description
`-v {1 ¦ 2}`	This optional parameter specifies whether you are going to use version 1 or version 2. SSH version 1 had some known vulnerabilities, so you should use version 2 whenever possible.
`-c {3des ¦ aes128-cbc ¦ aes192-cbc ¦ aes256-cbc}`	This optional parameter specifies the encryption you are going to use when communicating with the router. This value is optional; if you choose not to use it, the routers will negotiate the encryption algorithm to use automatically.
`-l username`	This specifies the username to use when logging in to the remote router.
`-m {hmac-md5 ¦ hmac-md5-96 ¦ hmac-sha1 ¦ hmac-sha1-96}`	This specifies the type of hashing algorithm to use when sending your password. It is optional and if you do not use it, the routers will negotiate what type of hashing to use.
`ip-address	hostname`	You need to specify the IP address or, if you have DNS or static hostnames configured, the name of the router you want to connect to.

For example, if you wanted to use SSH version 2 to connect to a router at IP address 192.168.0.1 with the username of Admin, using AES256-CBC encryption, and using SHA1 hashing, you would type the following:

```
Router#ssh -v 2 -l Admin -c aes256-cbc -m hmac-sha-1 192.168.0.1
```

The syntax may appear long at first, but after you start using it on a regular basis to manage your routers, it will become second nature to you.

CDP

Sometimes when you Telnet to another router, you might not know what its IP address is. If this is the case, you can use the CDP to discover the Layer 3 address of neighboring devices.

CDP is a Cisco proprietary layer 2 (data-link) multicast protocol that is enabled on all Cisco routers and switches. It can be used to discover information about directly connected devices. Although it is a Layer 2 protocol, it is not forwarded by Cisco switches. (It is by other vendors, however.)

To view what neighboring Cisco devices you have connected to your router or switch, execute the `show cdp neighbors` command from either user EXEC or privileged EXEC mode. Following is an example of this output:

```
Router#show cdp neighbors
Capability Codes: R - Router, T - Trans Bridge, B - Source Route Bridge
                  S - Switch, H - Host, I - IGMP, r - Repeater

Device ID       Local Intrfce   Holdtme   Capability  Platform  Port ID
CoreRouter        Ser 1           144         R          2500     Ser 0
```

Here you see that you are connected to a router named "CoreRouter." You are connected to it out of your local interface serial 1. The holdtime indicates how long it will take to flush this entry out should your router stop hearing CDP frames. CDP sends advertisements every 60 seconds by default and will flush out an entry if it fails to hear a CDP advertisement after 180 seconds. (Timers are manipulated with the `cdp timers` global configuration command.) The capability of this device is 'R,' which stands for router. In fact, from this output you can see that this is a 2500 series router and it is connected to your router out of its serial 0 interface.

Quite a bit of information gets generated from this command, but it did not tell you the IP address of the 2500 nor did it tell you the IOS version running on the 2500. The two commands you can enter through the Layer 3 IP address and IOS version are as follows:

▶ `show cdp neighbors detail`

▶ `show cdp entry *`

These two commands are functionally equivalent. You can look at a specific device in the **show cdp entry command** or use the wildcard asterisk character to view all entries. Following is the output of the **show cdp neighbors detail** command (the other show command would generate the same output):

```
Router#show cdp neighbors detail
-----------------.
Device ID: CoreRouter
Entry address(es):
  IP address: 10.0.0.1
Platform: cisco 2500,  Capabilities: Router
Interface: Serial0,  Port ID (outgoing port): Serial0
Holdtime : 171 sec

Version :
Cisco Internetwork Operating System Software
IOS (tm) 2500 Software (C2500-I-L), Version 12.1(20), RELEASE SOFTWARE (fc2)
Copyright (c) 1986-2003 by cisco Systems, Inc.
Compiled Thu 29-May-03 22:00 by kellythw
```

EXAM ALERT

If you need to Telnet into a router but do not know its IP address, use CDP. Remember, only the **show cdp neighbors detail** and **show cdp entry *** will show you the IP address and IOS version of neighboring devices.

ICMP

Another useful troubleshooting tool is the ICMP. ICMP is a layer 3 (network) protocol designed to carry status messages. CCNAs will exercise ICMP via two programs, Ping and Traceroute. The two messages used by the Ping program, Echo Request and Echo Reply, test both connectivity and integrity; the responding station's job is to reply and repeat the payload, thus testing the quality of the connection. The **ping** command followed by an IP address or name uses a default payload and primarily tests connectivity.

If a host is unreachable, you will get an ICMP Type 3 Destination Unreachable message. If a firewall or access-list is blocking ICMP, you will get an ICMP Type 3/Code 13 Destination Unreachable:Administratively Prohibited Message. Unreachables will show a "U" in the output on your screen, whereas a successful ping will show exclamation points (!). Timeouts will show a "." (period) in the output. The extended ping has options to test integrity, such as the capability to change the size and content of the payload to be echoed back. Cisco also supports an extended ping feature that is accessible from privileged EXEC. To access the extended ping feature, enter privileged EXEC and type **ping**. Do not enter an IP address, however; instead, press Enter, and you will be presented with a number of questions. With extended ping, you have the ability to set the size of your ping messages, source interface, number of pings, and timeout settings. Following is the output of the extended ping command. Note that the exclamation mark is an indication of a successful ping:

```
Router#ping
Protocol [ip]:
Target IP address: 10.0.0.1
Repeat count [5]: 1000
Datagram size [100]: 1024
Timeout in seconds [2]:
Extended commands [n]: y
Source address or interface: 172.16.0.1
Type of service [0]:
Set DF bit in IP header? [no]:
Validate reply data? [no]:
Data pattern [0xABCD]:
Loose, Strict, Record, Timestamp, Verbose[none]:
Sweep range of sizes [n]:
Type escape sequence to abort.
Sending 1000, 1024-byte ICMP Echos to 10.0.0.1, timeout is 2 seconds:
!!!!!!!!!!!!!!!!!!!!!!!!!!!!!!!!!!!!!!!!!!!!!!!!!!!!!!!!!!!!!!!!!!!!!
```

TIP

When bringing up a new wide area network circuit, you can do an extended ping and send out 10,000 pings with a size of 1,024 bytes. Watch the results and verify success. If some packets are lost, you know it is not a clean circuit and you should contact your provider.

Traceroute is a technique used when you suspect that a router on the path to an unreachable network is at fault. Traceroute sends out a packet to a destination with a Time To Live (TTL) of 1. If the first hop is not the destination, an ICMP type 11/Code 0 (ICMP Time Exceeded) message is sent back and the response time in milliseconds is recorded. Routers decrement TTL so that a packet will not circulate forever if there is a problem such as a routing loop (covered in Chapter 10, "Basic Routing"). When a TTL gets to 0, the router drops the packet and returns the unreachable message.

A second packet is then sent out with a TTL value of 2, and if it is not the destination, an unreachable message is sent back and the response time in milliseconds is recorded. This continues until the destination is reached or until the maximum TTL as defined by the vendor is reached. (Cisco uses 30 as its maximum TTL with traceroute, but this is configurable.)

Many devices support traceroute. On Windows machines, the command is **tracert**. On Cisco devices, the command is **traceroute**, but this can be abbreviated as **trace**.

EXAM ALERT

Make sure that you know what options are available with extended ping. Also, know why you would use the **traceroute** command.

Exam Prep Questions

1. Which of the following is included in the filename c1600-js-mz.120-9.bin? Select all that apply.

   ○ **A.** Platform

   ○ **B.** Feature set

   ○ **C.** IOS Version

   ○ **D.** Compression Type

2. You are trying to Telnet to a router, but do not know its IP address. What commands can you enter to see the IP address of a neighboring router? Select all that apply.

   ○ **A.** `show cdp neighbors detail`

   ○ **B.** `show cdp neighbors`

   ○ **C.** `show cdp entry *`

   ○ **D.** `show cdp`

   ○ **E.** `show cdp entry neighbors`

3. What is the command to back up your IOS to a TFTP server?

   ○ **A.** `copy nvram tftp`

   ○ **B.** `copy tftp nvram`

   ○ **C.** `copy tftp flash`

   ○ **D.** `copy flash tftp`

4. Which of the following commands can you enter to return to the last suspended Telnet session you were using? Assume that the session number is 1. Select all that apply.

   ○ **A.** `resume`

   ○ **B.** `return session`

   ○ **C.** `return 1`

   ○ **D.** `resume 1`

   ○ **E.** `Enter`

5. What command will show you the IOS you are currently using on your router?

- ○ **A.** `show nvram`
- ○ **B.** `show flash`
- ○ **C.** `show ios`
- ○ **D.** `show version`

6. What command can you enter to close out a suspended Telnet session?

- ○ **A.** `close session`
- ○ **B.** `disconnect`
- ○ **C.** `exit`
- ○ **D.** `quit`

7. The `show cdp neighbors detail` command will show you more output than just the show cdp neighbors command. What can you see with the `show cdp neighbors detail` command that you cannot see with the `show cdp neighbors` command? Select all that apply.

- ○ **A.** IOS version
- ○ **B.** Capabilities
- ○ **C.** Platform
- ○ **D.** Layer 3 address
- ○ **E.** Outgoing interface

8. An ICMP ping is composed of which two primary messages? Select two.

- ○ **A.** `traceroute`
- ○ **B.** `echo reply`
- ○ **C.** `chargen`
- ○ **D.** `echo request`
- ○ **E.** `Ping reply`

9. Which of the following commands is used to troubleshoot Layer 3 connectivity?

- ○ **A.** `telnet`
- ○ **B.** `ftp`
- ○ **C.** `ping`
- ○ **D.** `show cdp neighbors`

10. You suspect that the routing configuration on one of your routers is incorrect because you are unable to reach a remote network. What command can you use to detect which router has a problem routing to a remote network?

   ○ A. `telnet`

   ○ B. `ping`

   ○ C. `traceroute`

   ○ D. `show ip route`

Answers to Exam Prep Questions

1. Answers A, B, C, and D are the correct answers. C1600 refers to the platform that the IOS runs on. The 'js' refers to the enterprise plus feature set. The IOS version is 12.0(9) as indicated in the 120-9 section. Finally, the compression and execution area are indicated as 'mz,' which indicates that the image runs from RAM and is Zip compressed.

2. Answers A and C are correct. The commands **show cdp neighbors detail** and **show cdp entry** * are functionally equivalent and would show you the Layer 3 IP address of the neighboring router along with platform and IOS version. Answer B is incorrect because this would not give you the IP address of a neighboring router. Answer D shows global CDP statistics but will also not give you the output this question is asking about. Answer E is incorrect because it is not a valid command.

3. Answer D is the correct answer. This would copy the IOS in flash memory to a TFTP server. Answers A and B are incorrect because the IOS is stored in flash and not NVRAM. Answer C is incorrect because **copy tftp flash** would upgrade your IOS from a TFTP server rather than copy your IOS to a TFTP server.

4. Answers A, D, and E are correct. The **resume** command will resume you to the last Telnet session you were in. Typing **resume 1** will return you to session 1. Pressing the **Enter** key by itself will also return you to the last session you were using. Answers B and C are incorrect because these are not valid commands.

5. Answer D is the correct answer. The **show version** command will show you the current IOS you are using. Answer A is incorrect because this is not a valid command. Answer B will show you all the IOS images you have on your router but does not distinguish between different IOS images to tell you which one you are currently using. Answer C is incorrect because this is not a valid command.

6. Answer B is the correct answer. Disconnect will close the last Telnet session you had open. Answer A is incorrect because this is not a valid command. Answer C will close an active Telnet session but not a suspended session, so is therefore incorrect. Answer D will not close out a suspended Telnet session, so it is also incorrect.

7. Answers A and D are correct. The **show cdp neighbors detail** command will show you both the IOS version and the Layer 3 address of a neighboring device. Answers B, C, and E are incorrect because all of these are shown with both the **show cdp neighbors** and **show cdp neighbors detail** commands.

8. Answers B and D are correct. ICMP ping messages are composed of echo request (ICMP type 8) and echo reply (ICMP type 0) messages. Answers A, C, and E are wrong because these are not ICMP messages.

9. Answer C is correct. Ping uses ICMP, which operates at the third layer (Network) of the OSI model. Answers A and B are wrong because Telnet and FTP operate at Layer 7 (Application). Answer D is wrong because this operates at Layer 2 (Data-link).

10. Answer C is the correct answer. Traceroute is used when you try to pinpoint which router has problems getting to a network. Answer A, B, and D are wrong because they do not allow you to detect which router is unable to reach a network.

CHAPTER SIX

Basic Catalyst Switch Operations and Configuration

Terms you'll need to understand:

✓ Bridge

✓ Switch

✓ Store and Forward

✓ Cut Through

✓ Fragment Free

✓ Duplex

✓ Spanning Tree

Techniques you'll need to master:

✓ Differentiating between bridges and switches

✓ Identifying the benefits of bridges and switches

✓ Configuring switch ports

✓ Connecting switches

Introduction

This chapter introduces the concepts and modes of Layer 2 Switching and physical-layer connectivity between switches. We also introduce the Spanning Tree Protocol and its importance to switched systems.

Bridging and Switching

Bridges and switches are devices that segment (break up) collision domains. They are important parts of a network infrastructure, and the concepts presented here are heavily tested on the CCNA exam(s).

Functions of Bridges and Switches

When talking about LANs at the CCNA level, we are almost exclusively interested in ethernet. You have an idea from Chapter 1, "Networking Fundamentals," of how ethernet works. This chapter deals with how to make it work at a highly optimized level by using specialized devices to enhance the simple and adaptable ethernet technology.

In the early implementations of ethernet, every device connected to a single wire. Thicknet (10-BASE 5) and Thinnet (10-BASE 2) were the most common physical layer implementations. A little later, hubs were used. All these technologies did effectively the same thing: connect many hosts together so that one of them at a time could transmit on the wire. This created a single, often large, collision domain. As you recall from Chapter 1, the bigger the collision domain, the more collisions and the less data that actually gets sent. In these types of implementations, you can lose 50–60% of the available bandwidth just because of collisions. So if we had a 10-BASE T hub, not only did we actually end up with only about 4 or 5Mbs instead of 10Mbs, but that reduced bandwidth must also be shared by all the devices on that segment, instead of each device getting the full 10Mbs. Breaking up (segmenting) collision domains is necessary to make them small enough so that devices can reliably transmit data. We can segment using routers, but routers are expensive and difficult to configure; in addition, they don't typically have very many ports on them, so we would need a lot of them to segment effectively.

Bridges were developed to address this issue. A *bridge* isolates one collision domain from another while still connecting them and selectively allowing frames to pass from one to the other. A *switch* is simply a bigger, faster bridge. Every port on a switch or bridge is its own collision domain. The terms bridge and switch can be used interchangeably when discussing their basic operations; we use the term *switch* because switches are more modern and more common.

A switch must do three things:

- ▶ Address Learning

- ▶ Frame Forwarding

- ▶ Layer 2 Loop Removal

NOTE

All the descriptions and references in this book are to Transparent Bridging (Switching). By definition, a Transparent Bridge is invisible to the hosts connected through it. Other bridge types (for example, Source-Route, Source-Route Translational) are used in mixed-media networks, including Token Ring and FDDI, that are no longer relevant to the CCNA test.

Address Learning

Address learning refers to the intelligent capability of switches to dynamically learn the source MAC addresses of devices that are connected to its various ports. These addresses are stored in RAM in a table that lists the address and the port on which a frame was last received from that address. This enables a switch to selectively forward the frame out the appropriate port(s), based on the destination MAC address of the frame.

Anytime a device that is connected to a switch sends a frame through the switch, the switch records the source MAC address of the frame in a table and associates that address with the port the frame arrived on. Figure 6.1 illustrates a switch that has learned the MAC addresses of the three hosts connected to it, as well as the ports to which they are connected.

Frame Forwarding

After a switch has learned the MAC addresses of the devices connected to it, it can intelligently forward unicast frames to the correct host by comparing the destination MAC of the frame with the addresses in its MAC table; when it finds a match, it then sends the frame out the port associated with that entry. Figure 6.2 illustrates the forwarding decision made by the switch.

This is where switches create such a benefit to an ethernet network: If a switch knows the port to which the destination MAC is connected, the switch will send the frame out that port and only that port. This prevents the traffic from being unnecessarily sent to hosts that it is not intended for, significantly improving the efficiency of the network. This is in sharp contrast to the behavior of a hub, which always sends all frames out all ports except the one it came in on (to avoid a false collision detection by the sending station).

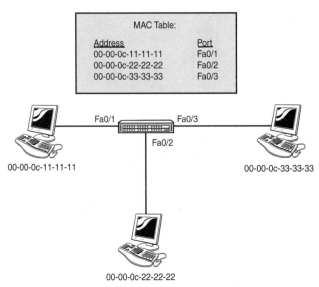

FIGURE 6.1 A switch with a complete MAC table.

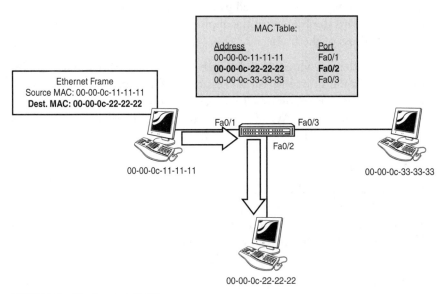

FIGURE 6.2 The forward decision.

There are some situations in which a switch cannot make its forwarding deci-sion, however. Consider the case in which one of the hosts sends out a broad-cast. The MAC address for a broadcast is FF-FF-FF-FF-FF-FF; this is effectively the MAC address of all hosts because every host in a broadcast domain must receive all broadcasts. When the switch receives a broadcast frame inbound on one of its ports, it will check that the source MAC is correctly listed in its MAC table (and update it if necessary) and check the destination MAC of the frame for a match in the table. Because FF-FF-FF-FF-FF-FF matches the MAC of all hosts, the switch must *flood* the frame—it sends it out every port (except the one it came in on) so that the broadcast frame will reach all possible hosts. At this point, the switch is behaving like a hub. This also illustrates why switches (by default) do not segment broadcast domains.

Another scenario in which a switch (by default) is unable to be optimally efficient in the delivery of frames is in the case of a multicast. A *multicast* is a message sent by one host and intended for a specific group of other hosts. This group could be a single host or a very large number of hosts in different places. The key here is that a single host transmits a stream of data (perhaps a video of a speech or event) to a group of hosts. By default, the switch will treat this the same way as a broadcast, flooding it out all ports to make sure that it reaches all the possible hosts in the group. This is inefficient because the traffic also hits those hosts who do not want the stream. There are several mechanisms and configurations to set it so that only the hosts in the multicast group receive the multicast, but that is well out of the scope of the CCNA exam; the CCNP Building Cisco Multilayer Switched Networks course covers this topic.

The switch will also flood a frame if it does not have an entry in its MAC table for the destination MAC in the frame. Although this happens rarely, if the switch doesn't know which specific port to send the frame out, it responds by doing the safest thing and flooding that frame so that it has the best chance of reaching the correct destination. Interestingly, after the destination host responds to that first frame, the switch will enter the missing MAC address into its table and the flood probably won't happen again.

The last situation we should examine is what happens if the sending and receiving hosts are both connected to the same port on the switch. This is most commonly seen when the two hosts are connected to a hub, which is in turn connected to a switch. From the switch's perspective, the two hosts are on the same port. When the sending host transmits a frame, the hub does its thing and floods it out all ports, including the ones connected to the intended receiver and the switch. The receiver simply receives it; the switch checks the source MAC of the frame, updates its MAC table if necessary, and then checks the destination MAC in its table to see which port it should be sent out. When it discovers that the two MACs are associated with the same port, it *filters* the frame: The switch does not transmit the frame out any ports and assumes that the frame will reach its intended recipient without help from the switch. Figure 6.3 illustrates this process.

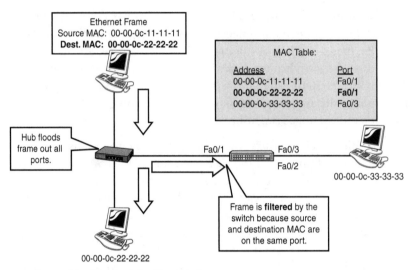

FIGURE 6.3 The filter decision illustrated.

You have seen how switching gives you a huge efficiency advantage over hubs and coaxial media. Even a low-end switch is preferable to any kind of hub or coax media. You want to be sure that you get the right equipment for the job; different switches run at various speeds, and have diverse limitations on the number of MAC addresses they can support. Although almost any switch is better than any hub, you should take stock of your network, how many hosts, how much and what kind of traffic you expect to support, and then choose the switch that best meets your performance and budget requirements.

The Differences Between Switches and Bridges

We have been using the term "switch" interchangeably with "bridge," but there are some significant differences that you need to know about. The key difference is in the technology. Bridges, which are older, do all the work of frame analysis and decision making in software, using the CPU to analyze data stored in RAM. Switches use ASIC (Application-Specific Integrated Circuit) chips.

ASICs are specialized processors designed to do one thing—in this case, switch frames. Depending on the model of switch, the speed difference can be astounding: A bridge typically switches around 50,000 frames per second, whereas a lowly 2950 switch can move an average of 12 million frames per second. (This, of course, depends on the frame size.) A big switch, such as the Catalyst 6500 series, could do 10 times that, depending on the hardware configuration.

Switches also tend to have many more ports than bridges; a bridge by definition has at least two ports, and they didn't get much bigger than 16 ports. Switches can have hundreds of ports if you buy the appropriate expansion modules.

Other differences include the following:

▶ Switches support half and full duplex, bridges only half duplex.

▶ Switches support different port speeds (10 and 100Mbs, for example), but a bridge's ports must all be the same speed.

▶ Switches support multiple VLANs and an instance of Spanning Tree for every VLAN (more on this soon).

Table 6.1 summarizes the differences between switches and bridges.

TABLE 6.1   Switches and Bridges Compared

Comparison	Switches	Bridges
Switching Technology	ASIC (Hardware)	Software
Speed	Fast	Slow
Port Density	High	Low
Duplex	Full and Half	Half Only
VLAN-Aware	Yes	No
Collision Domains	1 per Port	1 per Port
Broadcast Domains	1 per VLAN	1
STP Instances	1 per VLAN	1

EXAM ALERT

Know the differences between switches and bridges.

Switching Modes

Switches examine the source and destination MAC in a frame to build their MAC table and make their forwarding decision. Exactly how they do that is the topic of this section. You need to be aware of three switching modes: Store and Forward, Cut Through, and Fragment Free.

Store and Forward

Store and Forward is the basic mode that bridges and switches use. It is the only mode that bridges can use, but many switches can use one or more of the other modes as well, depending on the model. In Store-and-Forward switching, the entire frame is buffered (copied into memory) and the Cyclic Redundancy Check (CRC), also known as the FCS or Frame Check Sequence is run to ensure that the frame is valid and not corrupted.

> **NOTE**
>
> A CRC is a simple mathematical calculation. A sample of the data (in this case, a frame) is used as the variable in an equation. The product of the equation is included as the CRC at the end of the frame as it is transmitted by the source host. When it is received by the switch, the same equation is run against the same sample of data; if the product value is the same as the value of the CRC in the frame, the frame is assumed to be good. If the value is different, the frame is assumed to be corrupt or damaged, and the frame is dropped. This analysis happens before the forwarding decision is made.

Cut Through

Cut Through is the fastest switching mode. The switch analyzes the first six bytes after the preamble of the frame to make its forwarding decision. Those six bytes are the destination MAC address, which, if you think about it, is the minimum amount of information a switch has to look at to switch efficiently. After the forwarding decision has been made, the switch can begin to send the frame out the appropriate port(s), even if the rest of the frame is still arriving at the inbound port. The chief advantage of Cut-Through switching is speed; no time is spent running the CRC, and the frame is forwarded as fast as possible. The disadvantage is clearly that bad frames will be switched along with the good. Because the CRC/FCS is not being checked, we might be propagating bad frames. This would be a bad thing in a busy network, so some vendors support a mechanism in which the CRCs are still checked but no action is taken until the count of bad CRCs reaches a threshold that causes the switch to change to Store-and-Forward mode.

Fragment Free

Fragment-Free mode is a switching method that picks a compromise between the reliability of Store and Forward and the speed of Cut Through. The theory here is that frames that are damaged (usually by collisions) are often shorter than the minimum valid ethernet frame size of 64 bytes. Fragment-Free buffers the first 64 bytes of each frame, updates the source MAC and port if necessary, reads the destination MAC, and forwards the frame. If the frame is less than 64 bytes, it is discarded. Frames that are smaller than 64 bytes are called *runts*; Fragment-Free switching is sometimes called "runtless" switching for this reason. Because the switch only ever buffers 64 bytes of each frame, Fragment Free is a faster mode than Store and Forward, but there still exists a risk of forwarding bad frames, so the previously described mechanisms to change to Store and Forward if excessive bad CRCs are received are often implemented as well.

> **EXAM ALERT**
>
> Know the three switching modes and how they work.

Switch Connections

Switches have the capability of connecting to various types of devices: PCs, servers, routers, hubs, other switches, and so on. Historically, their role was to break up collision domains, which meant plugging hubs into them. This meant that the switch port had to be able to connect in the same way as the hub—using CSMA/CD, which in turn implies half duplex.

Half duplex means that only one device can use the wire at a time; much like a walkie-talkie set, if one person is transmitting, the other(s) must listen. If others try to transmit at the same time, all you get is a squawk, which is called a collision in network terms. Hubs can use only half-duplex communication. Some older NICs (network interface cards), whether for PCs or even for older routers such as the Cisco 2500 series, can use only half duplex as well.

Full duplex is more advanced. In this technology, a device can send and receive at the same time because the send wire is connected directly to the receive wire on both connected devices. This means that we get the full bandwidth of the link (whether 10Mbs, 100Mbs, or 1Gbs) for both transmit and receive, at the same time, for every connected device. If we have a 100Mbs FastEthernet connection using full duplex, it can be said that the total available bandwidth is 200Mbs. This doesn't mean 200Mbs up or 200Mbs down, but is the sum of the full 100Mbs up and 100Mbs down for that link; some sales documentation might gloss over this point in an effort to make the switch look better on paper.

Full duplex does give us a major boost in efficiency because it allows for a zero-collision environment: if every device connected to a switch can send and receive at the same time, they cannot collide with each other. The only possible conflict (collision is not the right term here) is within the switch itself, and this problem (should it even happen) is handled by the switch's capability to buffer the frames until the conflict is cleared. Setting up a switch so that every device connected to it is running full duplex (and therefore there are no collisions) is sometimes called *microsegmentation* because every device has been segmented into its own collision domain, in which there are no collisions. You might see a reference to the collision detection circuit being disabled on a switch as soon as full duplex is selected for a switch port. Note that full-duplex connections can be only point-to-point, meaning one full-duplex device connected to one switch port; half-duplex connections are considered multipoint, which makes sense when you consider that a hub might be connected to a switch port, and there might be several hosts connected to the hub.

Note that not every NIC, whether on a PC or a router, can support full duplex, although it is very rare these days to find a NIC that does not. Most newer NICs have the capability of full duplex, and virtually all switches do as well; furthermore, most NICs and some switches can perform an autosensing function to determine whether the link is full duplex and set themselves accordingly.

TIP

It is a good practice to set the duplex of certain connections manually to full duplex (or half where necessary), instead of using the Auto function. Connections to other switches, routers, or important servers should be stable and well known enough to set as full duplex. Doing so avoids potential problems in which the duplex negotiation fails, causing a degradation or loss of connectivity. For connections to hosts, where we don't necessarily have control over the NIC settings, the Auto function is useful.

Duplex Configuration

Setting the appropriate duplex mode is done at the interface configuration prompt. The choices you have are Auto, Full, or Half; the default is Auto, so your switch should work in most cases if you do not make any configuration changes at all. Note that if you manually set duplex to Half or Full, the interface(s) will be locked to that setting and will no longer use the Auto negotiation to dynamically determine the duplex setting of the link(s).

Following is an example of a configuration that sets Interface FastEthernet 0/1 to Full duplex/100Mbs, Interface 0/2 to Half Duplex/10Mbs, and Interface 0/3 to Auto Duplex/Auto speed:

```
2950#config terminal
2950(config)#interface fastethernet 0/1
2950(config-if)#duplex full
2950(config-if)#speed 100
2950(config-if)#interface fastethernet 0/2
2950(config-if)#duplex half
2950(config-if)#speed 10
2950(config-if)#interface fastethernet 0/3
2950(config-if)#duplex auto
2950(config-if)#speed auto
```

STP

Earlier, we mentioned that one of the functions of a switch was Layer 2 Loop removal. The Spanning Tree Protocol (STP) carries out this function. STP is a critical feature; without it many switched networks would completely cease to function. Either accidentally or deliberately in the process of creating a redundant network, the problem arises when we create a looped switched path. A *loop* can be defined as two or more switches that are interconnected by two or more physical links.

Switching loops create three major problems:

> ▶ Broadcast storms—Switches must flood broadcasts, so a looped topology will create multiple copies of a single broadcast and perpetually cycle them through the loop.

> ▶ MAC table instability—Loops make it appear that a single MAC address is reachable on multiple ports of a switch, and the switch is constantly updating the MAC table.

> ▶ Duplicate frames—Because there are multiple paths to a single MAC, it is possible that a frame could be duplicated in order to be flooded out all paths to a single destination MAC.

All these problems are serious and will bring a network to an effective standstill unless prevented.

Figure 6.4 illustrates a looped configuration and some of the problems it can create.

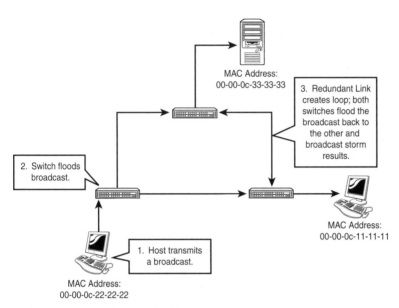

MAC Address:
00-00-0c-33-33-33

3. Redundant Link
creates loop; both
switches flood the
broadcast back to
the other and
broadcast storm
results.

2. Switch floods
broadcast.

MAC Address:
00-00-0c-11-11-11

1. Host transmits
a broadcast.

MAC Address:
00-00-0c-22-22-22

FIGURE 6.4 A Layer 2 (Switching) loop.

Other than simple error, the most common reason that loops are created is because
we want to build a redundant or fault-tolerant network. By definition, redundancy
means that we have a backup, separate path for data to follow in the event the first
one fails. The problem is that unless the backup path is physically disabled—
perhaps by unplugging it—the path creates a loop and causes the problems mentioned previously. We like redundant systems; we do not like loops and the problems they cause. We need a mechanism that automatically detects and prevents
loops so that we can build the fault-tolerant physical links and have them become
active only when needed. The mechanism is called the *Spanning Tree Protocol*; STP
is a protocol that runs on bridges and switches to find and block redundant looped
paths during normal operation. Spanning Tree was originally developed by the
Digital Equipment Corporation (DEC), and the idea was adopted and modified by
the IEEE to become 802.1d. The two are incompatible, but it is exceedingly rare
to find a DEC bridge these days, so the incompatibility is not usually a problem.

EXAM ALERT

STP eliminates Layer 2 loops in switched networks with redundant paths.

NOTE

We will discuss STP at length in the ICND2 section in Chapter 12, "Advanced Catalyst
Switch Operations and Configuration."

Exam Prep Questions

1. What is the most common Layer 2 device?

   ○ **A.** Hub

   ○ **B.** Repeater

   ○ **C.** Router

   ○ **D.** Switch

   ○ **E.** Bridge

2. What devices and functions can an administrator use to segment the network, assuming that no VLANs are used? Choose all that apply.

   ○ **A.** Routers to segment broadcast domains

   ○ **B.** Switches to segment broadcast domains

   ○ **C.** Switches to increase the number of collision domains

   ○ **D.** Bridges to segment collision domains

   ○ **E.** Hubs to segment collision domains

   ○ **F.** Bridges to segment broadcast domains

   ○ **G.** Repeaters to segment broadcast domains

3. How many collision and broadcast domains exist on a 12-port switch with default configuration?

   ○ **A.** 2 collision domains, 12 broadcast domains

   ○ **B.** 1 collision domain, 12 broadcast domains

   ○ **C.** 1 collision domain, 1 broadcast domain

   ○ **D.** 12 collision domains, 1 broadcast domain

4. Which of the following are true of switches and bridges? Choose all that apply.

   ○ **A.** Switches have fewer ports and switch in software.

   ○ **B.** Switches have a higher port density and switch using ASIC hardware.

   ○ **C.** Bridges are faster than switches.

   ○ **D.** Switches are faster than bridges.

   ○ **E.** Switches create only one broadcast domain by default.

   ○ **F.** Bridges create only one broadcast domain.

5. Which switching mode sacrifices speed for error-free switching?

    ○ **A.** Segment-Free

    ○ **B.** Store and Forward

    ○ **C.** Cut Throat

    ○ **D.** Fragment Free

    ○ **E.** Cut Through

6. What is the function of 802.1d STP?

    ○ **A.** Prevents routing loops in redundant topologies

    ○ **B.** Prevents Layer 2 loops in networks with redundant switched paths

    ○ **C.** Prevents frame forwarding until all IP addresses are known

    ○ **D.** Enables the use of multiple routed paths for load-sharing

    ○ **E.** Allows the propagation of VLAN information from a central source

7. What happens when a switch receives a frame with the destination MAC address of FF-FF-FF-FF-FF-FF?

    ○ **A.** The switch drops the frame and sends a "Destination Unreachable" message back to the source.

    ○ **B.** The switch forwards the frame out the port that connects to the host with that MAC address.

    ○ **C.** The switch filters the frame because the address is not valid.

    ○ **D.** The switch floods the frame out all ports except the one it came in on.

8. Which of the following is an advantage of switches over hubs?

    ○ **A.** Switches provide full-duplex microsegmentation of collision domains.

    ○ **B.** Switches' low cost compared to hubs makes them an attractive choice for growing businesses.

    ○ **C.** Although they cannot segment broadcast domains, switches' much greater speed still makes them a desirable upgrade.

    ○ **D.** Switches are impervious to security threats by definition and provide a secure Layer 2 solution out of the box.

9. Which of the following explains why full-duplex operation is desirable?

    ○ **A.** Full duplex allows for the detection of collisions so that data can be retransmitted when the wire is free.

    ○ **B.** Full duplex allows simultaneous transmit and receive functions, providing higher overall throughput.

    ○ **C.** Full duplex provides inter-VLAN routing capability.

    ○ **D.** Full duplex can take advantage of existing coaxial cabling.

10. You currently have seven hubs that form the LAN in your office, to connect 12 servers and 30 users. You have the budget to buy one 24-port switch. What is the most efficient way to utilize your limited switch resources?

    ○ **A.** Connect all the hubs to each other, and then connect the string of hubs to one switch port.

    ○ **B.** Connect each hub to a single switch port.

    ○ **C.** Connect each hub to a single switch port. Move the servers to their own switch ports. Move active user PCs to the remaining switch ports, leaving the less-active PCs attached to hubs. Distribute the remaining PCs evenly across the hubs.

    ○ **D.** Connect each hub to the switch with 2 or 3 cables to provide additional bandwidth.

Answers to Exam Prep Questions

1. Answer D is correct. Switches are by far the most common Layer 2 device in use. A, B, and C are incorrect because hubs, repeaters, and routers are not Layer 2 devices. (Hubs and repeaters are Layer 1; routers are Layer 3.) Answer E is incorrect because switches are much more common than bridges.

2. Answers A, C, and D are correct. Routers segment broadcast domains; switches and bridges segment (increase the number of) collision domains. Answers B, E, F, and G are incorrect. The question stipulates that VLANs are not in use, so a switch does not segment broadcast domains. Hubs and repeaters extend and enlarge, not segment, collision and broadcast domains. Bridges do not segment broadcast domains.

3. Answer D is correct. Each port on a switch is a collision domain. Answers A, B, and C are incorrect; with a default configuration (that is, a single VLAN), a switch creates one broadcast domain.

4. Answers B, D, E, and F are correct. Switches have more ports than bridges and are faster than bridges. Watch out for the trick: Both switches and bridges create only one broadcast domain. Answers A and C are incorrect.

5. Answer B is correct. Store and Forward is the slowest mode but has the advantage of fully error checking every frame for reliability. Answers A, C, D, and E are incorrect. There is no such thing as Segment-Free or Cut-Throat switching. Fragment Free examines the first 64B of every frame for increased reliability, but is not as fast as Cut-Through.

6. Answer B is correct. STP prevents Layer 2 loops if redundant paths exist. Answers A, C, D, and E are incorrect; STP is not concerned with routing loops, IP addresses, routing in general, or VLAN administration.

7. Answer D is correct. The MAC address shown is the broadcast address, so the switch will perform the flood operation. Answer A is what a router would do to a packet it has no route for. Answer B is what the switch would do with a frame whose address is in the MAC address table, and Answer C, the filter operation, happens only when the source and destination addresses are on the same port.

8. Answer A is correct. Switches, when they are configured correctly, can eliminate collisions from the LAN. This design of creating a single collision domain for each connected device is called *microsegmentation*. Answer B is incorrect; switches cost more than hubs. Answer C is incorrect; switches *can* segment broadcast domains through the use of VLANs. Answer D is incorrect; switches are *not* inherently secure and should have basic security measures applied.

9. Answer B is correct. Full duplex uses two pairs to establish separate send and receive circuits, effectively doubling potential throughput. Answer A is incorrect; full duplex disables the collision-detection circuit because it is no longer required. Answer C is incorrect; inter-VLAN routing capability is a Layer 3 function available only on certain switches and has nothing to do with duplex setting (Layer 1). Answer D is incorrect; full duplex cannot work on coaxial cabling because there is only one pair of conductors, and full duplex requires two.

10. Answer C is correct. Doing this will ensure that the most important devices have the best possible data access speed. Answer A is incorrect; this creates a single large collision domain with minimal bandwidth. Answer B is not wrong, it is just not the best answer; in doing this you create several collision domains, but do not make the best use of the switch resources. Answer D is incorrect; this could create nasty loops in your network, and to take advantage of the potential bandwidth both devices would need to be compatible switches—hubs can't do the intended function.

7

CHAPTER SEVEN

Introduction to Wide-Area Networks

Terms you'll need to understand:

✓ Challenge Handshake Authentication Protocol (CHAP)

✓ Password Authentication Protocol (PAP)

✓ Permanent Virtual Circuit (PVC)

✓ Committed Information Rate (CIR)

✓ Local Management Interface (LMI)

✓ Backward Explicit Congestion Notification (BECN)

✓ Forward Explicit Congestion Notification (FECN)

✓ High-Level Data Link Control (HDLC)

✓ Point-to-Point Protocol (PPP)

✓ Network Address Translation (NAT)

Concepts and techniques you'll need to master:

✓ Configuring PPP (point-to-point)

✓ Configuring Frame Relay

✓ Configuring NAT

Introduction

There are two major types of networking: local area network (LAN) and wide-area network (WAN). This chapter discusses WANs.

A WAN is a network that spans a broad geographical area and includes such technologies as ATM, frame-relay, leased lines, and ISDN. These wide-area networking services are leased from providers.

In its simplest definition, wide-area networking can be broken down into three categories:

▶ leased line

▶ circuit switched

▶ packet switched

Leased line WAN solutions use synchronous serial interfaces to connect two sites together. This is the easiest to configure and provides the best reliability. However, this is also the most expensive over long distances.

The second option is circuit-switched technologies. These technologies include both modems connected to asynchronous interfaces and ISDN technologies. With circuit-switched solutions, you establish a circuit between two sites using a telephone company.

The final option is packet-switched technologies, which also use synchronous serial interfaces similar to leased line solutions, but with these, a virtual circuit is established between two or more sites and your data packets are switched across a service provider's network. The service provider's network is transparent to the customer; you will not be able to see any of your provider's equipment. Packet switched technologies include frame-relay, ATM, and X.25. They are commonly used when leased line solutions become cost prohibitive.

Encapsulation Types

With each WAN solution, there is an encapsulation type. Encapsulations wrap an "information envelope" called a *frame* around your data; it is used to transport your data traffic. If you use leased line as your wide-area networking choice, you can encapsulate your data inside a High-level Data-Link Control (HDLC) frame, PPP frame, or Serial Line IP (SLIP) frame. For packet-switched networks, you can encapsulate or package your data in X.25 frames, frame-relay, or asynchronous transfer mode (ATM) frames. (ATM and frame-relay actually have multiple encapsulations—envelope formats—that you can use.) Finally, in circuit-switched environments, you have HDLC, PPP, or SLIP as you do with leased line, but with circuit-switched solutions, it is more common to use PPP as your choice. This is because of the options available with PPP that are catered to using telephone-based circuit-switched networks. These options include such things as authentication and compression. Table 7.1 illustrates the different encapsulations as they are used by various WAN technologies.

TABLE 7.1   WAN Encapsulations

	Leased Lines	Circuit-Switched	Packet-Switched
HDLC	X	X	
PPP*	X	X	
SLIP	X	X	
Frame Relay**			X
ATM***			X
X.25			X

* Technically, it is possible to have PPP run over ATM and frame-relay, but it is not necessary to know this for the CCNA exam.
** Frame Relay actually has two types of encapsulations: IETF and Cisco.
***ATM has several types of encapsulations, but it is not necessary to know these for the CCNA exam.

Cisco HDLC

The default encapsulation on a serial interface is HDLC. The original HDLC encapsulation was defined by the International Organization for Standards (ISO), those same folks who developed the OSI model. The ISO version of HDLC had one shortcoming, however; it had no options to support multiple Layer 3 routed protocols. As a result, most vendors have created their own form of HDLC. Cisco is no exception as it has its own proprietary form of HDLC to support various Layer 3 protocols such as IPX, IP, and AppleTalk. Figure 7.1 illustrates the difference between the ISO and Cisco HDLC frame formats.

EXAM ALERT

Vendors love to test your knowledge of the default settings for their products. Make sure you know that HDLC is the default encapsulation on a serial interface.

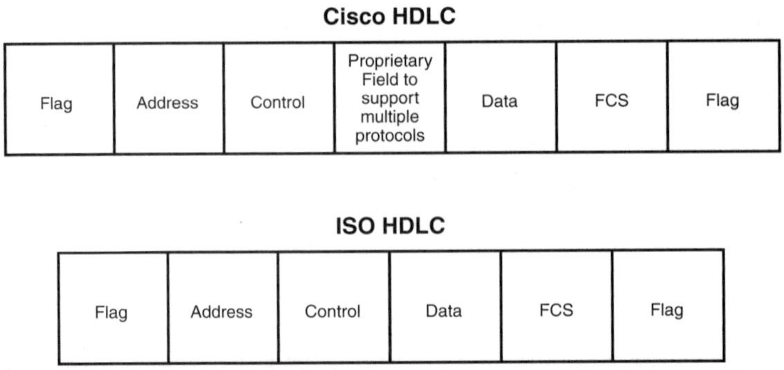

Cisco HDLC

Flag	Address	Control	Proprietary Field to support multiple protocols	Data	FCS	Flag

ISO HDLC

Flag	Address	Control	Data	FCS	Flag

FIGURE 7.1   Cisco and ISO HDLC formats.

PPP

Point-to-point protocol (PPP), defined in RFC 1661, is used to encapsulate network Layer protocols over point-to-point links. PPP can be used over asynchronous, synchronous, or ISDN links.

Components

PPP has two sublayers called network control protocol (NCP) and link control protocol (LCP).

NCP is responsible for supporting multiple Layer 3 protocols. Each protocol has its own NCP, such as the IPCP for IP communication and IPXCP for IPX communication. Think of NCP as the "packager," as it is responsible for packaging, or encapsulating, your packets into a control protocol that is readable by PPP.

The link control protocol is used for establishing the link and negotiating optional settings. These options include

- ▶ **Compression**—You can compress your data to conserve bandwidth across your wide-area network. Options for compression are Stacker and Predictor.

- ▶ **Callback**—With callback, you dial into a router using a modem or ISDN and then disconnect. The other router then calls you back at a predefined number. This option is used for centralized billing and security reasons.

- ▶ **Multilink**—Multilink allows you to bundle together more than one link to create more bandwidth. (Traffic will load balance across the links.) For example, you can bundle two 64K channels together to get a combined 128K.

▶ **Authentication**—You can use authentication to verify a router's identity when it is connecting into your router. Options for authentication include CHAP and PAP.

You can think of LCP as the "negotiator" because it is responsible for negotiating these options between two routers.

Authentication with PAP and CHAP

There are two types of authentications you can use with PPP:

▶ Password Authentication Protocol (PAP)

▶ Challenge Handshake Authentication Protocol (CHAP)

PAP uses a two-way authentication process where the username and password is sent followed by a response message indicating successful or failed authentication. CHAP, however, is much more paranoid about its authentication. It performs a three-way authentication process as shown in Figure 7.2, which takes place not only at the beginning of a connection, but also every two minutes. As if that wasn't paranoid enough, CHAP never sends the password across the link. Instead, an MD5 hash is used to mask the password.

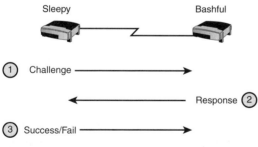

FIGURE 7.2 CHAP authentication.

Configuration

Configuring authentication is a four step process:

1. Configure your hostname.

2. Configure the username and password list for other routers to authenticate to your router.

3. Enable PPP encapsulation.

4. Enable PAP or CHAP authentication.

The hostname takes on a special significance with PPP as it is used as the username to authenticate to another router. For example, let's say that you had two routers named Sleepy and Bashful, as shown in Figure 7.3. For Sleepy, its hostname is used as the username to authenticate to Bashful. For Bashful, its hostname is used as the username to authenticate to Sleepy. Use the hostname command to configure the hostname on each router:

Sleepy:

```
Router(config)#hostname Sleepy
```

Bashful:

```
Router(config)#hostname Bashful
```

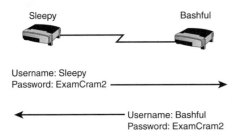

FIGURE 7.3 PPP configuration example.

Next, configure the username and password for other routers to authenticate to you. For the Sleepy router, you will need to configure a username and password for the Bashful router to authenticate to it. Likewise, you will need to configure a username and password for the Sleepy router to authenticate to the Bashful router. Both routers must use the same password. Use the global configuration **username** command to configure your username and password. The syntax for this command is

username *name* **password** *password*

For example,

Sleepy:

```
Sleepy(config)#username Bashful password ExamCram2
```

Bashful:

```
Bashful(config)#username Sleepy password ExamCram2
```

> **TIP**
>
> The hostnames and passwords are case-sensitive. The hostname **Sleepy** is different from the hostname **sleepy**. Make sure that you check the case of your letters when configuring PPP authentication.

The third step in configuring PPP is to enable PPP encapsulation on the interface using the **encapsulation** command. For example, to configure PPP encapsulation on the Serial 0 interface, type the following:

```
Sleepy(config)#interface serial 0
Sleepy(config-if)#encapsulation ppp
```

Finally, you will need to configure your authentication. The interface level command to do this is

```
ppp authentication [chap ¦ chap pap ¦ pap]
```

If you choose the **chap pap** option, it will try CHAP authentication first, and if that fails, it will try PAP. Newer IOS versions (12.3 and 12.4) will also support EAP, MS-Chap, and MS-Chap version 2. Following is the final configuration for the two routers using CHAP authentication:

Sleepy:

```
Router(config)#hostname Sleepy
Sleepy(config)#username Bashful password ExamCram2
Sleepy(config)#interface serial0
Sleepy(config-if)#encapsulation ppp
Sleepy(config-if)#ppp authentication chap
```

Bashful:

```
Router(config)#hostname Bashful
Bashful(config)#username Sleepy password ExamCram2
Bashful(config)#interface serial0
Bashful(config-if)#encapsulation ppp
Bashful(config-if)#ppp authentication chap
```

Verification and Troubleshooting

Verifying and troubleshooting PPP can be done with two commands:

- `show interfaces`

- `debug ppp authentication`

The `show interfaces` command will show you if the line protocol is up or down and the state of LCP. LCP will report in the closed state if it was unable to establish a connection to another router. Following is a sample output from the Sleepy router:

```
Sleepy(config)#show interfaces serial0
serial0 is up, line protocol is up
Hardware is QUICC
  MTU 1500 bytes, BW 64 Kbit, DLY 20000 usec, rely 255/255, load 1/255
  Encapsulation PPP, loopback not set, keepalive not set
 LCP Open
Closed: IPXCP
Listen: CCP
Open: IPCP, CDPCP
<...output omitted...>
```

The `debug ppp authentication` command will show you your authentication as it happens. Following is the output of this command on a router using CHAP authentication:

```
Sleepy#debug ppp authentication
PPP serial0: Send CHAP challenge id=34 to remote
PPP serial0: CHAP challenge from Bashful
PPP serial0: CHAP response received from Bashful
PPP serial0: CHAP response id=34 received from Bashful
PPP serial0: send CHAP success id=34 to remote
```

Frame Relay

Frame Relay is a scalable WAN solution that is often used as an alternative to leased lines when leased lines prove to be cost prohibitive. With frame-relay, you can have a single serial interface on a router connecting into multiple remote sites through virtual circuits.

Concepts and Terminology

You should be familiar with many terms when working with frame-relay. The following sections introduce you to these terms and their definitions.

Virtual Circuits and Network Design

Your virtual circuits can be either permanent or switched. A permanent virtual circuit (PVC) is always connected and, once up, operates very much like a leased line. A switched virtual circuit (SVC) is established only when it is needed. Of these two, PVCs are much more common.

DLCI

Circuits are identified by data-link connection identifiers (DLCI). DLCIs are assigned by your provider and are used between your router and the frame-relay provider. In other words, DLCIs are locally significant.

For example, in Figure 7.4, there are three routers named Sleepy, Grumpy, and Bashful. The Sleepy router is connected to a frame-relay provider that provides permanent virtual circuits to both the Bashful and Grumpy routers. DLCI 100 defines the PVC to Bashful, and DLCI 200 defines the PVC to Grumpy. Although it is not shown in the figure, Bashful and Grumpy will likewise have DLCIs to define their PVCs back to Sleepy.

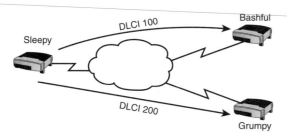

FIGURE 7.4 Frame Relay PVCs.

As an analogy, DLCIs are like shipping docks. If you work for a shipping company, you might have several ships attached to docks that are each going to a different destination. When you have a package to ship, you just need to take it to the ship headed for the destination. It is the captain's job to know how to reach the destination.

DLCIs are like these docks. They are significant only on your side. You send your packet out the relevant DLCI, and the provider's job is to figure out how to get that frame to its destination.

LMI

Behind-the-scenes is a little helper called the local management interface (LMI) that works as a status enquiry and reporting message. LMI messages are sent between your router and the frame-relay provider's equipment to verify and report on the status of your PVC. The three possible states that your PVC can be in are

▶ **Active**—Active is good. Active means that everything is up and operational.

▶ **Inactive**—Inactive is bad. Inactive means that you are connected to your frame-relay provider, but there is a problem with the far-end connection. The problem is most likely between the far-end router and its connection to the frame-relay provider. You should contact your provider to troubleshoot the issue.

▶ **Deleted**—Deleted is also bad. Deleted means that there is a problem between your router and the frame-relay provider's equipment. You should contact your provider to troubleshoot this issue.

Because of the frequency of LMI messages sent between your router and the frame-relay provider, LMI is also used as a keepalive mechanism. Should your router stop hearing LMI messages it will know that there is a problem with your PVC.

There are three types of LMI. These can be manually configured (discussed later in the configuration section) or, with IOS 11.2 and higher, can be auto-detected. The three types of LMI are

▶ Cisco

▶ ANSI

▶ Q933A

CIR

The committed information rate (CIR) is the guaranteed rate at which you are allowed to pass data for a particular PVC. When ordering a PVC, you will request a local access rate (the bandwidth of the physical connection) and the CIR for a PVC. For example, you may order a T1, which has a local access rate of 1.544Mb, for the Sleepy router and a CIR of 128K for the PVC to Bashful, and a CIR of 512K for Grumpy.

BECN and FECN

Frame Relay is generous with its bandwidth. If there is no congestion on your link, you are allowed to burst above the CIR rate. Any traffic sent above your CIR is marked as being Discard Eligible (DE) and, in the event of congestion, will be dropped.

When congestion does occur, congestion notification messages are sent out to notify both the sending and the receiving routers that congestion has occurred and that they should slow down their transmission rates. A Backward Explicit Congestion Notification (BECN) is sent back to the sender and a Forward Explicit Congestion Notification (FECN) is sent forward to the destination to notify them of congestion.

A BECN message is only sent back to the source when the destination sends a frame back. Because the provider must wait for a message to return in order to set the BECN bit in the frame header, the FECN bit is sent to the destination to request some traffic to be sent back in the reverse direction. Without this, the source might never know that congestion has occurred.

In Figure 7.5, traffic is congested going from the Sleepy router to the Bashful router. A FECN is sent to the Bashful router, and a BECN is sent back to the Sleepy router.

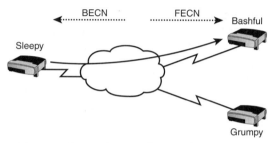

FIGURE 7.5 Congestion on a Frame Relay network.

Inverse-Arp

Frame Relay needs a mechanism to map Layer 3 addresses with Layer 2 frame-relay DLCIs. This can be done through a static map command (shown later in the configuration section) or through inverse-arp. Just like Ethernet ARP, inverse-arp is used to map a Layer 3 address to a Layer 2 address. However, Ethernet ARP maps an IP address to a MAC address and inverse-arp works to map an IP address (or other protocol) to a DLCI.

In Figure 7.6 Sleepy will need a Layer 3 to Layer 2 map to connect to Bashful, which has IP address 10.0.0.2. Using inverse-arp, Sleepy will automatically create a map telling it to use DLCI 100 to get to IP address 10.0.0.2.

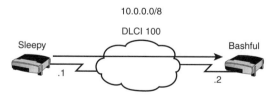

FIGURE 7.6 Inverse-arp example.

NBMA

Frame Relay is a nonbroadcast multi-access (NBMA) medium, which means that broadcast traffic is not allowed to traverse frame-relay traffic. There are ways, however, to circumvent the NBMA nature of frame-relay to allow broadcasts to cross the frame-relay cloud. These are discussed in the configuration section.

The Split Horizon Problem

The split horizon rule (described in Chapter 10, "Basic Routing") states that a route learned on an interface should not be advertised back out that same interface. This poses a problem in NBMA networks where multiple circuits can connect to a single interface in a hub-and-spoke topology.

Hub-and-spoke topologies are commonly used to connect multiple branch offices to a headquarters office. For example, in Figure 7.7, the Bashful and Grumpy routers have circuits to the Sleepy router but not to each other. In this example, Sleepy is operating as the headquarters office. When Grumpy advertises its 13.0.0.0/8 network to the Sleepy router, it is sent into serial 0/0, but the Sleepy router is not allowed to send it back out serial0/0. This causes a problem because serial0/0 is also connected to the Bashful router. As a result, the Bashful router will never know about the 13.0.0.0/8 network.

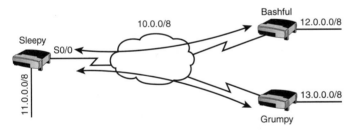

FIGURE 7.7 Split horizon problem.

You have four options to get around the split-horizon problem:

- ▸ Disable split horizon with the no **ip split-horizon** command. If you are not careful, this could create a loop.

- ▸ Have a fully meshed topology where every router has a PVC to every other router. This can get expensive.

- ▸ Use static routes instead of dynamic routing protocols. This is not a scalable solution.

- ▸ Use subinterfaces. This is your best option.

Subinterfaces

A *subinterface* is a subset of an existing physical interface. As far as the router is concerned, the subinterface is a separate interface. By creating subinterfaces, each circuit can be on its own subnet.

There are two types of subinterfaces:

▶ `point-to-point`—This maps a single IP subnet to a single subinterface and DLCI.

▶ `multipoint`—This maps a single IP subnet to multiple DLCIs on a subinterface.

Of these two, only point-to-point subinterfaces address the issue of split horizon. In Figure 7.8, subinterfaces are used on the Sleepy router. Subinterface serial0/0.1 is connected to the Bashful router and subinterface serial0/0.2 is connected to the Grumpy router. Now when Grumpy advertises the 13.0.0.0/8 network to Sleepy, it is sent to the subinterface. Sleepy can forward that information on to the Bashful router because the Bashful router is connected to a different subinterface—a logically (but not physically) different interface.

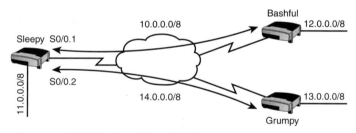

FIGURE 7.8 Split horizon with subinterfaces.

Configuration

Configuring frame-relay involves the following steps:

▶ Changing the encapsulation for frame-relay

▶ Configuring the LMI type (optional for IOS 11.2 or higher)

▶ Configuring the frame-relay map (optional unless you are using subinterfaces)

▶ Configuring subinterfaces (optional)

▶ If using a point-to-point subinterface, configuring your DLCI

To begin, select the frame-relay encapsulation on the interface. There are two types of frame-relay encapsulations: Cisco and IETF. Cisco is the default. The syntax to set your encapsulation is

`encapsulation frame-relay [ietf]`

Next, you can configure the LMI type. The three LMI types are Cisco, Ansi, and Q933a. For IOS 11.2 and higher, the LMI type is automatically detected. For earlier IOS versions, enter the following command under the interface:

`frame-relay lmi-type [cisco ¦ ansi ¦ q933a]`

The third option, configuring a static frame-relay map, is optional unless you are using subinterfaces. The frame-relay map will map a Layer 3 address to a local DLCI. This step is optional because inverse-arp will automatically perform this map for you. The syntax for a frame-relay map is as follows:

`frame-relay map protocol address dlci [broadcast] [cisco ¦ ietf]`

Table 7.2 describes each of these parameters.

TABLE 7.2 frame-relay map Command

Parameter	Description
Protocol	Layer 3 protocol such as IP or IPX.
Address	The Layer 3 address of the remote router (such as an IP address or IPX address).
DLCI	Your local DLCI defining your PVC to the remote router.
Broadcast	Optional, this allows for broadcasts and multicasts to traverse your Nonbroadcast Multiaccess (NBMA) frame-relay network.
Cisco | IETF	Optional, this allows you to change your frame-relay encapsulation per DLCI.

For example, if you were connected to another router using DLCI 100 and the router had the IP address of 10.0.0.2, your frame-relay map statement would be

`Router(config-if)#frame-relay map ip 10.0.0.2 100`

If you want to use a routing protocol across your Frame Relay network, you will need to add the keyword **broadcast** to the end of this command. Routing protocols use broadcasts and multicasts by default, and Frame Relay does not enable broadcasts and multicasts without the use of the broadcast keyword. If you are using inverse-arp to create your maps for you, inverse-arp assumes that you want to use routing protocols and adds the broadcast feature for you.

If you are using a routing protocol in a hub-and-spoke topology, you will probably want to use subinterfaces to avoid the split horizon problem. To configure a subinterface, remove the IP address off the main interface and put it under the subinterface. Configuring a subinterface involves assigning it a number and specifying the type. The following command creates point-to-point subinterface serial0/0.1:

```
Router(config)#interface serial0/0.1 point-to-point
```

To create a multipoint subinterface, enter multipoint instead:

```
Router(config)#interface  serial0/0.1 multipoint
```

After entering one of these commands you will be taken to the subinterface configuration mode where you can enter your IP address:

```
Router(config-subif)#ip address 10.0.0.2 255.0.0.0
```

If you are using a multipoint subinterface, you will need to configure Frame Relay maps and you cannot rely on inverse-arp.

If you are using a point-to-point subinterface, you will need to assign a DLCI to the subinterface. This is only for point-to-point subinterfaces; this is not needed on the main interface or on multipoint subinterfaces. To assign a DLCI to a point-to-point subinterface, enter the following command under the subinterface:

```
frame-relay interface-dlci dlci
```

Now let's put the entire configuration together. The following configuration will configure frame-relay for the Sleepy router using a point-to-point subinterface to connect to the Bashful router and a multipoint subinterface to connect to the Grumpy router. (A point-to-point could also have been used, but we'll use multipoint so you can see both methods.) Figure 7.9 shows the topology for the configuration.

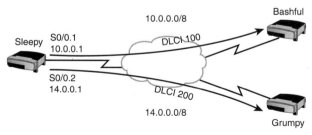

FIGURE 7.9 Frame Relay configuration.

```
interface serial 0/0
encapsulation frame-relay
!
! Take the IP address off the main interface:
no ip address
!
! Configure the connection to the Bashful router
interface serial 0/0.1 point-to-point
ip address 10.0.0.1 255.0.0.0
frame-relay interface-dlci 100
!
! Configure the connection to the Grumpy router
interface serial 0/0.2 multipoint
ip address 14.0.0.2 255.0.0.0
frame-relay map ip 14.0.0.3 200 broadcast
```

> **TIP**
>
> Many engineers like to configure their subinterface number to be the same as the DLCI. For example, if you had a subinterface connected to DLCI 100, your subinterface may be serial 0/0.100.

Verification and Troubleshooting

There are three verification commands and one troubleshooting command you should be familiar with for the exam.

The three commands you can use to verify your configuration are

▶ `show frame-relay lmi`

▶ `show frame-relay pvc`

▶ `show frame-relay map`

`show frame-relay lmi` (displayed in the following) will show LMI statistics, including the number of status enquiries sent and received. Because the status enquiries and responses are used as continuous keepalives, these should be incrementing.

```
LMI Statistics for interface Serial1 (Frame Relay DTE) LMI TYPE = ANSI
   Invalid Unnumbered info 0            Invalid Prot Disc 0
   Invalid dummy Call Ref 0             Invalid Msg Type 0
   Invalid Status Message 0             Invalid Lock Shift 0
   Invalid Information ID 0             Invalid Report IE Len 0
   Invalid Report Request 0             Invalid Keep IE Len 0
   Num Status Enq. Sent 140             Num Status msgs Rcvd 139
   Num Update Status Rcvd 0             Num Status Timeouts 0
```

show frame-relay pvc (displayed in the following) will inform you to the status of your PVC. The status should read ACTIVE. This is also where you will see if your router is receiving BECN and FECN messages.

```
DLCI = 100, DLCI USAGE = LOCAL, PVC STATUS = ACTIVE, INTERFACE = Serial0/0

    input pkts 120          output pkts 70          in bytes 5122
    out bytes 3366          dropped pkts 0          in FECN pkts 0
    in BECN pkts 0          out FECN pkts 0         out BECN pkts 0
    in DE pkts 0            out DE pkts 0
    out bcast pkts 7          out bcast bytes 1366
    pvc create time 1d04h, last time pvc status changed 00:30:32
```

show frame-relay map (displayed in the following) will show you any static maps configured and maps created by inverse-arp. This command will also show you the status of your PVC.

```
Serial0/0 (up): ip 10.0.0.1 dlci 100(0x64,0x1840), dynamic,
            broadcast,, status defined, active
```

EXAM ALERT

Remember, the three **show frame-relay** commands and what they do. show frame-relay lmi shows your LMI statistics while show frame-relay pvc and show frame-relay map will show your PVC status.

For troubleshooting, you can execute the **debug frame-relay lmi** command. This command shows you LMI messages in real-time:

```
Serial 0/0 (out) : StEnq, clock 202121241, myseq 120, mineseen,
119, yourseen 140, DTE up
PVC IE 0x64, length 0x6, dlci 100, status 0, bandwidth 64000
```

Network Address Translation

Network Address Translation (known as NAT in network lingo) has become a generic term for several related but different processes. The basic principle involves changing the source IP of a host in the packet header as its traffic crosses the NAT device. We examine the three main implementations of NAT on Cisco routers, along with the applications, advantages, and disadvantages of the NAT service, and finally the configuration commands to implement, verify, and troubleshoot it.

NAT Terminology

A number of unfortunately confusing terms are associated with NAT that in a typically evil plot are usually testable. Figure 7.10 diagrams a typical, simple NAT setup and accurately locates the terms you need to know.

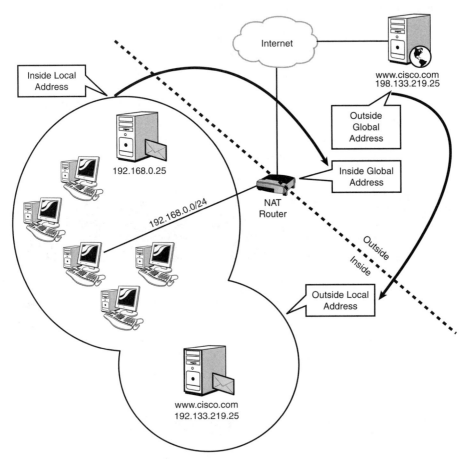

FIGURE 7.10 NAT terminology put into context.

The terms you need to be familiar with are as follows:

▶ `Inside`: This refers (typically) to the private side of the network, usually the source of addresses that are being translated.

▶ `Outside`: This is typically the public side of the network, the address space to which inside hosts are being translated.

- **Inside Local**: These addresses are assigned to inside hosts and are the ones being translated. Inside Local IPs are often RFC 1918 private IPs such as 192.168.x.x, 172.16–31.x.x and 10.x.x.x, but this is by no means a requirement.

- **Inside Global**: These are the addresses to which Inside Locals get translated; often registered IPs obtained from the ISP.

- **Outside Global**: These are typically registered IPs assigned to web servers, mail servers, or any host that is reachable on the public network (Internet, usually) itself.

- **Outside Local**: These are the addresses of Outside Global hosts as they appear on the Inside network; they might or might not have been translated from Outside to Inside, depending on the configuration.

These terms are confusing, and explaining them tends to make things worse.

As a simplification, start with Local and Global: Local addresses are most often the RFC 1918 private ones that we are so familiar with; these will be on the private side of an Internet router. Global addresses are usually real, live, registered IPs, such as www.cisco.com, which at the time of this writing was 198.133.219.25. From this toehold on the terms, you should be able to reconstruct the others—an outside host with a local IP; an inside host with a global IP, and so on.

EXAM ALERT

You must know these terms and where they fit in the NAT system; furthermore, you must be able to apply these terms to the output of some of the NAT verification and troubleshooting commands.

Applications, Advantages, and Disadvantages of NAT

NAT has three main applications:

- If you have more inside hosts than you have outside IP addresses, the NAT service can translate multiple inside hosts to a single outside IP. The two most common scenarios for this are a typical Internet access router, where all the hosts on the inside are granted Internet access using very few—or even just one—outside IP address, or a modification of that example in which a lot of IPs are available, but not enough for our requirements. In both cases, the problem that NAT solves is the depletion of IP addresses; the fact is that very few registered IPs are available any more, so being able to "reuse" them by NATing many hosts to a few of them is very helpful in extending the lifespan of the Internet address space.

▶ NAT can be used to solve two related and vexing network issues: The Overlapping Address Space and the Well-Meaning Admin Error. The Overlapping Address Space happens when we connect to another network that uses the same IP address range as we do; typically, this happens when we merge with another company. The problem is that we will have duplicate routes in different locations when the routers start updating each other, leading to instability, misrouting, and general mayhem.

The Well-Meaning Admin Error happens when the person responsible for the network design either fails to plan for future growth of his network, or simply makes a mistake because of ignorance or arrogance. This most often takes the form of a private network being addressed with public IPs that belong to someone else.

A real-world example of this occurred when a representative from the ISP told their customer (a credit union where I worked) to use the address space of 191.168.0.0 /24 for the inside network. This worked fine until Internet connectivity was required; at which time, it was pointed out that the 191.168.0.0 network was a registered Internet range belonging to an insurance firm in the Carolinas. This did cause some issues (for example, when one wanted to ping a domain controller in the head office in Vancouver, the replies came back from a large router somewhere on the East Coast), but the problem was largely hidden by the NAT service, which translated all those inside local IPs (which were incorrectly using outside global addresses) to appropriate outside global addresses.

▶ NAT can also be used to give a whole cluster of machines (each with different inside local IPs) a single IP address that the clients can use. This is called Load Distribution, and works well for high-volume server clusters such as databases or web servers in which all the clients can use a single virtual IP to reach the service, and that single IP is NATed to all the real IPs of the physical servers.

The advantages of NAT are first and foremost that it conserves the registered IP address space. There is a critical shortage of IPs now, so being able to connect hundreds of hosts to the Internet through a single address is a huge benefit. NAT also provides a certain degree of security because it hides the originating IP address and, if configured properly, prevents bad guys on the Internet from connecting to inside hosts. (The usual caveats here… NAT alone does not provide adequate security, but it can form a part of a secure configuration.) It also helps as a workaround alternative to having to readdress entire networks when address schemes overlap, and makes it easy to change ISP addresses without having to readdress all the inside hosts.

The disadvantages of NAT are primarily that by its very nature, it changes the source IP of traffic, from the actual IP of the host to the Inside Global IP to which it is translated. Some applications do not like this loss of end-to-end IP traceability and stop working. NAT also makes it more difficult when troubleshooting because of that source IP change—and you might be NATed a couple times or more on the journey through the internetwork. Last, the NAT process introduces a certain delay in the transmission of packets as they are rewritten and the translation information is looked up. Spending more money on your NAT box might help speed this up. Call your authorized Cisco VAR, quick!

> **EXAM ALERT**
>
> Know the applications, advantages, and disadvantages of NAT.

Let's look now at the three main NAT implementations.

Static NAT

Static NAT refers to the creation of a one-to-one mapping of an Inside Local IP to an Inside Global IP. Note that this type of NAT does not conserve IP addresses at all because we need one outside IP for every inside IP. Static NAT gives hosts such as mail or web servers access to the Internet even though they are physically on the private network. Perhaps more importantly, it allows us to access that web server from the Internet by creating a static NAT entry from an outside global IP to the server's inside local IP.

Configuring a static NAT entry is easy. The only trick is to make sure that you get NAT working in the right direction: You must be very clear when identifying the Inside interface and the Outside. Figure 7.11 shows a simple network that we use to learn NAT configuration.

Let's create a static NAT entry for the MX (Mail Exchanger) server with the IP of 192.168.0.25. The ISP has told us that we can use a block of IP addresses as shown, from 24.1.1.2 through 24.1.1.6, for our Inside Global addresses. We have decided to use 24.1.1.2 for the Inside Global IP of the MX host.

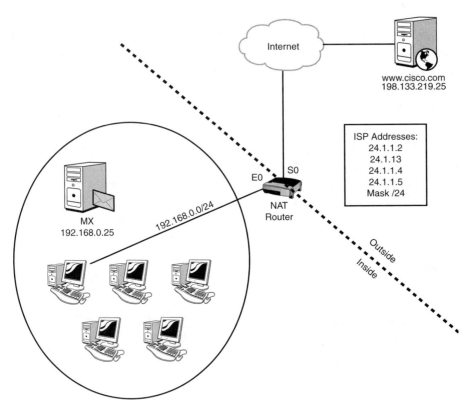

FIGURE 7.11 Sample NAT network.

The global config Static NAT command uses fairly logical syntax:

```
ip nat inside source static <inside local IP> <inside global IP>
```

For our example, the command to enter on the NAT Router would look like this:

```
NAT(config)#ip nat inside source static 192.168.0.25  24.1.1.2
```

Next, we have to identify the Inside and Outside interfaces:

```
NAT(config)#interface e0
NAT(config-if)#ip nat inside
NAT(config-if)#interface s0
NAT(config-if)#ip nat outside
```

And that's all there is to creating a static NAT entry. Remember that static NAT entries use up one outside IP for every inside IP, so they do not conserve the IP address space at all.

Dynamic NAT

Dynamic NAT enables an inside host to get an outside address when needed; this saves us the trouble of creating multiple static maps, one for each host that wants to use the Internet. Dynamic NAT entries still don't conserve IPs, since we still need one IP for every host that wants to connect to the Internet. Remember that if you have more hosts than outside IPs, some hosts will not get a translation entry and will not be capable of using the Internet. For this reason, it is not used much for Internet connectivity.

One of the interesting concepts introduced with Dynamic NAT is that of the NAT Pool: A *Pool* is a defined group of addresses that are available for translation. Configuring Dynamic NAT involves identifying which hosts are to be translated, and to which addresses they should be translated. Both of these steps can use the pool command, but it is more common to use an access list for the inside source and a pool for the outside addresses. The syntax to build a NAT pool looks like this:

```
ip nat pool [pool-name] [first-IP] [last-IP] netmask [mask]
```

The pool name is arbitrary. You can pick something that is meaningful to you. The first-IP and last-IP are the first and last IPs in the pool range, and the mask is the subnet mask of the network those outside IPs are on. Note that you must have the word netmask in the syntax! Here's what this command would look like if we used the same network shown in Figure 7.11 and wanted to use the last four IPs in the range that the ISP gave us:

```
NAT(config)#ip nat pool MyPool 24.1.1.3 24.1.1.6 netmask 255.255.255.0
```

Next, we need to identify what hosts get to be translated; we could build another pool to do this, but it is more commonly done with a standard access list:

```
NAT(config)#access-list 1 permit 192.168.0.0 0.0.0.255
```

This list permits any address that starts with 192.168.0.x. Note that in this case, the list is not permitting traffic to or from the hosts; rather, it is identifying those hosts that can be translated.

> **TIP**
>
> It is a good idea (a best practices) to specifically deny any hosts that you do not want translated, using your access list. For example, because we already have a static NAT entry for the MX server in our example, we don't want it to get another Dynamic translation, so we would start the access list with the line
>
> NAT(config)#`access-list 1 deny host 192.168.0.25`

So at this point, we have built the pool of addresses that we will be translating to, we have identified which hosts can be translated (and possibly those that cannot), and all that is left is to configure the NAT process itself:

```
NAT(config)#ip nat inside source list 1 pool MyPool
NAT(config)#interface e0
NAT(config-if)#ip nat inside
NAT(config)#interface s0
NAT(config-if)#ip nat outside
```

The first line tells the router to use List 1 (which we built previously) to identify which hosts can be translated (these are the Inside Source addresses), and then identifies the pool called MyPool as the addresses to which the Inside Source Addresses should be translated.

The next lines, as before, tell the router which interface should be Inside and Outside. Remember, if you get these backwards, you will be translating the Internet into your private network…that could be bad.

Note that with a pool of only four addresses, the first four hosts who request a translation will get one (which they keep for 24 hours by default), and any additional hosts who request a translation will not be able to get one. The next section shows how PAT resolves this limitation.

> **EXAM ALERT**
>
> **Know the syntax to create a pool of addresses to which hosts can be translated!**

PAT

PAT (Port Address Translation, also known as an **extended NAT entry**) leverages the nature of TCP/IP communication by using the source ports of hosts to distinguish them from each other when they are all being translated, possibly to a single outside address.

With PAT, an inside host is given a translation entry that uses not only the host's IP address, but also its source port. Figure 7.12 illustrates the process as three inside hosts are translated to a single outside IP address as they contact different web servers.

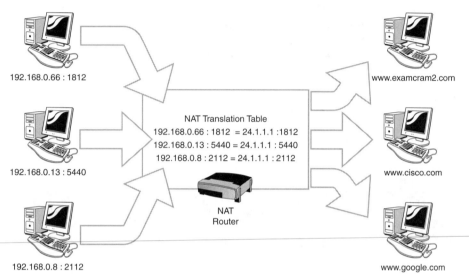

FIGURE 7.12   The mechanics of PAT.

So you can see now how PAT can hugely extend the registered Internet address space: We could in theory translate thousands of private IPs to a single IP (often, the IP assigned to our Outside interface) using PAT, by extending the Inside Local IP with the randomly-generated source port and mapping that to the Inside Global IP extended by the same port number. With more than 64,000 ports available for this *extended translation entry*, the chances of two hosts randomly choosing the same source port are slim; if it does happen, the conflicting hosts are forced to reset and choose a different port number. We can further reduce the chances of this conflict happening by using a pool for PAT, which makes it very unlikely indeed that two hosts would get the same port *and* Inside Global IP from the pool.

The Cisco term for PAT is *overload* because we are overloading a single Inside Global IP with many Inside Local+Port mappings.

Configuring PAT is very easy; the commands are very similar to Dynamic NAT, with the addition of the keyword **overload** as shown:

```
NAT(config)#access-list 1 permit 192.168.0.0 0.0.0.255
NAT(config)#ip nat inside source list 1 interface serial 0 overload
NAT(config)#interface e0
NAT(config-if)#ip nat inside
NAT(config)#interface s0
NAT(config-if)#ip nat outside
```

Note that we have used the parameters interface serial 0 overload at the end of the NAT command; the keyword overload turns on PAT, and the interface serial 0 parameter simply instructs the NAT service to use the existing IP of Serial 0 as the Inside Global IP for the translation. Here is a sample configuration that ties together a Static NAT entry, creates a pool, and overloads that pool to enable PAT:

```
NAT(config)#access-list 1 deny host 192.168.0.25
NAT(config)#access-list 1 permit 192.168.0.0 0.0.0.255
NAT(config)#ip nat inside source static 192.168.0.25  24.1.1.2
NAT(config)#ip nat pool MyPool 24.1.1.3 24.1.1.6 netmask 255.255.255.0
NAT(config)#ip nat inside source list 1 pool MyPool overload
NAT(config)#interface e0
NAT(config-if)#ip nat inside
NAT(config)#interface s0
NAT(config-if)#ip nat outside
```

> **EXAM ALERT**
>
> This configuration, because it is such a fundamental and important one for Internet-connected networks, is highly tested. You should practice entering this configuration on a real router or router sim until you are totally comfortable with the commands.

Verification and Troubleshooting NAT and PAT

The main command used to verify that your NAT configuration is working is **show ip nat translations**. The following sample output demonstrates which could have come from the NAT router in our previous examples.

```
NAT#show ip nat translations
Pro   Inside Global      Inside Local       Outside Local     Outside Global
tcp   24.1.1.1:1812      192.168.0.66:1812  63.240.93.157     63.240.93.157
tcp   24.1.1.1:5440      192.168.0.13:5440  198.133.219.25    63.240.93.157
tcp   24.1.1.1:2112      192.168.0.8:2112   64.233.187.104    64.233.187.104
```

Note that all three inside hosts have been translated to the same Inside Global IP (which likely means that we have overloaded the S0 interface). We have proved that the PAT service is functioning because we can see the different port number extensions listed for each host. Note that the Outside Global and Outside Local IPs are the same; this is because we are not translating those IPs back into our inside network. If we were trying to solve the overlapping address space problem, those two IPs would be different for each outside host.

The command **show ip nat statistics** gives us a snapshot of how many translations have been performed, a general overview of how the NAT device is configured, and how much of our pool has been used, as demonstrated in the following output.

```
NAT#show ip nat statistics
Total translations:  3 (0 static, 0 dynamic, 3 extended)
Outside interfaces:  Serial0
Inside interfaces:  Ethernet)
Hits: 38  Misses:  3
Expired Translations:  0
Dynamic Mappings:
— Inside source
access-list 1 pool MyPool refcount 3
Pool MyPool:  netmask 255.255.255.0
Start 24.1.1.3 end 24.1.1.6
Type generic, total addresses 4, allocated 3 (75%), misses 0
```

If you can successfully ping a remote host, chances are good that your NAT / PAT config is at least partially functional.

If you do run into problems, it is possible to clear the NAT translations from the router, using **clear ip nat translation ***. This command clears all dynamic and extended translation entries. To clear a static entry, you must remove the command from your running-config.

Exam Prep Questions

1. Frame Relay NBMA networks present problems with split-horizon if the topology is not a full mesh. What could you do to get around issues of split-horizon in frame-relay networks? Select the best answer.

   ○ **A.** Enable the command `split-horizon frame-relay` on each serial interface.

   ○ **B.** Create subinterfaces and put each DLCI on its own subinterface.

   ○ **C.** Disable routing protocols on frame-relay interfaces.

   ○ **D.** Create static routes on your spoke routers.

2. Which of the following are components of the LCP phase of PPP? Select all that apply.

   ○ **A.** Compression

   ○ **B.** Authentication

   ○ **C.** QoS

   ○ **D.** Multilink

3. What are the three frame-relay LMI types? Select three.

   ○ **A.** HDLC

   ○ **B.** Cisco

   ○ **C.** Q933A

   ○ **D.** IETF

   ○ **E.** ANSI

4. Given the following configurations, why is the router not routing traffic?

```
router rip
network 10.0.0.0
network 11.0.0.0
!
interface fastethernet0/0
ip address 10.0.0.1 255.0.0.0
!
interface serial0/0
ip address 11.0.0.1 255.0.0.0
encapsulation frame-relay
frame-relay map ip 11.0.0.2 255.0.0.0
```

○ **A.** RIP configuration is incorrect.

○ **B.** IP addresses are incorrect.

○ **C.** The `frame-relay map` statement is incorrect.

○ **D.** Router is missing a static route statement.

5. You have a Cisco router set to the default encapsulation. You connect it to a Juniper router running HDLC encapsulation. Why are the two routers unable to communicate?

○ **A.** The default encapsulation on the Cisco router is PPP. You must change it to HDLC.

○ **B.** The default encapsulation on the Cisco router is IETF. You must change it to HDLC.

○ **C.** Cisco's HDLC implementation is proprietary and is therefore incompatible with other vendor's HDLC implementations.

○ **D.** Cisco routers can connect only to other Cisco routers. You must replace the Juniper router with a Cisco router.

6. What commands can you enter to check the state of your frame-relay PVC? Select all that apply.

○ **A.** `show frame-relay lmi`

○ **B.** `show frame-relay pvc`

○ **C.** `show frame-relay map`

○ **D.** `show frame-relay status`

○ **E.** `show frame-relay`

Answers to Exam Prep Questions

1. Answer B is correct. You should create a subinterface for each DLCI. This will require a different subnet on each subinterface, but you resolve split-horizon issues. Answer A is incorrect because there is not a "split-horizon frame-relay" command. Answers C and D would technically resolve your problem, but they would limit the functionality of your routers. Therefore, answers C and D are not the best answers.

2. Answers A, B, and D are all correct. The LCP phase is responsible for the initial link-setup and negotiating options such as compression, callback, multilink, and authentication. Answer C is incorrect because this is not a component of LCP.

3. Answers B, C, and E are correct. Answer A is incorrect because HDLC is a wide-area network Layer 2 encapsulation, not a frame-relay LMI type. Answer D is incorrect because IETF is a frame-relay encapsulation type, not a frame-relay LMI type.

4. Answer C is correct. If you were not using routing protocols, the **frame-relay map** statement would be correct. However, because you are using a routing protocol, you must have the broadcast keyword at the end for the routing protocols to exchange route information across the Frame Relay link. Answer A is incorrect because RIP is configured correctly. Answer B is incorrect because the IP addresses are correct. Answer D is incorrect because the router is running RIP and does not need a static route.

5. Answer C is correct. Cisco's HDLC contains a proprietary data field that makes it incompatible with other vendor's implementation of HDLC. Answers A and B are incorrect because the default encapsulation is HDLC, not PPP or IETF. Although answer D would make some Cisco salespeople happy, answer D is not the correct answer either. Cisco can communicate with other vendors but not with the default encapsulation.

6. Answers B and C are correct. Answer A is incorrect because **show frame-relay lmi** shows your LMI statistics and not your PVC status. Answers D and E are incorrect because these are invalid commands.

CHAPTER EIGHT

Wireless LANs

Terms you'll need to understand:

- ✓ ISM and U-NII
- ✓ Wi-Fi , 802.11, 802.11a, 802.11b, 802.11g
- ✓ Ad-Hoc mode and Infrastructure mode
- ✓ BSS and ESS
- ✓ FHSS, DSSS and OFDM
- ✓ SSID
- ✓ Authentication, Encryption, and Intrusion
- ✓ WEP, EAP, WPA and WPA2/802.11i

Concepts and techniques you'll need to master:

- ✓ Identify the differences between wireless LAN standards
- ✓ Describe the differences between WLAN modes
- ✓ Identify the differences between BSS and ESS
- ✓ Identify security threats specific to WLANs and techniques to mitigate them
- ✓ Identify the four WLAN security implementations, their operation, strengths, and weaknesses
- ✓ Identify the basic configuration steps for installing and using a wireless access point

Introduction

This chapter introduces Wireless LAN (WLAN) technology. We will discuss the standards associated with WLANs, how WLANs are deployed and the basics of how they operate, security threats specific to WLANs and measures to mitigate them, and the essential steps to connect and configure an access point (AP) and a client.

WLAN Standards

WLAN technology has made rapid advancement in the past few years. The reasons for this are pretty simple: It is very convenient for users; it's usually less trouble and cost to deploy (because there are no wires to buy and install); and as the technology improves, the speeds attainable are pretty respectable, even in today's bandwidth-hungry world.

As with any networking technology, some implementations are vendor-proprietary, but most are compliant with a standard, especially after some time has passed and the standard is ratified, allowing all the vendors to build equipment that is compliant. WLANs are defined by a series of standards that are the result of cooperative work between the International Telecommunication Union-Radio Communication Sector (ITU-R), the Institute of Electrical and Electronics Engineers (IEEE), the Wi-Fi Alliance and the Federal Communications Commission (FCC) (or its equivalent in other countries). So many regulatory bodies are in on this because unlike an Ethernet switch, for example, a wireless AP could really interfere with other radio functions if it did not stick to its allocated frequencies and transmission strength. Imagine if you set up your AP and discovered that you had just jammed all radio contact between an airport tower and the aircraft it was controlling. That would be bad. It would be worse for the people on the planes, though.

Unlicensed Radio Bands

WLANs operate in one of the unlicensed radio frequency bands under the regulation of the FCC (or its equivalent in other countries). These bands are called the Industrial, Scientific, Medical (ISM) and the Unlicensed National Information Infrastructure (U-NII) bands. These bands are reserved for use by low-power radio equipment that does not require a radio operator's license to use (some WLANs can be operated in the ISM band at much higher power if the operator acquires a license). Table 8.1 lists the information of interest.

TABLE 8.1 Frequency Bands, Names and Related Standards

Frequency Band	Name	Application
900MHz	ISM	Older cordless phones, Global System for Mobile Communications (GSM) cell phones
2.4GHz	ISM	802.11, 802.11b, 802.11g, 802.11n WLANs
5GHz	U-NII	802.11a, 802.11n WLANs

EXAM ALERT

Know the information in Table 8.1.

802.11

The core WLAN standard is IEEE 802.11, sometimes known as Wi-Fi because this was the first standard championed by the Wi-Fi Alliance. Wi-Fi is short for Wireless Fidelity, a retro/hip reference to Hi-Fi. The IEEE ratified 802.11 in 1997.

In much the same way that ethernet was standardized by 802.3 with subsequent iterations of improved ethernet getting extra letters to distinguish them from the original (such as 802.3u, 802.3z, 802.3ae, and so on), the subsequent variations and improvements to 802.11 are distinguished by a letter as well. The ones you want to remember are 802.11a, 802.11b, and 802.11g. There are a couple others in the works; you have probably seen 802.11n gear in stores. The CCENT and CCNA tests are not talking about 802.11n yet, but we've included a little of it here for interest and perspective, and because we think it will be included on the exam one of these days.

Table 8.2 lists the WLAN standards you should know, and some of the relevant info about each. (Some of the terms and acronyms will be explained in later sections).

TABLE 8.2 WLAN Standards (North American Version)

Characteristic	802.11	802.11a	802.11b	802.11g	802.11n
Date of Standard	1997	1999	1999	2003	2008?
Max Speed (DSSS)	n/a				
11-Mbps FHSS	n/a	11Mbps	n/a		11 Mbps per stream
Max Speed(OFDM)	n/a	54Mbps	n/a	54Mbps	600Mbps
Assigned Frequency Band	2.4GHz	5GHz	2.4GHz	2.4GHz	2.4 and/or 5.0GHz
Available Channels	11	23	11	11	11 or 23
Approx. Range	75 feet	75 feet	150 feet	150 feet	500 feet

802.11, sometimes known as *legacy*, specifies an 11Mbps maximum speed, using 11 channels in the 2.4GHz band. The 11 channels available were used in a random, rapid sequence to statistically avoid interference from other devices using the same frequencies. This "skipping around" the channels is called Frequency Hopping Spread Spectrum (FHSS). In reality, a lot of the data was lost to interference anyway, and a more sophisticated system was engineered for 802.11a.

802.11a

802.11a uses a much higher frequency (5GHz) and a fancy method of using the available channels, called Orthogonal Frequency Division Multiplexing (OFDM). The science of how OFDM works is well beyond the scope of this exam, but you should know the term and which standards it applies to. A big advantage of the 5GHz band is that it is immune to common 2.4GHz emissions, such as from cordless phones, baby monitors, microwave ovens, and many of the wireless conveniences we take for granted that can really interfere with WLAN transmissions in the 2.4GHz range. A disadvantage is that the higher frequencies are more easily absorbed by structures and furniture, reducing the effective range. However, the way OFDM works actually gives it a range advantage in these office-type surroundings; in addition, higher frequencies mean smaller antennas, which means we can increase the antenna gain (sort of like turning up the listening volume). These things improve the range and so balance out the range loss of the higher frequencies. It was mostly enterprise customers who liked (and often still like) 802.11a, in part because it never caught on with the general public so the risk of interference and security breaches was reduced.

TIP

On the topic of high and low frequencies and transmission range, here's a little lesson to help you remember what happens. Did you ever wonder why foghorns are really low notes, instead of a shrill whistle? It's because the low frequency travels much farther, especially through fog, than a high one would. This is useful if you don't want to drive your boat onto a rock. For those who have never heard a foghorn, think of a car with a big stereo system: What do you hear from a block away? *Boooom... Boooom.* Not the tweeters—the subwoofer. Low frequency, longer range.

802.11b

802.11b, although later in the standards list, was actually in the market before 802.11a. 802.11b is back in the 2.4GHz range, so interference sources are a concern, but now we have another method of using the available channels called Direct Sequence Spread Spectrum (DSSS). Again, the complex science behind how it works is not of concern for the CCNA exams, but you need to understand a little about it. There are eleven channels within the frequency band assigned to this standard by the FCC. Typically, only three of these channels (channels 1, 6, and 11) are ever used because all 11 channels overlap each other. When two APs use channels that are adjacent or close together (say, 2 and 3) or the APs themselves are close enough together to "jam" each other, the signals from one channel get stepped on, interfered with, and generally disrupted by the other. Channels 1, 6, and 11 do not overlap each other, as shown in Figure 8.1.

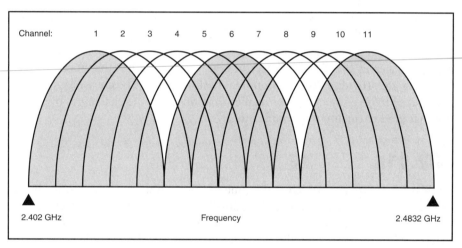

FIGURE 8.1 2.4GHz DSSS 11-channel overlap showing channels 1, 6, and 11 nonoverlapping.

By sticking to these three channels, the frequencies are far enough apart that it is very unlikely that they will interfere with each other, so less data is lost. In an environment where you have multiple APs (as in most business implementations), you take advantage of this by having your different access points using different channels, consequently overlapping their coverage area without overlapping the channels they use that could cause interference. We'll mention this again when we talk about BSS and ESS a little later.

802.11g

802.11g is currently the most popular standard, mostly because the home market has significantly driven demand. Consumers wanted more speed and backward compatibility with the wireless devices they already had, and they wanted it quickly and cheaply, well before the standard was ratified. The home market exploded, but the business market held back until that ratification happened to avoid deploying immature technology (another reason that you will find more 802.11a than 802.11g in business environments). 802.11g is backward compatible with 802.11b and uses the same 2.4GHz frequency band, but provides the same higher speeds of 54Mbps and slightly longer range. This was a difficult engineering feat to achieve, and if 802.11b and 802.11g do coexist in the same system, the 802.11b tends to impair the performance of the 802.11g system. 802.11g uses OFDM for most of its possible data speeds, but reverts to an 802.11b-compatible system for others. Many wireless devices now provide a, b, and g capability in a single unit.

The problem with the popularity of 802.11g goes back to overcrowding and interference. As I sit here in my home office, I can pick up no less than 12 wireless APs, and all of them are using the same channel. Add in all the other interfering devices in the 2.4GHz spectrum, and it's a safe bet that these wireless networks are providing less than optimal performance. A business-class WLAN is expected to be of much higher quality than that, and the challenges of providing that kind of quality are significant.

802.11n

Table 8.2 lists 802.11n, which at the time of this writing is not yet ratified by the IEEE but is expected to be so in 2008, possibly as late as 2009. Manufacturers are already selling "prestandard" 802.11n devices that comply with the draft standard, which will presumably be upgradeable if the standard should substantially change. The big draw is, of course, speed, with theoretical speeds of 600Mbps. This opens up the exciting possibility of wirelessly streaming HD-format movies from your media center to the TV in the bedroom without excessive delay. In addition to OFDM and the use of the 5GHz band, 802.11n uses a feature called Multiple Input Multiple Output (MIMO), which requires two sending antennae and two receiving antennae, and allows for up to four send and four receive. Effectively, you use multiple concurrent streams to achieve the high data rates. That's why the 802.11n APs often have several antennae on the box.

802.11n is exciting because it is fast, has great range, uses the 5GHz band (reducing the interference and overcrowding problem) and is backward compatible with a, b, and g. The only caution is that all of this is still prestandard; if you are going to buy something, make sure the box at least says it is compliant with the 802.11n draft standard.

WLAN Operational Modes

A wireless device can operate in either Ad Hoc mode or in Infrastructure mode. The following sections describe these modes.

Ad Hoc Mode

Ad Hoc is Latin for "this purpose"; in this case, it refers to a connection between wireless devices (such as two laptops, for example) for a temporary high-speed link, perhaps to share files or play a game. No AP is required; indeed, no network devices other than the two client machines are needed. Ad Hoc mode is not usually associated with business-class networks.

Infrastructure Mode

In Infrastructure mode, an AP is required because the client devices cannot send directly to each other; they must send through the AP. The AP, in turn, handles all the wireless client data and provides the connection to the wired LAN by way of its connection to the switch. Infrastructure mode is what you will find in business environments. With the use of an AP, many devices can connect to the network, and you can provide authentication and encryption for wireless connections to help secure the WLAN.

Autonomous Mode

Within the Infrastructure mode of operation, Cisco makes a distinction between Autonomous and Lightweight modes. The difference is simple: in Autonomous mode, each AP is managed separately and sends wireless client data into the network itself. This is a suitable mode for small networks where management and security issues are not overwhelming.

Lightweight Mode

Cisco has put a lot of work into making WLANs manageable and secure. In Lightweight mode, each AP associates with a WLAN controller, a special device that provides a single point for management and security of multiple APs in the network. The APs and WLAN controllers communicate using the Lightweight Access Point Protocol (LWAPP), a Cisco-proprietary protocol built for this system. In addition, all wireless client traffic from each AP is tunneled through the WLAN controller. It's more complicated and more expensive, but tremendously powerful for managing and securing many APs in a centralized fashion.

Basic Service Set and Extended Service Set

Basic Service Set (BSS) and Extended Service Set (ESS) are terms that describe how clients can associate with and use the available APs and network infrastructure. The following sections describe these terms.

BSS

BSS is defined as a single AP that provides network connectivity for its associated clients. You could have several APs in your system, but they would each be offering a separate WLAN, and you could not "roam" between the APs; your laptop would need to associate itself with each new AP when you lost signal from the old one as you walked around the building.

ESS

ESS is more typical of a business environment. With ESS, each AP still defines a BSS, but the group of APs and their BSSs form the ESS. The main advantage is that clients can roam between the overlapping coverage areas of the individual APs' BSSs, without losing the functionality of their connection to the ESS and thus to the network. To form an ESS, all the APs use the same Service Set Identifier (SSID). An SSID is just a name (technically, it is a string of up to 32 alphanumeric characters) that identifies the WLAN. You might have three APs for the office area, all configured with the same SSID, with overlapping coverage areas. Each wireless client changes its association to the AP with the strongest signal, which will change depending on where you are in the office and where you move to. It is typical to have the APs use different channels, to reduce interference and keep the throughput speed up. As you move, even though your association to the BSS of the AP changes to that of the next one, your association to the ESS provided by the three APs together does not, so your perception is that you never lose your connection to the network. Figure 8.2 shows what an ESS system might look like; there are two APs, each using the same SSID but on different channels. Mobile devices such as laptops, PDAs, or a wireless IP Phone can move between the two APs without losing connectivity to the network. In the diagram, the wireless IP Phone is roaming between the APs.

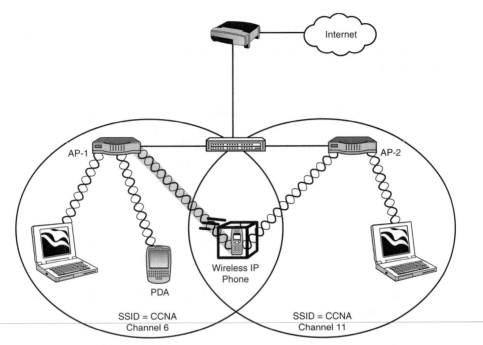

FIGURE 8.2   Two APs in Infrastructure mode using the same SSID form an ESS to allow devices to roam.

WLAN Security

This section takes a brief look at some of the security threats that target WLANs and the methods available to mitigate those threats.

WLAN Security Threats

Any network is vulnerable to attack. A wired network requires that you physically connect to a cable to execute an attack. If there is no possibility of an outside connection to your wired system, an attack must come from an available wired connection and is much easier to find and stop.

A WLAN's versatility and convenience makes it a huge security vulnerability. By adding an AP to your network, you are making it possible for people to connect to your network without being in physical contact with it. The following are just some of the more common WLAN threats that we need to guard against:

▶ **War Driving**—Refers to driving around with a laptop, looking for unsecured APs to connect to and get free Internet access. Of those 12 APs in my neighborhood, 4 of them are completely unsecured and I could connect, use their Internet service, or snoop around their home network if I chose to.

▶ **Hackers**—Hackers usually want more than free Internet access; they are looking for interesting or useful information such as credit card numbers or other protected data, or else they just want to mess up someone's network out of malice or boredom. Being able to claim that they took down Yahoo for an hour gives them bragging rights; putting their former employer offline is an act of revenge.

▶ **Internal**—These attacks are the result of malicious or ignorant actions by the company's own employees. The classic example is the employee who buys a little AP and plugs it into the network drop in their office. The defaults on consumer APs are typically no security at all; now a hacker can connect easily and steal access or information. The hacker does not even need to actively seek information; the hacker can simply intercept the unencrypted traffic and possibly get useful or private information. The FBI estimates that more than 75% of network attacks come from internal sources.

▶ **Rogue APs**—These are APs put in place in a WLAN without authorization. Usually, the hacker has spent some time with easily available software tools intercepting the signaling between existing APs and clients. Even if there is some security in place, given enough time, weak authentication and encryption can be cracked. After the hacker has the necessary information, the hacker can set up a rogue AP with the correct SSID and authentication keys. Clients then associate with the device, and now the hacker has direct access to all the information coming through that AP.

These scenarios make a business network admin freak out. For quite a while, businesses were not implementing WLANs because they knew that the lack of security was a major issue.

WLAN Security Methods

There are three main ways to apply security to WLANs:

▶ **Authentication**—Requires all clients connecting to an AP to provide some (hopefully secret) information called a *key* to prove that they are authorized to connect. Ideally, we want to use *mutual authentication*, where the AP also has to prove to the client that it is a legitimate (that is, not rogue) AP. Strong cryptography allows the exchange of proof of the correct key without actually sending the key; this small mathematical miracle means that hackers can't simply intercept the key and use it to gain access.

▶ **Encryption**—Applies a mathematical formula and a secret key to the raw data, encrypting it into a stream of gibberish that only another device with the correct key and decryption formula can unscramble. If hackers intercept encrypted data, they are unlikely to be able to decrypt it without the key. I didn't say it was impossible—there are some weak encryption schemes out there that can be cracked relatively quickly. The strong encryption schemes are strong enough that it would take years to crack them, at which point most data would no longer be worth the trouble.

▶ **Intrusion Detection/Intrusion Prevention**—These systems guard against unauthorized use of the WLAN. These systems are typically implemented as part of a Lightweight architecture. One of my favorites is a system that detects a new AP in the system, interrogates it, and causes it to shut down if it is classified as a rogue AP. Cisco's Structured Wireless-Aware Network architecture (SWAN) includes several devices and tools that improve the manageability and security of WLANs. Learn more about SWAN at www.cisco.com/go/swan.

As usual, different vendors were keen to get their product to market and start making money, so there were some nonstandardized security systems in place before the standards came out, but things have settled down somewhat into a fairly consistent and pretty secure standard that most vendors are supporting. It goes without saying that if you do not actually apply the security, it is not secure!

WLAN Security Standards

The next section describes the four WLAN security standards you need to know for the exam.

WEP

The Wired Equivalent Privacy (WEP) standard was introduced as part of 802.11. WEP uses a static preshared key system, meaning that all the APs and all the clients must have the same key string configured in order to authenticate and transmit encrypted data. The problems with this are that it is an administrative headache to change the keys, which means they don't change often, which is not good. On top of that, the encryption method used was pretty weak. These factors meant that a hacker could intercept lots of authentication attempts, with all the clients using the same key over and over, all of it using weak encryption. From that point it is a pretty simple matter to crack the encryption, read the data, or connect to the network at will.

Some additional (not part of the standard) features were introduced by manufacturers to bolster the flaws in WEP. Most APs allow you to choose not to broadcast the SSID, which means that a client wanting to connect must know the SSID. This is not going to fool a serious hacker; it is still perfectly possible to capture WLAN traffic and determine the SSID in use. Another supplementary security feature was the capability to filter which Media Access Control (MAC) addresses (of client wireless NICs) could connect to the AP. The premise was that no two MACs are the same, so only a short list of authorized MACs needed to be added to the APs list. Unfortunately, it is a trivial matter to change the source MAC with software, so after we learn an authorized MAC, we can pretend to be that MAC.

Because its security features really deter only honest people, WEP should not be considered a viable security method in current WLAN deployments.

The Cisco Interim Solution

Being one of the major stakeholders in the success of wireless for enterprise customers, Cisco worked out an interim set of solutions to the problems WEP had. In cooperation with the Wi-Fi Alliance, Cisco utilized components of the IEEE 802.1x authentication protocol and its own Extensible Authentication Protocol (EAP) to significantly increase WLAN security. The three key improvements that Cisco's solution offered were the following:

▶ **Dynamic Key Exchange**—This system utilizes an elegant cryptographic solution to the problem of keying. Instead of a preshared key that all devices must be manually configured with (and that as a consequence seldom changes), dynamic keying allows the key to be secretly agreed upon by the devices themselves, without administrative effort beyond setting it up. Cisco used a proprietary method of dynamic keying.

▶ **User Authentication with 802.1x**—This component leveraged an existing IEEE authentication scheme, requiring the user to supply a username/password package when attempting to connect. This added another layer of complexity to the task of hacking in, because somehow the username and password had to be learned. 802.1x is quite difficult to circumvent if it's properly configured, but it is somewhat complex to set up.

▶ **Unique Key per Packet**—With the use of dynamic keying, the encryption key could change with every packet sent, so that even if the hacker figures out the key, all the hacker can read is that one packet. This operation obviously adds significant overhead to packet processing, but processing power was getting better and cheaper all the time, so the benefits outweighed the drawbacks.

WPA

Cisco was out of the gate fast with a hybrid of proprietary and standards-based protocols to address WLAN security, because the IEEE standards ratification process was slower than the market demand. While Cisco was doing their own thing on their products, the Wi-Fi Alliance kept one eye on what the IEEE was likely to implement, so that they weren't too far off base when the standard did come out, and put forth a WLAN industry-standard (in contrast to IEEE standard) security scheme called Wi-Fi Protected Access (WPA).

WPA set the same basic goals as Cisco's solution, but with differences in how it was executed. Dynamic keying was achieved using the Temporal Key Integrity Protocol (TKIP) standard. WPA does device authentication either with simple preshared keying or 802.1x authentication. This worked well for both the consumer and business markets because the typical consumer could not set up an 802.1x system, whereas most businesses could and wanted the extra security.

One other benefit of WPA was its sponsorship by the Wi-Fi Alliance, which had proved that its certification program could guarantee that Wi-Fi–certified devices would work together reliably.

802.11i/WPA2

In 2005, the IEEE ratified the 802.11i security standard, which included features for dynamic keying, authentication, and very strong encryption using the Advanced Encryption Standard (AES) algorithm. Although functionally similar to the Cisco and WPA systems, 802.11i is not backward compatible, and provides much stronger encryption.

The Wi-Fi Alliance continues to certify equipment for compliance with the 802.11i standard, but they call it WPA2. This continues the positive association with the success of WPA in the minds of consumers and IT managers, but causes some confusion as to whether they are two different standards. They aren't.

Basic WLAN Configuration Steps

Installing a WLAN is relatively simple, but you should bear in mind the following procedure, both to make your life simpler and to stick close to what Cisco wants you to know as a CCNA.

The steps to implementing a WLAN are as follows:

1. Verify the existing wired network—Check that Dynamic Host Configuration Protocol (DHCP) is working and that the virtual LAN (VLAN) assigned to the access port is configured as required. If a client connected to the port that the AP will use can get an IP address and communicate with other network resources, the AP should be able to as well.

2. Install the first AP—Assign the AP an IP address and mask and a Default Gateway for management purposes. Connect to the switch access port with a straight-through cable.

3. Configure the wireless settings—Change the default SSID to something in accordance with your local Security Policy (typically *not* the company name or phone number). Enable the radio, but do not enable any security yet. Choose which standard(s) the radio will support (802.11a/b/g). Choose the channel the AP will use (check what channels are in use nearby). Choose the transmit power setting.

4. Install and configure one wireless client—Verify that it can connect. Many current operating systems and NIC software products will automatically discover APs and connect to the strongest signal.

5. Verify that the client works—In the absence of security configuration, the simplest way to check is to try to browse the Internet. If the client does not function properly, check the following:

   ▶ Is the AP close to the center of the area where the clients are?

   ▶ Is there an interference source close by (microwave, cordless phone, or the like)?

   ▶ Is the AP or the client close to a large metal structure (filing cabinet, steel door, reinforced concrete wall, steel-stud wall, heating/cooling duct)? If so, move it to an area free of metal.

   ▶ Is the AP's coverage area adequate to reach the client? Try moving closer to the AP.

6. Configure the desired security features on both AP and client (it's recommended to use the strongest available security method).

7. Verify that the client can still connect to resources in the presence of security configuration.

The configuration of security is beyond the scope of the exam, but you should understand the process: If it works without security but stops working when you add security, the security configuration is the likely problem.

Exam Prep Questions

1. Which of the following frequency bands is used by 802.11a ?

   ○ **A.** 2.4MHz

   ○ **B.** 2.4GHz

   ○ **C.** 5KHz

   ○ **D.** 5GHz

2. Which of the following are true of WLAN standards?

   ○ **A.** 802.11b uses DSSS to achieve speeds of 54Mbps

   ○ **B.** 802.11b uses OFDM to achieve speeds of 11Mbps

   ○ **C.** 802.11g uses only OFDM in the 5GHZ range

   ○ **D.** 802.11a uses only OFDM to achieve speeds of 54Mbps

3. You have been given an 802.11b-compliant AP to install in your location in San Jose, California. Which three channels will you be able to use without interference due to overlapping?

   ○ **A.** a, b, g

   ○ **B.** 21, 22, 23

   ○ **C.** 1, 5, 10

   ○ **D.** 1, 6, 11

4. You want to be able to walk around your production floor with a tablet PC, checking inventory and order status on the database. The shop floor will need four APs to provide adequate coverage area. What mode will allow you to stay wirelessly connected as you move between the four APs?

   ○ **A.** Ad Hoc

   ○ **B.** 802.1q

   ○ **C.** BSS

   ○ **D.** ESL

   ○ **E.** ESS

5. Which of the following is not a security scheme for WLANs?

   ○ **A.** WEP

   ○ **B.** WPA

   ○ **C.** 802.11i

   ○ **D.** MIMO

6. True or False: Multiple APs in the same ESS WLAN should be in the same VLAN.

   ○ **A.** True

   ○ **B.** False

7. Which of the following could interfere with your AP's transmissions?

   ○ **A.** A large magnet nearby

   ○ **B.** An AM radio nearby

   ○ **C.** A baby monitor nearby

   ○ **D.** A CDMA cell phone nearby

8. Which standards-based WLAN security scheme includes dynamic keying and strong encryption using AES?

   ○ **A.** WPA

   ○ **B.** Cisco EAP/802.1x

   ○ **C.** 802.1i

   ○ **D.** 802.11i

9. What is a rogue AP?

   ○ **A.** An AP that has a faulty component, causing it to "jam" other APs by transmitting collision frames at maximum power

   ○ **B.** An AP that can be easily moved to any location in the building

   ○ **C.** An unauthorized AP that is installed to facilitate the capture of information

   ○ **D.** An AP that does not follow the accepted WLAN standards, but uses proprietary protocols instead

10. Which option will you configure last when setting up your AP?

   ○ **A.** 802.11i settings

   ○ **B.** IP address and Mask

   ○ **C.** a/b/g mode

   ○ **D.** SSID

Answers to Exam Prep Questions

1. Answer D is correct. 802.11a uses the 5GHz range, not 2.4GHz, and certainly not anything in the MHz or KHZ range!

2. Answer D is correct. Answer A is incorrect; 802.11b cannot send faster than 11Mbps. Answer B is incorrect; 802.11b does not use OFDM. Answer C is incorrect; 802.11g does not use the 5GHz band.

3. Answer D is correct. In North America, the regulatory agencies have allotted the non-overlapping channels 1, 6, and 11 for use by 802.11b APs. Answer A is wrong because the channels are numbered, not lettered, and these letters refer to the 802.11 standards as a way to trick you. Answers B and C are the wrong channels.

4. Answer E is correct. The Extended Service Set allows you to roam between APs with the same SSID. Answer A is wrong; Ad Hoc refers to a client-to-client temporary connection. Answer B is wrong; the 802.1q standard refers to a switch trunking protocol. Answer C is wrong; Basic Service Set does not allow roaming, it provides association to a single AP with a unique SSID. Answer D is wrong; English as a Second Language is of almost no use in allowing you to roam wirelessly.

5. Answer D is correct. Multiple Input Multiple Output is a feature of 802.1n APs that increases the data rate. WEP, WPA, and 802.1i are all security schemes for WLANs.

6. True. Multiple APs should be in the same VLAN, which is determined by the switchport setting on the access switch that the AP connects to.

7. Answer C is correct. Baby monitors often use the 2.4GHz band, as do many APs, and could easily cause interference. Magnets do not themselves cause interference (an electromagnet might, or a fixed magnet that is part of an energized speaker might). An AM radio is just a receiver and will not cause interference (unless there is a faulty component "leaking" EMR). CDMA cell phones are usually down in the 800 or 1900MHz band and are not likely to interfere.

8. Answer D is correct. 802.11i defines a set of standard protocols for authentication, dynamic key exchange, and encryption using AES. WPA does not use AES; Cisco's EAP/ 802.1x solution is not fully standards-based and does not use AES; 802.1i is a distracter to fool you.

9. Answer C is correct. A rogue AP is usually put in place by a hacker or an inside facilitator to capture information from clients that associate to it unknowingly. Answers A, B, and D sound good, but are just wrong.

10. Answer A is correct. Security settings should be the last component you configure, after you have ensured that the AP works properly without security applied. Answers B, C, and D are all part of the steps to set up the AP for client testing without security.

CHAPTER NINE

Basic Network Security

Terms you'll need to understand:

✓ Confidentiality

✓ Integrity

✓ Availability

✓ Intruder Prevention System

✓ Adaptive Security Appliance

✓ Anomaly Guard

✓ Cisco Secure Agent

✓ Network Admission Control

✓ Monitoring, Analysis, and Response System

Concepts and techniques you'll need to master:

✓ Importance of security policies

✓ Basic mitigation steps

Introduction

To say that security is important is to state the obvious. With Cisco routers and switches forming the backbone to today's network infrastructures, it becomes especially important to keep security in mind. Should your backbone be breached, the entire network could be crippled, sensitive information could be eavesdropped on, and data could be corrupted or altered in a way that could have drastic effects on your operations. For this reason, Cisco expects you to have a general understanding of network security, which includes

- Describing the increase in security threats and the need for a security policy

- Explaining general methods to mitigate threats

- Describing the functions of common security appliances/applications

- Describing the recommended practices of securing network devices

The Need for Security

The goal of security is to keep that which is vulnerable from being exploited. Servers, network devices, operating systems, and applications can all contain vulnerabilities that you may be responsible for protecting against attacks. These vulnerabilities exist because of coding errors and configuration problems. Today's networks are becoming increasingly complex and more difficult to manage. As networks become more complex, the number of vulnerabilities in a network increases.

A second reason for the rise of threats is the constant challenge of software developers balancing features and ease of use and at the same time providing a secure product. People want software and hardware that contains many features and is easy for them to operate; introducing security into their software often limits the amount of features that can be offered and introduces more configuration steps.

No matter what software or hardware you decide to use in your environment, securing your network is a never-ending task that involves addressing three key goals:

- Confidentiality

- Integrity

- Availability

Table 9.1 describes each of these goals and the general ways to mitigate threats against them.

TABLE 9.1 Security Goals

Goal	Description	Examples	Mitigation Steps
Confidentiality	Keeping your data private from eavesdropping	Packet capturing and replaying	Use encryption to hide the contents of the data in transit
Integrity	Keeping your data from being altered	Man-in-the-middle (MiTM) attacks	Use hashing to take a fingerprint of your data so you can verify it has not changed from its original form
Availability	Keeping your data, hosts, and services available for their intended purposes	Denial of service (DoS) attacks	Use rate limiting to stop an excessive flow of traffic and install the latest patches

EXAM ALERT

Be sure to memorize Table 9.1 for the exam. You should be familiar with the terms confidentiality, integrity, and availability, examples of each, and the mitigation steps.

At this point it might appear that all the security problems and solutions are technology related. In reality, this could not be further from the truth. At the end of the day, the problem of security is not with technology, but with the existence and enforcement of security policies. Wherever security measures are lacking, the security policy is either lacking or is not enforced. For example, if you do not have a policy stating that only management-approved software may be installed on a user's computer, a user may install software that contains malicious code that could have drastic effects on your network. Your security policy should include a high-level overview as to your organization's stance on security.

EXAM ALERT

Remember that security always starts with a corporate security policy and not technology.

Mitigation Steps

A security policy is good at detailing an organization's overall position on security, but it does not define the specific processes for how threats should be handled. You should have a plan before an attack occurs for how you will mitigate any infrastructure threats.

Attacks against your Cisco infrastructure can fall into one of three categories:

- Reconnaissance attacks

- Access attacks

- Denial of service attacks

Reconnaissance Attacks

The first type of attack is a reconnaissance attack. Before a malicious hacker attempts to gain access into your network, he or she will begin with trying to discover as much information as possible about your network. The information may include such things as IP addresses, types of devices, and software revisions. Attacks may take the form of packet-capturing software, ping sweeps, and Internet information queries, to name a few.

Packet-capturing software allows a hacker to sit back and capture all packets of data or voice as they traverse the network. The attacker can use information in these packets to learn about the type of traffic on the network. For example, if a hacker captures a number of packets that include web traffic to a particular type of web server, the hacker can use that information to look for attacks against that version of web server.

Ping sweeps are when a hacker attempts to ping all possible IP addresses on a subnet. Successful responses to the ping will tell the hacker which hosts are up. The attacker can then follow that up with attempting to scan the listening ports on the hosts to discover what type of services may be running on them. After an attacker learns of the services on a system, he or she can try to exploit the vulnerabilities associated with those services.

Internet information queries are used by hackers to discover information about public hosts on the Internet. These are done using domain name system (DNS) lookups with such tools as nslookup (Windows and Linux), Dig (Linux), and Host (Linux), among others. These tools will query a regional Internet registrar (RIR) such as American Registry for Internet Numbers (ARIN) or Réseaux IP Européens (RIPE) for information about a particular public DNS domain. The registrars will respond with telling the hacker about internal technical contacts (which can be used for social engineering attacks), public host IP addresses, and email servers.

Attackers will use all these techniques to map out your infrastructure in preparation for an attack to gain access.

You can reduce the threat of reconnaissance attacks in a couple of ways. First, you should use cryptographic protocols (such as IPsec, Secure Sockets Layer [SSL], or Secure Shell [SSH]) as much as possible to protect the confidentiality of your data in transit. Second, you can protect against packet capturing by using switches instead of hubs. Because a switch with a populated and accurate MAC address table will only forward data out the respective port to reach a destination host, traffic will not be sent out other ports that might be connected to a malicious hacker. This prevents the malicious hacker from capturing traffic sent to hosts other than the hacker's machine.

TIP

Using Switches as a Means to Protect Against Reconnaissance Attacks Using switches is the first step, but not the only step, you should take to prevent against packet capturing. There are many methods to get around switched networks to capture traffic. Implementing switches just adds to the steps an attacker must take to capture your traffic; it does not prevent the attacker from doing it. Other countermeasures are covered in the Cisco Certified Network Professional (CCNP) and Cisco Certified Security Professional (CCSP) exams.

Access Attacks

If a reconnaissance attack is like finding the doors and locks on a house, an access attack is like trying to break the locks and get into a house. Examples of access attacks include

- ▶ Password attacks
- ▶ Trust exploitation
- ▶ Man-in-the-middle

Your routers and switches can—and should—be configured with passwords. If an attacker can crack the password to your router or switch, he or she can subsequently gain access to configurations and change them to either take down your network or redirect all traffic to another computer where the attacker can read, replay, alter, or destroy the data.

Trust exploitation is when an attacker elevates his or her privileges. An example would be a user on your network that has limited access but is able to exploit an application to have administrator access.

Man-in-the-middle (MiTM) attacks involve capturing data in transit and changing it or using that data to launch another attack. This is similar to the packet-capturing reconnaissance attack. For example, in Figure 9.1 a user named Chris is sending an email to Brian, and he is offering him a raise in salary. However, Tami is a malicious hacker who intercepts the email and alters it so that it reads that there is a reduction in salary. If Tami can successfully intercept the email, alter it, and forward it on to Brian while still making it appear as if it came from Chris, she will have successfully carried out a man-in-the-middle attack.

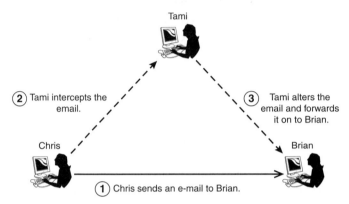

FIGURE 9.1   Man-in-the-middle (MiTM) attack.

Many of the access attacks may use malicious software, called malware, to exploit a system. Examples of malware include viruses and worms. Although the terms virus and worm are often used interchangeably, there is a difference. A *virus* is malware that cannot spread to another computer without human assistance. In comparison, a *worm* does not require human assistance to spread from computer to computer.

There are almost as many countermeasures against access attacks as there are exploits. A good countermeasure that you should always employ to defend against access attacks is to keep your operating system and applications current with the latest vendor patches.

Denial of Service Attacks

A denial of service attack is when a malicious attacker attempts to deny legitimate access to a network, system, or application. A variation of this is a distributed denial of service attack (DDoS) where an attacker will first compromise a number of zombie hosts before launching an attack on a victim host, application, or network (see Figure 9.2). In addition to increasing the severity of the attack by using multiple attacking hosts, it also makes it difficult to trace the attack back to the original attacker because there may be thousands of compromised computers used in the attack.

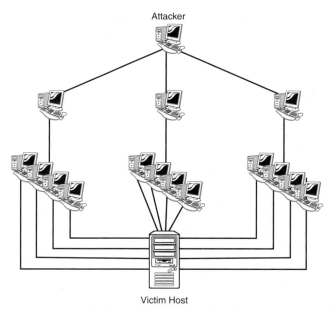

Attacker

Victim Host

FIGURE 9.2 Distributed denial of service (DDoS) attack.

Protecting against DoS and DDoS attacks is similar to protecting against access attacks in that you should always keep your systems up to date with the current patches. A second step to protecting against DoS and DDoS attacks is to configure rate limiting on our Internet facing routers to prevent against traffic floods. (Rate limiting configuration is covered in the Cisco Certified Network Professional track).

EXAM ALERT

Be sure to recognize a description of a denial of service attack on the exam. For example, flooding a system with malformed packets in an effort to crash a server is an example of a denial of service attack.

Common Security Appliances

Networks must be able to absorb attacks and remain operational much like a person's immune system functions when infected with a virus. The rate of increased security threats makes it difficult for information technology professionals to maintain control over their networks. Cisco recognizes the importance of security for your organization's network infrastructure. Their self-defending network (SDN) initiative integrates security into your network to identify, prevent, and adapt to threats. Cisco SDN solutions include

- ▶ Intruder Prevention Systems (IPS)

- ▶ Adaptive Security Appliance (ASA)

- ▶ Cisco DDoS Guard

- ▶ Anomaly Guard and Protector

- ▶ Cisco Secure Agent (CSA)

- ▶ Network Admission Control (NAC)

- ▶ Monitoring, Analysis, and Response System (MARS)

The Cisco Intruder Prevention System (IPS) listens to all traffic on your network to detect an attack. When an attack is matched against a signature, the IPS can automatically modify firewall and access control lists on your routers to block the attacker. An IPS can be a standalone device or can be integrated into the IOS of a router and into Cisco's Adaptive Security Appliance.

The Cisco Adaptive Security Appliance (ASA) is the replacement to the Cisco PIX firewall. It not only operates as a firewall but can also support antivirus, IPsec, network admission control, IPS, and virtual private network (VPN) technologies into a single device.

Cisco DDoS Guard protects against distributed denial of service (DDoS) attacks. A DDoS attack is a DoS attack involving many distributed systems (often thousands) that are working in sync to attack a single system or service. Cisco DDoS Guard will detect the presence of a potential DDoS attack and block malicious traffic in real-time while not affecting the flow of legitimate, mission-critical transactions.

The Anomaly Guard and Protector (also called the Cisco Anomaly Guard) works in conjunction with the DDoS Guard. The DDoS Guard matches only known DDoS signatures; it cannot detect new forms of attacks for which there is no signature. The Anomaly Guard uses behavior analysis to maintain a profile for normal traffic and detect any deviations from the normal traffic profile. It can send alerts or interact with the DDoS guard to mitigate the attack.

The Cisco Secure Agent (CSA) is software installed on endpoint systems such as desktop clients, servers, and point-of-sale (POS) systems. It defends against targeted attacks, spyware, rootkits, and day-zero attack (a threat for which no patch has been written). CSA features include a built-in IPS, malicious mobile code protection, OS patch assurance, and audit logs.

Network Admission Control (NAC), formerly called Cisco Clean Access, allows administrators to authenticate, authorize, evaluate, and remediate wired and wireless users prior to allowing the users on the network. It can quarantine and prevent noncompliant end stations from accessing the network until they achieve security policy compliance.

Finally, the Security Monitoring, Analysis, and Response System (MARS) provides security monitoring for security devices and host applications. It offers event aggregation, device discovery, compliance reporting, and notifications. Using MARS can greatly assist with analysis and response of threats on your network.

Although no one can claim to secure your network entirely, Cisco has made great strides with its self-defending network solutions to give you peace of mind that your network is guarded and protected against most current and future threats.

Best Practices

With all the attacks occurring today, it may be tough to know where to begin protecting your network. No matter what your level of experience is with Cisco routers, there are a few basic best practices that you should use whenever setting up a new Cisco router. These include the following:

- ▶ Use SSH instead of Telnet.

- ▶ Configure access lists to permit only necessary traffic.

- ▶ Use difficult passwords that do not use words found in a dictionary.

- ▶ Use current Cisco IOS Software.

- ▶ Encrypt all passwords in the configuration.

- ▶ Disable services that you do not need.

After you have taken these initial steps, you can then decide what additional steps you may need to take to protect your network.

Exam Prep Questions

1. Which of the following is an example of an attack against confidentiality?

   ○ **A.** An attacker attempts to crash a mission-critical server.

   ○ **B.** An attacker uses the nslookup utility to determine the IP addresses of public hosts.

   ○ **C.** An attacker attempts to read an email.

   ○ **D.** An attacker attempts to change an email.

2. Which of the following can be used to quarantine and prevent noncompliant end stations from accessing the network?

   ○ **A.** MARS

   ○ **B.** NAC

   ○ **C.** CSA

   ○ **D.** ASA

3. What is the first step in protecting against security threats?

   ○ **A.** Install the latest operating system patches.

   ○ **B.** Configure rate limiting.

   ○ **C.** Use switches.

   ○ **D.** Create a security policy.

4. You notice an excessive number of pings on your network. What type of attack might someone be doing on your network?

   ○ **A.** Reconnaissance attack

   ○ **B.** Denial of service attack

   ○ **C.** Access attack

   ○ **D.** Social engineering attack

5. What type of device is used to listen to all traffic on your network and automatically configure your firewall or router to block an attack when it is matched against a signature?

   ○ **A.** MARS

   ○ **B.** NAC

   ○ **C.** IPS

   ○ **D.** Anomaly Guard

6. Which of the following is a way to protect the confidentiality of your data?

   ○ **A.** Make a hash of each packet that can be verified when the packet is received.

   ○ **B.** Encrypt the payload of each packet.

   ○ **C.** Use rate limiting to prevent an excessive number of packets.

   ○ **D.** Install the latest patches to protect against worms and viruses.

7. Which of the following is a reason why security vulnerabilities are on the rise?

   ○ **A.** End users are not knowledgeable about the latest security threats.

   ○ **B.** CPU and memory resources are not available to protect against denial of service attacks.

   ○ **C.** Computer networks are becoming increasingly complex.

   ○ **D.** There are not enough certified professionals.

8. Which of the following is not a general best practice for securing your network infrastructure?

   ○ **A.** Use Telnet instead of SSH.

   ○ **B.** Use complex passwords consisting of special characters, numbers, and letters.

   ○ **C.** Encrypt all passwords in the configuration.

   ○ **D.** Disable unnecessary services.

9. One of your employees has been unhappy with her job because she is unable to change the wallpaper on her computer because of not having the right permissions. She tries to find a vulnerability in which she can elevate her privileges so that she can change her desktop wallpaper. What type of attack does she want to do?

   ○ **A.** Man-in-the-middle attack

   ○ **B.** Denial of service attack

   ○ **C.** Password attack

   ○ **D.** Trust exploitation attack

Answers to Exam Prep Questions

1. Answer C is correct. Confidentiality attacks attempt to read data by someone other than the intended receiver(s). Answer A is incorrect because this describes a denial of service/availability attack. Answer B is incorrect because this is a type of reconnaissance attack. Answer D is incorrect because this describes a man-in-the-middle (MiTM)/integrity attack.

2. Answer B is correct. Network Admission Control (NAC) checks all end stations before they attach to a network to ensure policy compliance. Answers A, C, and D are incorrect because these security solutions do not quarantine and prevent noncompliant security devices from joining the network.

3. Answer D is correct. You should always start with creating a security policy for your organization before you implement any technical solution. Answers A, B, and C will all help protect against attacks but are not the first step.

4. Answer A is correct. A ping sweep is an example of a reconnaissance attack where a malicious attacker will attempt to ping all IP addresses on a subnet in hopes of determining which hosts are on. Answer B is incorrect because a ping sweep is used to collect information about a network and not to crash an application. Answer C is incorrect because access attacks include password and man-in-the-middle attacks but not ping sweeps. Finally, answer D is incorrect because social engineering attacks are typically done via email, telephone, or in person, but not through ping sweeps.

5. Answer C is correct. The Cisco Intruder Prevent System will match attacks to a signature database and can optionally automatically configure your firewalls and routers to block the attacker. All the other options are Cisco security solutions but do not have all the features of the Cisco IPS appliance.

6. Answer B is correct. The best defense against confidentiality attacks is to use encryption. Answer A is incorrect because hashing is used to protect against integrity/access attacks, not confidentiality. Answer C is incorrect because this is used to protect against availability/denial of service attacks. Answer D is incorrect because this is used to protect against access attacks.

7. Answer C is correct. Computer networks are becoming increasingly complex and new vulnerabilities are introduced with this added complexity. Answer A is incorrect because although end users should be somewhat knowledgeable about basic security risks, they do not need extensive training in information technology security. Answer B is incorrect because most denial of service attacks have little to do with flooding your processor or memory. Answer D is incorrect because having certified professionals is not the cause for increased threats.

8. Answer A is correct. You should use SSH instead of Telnet, not the other way around. Answers B, C, and D are incorrect because these are all general best practices for securing your network infrastructure.

9. Answer D is correct. A trust exploitation is an example of an attack where a user attempts to escalate his or her privileges. Answers A, B, and C are incorrect because they do not require elevated privileges.

CHAPTER TEN

Basic Routing

Terms You'll Need to Understand

✓ Static routes

✓ Default routes

✓ Distance Vector

✓ Link State

✓ Administrative Distance

✓ Routing Information Protocol (RIP)

Concepts and Techniques You'll Need to Master

✓ Understanding dynamic routing algorithms

✓ Understanding the use of Administrative Distances

✓ Configuring static routes

✓ Configuring RIP

Introduction

Routing is the process by which a packet gets from one location to another. To route a packet, a router needs to know the destination address and on what interface to send the traffic out (egress interface). When a packet comes into an interface (ingress interface) on a router, it looks up the destination IP address in the packet header and compares it with its routing table. The routing table, which is stored in RAM, tells the router which outgoing, or egress, interface the packet should go out to reach the destination network.

There are three ways to control routing decisions on your router:

▶ Static routes

▶ Default routes

▶ Dynamic routes

Static Routes

Use a static route when you want to manually define the path that the packet will take through your network. Static routes are useful in small networks with rarely changing routes, when you have little bandwidth and do not want the overhead of a dynamic routing protocol, or when you want to manually define all of your routes for security reasons.

Static routes are created in global configuration mode. The syntax for the static route is as follows:

```
ip route destination network address [subnet mask]
{next-hop-address ¦ interface] [distance]
```

For example, in Figure 10.1, Carol is trying to get to a web server on a different network. Her computer will be configured to use the Cancun router as its default gateway, but the Cancun router needs to know how to get to the 192.168.100.0/24 network where the web server resides.

Using the Honolulu router as your next hop in the path to the web server, type the following to create a static route on the Cancun router:

```
ip route 192.168.100.0 255.255.255.0 172.16.0.2
```

Instead of routing to the next-hop router, you could also create a static route out of an interface. If you did not know the address of the Honolulu router, you could tell the Cancun router to use interface serial 0/0 to get to the 192.168.100.0 network. The syntax would then be **ip route 192.168.100.0 255.255.255.0 serial 0/0**.

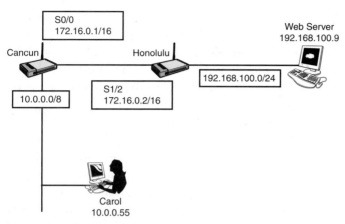

FIGURE 10.1 Static route example.

At this point, you have created a route to get to the 192.168.100.0 network
attached to the Honolulu router. That will get Carol's data to the web server, but
the Honolulu router will also need a route to get traffic back to Carol's network.
Using the Cancun router as the next hop, the syntax would be:

```
ip route 10.0.0.0 255.0.0.0 172.16.0.1
```

Remember that when entering the static route, the destination is a network
address, whereas the next-hop address is a specific IP address assigned to another router's interface. As noted previously, you can also create a static route to
direct your traffic through a specific interface.

Default Routes

A default route is similar to a static route, but instead of configuring a route to
a specific network, you are configuring the router to know where to send traffic
for any network not found in its routing table. Default routes are used to establish a gateway of last resort for your router.

There are two ways to create a default route. The first is to use the same command that you used for a static route but use the 0.0.0.0 network as your destination with a subnet mask of 0.0.0.0. For example, to establish a default route to
send traffic out serial 0/0 destined for any network not learned through dynamic or static means, type the following:

```
ip route 0.0.0.0 0.0.0.0 serial 0/0
```

If you chose to specify the next-hop IP address of the router, you could type the
following instead (assuming a next-hop address of 192.168.1.1):

```
ip route 0.0.0.0 0.0.0.0 192.168.1.1
```

The second method of creating a default route is to use the **ip default-network** command. With this command, any traffic destined for networks not found in the routing table will be sent to the default network. Figure 10.2 illustrates the use of the default network. If Carol is trying to access the Internet, a default route could be configured with the following global configuration command on the Honolulu router:

```
Honolulu(config)#ip default-network 192.168.100.0
```

Note that you do not include the subnet mask in this command. Routing protocols, such as RIP, can propagate this default network to other routers. When Carol attempts to access the Internet, her computer sends traffic to the Cancun router, which is her default gateway. The Cancun router will see a default network of 192.168.100.0, look up this destination in its routing table, and forward her packets to the Honolulu router. The Honolulu router, in turn, will forward the traffic out its interface connected to the 192.168.100.0 network and onto the Internet.

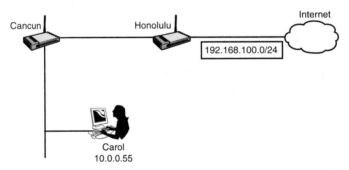

FIGURE 10.2   Default network example.

> **EXAM ALERT**
> Know how to configure a static route, default route, and default network.

Dynamic Routes

Static and default routes are nice, but they are not scalable. If you need a scalable solution, you need to experiment with dynamic routing protocols. For the ICND1 exam, you need to know how to configure RIP, static, and default routing. For the CCNA and ICND2 exams, you will need to understand the operation and configuration of EIGRP and OSPF as well. EIGRP and OSPF are covered in Chapter 14, "Routing."

Before we get into the details of each of these routing methods, you should first understand some of the characteristics of all routing protocols. These characteristics include administrative distances, metrics, distance vector, and link state operations.

Administrative Distance

Administrative distance is the measure of trustworthiness that a router assigns to how a route to a network was learned. A route can be learned if the network is directly connected, there is a static route to the network, or by various routing protocols as they exchange information about networks between routers. For example, in Figure 10.3, the Jupiter router needs to determine the best route to get to the 10.0.0.0/8 network attached to the Earth router. It has learned of two separate paths; one is learned through EIGRP and the other through OSPF. EIGRP has decided that the best path for a packet destined to the 10.0.0.0/8 network is through Saturn, Mars, and finally Earth. On the other hand, OSPF has determined that the best path is through Pluto and then Earth. The Jupiter router needs to decide which routing protocol it should trust, or prefer, over the other. The one preferred will be the one the router listens to when making decisions on how to route.

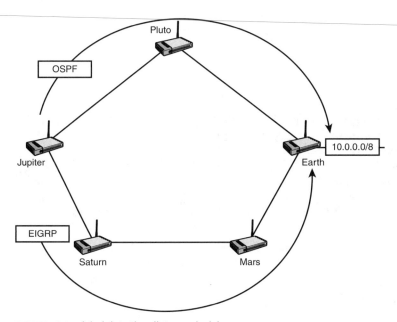

FIGURE 10.3 Administrative distance decisions.

To determine which routing source is preferred, Cisco has assigned administrative distances to sources of routing information. A router will choose the route that is learned through the source with the lowest administrative distance. Table 10.1 illustrates the default administrative distance value.

EXAM ALERT

It is possible to change the administrative distance of a static route by appending a different administrative distance to the end of the command. For example, the following command assigns the administrative distance of 130 to a static route:

```
ip route 10.0.0.0 255.0.0.0 serial 0/0 130
```

Changing the administrative distance of a static route is commonly used when configuring a backup route, called a *floating* static route. If you do not specify an administrative distance at the end of the static route, the default is being used. For the exam, you should be able to look at the syntax of a static route and know what administrative distance is being used.

TABLE 10.1   Administrative Distances

Routing Source	Administrative Distance
Connected	0
Static	1
EIGRP (internal)	90
OSPF	110
RIP (version 1 and 2)	120
EIGRP (external)	170

EXAM ALERT

Make sure that you memorize this table. You should know both the values and understand the concept of administrative distances. Remember, the lowest number is preferred. It might help you to memorize these by remembering the word "Eeyore"— E-OR, for EIGRP, OSPF, and RIP. This is the order of the dynamic routing protocols. (EIGRP external routes are discussed in Chapter 14, "Routing.") They are also alphabetical in order.

In Figure 10.3, the Jupiter router would take the EIGRP learned path through Saturn and Mars to get to the 10.0.0.0/8 network attached to the Earth router. EIGRP has a lower administrative distance (90) than OSPF (110) and is therefore preferred.

Metrics

In the previous example, two routing protocols run on the routers, but OSPF and EIGRP chose two different paths to get to the Earth router. Each routing protocol has its own algorithm to determine what they consider to be the best path to a destination network. The main factor in deciding the best path is the routing protocol's *metric*.

A metric is the variable used in the algorithm when making routing decisions. Each routing protocol uses a different type of metric. Table 10.2 illustrates the different metrics used by routing protocols.

TABLE 10.2   Routing Metrics

Routing Protocol	Metric	Description
RIP	Hop Count	The number of hops, or routers, that a packet has to pass through to reach a destination. The route with the lowest hop count is preferred.
EIGRP	Bandwidth, Delay	Uses Bandwidth and Delay by default, but also can factor Reliability, Load, and Maximum Transmission Unit (MTU).
OSPF	Cost	Cost is defined as 10^8/bandwidth.

Metrics are not the only thing that distinguishes the routing protocols. Routing protocols can be further classified into two categories:

▶ Distance vector routing protocols

▶ Link state routing protocols

Distance Vector Routing Protocols

Distance vector routing protocols include RIP and the now unsupported legacy protocol, Interior Gateway Routing Protocol (IGRP). EIGRP is a hybrid that contains many of the characteristics of a distance vector protocol. Characteristics of distance vector routing protocols are as follows:

▶ Periodically broadcasts entire routing table out of all interfaces.

▶ Trusts what the other router tells it. (For this reason, distance vector routing is sometimes called "routing by rumor.")

Controlling Routing Loops

Because distance vector routing protocols trust the next router without compiling a topology map of all networks and routers, distance vector protocols run the risk of creating loops in a network.

This is analogous of driving to a location without a map. Instead, you trust what each sign tells you. Trusting the street signs might get you where you want to go, but I've been in some cities where trusting what the signs say will lead you in loops. The same is true with distance vector routing protocols. Simply trusting what the next router tells it can potentially lead the packets to loop endlessly. These loops could saturate a network and cause systems to crash. This, in turn, makes managers very upset and means that you have to work late into the evening to fix it.

Luckily, distance vector protocols have some mechanisms built in to them to prevent loops. These mechanisms are as follows:

- Maximum hop count
- Split-horizon
- Route poisoning
- Poison reverse
- Hold down timers
- Triggered updates

Routers maintain a routing table which is stored in RAM. The routing table lists every network the router has learned about and the number of hops, or routers, it takes to go through to get to a destination network. For example, if a packet sent from a router needs to go through two other routers to get to the destination network, a hop count of two would be recorded. All distance vector routing protocols maintain a record of hop count even if they do not use hop count in their routing decisions.

Examine Figure 10.4. Through the use of a dynamic routing protocol, each router will exchange information with the next router. Mars will learn of the networks known by Saturn and Jupiter, and Mars will let Saturn and Jupiter know of the networks that Mars knows about. Table 10.3 shows the networks and associated hop counts for each router.

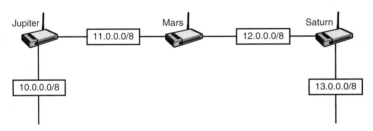

FIGURE 10.4 Avoiding loops.

TABLE 10.3   Hop Count

	Network 10.0.0.0	Network 11.0.0.0	Network 12.0.0.0	Network 13.0.0.0
Jupiter	0	0	1	2
Mars	1	0	0	1
Saturn	2	1	0	0

Distance vector routing protocols keep track of hop counts because if a route exceeds a maximum hop count limit (determined differently by each routing protocol), the network is considered unreachable. This prevents packets from cycling endlessly across your networks. Table 10.4 shows the maximum hop count for distance vector protocols.

TABLE 10.4   Maximum Hop Count Values

Routing Protocol	Maximum Hop Count
RIP	15
EIGRP	224

EXAM ALERT

Make sure that you know the maximum hop count for all routing protocols. Note that OSPF is not mentioned here. OSPF is a link-state protocol and has an unlimited hop count.

Having a maximum hop count should be enough to prevent loops, but because loops are so dangerous, other methods are used as well. The second method to prevent routing loops is split-horizon. The split-horizon rule states that information about a route should not be sent back in the direction in which it was learned.

Look back at Figure 10.4. The split-horizon rule states that if Saturn tells Mars about the 13.0.0.0/8 network, Mars should not advertise it back to Saturn. If it did, Saturn would be confused and think that it could possibly use Mars to get to the 13.0.0.0 should its interface to that network ever go down. This would cause a packet to loop endlessly as the packet would go to Mars, which would in turn send it back to Saturn. Split-horizon resolves this issue by ensuring that the Mars router never sends information about the 13.0.0.0 network back to the Saturn router that it heard it from.

To make absolutely sure that no loops are created, route poisoning and poison reverse are also implemented. With route poisoning, as soon as a network is thought to be down, it is advertised out with a hop count that is one greater than what is allowed. This would declare the route as being inaccessible. Poison reverse does the same thing but in reverse. The router that hears about a down network, violates split-horizon, and sends back an update with the network being unreachable. Figure 10.5 illustrates how this would look if the routers were running RIP, where the maximum hop count is 15 and a hop count of 16 declares the route inaccessible.

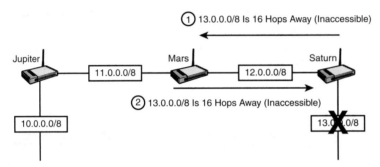

FIGURE 10.5 Poison reverse and route poisoning.

The next mechanism to prevent loops is holddown timers. When a router receives information that a network is possibly down from a neighbor router, it will not accept any new information from that router for a specified period of time. This is to prevent regular update messages from reinstating a down route. The default hold down timer for RIP is 180 seconds.

Finally, triggered updates are used to prevent loops by exchanging routing information whenever there is a change. In other words, a change in the routing topology will trigger routers to update each other. Without triggered update, a router would have to wait for the next update interval to learn of a changed route. During that period of when a route is changed and when the next routine update is sent out there is a potential of a loop. To lessen the risk of a loop during this waiting period, routers will not wait for the update interval to send out the information about a changed network but will instead send out the information immediately. This way all routers can learn of the change as soon as possible.

Link State Routing Protocols

If distance vector routing protocols are like trusting the highway signs when you are on a road trip, link state routing protocols are like having the map in front of you. With link-state routing protocols such as OSPF, your router will know all the networks and the various paths to the networks.

The Cisco Hybrid: EIGRP

Extra! Extra! Read all about it! EIGRP solves the world's problems. It's the best of both worlds! You get the best of link state and distance vector routing all built in to one protocol!

Okay, so perhaps that's a little more hype than necessary, but it is not that far from the truth. EIGRP is a Cisco proprietary protocol that combines characteristics of link state and distance vector routing protocols. For example, like a link state routing protocol, it sends out hello messages to discover its neighbors. However, it does not have a built-in hierarchical design like OSPF, thus making it more like a distance vector. The operations and configurations of EIGRP and OSPF are not tested on in the ICND1 exam, but you will want to know the differences between link state and distance vector protocols. You read more about EIGRP later, but for now let's start with a very simple protocol, RIP.

EXAM ALERT

Know the characteristics of distance vector and link state routing protocols and know which of these categories each routing protocol falls into.

RIP

The Routing Information Protocol (RIP) uses the Bellman-Ford algorithm, which simply counts the number of hops, or routers, to a destination network and chooses the path that is the fewest number of hops. Any destination that is more than 15 hops away is considered inaccessible.

Characteristics of RIP

RIP routers exchange information by broadcasting the entire routing table every 30 seconds out all interfaces with RIP enabled. RIP version 2 also sends out updates every 30 seconds but sends out updates using the multicast address of 224.0.0.9 (can be configured to do unicast as well). In addition, version 2 provides the following benefits not available in version 1:

- ▶ Routing Authentication
- ▶ Classless routing
- ▶ Summarization

Implementing RIP

Configuring RIP is straightforward. The four steps to configuring a routing protocol are as follows:

1. Enable the routing protocol.

2. Activate it on interfaces.

3. Advertise directly networks.

4. Configure optional parameters.

The first step, enable the routing protocol, is done from global configuration mode by typing **router rip**. The next two steps, activating RIP on interfaces and advertising networks, is done with a single command, the `network` command.

If you look at Figure 10.6 you see three routers named Larry, Curly, and Moe. For the Moe router, you need to enable RIP and enter the networks you want to advertise. The Moe router has the 192.168.10.0/24 and 192.168.20.0/24 networks directly connected to it. Moe's configuration would be

```
Moe(config)#router rip
Moe(config-router)#network 192.168.10.0
Moe(config-router)#network 192.168.20.0
```

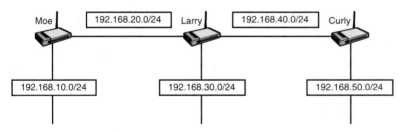

FIGURE 10.6 RIP example.

Larry has three networks attached to his router. His configuration would be

```
Larry(config)#router rip
Larry(config-router)#network 192.168.20.0
Larry(config-router)#network 192.168.30.0
Larry(config-router)#network 192.168.40.0
```

Finally, we can't forget Curly. Curly's configuration would be

```
Curly(config)#router rip
Curly(config-router)#network 192.168.40.0
Curly(config-router)#network 192.168.50.0
```

When you enter your networks in your RIP configuration, RIP is activated on the interfaces that are assigned those networks. All networks that you listed in your configuration are then sent out all RIP activated interfaces. Thus, the networks that you entered on Curly's router will be sent out to Larry. Larry will take what he learned from Curly, add his own networks, and send them out to Moe. Larry will also learn networks from Moe, add his own networks, and send them out to Curly.

Remember to enter only your directly connected networks. Curly, for example, should not enter 192.168.10.0/24 in his configuration because that network is not directly connected to his router. Also, you should enter classful networks only. A classful network is the major class A, B, or C network with the default masks of /8, /16, or /24. This means that even if you are subnetting, you should enter the major class A, B, or C address. In Figure 10.7, our three friends have new networks that are taken from a major class A network. Even though multiple networks are attached to them, enter only the major 10.0.0.0/8 network. Thus, all three routers would have the same configuration:

```
Router(config)#router rip
Router(config-router)#network 10.0.0.0
```

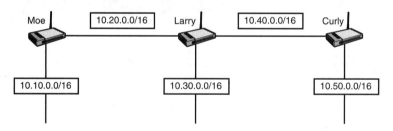

FIGURE 10.7   RIP example with subnetting.

Finally, you may enter some optional commands. The two optional commands that you should be familiar with for the exam are as follows:

▶ **version 2**

▶ **no auto-summary**

Both commands are entered under the RIP routing process. The first command, **version 2**, enables RIP version 2 on your router. RIP version 2 adds the benefits of optional authentication, multicast updates, summarization, and classless routing. Although RIP version 2 does support classless routing, it still automatically summarizes all networks on the default class A, B, and C boundaries. In our previous example in Figure 10.7, RIP version 2 still summarizes the networks at the major 10.0.0.0/8 boundary. (/8 is the default mask for a class A network.) To disable automatic summarization, enter the **no auto-summary** command under the routing process. Using Figure 10.7 again, the complete configuration for Larry's router, assuming that you wanted RIP version 2 with no automatic summarization, is

```
Larry(config)#router rip
Larry(config-router)#network 10.0.0.0
Larry(config-router)#version 2
Larry(config-router)#no auto-summary
```

Note that even though we disabled automatic summarization, we still put the default classful networks in our configuration. RIP is smart enough to go on the interfaces and discover the individual subnetworks and their associated subnet masks.

EXAM ALERT

The three classless routing protocols in this chapter are RIPv2, EIGRP, and OSPF. Remember these three protocols. Also, classless routing, VLSM, summarization, supernetting (another term for summarization), and route aggregation are all related, so if you are asked which routing protocols support these, remember RIPv2, EIGRP, and OSPF.

Verifying and Troubleshooting RIP

Now that RIP is configured, you should verify your configuration. There are two commands that you can use to verify proper operation of RIP:

- ▶ `show ip route`

- ▶ `show ip protocols`

The first command displays your routing table. For the sake of simplicity, we'll go back to our original example of our three friends before they got creative and started subnetting. Figure 10.8 shows the Larry, Curly, and Moe routers before they subnetted. This time, the names of the interfaces have been included.

After executing the `show ip route` command on Larry's router, you should see the following:

```
Gateway of last resort is not set.
R    192.168.10.0 [120/1] via 192.168.20.1 00:00:08, Serial 0/0
R    192.168.50.0 [120/1] via 192.168.40.2 00:00:16, Serial 0/1
C    192.168.30.0 is directly connected, FastEthernet 0/0
C    192.168.20.0 is directly connected, Serial 0/0
C    192.168.40.0 is directly connected, Serial 0/1
```

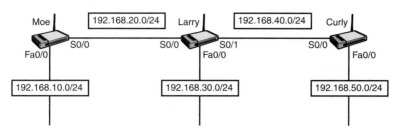

FIGURE 10.8 RIP example—before subnetting.

You should be comfortable reading the output of this command. Figure 10.9 provides a legend to understand the important elements that make up the output.

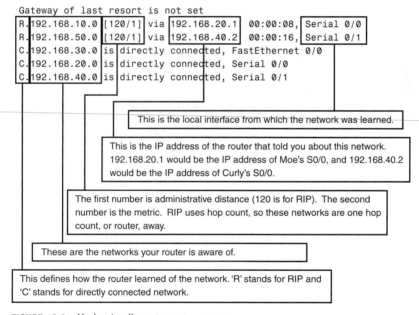

FIGURE 10.9 Understanding `show ip route`.

On Moe's router, the output looks as follows:

```
Gateway of last resort is not set.
R    192.168.30.0 [120/1] via 192.168.20.2 00:00:20, Serial 0/0
R    192.168.40.0 [120/1] via 192.168.20.2 00:00:20, Serial 0/0
R    192.168.50.0 [120/2] via 192.168.20.2 00:00:20, Serial 0/0
C    192.168.10.0 is directly connected, FastEthernet 0/0
C    192.168.20.0 is directly connected, Serial 0/0
```

Notice how the hop count for the 192.168.50.0 network is 2 because that network is two hops away. You must go through the Larry and Curly router to get to this network.

Curly's router has the following output:

```
Gateway of last resort is not set.
R     192.168.10.0 [120/2] via 192.168.40.1 00:00:4, Serial 0/0
R     192.168.20.0 [120/1] via 192.168.40.1 00:00:4, Serial 0/0
R     192.168.30.0 [120/1] via 192.168.40.1 00:00:4, Serial 0/0
C     192.168.50.0 is directly connected, FastEthernet 0/0
C     192.168.40.0 is directly connected, Serial 0/0
```

The second RIP command you should use is the **show ip protocols** command
to verify the operation of RIP on your router. Among other things, this command shows you the timers and the networks you are routing. These networks
are the same ones you entered under the RIP routing process. Following is the
output of this command on the Larry router:

```
Larry# show ip protocols
Routing Protocol is "rip"
Sending updates every 30 seconds, next due in 19 seconds
Invalid after 180 seconds, hold down 180, flushed after 240
Outgoing update filter list for all interfaces is
Incoming update filter list for all interfaces is
Redistribution: rip
Default version control: send version 1, receive any version
Interface        Send Recv Triggered RIP Key-chain
FastEthernet0/0  1    1         2
Serial0/0        1    1         2
Serial0/1        1    1         2
Routing for Networks:
192.168.20.0
192.168.30.0
192.168.40.0
Routing Information Sources:
Gateway Distance Last Update
192.168.20.1 120 00:00:02
192.168.40.2 120 00:00:26
```

Sometimes things do not work the way you anticipated. If this happens, you may
want to turn on debugging. Use the **debug ip rip** command to debug the routing process.

> **CAUTION**
>
> You should be very careful when using debug commands. If there is a significant amount
> of output being generated, it can crash your router. Only turn on debugging if you know it
> is safe in your environment. If you are not sure, contact Cisco's Technical Assistance
> Center (TAC) before debugging.

Executing this command on Moe's router generates the following output:

```
Moe#debug ip rip
1. RIP: received v1 update from 192.168.20.2 on Serial0/0
2.       192.168.30.0 in 1 hops
3.       192.168.40.0 in 1 hops
4.       192.168.50.0 in 2 hops
5. RIP: sending v1 update to 255.255.255.255 via Serial0/0
(192.168.20.1)
6.       network 192.168.10.0, metric 1
7. RIP: sending v1 update to 255.255.255.255 via FastEthernet0/0
(192.168.10.0)
8.       network 192.168.20.0, metric 1
9.       network 192.168.30.0, metric 2
10.      network 192.168.40.0, metric 2
11.      network 192.168.50.0, metric 3
```

For sake of clarity, each line of this output has been numbered.

The metric is added as it leaves the router. By looking at the networks being sent out with a metric of 1, we can glean that this router is configured to route for networks 192.168.20.0 and 192.168.10.0 (lines 6 and 8). You can also look at the interface IP addresses to see what networks are directly connected to the router (lines 5 and 7).

From this output, you can also tell that split-horizon works. The split-horizon rule states that you never advertise a route out of the interface through which it was learned. This router has learned three networks on interface serial 0/0 (lines 2, 3, and 4), but has not advertised out of any of them (line 6).

EXAM ALERT

You need to feel comfortable reading the output of the debug IP RIP command. Remember, it is not useful to send information back in the direction from which it came or to the source from which it came. If the learned route is not returned through the same interface on which it was received, the split horizon rule is in effect.

Exam Prep Questions

1. Given the exhibit in Figure 10.10, how would you configure RIP version 1 on the Chicago router?

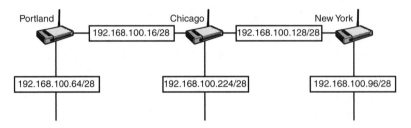

   ○ **A.** Chicago(config)#router rip

   Chicago(config-router)#**network 192.168.100.16 255.255.255.240**

   Chicago(config-router)#**network 192.168.100.224 255.255.255.240**

   Chicago(config-router)#**network 192.168.100.128 255.255.255.240**

   ○ **B.** Chicago(config)#**router rip**

   Chicago(config-router)#**network 192.168.100.0**

   ○ **B.** Chicago(config)#**router rip**

   Chicago(config-router)#**network 192.168.100.16**

   Chicago(config-router)#**network 192.168.100.224**

   Chicago(config-router)#**network 192.168.100.128**

   ○ **D.** Chicago(config-router)#**network 192.168.100.0 255.255.255.0**

2. Which of the following are methods used by distance vector routing protocols to prevent loops? Select all that apply.

   ○ **A.** Triggered holddowns

   ○ **B.** Triggered updates

   ○ **C.** Split horizon

   ○ **D.** Split updates

   ○ **E.** Holddown timers

3. Given the exhibit shown in Figure 10.11, what is the correct configuration for the Iceland router?

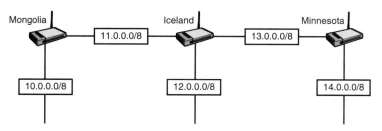

- ○ **A.** Iceland(config)#router rip

    Iceland(config-router)#**network 10.0.0.0**

    Iceland(config-router)#**network 11.0.0.0**

    Iceland(config-router)#**network 12.0.0.0**

    Iceland(config-router)#**network 13.0.0.0**

    Iceland(config-router)#**network 14.0.0.0**

- ○ **B.** Iceland(config)#**router rip 100**

    Iceland(config-router)#**network 11.0.0.0**

    Iceland(config-router)#**network 12.0.0.0**

    Iceland(config-router)#**network 13.0.0.0**

- ○ **C.** Iceland(config)#**router rip**

    Iceland(config-router)#**network 11.0.0.0**

    Iceland(config-router)#**network 13.0.0.0**

- ○ **D.** Iceland(config)#**router rip**

    Iceland(config-router)#**network 11.0.0.0**

    Iceland(config-router)#**network 12.0.0.0**

    Iceland(config-router)#**network 13.0.0.0**

4. What does RIP version 2 add that is not found in RIP version 1? Select all that apply.

Router	Fa0/0	Fa0/0
New Delhi	10.7.16.13/29	10.98.43.66/28
Shangai	10.98.43.66/28	10.100.0.131/26
Atlantic City	10.100.0.131/26	10.7.16.13/29

○ **A.** Authentication

○ **B.** Summarization

○ **C.** Multicast updates

○ **D.** VLSM

For questions 5-7, refer to Figure 10.12.

5. What would be the syntax to create a static route to the Atlantic City Fa0/1 network from the New Delhi router?

○ **A.** Router(config)#`ip route 10.7.16.16/29 Fastethernet0/1`

○ **B.** Router(config)#`ip route 10.7.16.16 255.255.255.248 fastethernet0/0`

○ **C.** Router(config)#`ip route 10.7.16.16 255.255.255.248 10.98.43.66`

○ **D.** Router(config)#`ip route 10.7.16.16 mask 255.255.255.248 gw 10.98.43.66`

○ **E.** Router(config)#`ip route 10.7.16.16 255.255.255.240 fa0/1`

6. What is the command to enter a default route on Shanghai's router to send all traffic to the New Delhi router?

   ○ **A.** `Router(config)#ip default-route fastethernet0/0`

   ○ **B.** `Router(config)#ip route default fastethernet0/0`

   ○ **C.** `Router(config)#ip route 0.0.0.0 fasthernet0/0`

   ○ **D.** `Router(config)#ip route 0.0.0.0 0.0.0.0 f astethernet0/0`

   ○ **E.** `Router(config)#ip route 0.0.0.0 255.255.255.255 fastethernet0/0`

7. You have replaced your static routes with RIP. You enter the following configuration for all three routers:

   ```
   Router(config)#router rip
   Router(config-router)#network 10.0.0.0
   ```

   Users are complaining that they are unable to communicate between the different networks. What is wrong? (Choose all that apply.)

   ○ **A.** Nothing. You cannot use subnetted networks with RIP.

   ○ **B.** You must specify the specific networks along with their respective masks.

   ○ **C.** You must specify the specific networks but do not need to specify the subnet masks.

   ○ **D.** You must type the no auto-summary command under the router process.

   ○ **E.** You must type the ip classless command.

   ○ **F.** You must type the **version 2** command under the router process.

8. Your network is running EIGRP, OSPF, RIP, and static routes. Which routing source will be the least preferred?

   ○ **A.** EIGRP

   ○ **B.** OSPF

   ○ **C.** RIP

   ○ **D.** Static

For questions 9 through 12, refer to the following output.

```
Router#debug ip rip
RIP: received update from 172.16.0.1 on FastEthernet0/0
 172.17.0.0 in 1 hops
 172.18.0.0 in 2 hops
 172.19.0.0 in 16 hops (inaccessible)
 0.0.0.0 in 4 hops
RIP: sending update to 255.255.255.255 via Fastethernet0/0 (172.16.0.2)
 172.20.0.0, metric 1
RIP: sending update to 255.255.255.255 via Serial0/0/0 (172.20.0.1)
 172.17.0.0 in 2 hops
 <output omitted>
```

9. Which version of RIP is being used on this router?

   - ○ **A.** Version 1
   - ○ **B.** Version 2
   - ○ **C.** Impossible to tell from the output
   - ○ **D.** Version 1 on interface FastEthernet0/0 and version 2 on Serial 0/0/0

10. What will happen to a packet destined for the 172.19.0.0 network?

   - ○ **A.** It will be forwarded out the FastEthernet0/0 interface.
   - ○ **B.** It will be forwarded out the Serial0/0/0 interface.
   - ○ **C.** It will be dropped.
   - ○ **D.** It will be sent to the default route.

11. Which networks are directly attached to this router? (Choose all that apply.)

   - ○ **A.** 172.16.0.0
   - ○ **B.** 172.17.0.0
   - ○ **C.** 172.18.0.0
   - ○ **D.** 172.19.0.0
   - ○ **E.** 172.20.0.0

12. How many hops away will the 172.20.0.0 network be for the router located at IP address 172.16.0.1?

   - ○ **A.** one
   - ○ **B.** two
   - ○ **C.** three
   - ○ **D.** four

Answers to Exam Prep Questions

1. Answer B is correct. RIP version 1 is a classful routing protocol, which means that it does not send out the subnet mask in its update. When configuring RIP, you must put in the default classful networks, even if you are subnetting. In this example, a class C network has been subnetted, but you should enter the network statement using the full class network of 192.168.100.0. Answer A is incorrect because it enters all three networks, and it uses subnet masks. Answer C is incorrect because it enters all three networks. Answer D is incorrect because it enters a subnet mask, which is not used in RIP.

2. Answers B, C, and E are correct. Triggered updates send out updates whenever there is a change in an effort to speed up convergence. Split horizon tells the router not to send back route information in the direction it received it from. Holddown timers hold on to route information for a period of time to wait for other routers to converge. Answers A and D are incorrect because these do not exist.

3. Answer D is correct. When configuring RIP, remember that you should configure it for all directly connected classful networks only. Answer A is incorrect because it configures more networks than necessary. Answer B is incorrect because no number is added to the end of the router rip command. Answer C is incorrect because it is missing a network.

4. Answers A, B, C, and D are correct. RIP version 2 supports MD5 authentication between routers, summarization, multicast updates to 224.0.0.9 instead of broadcast updates, and variable length subnet masks (VLSM). Remember, if a routing protocol is classless, this means that it supports VLSM and summarization. RIPv2, EIGRP, and OSPF are all classless.

5. Answer is C. The syntax for a static route is **ip route** <*destination network address*> [*subnet mask*] {*next-hop-address* | *interface*} [*distance*]. Answer A is wrong because you can not use slash notation (/29) in the command. Answer B is wrong because the wrong interface is being used. Answer D is wrong because it is using the wrong syntax. Finally, Answer E is incorrect because it is using the wrong subnet mask.

6. Answer D is correct. A default route has 0.0.0.0 for the network and 0.0.0.0 for the mask to specify any network and any mask. Answers A and B are incorrect because they are not valid commands. Answer C is incorrect because it is missing a subnet mask. Answer E is incorrect because it is using the wrong subnet mask value.

7. Answers D and F are correct. Only RIP version 2 supports classless routing with variable length subnet masks (VLSM). Once you enable version 2, you must follow that up with the no auto-summary command to disable automatic summarization. Answer A is wrong because there is a problem with the configuration. Answers B and C are wrong because you use the classful networks and do not specify a subnet mask. Answer E is wrong because the ip classless command is irrelevant.

8. Answer C is correct. RIP has the highest administrative distance so it is the least preferred routing information source. Answers A, B, and D are incorrect because their administrative distances are lower than that of RIP.

9. Answer A is correct. RIP version 1 sends out broadcasts to 255.255.255.255. RIP version 2 sends out multicast packets to 224.0.0.9. All other answers are therefore incorrect.

10. Answer C is correct. According to the output, the network is inaccessible and therefore any traffic to it will be dropped by the router.

11. Answers A and E are correct. If you look at the IP addresses assigned to the FastEthernet0/0 and the Serial0/0/0 interfaces you will see that they are on the 172.16.0.0 and 172.20.0.0 networks respectively. All other answers are incorrect because they are not local to the router but are instead learned through routing updates.

12. Answer A is correct. The local router in the output is advertising the network as one hop away. When the router at IP address 172.16.0.0 receives this information, it will populate its routing table with that information.

11

CHAPTER ELEVEN

Small-Office Internet Connection

Terms you'll need to understand:

✓ Security Device Manager (SDM)

✓ DHCP

✓ NAT

✓ VLAN1

✓ Access Port

✓ Default Gateway

✓ Default Route

Concepts and techniques you'll need to master:

✓ Using the Cisco SDM Express interface for initial router configuration

✓ IP Subnetting

✓ Using the Cisco SDM interface to configure NAT

✓ Using the Cisco SDM interface to configure DHCP

✓ Using the SDM interface to configure a default route

✓ Testing and troubleshooting LAN and WAN connectivity

Introduction

This chapter walks you through one of the tasks expected of a CCENT: Connecting a small office to the Internet. In our example, we will be using a Cisco 2821 router and a Catalyst 2960 switch, and our Internet connection will be an ADSL modem with an ethernet interface we can connect the router to.

We will learn a few new things, but most of what you will see here are applied concepts that previous chapters have covered.

To set the stage for this exercise, assume that your head office has shipped a brand new router and switch to you. You have access to some guidance from your boss at the head office, a PC to work with, and all the cables and software you need. (I could make a joke here about this scenario not being very realistic, but that would be gratuitous).

All right—let's get started.

Basic Configuration Using the Cisco Router and Security Device Manager (SDM)

You have unpacked the router and switch and set them on your desk, ready to be plugged in.

New Cisco gear has a graphical user interface (GUI) that simplifies some of the more basic configuration tasks and provides useful dashboard views of the current status of the device. The software runs on the built-in web server on new devices and requires Internet Explorer and Java. You will also need to turn off pop-up blockers.

Your boss has sent you some useful information: This new router comes with a factory configuration that allows you to use the SDM right out of the box—it's perfect for our scenario. When you use SDM for the first time on a router with factory-default settings, it starts with SDM Express, which is a quick-start GUI. We'll use SDM Express to get to the full SDM. The email from your boss says to do the following to use the factory-configured SDM Express interface:

1. Connect a crossover cable from interface Gigabit 0/0 to your PC's network interface card (NIC).

2. Statically set your PC's IP address to 10.10.10.2 and the mask to 255.255.255.248.

3. Point your web browser to http://10.10.10.1.

Figure 11.1 shows the results of this three-step operation.

FIGURE 11.1 SDM Express Login screen.

Your instructions say to use the username of **cisco** and the password **cisco**. Those are the defaults included from the factory to allow you to use the SDM interface. When you enter those, you are taken to the next screen, as shown in Figure 11.2.

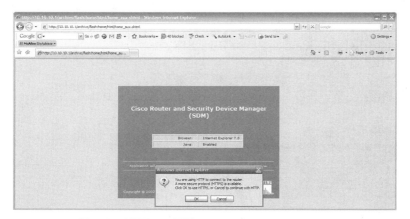

FIGURE 11.2 Choosing HTTP or HTTPs.

Choose HTTP for now. If the next screen warns about the website's security certificate, click Continue to This Website. The next window (see Figure 11.3) is another login prompt; enter **cisco** and **cisco** again. Don't worry, we'll be changing these pretty soon!

FIGURE 11.3 Logging in to SDM Express.

> **NOTE**
>
> You really will need to disable any pop-up blockers, or the Java interface will not work. Along the same lines, whenever you get a security warning from the SDM router, it's safe to allow access when your brand-new router is sitting on your desk, connected by a crossover cable. You may want to be more cautious when connecting to a router that is remote or that may have been compromised. For our purposes here, this kind of security is not a concern—yet.

You will probably get a couple security messages; it's OK to allow access and run applications as long as you are in this lab context. Figure 11.4 shows yet another login screen. Use the same password again. Notice that this one is giving you level_15 access; that's the same as Privileged EXEC.

FIGURE 11.4 Privileged EXEC level access to SDM Express.

TIP

You might find it confusing or even irritating that SDM prompts you for passwords so often. Unfortunately, it's a function of the Java interface. There is a way around it, though: If you have a CCO login account, you can download and install a local copy of the Cisco ASDM Launcher, which replaces the Java interface and stops the duplicate login screens. It's not strictly necessary, but it is useful.

After you press Enter, the SDM Express interface loads the router config, checks a couple things, and then presents you with the screen shown in Figure 11.5.

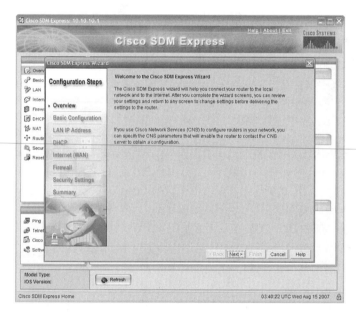

FIGURE 11.5 The SDM Express Wizard welcome screen.

SDM Express is the name for a stripped-down SDM interface that asks you to configure the bare essentials to get your router working, addressed, using DHCP, and connected to the Internet —which is exactly what we want to do here. It also allows you to set up a router firewall, if your IOS version has the capability. That's a little beyond what we want to do here, but I will say that in the real world you should never connect a router directly to the Internet unless it has a properly configured firewall protecting it!

Setting Hostname, Domain, and Login Credentials

The first screen as shown in Figure 11.6 asks for the basics of the router hostname, the domain name, and new usernames and passwords. The hostname we'll use is **Branch_2821**, the domain name will be **ExamCram2.net**, and we'll use the username of **admin** and the password **ciscocisco**. (The SDM Express security requirements mandate a minimum six-character password.) We'll use the same password for the enable secret as well, just to save confusion.

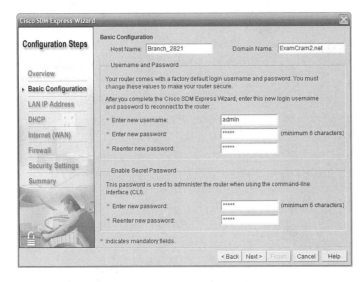

FIGURE 11.6
Supplying hostname, domain name, and user credentials.

Clicking Next brings us to a screen that asks how we want to configure this router (see Figure 11.7). We'll choose SDM Express and do it ourselves; the other choices are well beyond our scope but refer to methods of automated configuration in highly managed networks.

Configuring IP Addressing Using SDM Express

The next step is interesting. In it, we are going to change the IP address of the interface that we are actually connected to. That, of course, will break our connection, because we have to also change the address of the PC to match. It's a bit of a cliffhanger—"Did I do it right?" Don't panic. We always have the console cable.

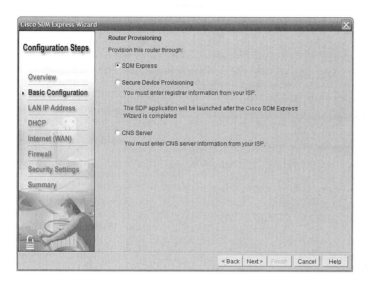

FIGURE 11.7
Choosing SDM Express as the configuration method.

Your boss has told you that this branch office LAN will use the last subnet created from 192.168.100.0/28. Because this is a new router, the zero subnets are available. The first IP address in this subnet will be assigned to the router.

> **NOTE**
>
> This router, a Cisco 2821, has two gigabit ethernet interfaces. Gi0/0 is factory configured with the IP address and mask that SDM uses. This will become our LAN interface. Gi0/1 will become our WAN (Internet) interface, but we will have the ADSL modem assign it a dynamic IP address using DHCP.

You didn't think you were going to get away without subnetting, did you? Try and figure this out without cheating by reading ahead.

OK, for all you cheaters, here's the solution:

192.168.100.0/28 uses an increment of 16 in the fourth octet. That means we will make 16 subnets from this Class C address, each of which has 14 host IPs available. (We get to keep all 16 subnets because the zero subnets are available.)

The first subnet is 192.168.100.0/28; the last one is 192.168.100.240/28. We can't use the first and last IPs (.240 and .255) because they are reserved for the NetID and Broadcast ID. So, the first host ID, which we will give to our router, is 192.168.100.241/28. Notice that in the SDM interface shown in Figure 11.8, you can either type in the mask in decimal or just select the number of mask bits with the arrows.

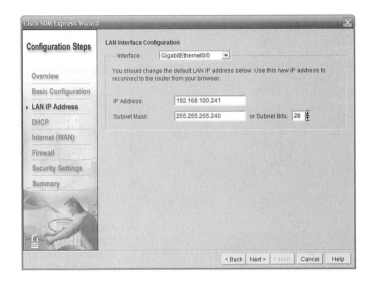

FIGURE 11.8 IP address and mask setting for interface Gi0/0.

Configuring the DHCP Server Using SDM Express

The next screen deals with setting up this router to be a DHCP server. Remember that DHCP assigns IP addresses, subnet masks, default gateway, and several other options (for example, DNS Server IPs) to hosts on the LAN. This is often a role assigned to a server on the LAN, but because our little branch office doesn't have a server, we'll take advantage of Cisco's built-in DHCP service.

To configure the DHCP server, first click the check box that says Enable DHCP Server on the LAN Interface. (In the previous screen, we set Gi0/0 as the LAN interface by not choosing the LAN IP to be on some other interface). We now have to specify what addresses the DHCP server should hand out by giving it a starting and ending range.

We need to remember that we must stay within the boundaries of our LAN subnet—but notice that SDM has already figured that out for you. By giving an IP address and mask to the LAN interface, SDM calculated our subnet IPs and starts with that whole range as its default. No cheating required!

Often with DHCP we want to exclude certain addresses—such as the router itself, and maybe servers or printers that are already statically configured. In our case, we don't have a server to worry about, but our switch will need an IP for management; we will give it 192.168.100.242/28. After taking the router's Gi0/0 and the switch into account, that means we must start the range of DHCP addresses (called a *scope*) at 192.168.100.243; we can let it run all the way to the end of the subnet, to the last available IP of 192.168.100.254.

The ISP will advise us of the correct DNS server IP addresses. For the time being, we'll use 4.2.2.2 in the first entry. Figure 11.9 shows the result.

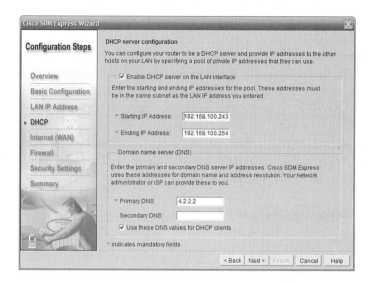

FIGURE 11.9
Configuring the
DHCP server.

Setting Up the Wan Interface in SDM Express

The next screen, shown in Figure 11.10, asks us to choose our WAN interface. You'll notice that this router has discovered and listed two interfaces: GigabitEthernet0/1 and Serial0/0/0. The serial interface will be used at a later date for the planned VoIP implementation; the boss has asked us to leave it unconfigured for now. We have selected GigabitEthernet0/1 as our WAN interface; highlight it and click Add Connection.

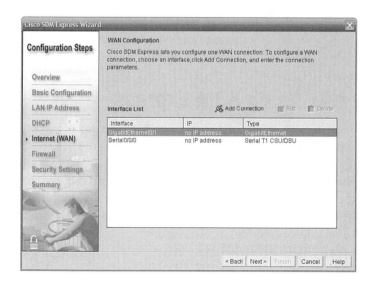

FIGURE 11.10
Choosing the WAN
interface.

The window that comes up asks us to choose how our WAN interface will get its IP address; our choices are either Static IP Address or Dynamic IP Address. Static IP Address means we have to know what the IP and mask should be and set them manually (the ISP tells us this info). Dynamic IP Address means that we want the interface to get its IP automatically from the ADSL modem. We'll choose Dynamic IP Address here; in the real world we might well choose Static IP Address if we wanted to access this router remotely or if there were servers in the office that we wanted to reach from the Internet. Usually we would need to specify in the ISP contract that we wanted one or more static IPs, and it might cost a little extra. Figure 11.11 shows the dialog box in action.

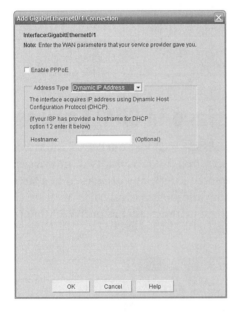

FIGURE 11.11 Choosing the WAN interface addressing method.

Configuring NAT Using SDM Express

Network Address Translation (NAT) is a vital function for Internet-connected routers. The SDM Express NAT interface allows you to configure static NAT entries, but not NAT Overload (PAT). Because our exercise needs PAT and not a static setup, we'll leave NAT disabled in the SDM for now. You can go back later and either use the command-line interface (CLI) or the full SDM interface (that is, not SDM Express) to configure it. Figure 11.12 shows the NAT screen with the Enable NAT box deselected.

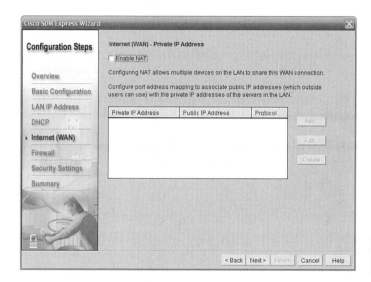

FIGURE 11.12
Disabling static NAT in SDM Express.

Firewall Option

SDM Express gives you the option to configure a firewall on the router (see Figure 11.13). SDM Express automatically creates a basic firewall that assumes one inside and one outside interface. Customizations can be made either from the full SDM version or preferably from the CLI.

Firewall configuration is well beyond our scope, but we do want to emphasize the importance of a firewall associated with an Internet-connected router. If your IOS feature set does not support firewall functions, you will not be able to configure one on your router at all, and you should instead have an external firewall such as a Cisco Adaptive Security Appliance (ASA) or a device from another reputable vendor. We'll point out the configurations that SDM Express added without delving into their meaning.

For now, we'll let SDM Express do its thing by selecting Yes, I Want to Protect My Network with a Firewall, as shown in Figure 11.13.

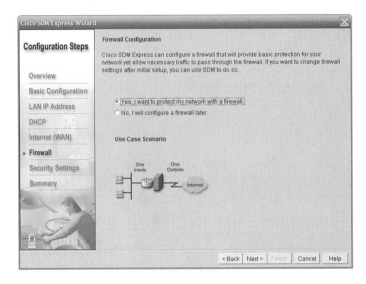

FIGURE 11.13
Enabling automatic firewall configuration in SDM Express.

Security Configuration Checklist

SDM Express can automatically prepare configurations for you that follow some of the best-practices recommendations for securing a router. Many of the terms seen in Figure 11.14 will be familiar from Chapter 9, "Basic Network Security," but some will be unfamiliar. We will leave the settings at their defaults (shown), but be aware that these settings will restrict how you can access the router (for example, requiring the use of SSH and strong passwords).

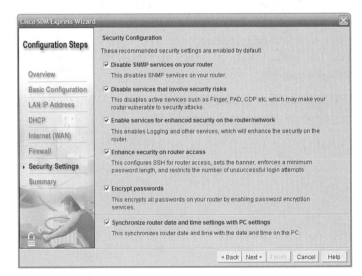

FIGURE 11.14
Enabling automatic security configuration in SDM Express.

SDM Express Configuration Summary

The screen in Figure 11.15 summarizes what we have told SDM Express to do. Here you can review your decisions, and you can click Back if you want to change anything.

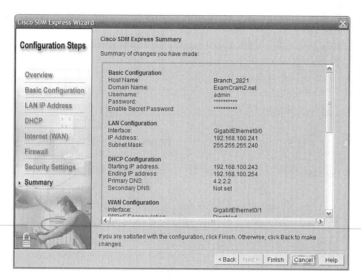

FIGURE 11.15
Cisco SDM Express Summary.

Reconnecting After SDM Express Applies Changes

One of the scarier moments is when SDM reboots the router with its new config and you can't connect to it anymore. You need to reconfigure your PC's NIC to connect using the new settings; the screen shown in Figure 11.16 is popped up when you click Finished in the previous screen. It's probably a good idea to save those instructions to a file by leaving the check box selected.

Because of the combination of settings we have chosen in SDM Express, the message shown in Figure 11.17 pops up. We will need to allow DHCP traffic, or else the Internet interface will not be able to get an IP address—the firewall basically prevents itself from doing so!

Figure 11.18 shows our "last warning" before the SDM configuration is applied and we lose connectivity. Clicking OK closes the SDM and Internet Explorer windows, and as the IP address of the web interfaces changes, connectivity to the router is (temporarily) lost.

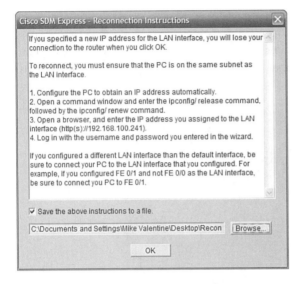

FIGURE 11.16 SDM Express Configuration Summary—Reconnection Instructions.

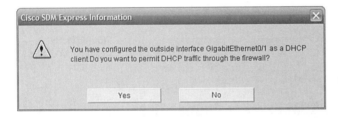

FIGURE 11.17 Firewall configuration query for DHCP.

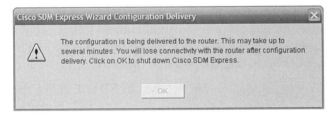

FIGURE 11.18 Configuration commit and disconnect warning.

Reconnecting to the SDM Interface

When you have reconfigured your PC's NIC as instructed by SDM, go to the address https://192.168.100.241 (this is the address in our exercise—obviously it could be different in your lab or reality!) We have specified the use of HTTPs, which is supported as a security option by SDM (as shown in Figure 11.16), but we could use HTTP instead.

Figure 11.19 shows the SDM home page after you have logged in (using the new username and password we specified) and accepted the same security warnings we saw before. Remember to disable pop-up blockers, or at least allow pop-ups from the new address of the router.

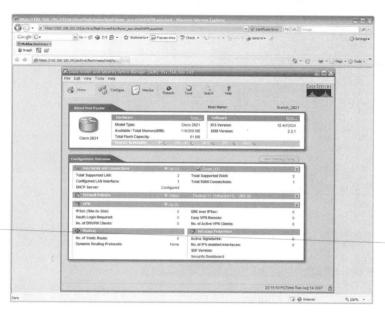

FIGURE 11.19   Home page of the full SDM interface.

We still need to set up Overload NAT and a default route; we can use the SDM interface to do this (SDM Express does not have this advanced capability). In Figure 11.20, we have clicked first on the Configure button at the top of the page; then when the page changes, we clicked NAT in the column on the left. We will configure Basic NAT because we do not need to specify servers and applications that must be reachable. Clicking the Launch the Selected Task button starts the Basic NAT Wizard.

The Basic NAT Wizard (see Figure 11.21) walks you through the configuration of Overload NAT on the router.

In Figure 11.22 we have selected the GigabitEthernet0/1 interface as our Internet interface (because it is) and selected the network that will be NATed to that interface.

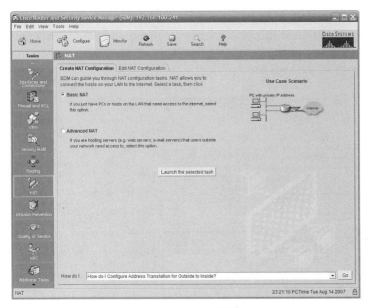

FIGURE 11.20 Configure Basic NAT in full SDM interface.

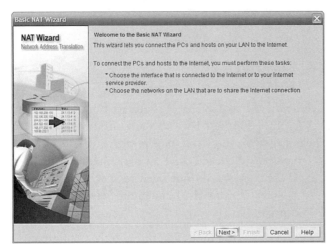

FIGURE 11.21 SDM Basic NAT Wizard start screen.

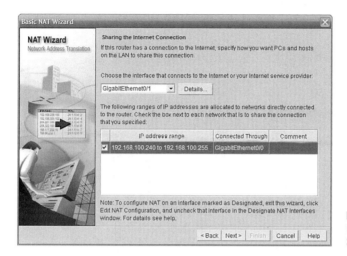

FIGURE 11.22 Setting up Overload NAT in SDM.

Figure 11.23 shows us the Finish screen of the Basic NAT Wizard and the settings we have selected.

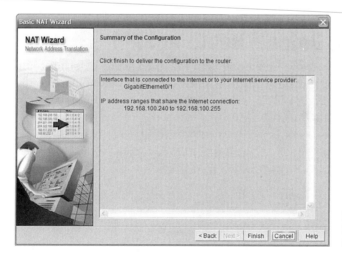

FIGURE 11.23 Basic NAT Wizard finish screen.

Figure 11.24 shows the updated SDM NAT page after our changes.

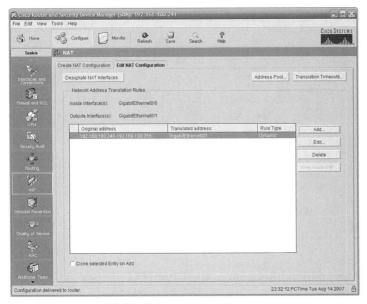

FIGURE 11.24 Updated SDM NAT page.

Configuring a Default Route in SDM

Our connection is almost ready. One thing left to do is to define a default route out to the Internet. Using the SDM interface, click Routing in the column on the left. The page shown in Figure 11.25 is displayed. There are no routes listed.

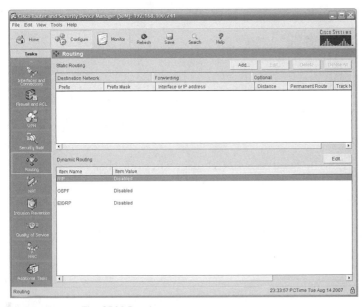

FIGURE 11.25 The SDM Routing page.

Clicking Add near the top pops up the route configuration dialog box. In Figure 11.26, we have chosen to create a default route by specifying the network 0.0.0.0, the mask 0.0.0.0, and selecting the Make This as the Default Route check box. We also specified GigabitEthernet0/1 as the next-hop interface because this is our Internet interface. If we were using a static IP from our ISP, we would specify the IP instead. I chose to check the Permanent Route box so that the route would stay in the route table even if the next hop is unavailable.

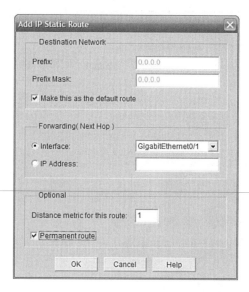

FIGURE 11.26 Enabling the default route in SDM.

Figure 11.27 shows the Routing page after our update. The default route is shown.

Testing Connectivity Using the SDM Interface

The SDM interface includes some very useful tools to check your connectivity. From the SDM home page, click the Monitor button near the top. Then click Interface Status on the left.

Near the top of the main pane in the screen is a list of interfaces. Click the Internet interface (in our case, GigabitEthernet0/1) to highlight it. Then, click the Test Connection button at the top right. Figure 11.28 shows the page that comes up when you do so.

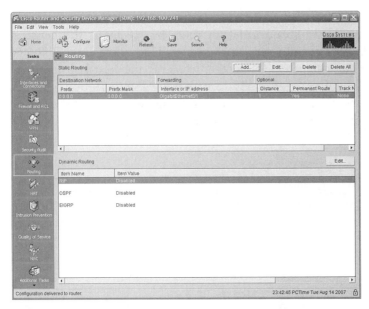

FIGURE 11.27 The SDM Routing page with default route shown.

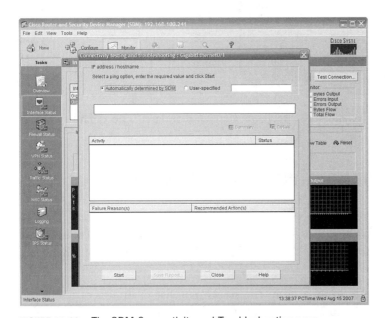

FIGURE 11.28 The SDM Connectivity and Troubleshooting page.

You have the option of letting SDM choose a host to ping, or you can specify one. Clicking Start at the bottom of the page starts a series of tests, and lists what the outcome was, as shown in Figure 11.29.

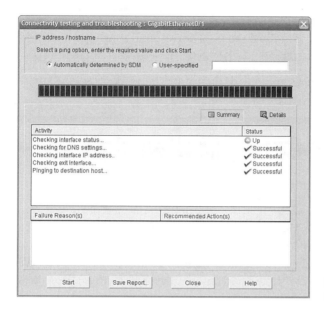

FIGURE 11.29 Output from a successful test.

You can click the Details button to see the specifics of what was tested.

Let's take a quick look at the DHCP configuration page in SDM to see the result of what we did in SDM Express. From the SDM home page, click Additional Tasks in the left (Tasks) pane. In the middle pane, click the plus sign to expand DHCP. Next, click DHCP Pools in the expanded list. Figure 11.30 shows the resulting view.

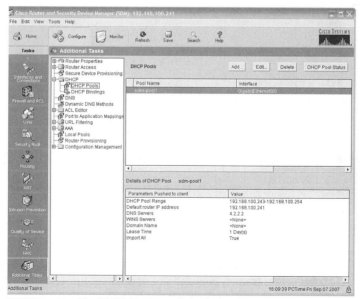

FIGURE 11.30 The DHCP Pools configuration page.

We can see that the pool named **sdm-pool1** is associated with Interface GigabitEthernet0/0, and the details of the pool correspond to what we entered into SDM Express earlier.

That is pretty much all we need to do with the router. Now let's turn our attention to the switch.

Basic Switch Configuration Using the CLI

Our switch is a new Catalyst 2960, with 24 10/100 ethernet ports and two 10/100/1000 ethernet ports. We will configure our switch from the CLI. We need to give the switch a management IP address and a default gateway; we also want to apply passwords and restrict remote access to Secure Shell (SSH). We will leave all interfaces in VLAN1 for now; more advanced configurations will be made later.

Plug in your console cable and make sure your terminal application is configured properly as follows:

- ▶ 9600 baud
- ▶ 8 data bits
- ▶ 1 stop bit
- ▶ No Parity
- ▶ Flow Control = OFF

Because this is a new switch, we will be prompted to enter the Initial Configuration dialog; we can bypass this and go straight to the command line. By default, there is no password to enable the switch.

Securing the Switch

We are going to configure some basic security on the switch. Our first tasks are the following:

1. Set the hostname to **Branch_2960**:

```
Switch>enable
Switch#config t
Switch(config)#hostname Branch_2960
Branch_2960(config)#
```

2. Configure a console password of **ciscocisco**

```
Branch_2960(config)#line con 0
Branch_2960(config-line)#password ciscocisco
Branch_2960(config-line)#login
Branch_2960(config-line)#
```

3. Configure a VTY line password of **ciscocisco** on the first five VTY lines.

4. Restrict access to the VTY lines to SSH only.

   To complete tasks 3 and 4, we need to go back to the Global Config prompt. SSH requires a hostname (we already set one), a domain name, and the generation of an RSA keypair. We will also create a username and password for local authentication. Then we will go back to the VTY lines and require a password to log in, configure the switch to use the username and password we gave it, and further restrict the VTY lines to SSH only.

```
Branch_2960(config-line)#exit
Branch_2960(config)#ip domain-name ExamCram2.net
Branch_2960(config)#crypto key generate rsa
Branch_2960(config)#username admin password ciscocisco
Branch_2960(config)#line vty 0 4
Branch_2960(config-line)#login
Branch_2960(config-line)#login local
Branch_2960(config-line)#transport input ssh
Branch_2960(config-line)#exit
Branch_2960(config)#
```

5. Set an encrypted Privileged EXEC password of **ciscosecret**:

```
Branch_2960(config)#enable secret ciscosecret
```

6. Encrypt console and VTY line passwords:

```
Branch_2960(config)#service password-encryption
```

Configuring a Management IP and Default Gateway

Setting the management IP on a switch involves configuring a VLAN interface. A Layer 2 switch such as the 2960 will support one VLAN interface at a time; the default is to use Interface VLAN1.

NOTE

Many students seem to have trouble grasping the difference between a VLAN and VLAN *interface*. A VLAN divides a switch, at Layer 2, into separate broadcast domains. Switch ports are assigned to VLANs. A VLAN *interface* is a virtual (software) interface that will accept an IP address and mask, and it is the only place on a Layer2 switch you can assign an IP. VLAN1 is the default ethernet VLAN; Interface VLAN1 is the default VLAN Interface and is usually the one used for managing the switch remotely.

To set the management IP on Interface VLAN1, the commands are

```
Branch_2960(config)#interface vlan1
Branch_2960(config-if)#ip address192.168.100.242 255.255.255.240
Branch_2960(config-if)#no shut
Branch_2960(config-if)#exit
Branch_2960(config)#
```

Setting the switch's default gateway allows the switch to send packets destined for any subnet that is not on its VLAN1 subnet to our router, which can then route the packet wherever it needs to go. A single command will do this:

```
Branch_2960(config)#ip default-gateway 192.168.100.241
```

That completes the switch configuration, At this point, to test whether it is all working, you can perform the classic troubleshooting methodology:

1. Plug in a PC to the switch; make sure the PC is set to use DHCP.

2. Check that link lights are lit on switchport and PC NIC.

   If this step fails, check your cables and connections.

3. Check that PC obtains an IP address and mask in the expected subnet from DHCP.

   If this step fails, try the command **ipconfig /renew** from the command prompt on the PC. If it still will not get an IP address, make sure that the connection to the router is working and verify that the DHCP server on the router is active. You may also want to try disabling and reenabling the PC NIC.

4. On the PC, ping its own IP address.

   If this step fails, there is a problem with the PC's NIC. Try replacing it, or try a different PC.

5. On the PC, ping the router's IP address.

   If this step fails, check that the router's interface is up/up and that the IP address is correct.

6. On the PC, ping an Internet IP address.

If this step fails, check the default route. Ensure that the Internet interface is up/up and that the Internet connection is working properly.

That is all we really need to do to set up and test a small office Internet connection. There are, of course, many more advanced configurations that might be required, depending on the circumstances.

Exam Prep Questions

1. Which element does not need to be configured to support SSH connections to a router or switch?

   ○ **A.** At the VTY lines, enter **transport input ssh**

   ○ **B.** A username and password for local authentication

   ○ **C.** A domain name

   ○ **D.** A hostname

   ○ **E.** An RSA key

2. On your new Catalyst 2960 switch, what configuration is required to put all switch ports into VLAN 1?

   ○ **A.** `Switch(config)#`**`switchport VLAN 1 default`**

   ○ **B.** `Switch(config-if)#`**`switchport VLAN 1 default`**

   ○ **C.** `Switch(config)#`**`switchport access vlan 1`**

   ○ **D.** No configuration is required.

3. Why would a Catalyst 2960 switch need an IP address?

   ○ **A.** To represent connected networks to the internal route table

   ○ **B.** To protect switch ports with SSH

   ○ **C.** To allow remote management of the switch

   ○ **D.** To activate inter-VLAN routing

4. You have configured your branch office switch with an IP address and verified that it can ping the router it is connected to. Later that day, you are back at head office and cannot ping, Telnet, or SSH to the switch back at the branch, although you can ping the servers at the branch that are connected to the switch. What could be the problem?

   ○ **A.** The firewall ports for the switch must be opened.

   ○ **B.** The WAN link to the branch is down.

   ○ **C.** The command **ip default-gateway** must be configured on the branch switch.

   ○ **D.** The router must be reloaded.

5. What is likely the problem if you get no reply to a ping to 127.0.0.1 on your PC?

- ○ **A.** Your router is not connected to the Internet.

- ○ **B.** That address is reserved as unpingable.

- ○ **C.** The switch is down.

- ○ **D.** Your PC has a problem with its TCP/IP protocol software.

6. Examine the figure that follows. Users are complaining that they cannot access resources on the LAN, nor can they access the Internet. What could be the problem?

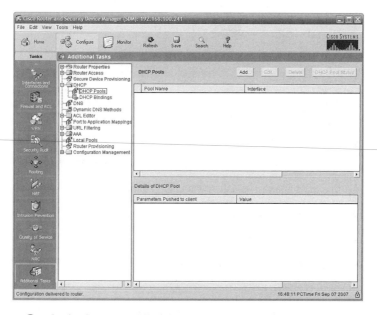

- ○ **A.** Inadequate user training.

- ○ **B.** The SDM router has run out of DHCP addresses.

- ○ **C.** The SDM interface has failed.

- ○ **D.** Client PCs are not receiving IP addresses from the SDM router because of missing configuration.

7. Examine the figure that follows. Users are not able to access the Internet, but are able to ping the default gateway and use LAN resources. What could be the problem?

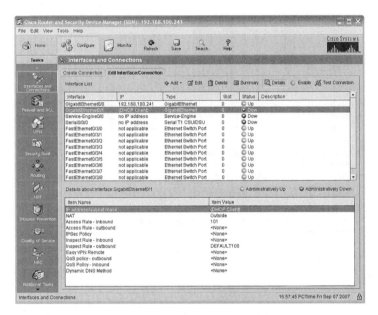

○ **A.** The SDM interface is listing unconfigured interfaces.

○ **B.** The Internet interface needs to be enabled.

○ **C.** The LAN interface needs to be enabled.

○ **D.** The firewall is interpreting HTTP traffic as an internal attack and blocking it.

Answers to Exam Prep Questions

1. Answer A is correct. You can add this command to allow *only* SSH (instead of Telnet *and* SSH), but it is not needed to make SSH work. Answers B, C, D, and E are required.

2. Answer D is correct. All switchports on a new switch are in VLAN 1 by default. Answers A and B are invalid syntax; answer C is correct syntax but at the wrong configuration prompt (this command is entered at the config-if prompt); also, answer C misses the key point that all switch interfaces are in VLAN 1 by default.

3. Answer C is correct; the IP address is what we use to Telnet/SSH to or from the switch. The IP is also needed for SNMP. Answer A is wrong because the 2960 is not capable of routing and therefore has no route table. Answer B is wrong because switch ports are not protected by SSH; remote management traffic to the VTY lines is encrypted by SSH. Answer D is wrong because the 2960 is not capable of inter-VLAN routing; we need an external router to do this.

4. Answer C is correct; without the `ip default-gateway` command, the switch does not know where to send traffic from a different network. Answer A is wrong; if you can ping hosts on the branch LAN, the firewall is probably not the problem. Answer B is wrong; if you can ping hosts in the branch over the WAN, the WAN cannot be down. Answer D is wrong; the router is apparently working just fine.

5. Answer D is correct; if you get no answer from the Loopback (localhost) IP, the problem is almost certainly with the TCP/IP software. Answer A is wrong because this is not an Internet IP, so whether the Internet router is working correctly is irrelevant. Answer B is wrong; there is no such classification as "reserved as unpingable" although it sounds official. Answer C is wrong; this test does not involve the switch at all.

6. Answer D is correct. The figure shows the SDM DHCP Pools configuration page, with no pools configured. This means that no DHCP addresses will be assigned to hosts, preventing them from accessing resources on the LAN or Internet. Answer A may well be correct, but it is not related to the issue at hand. Answer B could cause the same behavior for some clients, but the figure does not support the answer. Answer C is wrong; we are looking at the SDM interface, and in any case, this would not cause the user issues stated.

7. Answer B is correct; the SDM is showing the Gi0/1 is Administratively Down. Enabling it will almost certainly solve the reported problem. Answer A is wrong. There are several unconfigured interfaces listed, but that does not affect the functionality of the others; we're just not using them. Answer C is wrong. If the clients can ping the router, the LAN interface is working; in addition, SDM lists it as Up. Answer D is wrong; the figure gives no indication that this unlikely possibility is at fault.

CHAPTER TWELVE

Advanced Catalyst Switch Operations and Configuration

Terms you'll need to understand:

✓ Spanning Tree

✓ Root

✓ Designated

✓ Blocked

✓ VLAN

✓ Trunk

✓ ISL

✓ 802.1Q

✓ VTP Server, Client, Transparent

✓ VTP Domain

✓ Inter-VLAN routing

✓ Layer 3 Switching

Concepts and techniques you'll need to master:

✓ Identifying the Root switch in a system

✓ Identifying Root, Designated, and Blocked ports in a system

✓ Creating and naming VLANs

✓ Assigning Switch Ports to VLANs

✓ Configuring Trunk links

✓ Creating and joining a VTP Domain

✓ Troubleshooting VTP and Inter-VLAN routing

Introduction

This chapter introduces the Spanning Tree Protocol (STP) and reviews some of its enhanced features. We then move into the theory, benefits, applications, and implementation of VLANs. Inter-switch connectivity using trunks and the characteristics of different trunking protocols are explained. Finally, Inter-VLAN routing options are described, and troubleshooting tips are reviewed.

Spanning Tree Protocol

Earlier, we mentioned that one of the functions of a switch was Layer 2 Loop removal. This is a critical feature, as without it many switched networks would completely cease to function. Either accidentally or deliberately in the process of creating a redundant network, the problem arises when we create a looped switched path. A *loop* can be defined as two or more switches that are interconnected by two or more physical links.

Switching loops create three major problems:

 ▸ **Broadcast Storms**—Switches must flood broadcasts, so a looped topology will create multiple copies of a single broadcast and perpetually cycle them through the loop.

 ▸ **MAC table instability**—Loops make it appear that a single MAC address is reachable on multiple ports of a switch, and the switch is constantly updating the MAC table.

 ▸ **Duplicate frames**—Because there are multiple paths to a single MAC, it is possible that a frame could be duplicated to be flooded out all paths to a single destination MAC.

All these problems are serious and will bring a network to an effective standstill unless prevented.

Figure 12.1 illustrates a looped configuration causing a broadcast storm:

Other than simple error, the most common reason that loops are created is because we want to build a redundant or fault-tolerant network. By definition, redundancy means that we have a backup, separate path for data to follow in the event the first one fails. The problem is that unless the backup path is physically disabled—perhaps by unplugging it—the path creates a loop and causes the problems mentioned previously. We like redundant systems; we do not like loops and the problems they cause. We need a mechanism that automatically detects and prevents loops so that we can build the fault-tolerant physical links and have them become active only when needed. The mechanism is called the *Spanning Tree Protocol* (STP). STP is a protocol that runs on bridges and switches to find and block redundant looped paths during normal operation. Spanning Tree was originally developed by the Digital Equipment Corporation (DEC), and the idea was adopted and modified by the IEEE to become 802.1d. The two are incompatible, but it is exceedingly rare to find a DEC bridge these days, so the incompatibility is not usually a problem.

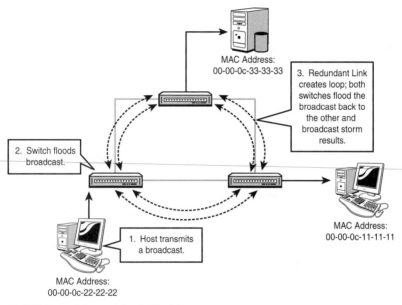

MAC Address:
00-00-0c-33-33-33

3. Redundant Link creates loop; both switches flood the broadcast back to the other and broadcast storm results.

2. Switch floods broadcast.

MAC Address:
00-00-0c-11-11-11

1. Host transmits a broadcast.

MAC Address:
00-00-0c-22-22-22

FIGURE 12.1 A Layer 2 (switching) loop.

EXAM ALERT

STP eliminates Layer 2 loops in switched networks with redundant paths.

Root Election

STP's basic function is to create a loop-free path to a *root bridge*. The root bridge is the bridge or switch that is the root of the Spanning Tree, with the branches being loop-free paths to the other switches in the system. The Root is the switch with the lowest Bridge ID; the ID is determined by a combination of an administrative Priority and the MAC address of the switch. The Priority is set to 32,768 (8000 hex) by default; if we leave the Priority at the default, whatever switch has the lowest MAC will be the Root. Figure 12.2 illustrates a simple Root selection when all switches are using the default Priority.

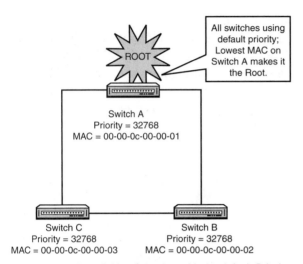

FIGURE 12.2 Root Bridge Selection with the default Priority.

We cannot change the MAC address of a switch, so what happens if Switch A in the previous example happens to be an old, slow Catalyst 1900? It might get elected the Root because it has a low MAC address, but we really don't want it to be the Root: Usually, we would choose a big, fast switch at the core of the network as the Root. Let's say that Switch C is a hot new switch and we want it to be our Root; how do we override the existing election? The answer is to change the default Priority—remember, the lowest ID wins the election, and the ID is the Priority prepended to the MAC. The ID is one long string, so lowering the Priority makes the ID lower. Thus, if we change the Priority of Switch C to a low value, it will win the election despite the fact that it has a higher MAC than A. Figure 12.3 illustrates this.

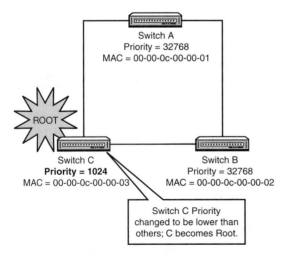

FIGURE 12.3 Root Election with a modified Priority.

EXAM ALERT

The Root is elected based on the Bridge ID and the Priority. The switch with the lowest Priority will always be the Root.

STP Communication with BPDUs

To determine the presence of loops and to block loops, switches must be capable of communicating with each other about the various connections they have. This communication in STP is carried out by the exchange of Bridge Protocol Data Units (BPDUs). The 802.1d BPDU is multicasted every two seconds and includes information the switches need to decide if there are loops, how to fix them, and which switch is the Root. Figure 12.4 shows the fields in an 802.1d BPDU; note the fields for the Bridge ID, the Root ID, and the Root path cost.

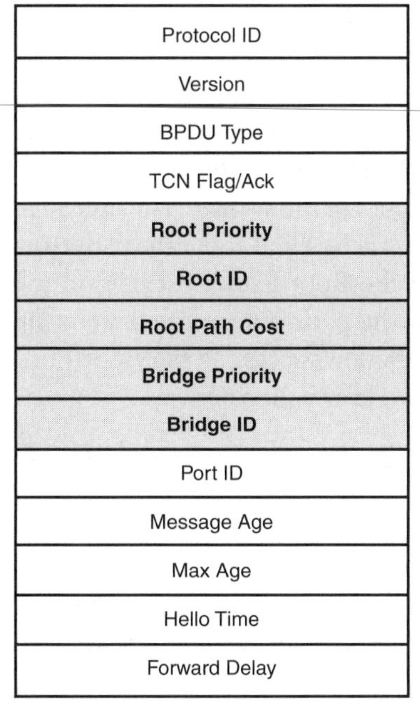
Protocol ID
Version
BPDU Type
TCN Flag/Ack
Root Priority
Root ID
Root Path Cost
Bridge Priority
Bridge ID
Port ID
Message Age
Max Age
Hello Time
Forward Delay

FIGURE 12.4 Detailed contents of 802.1d BPDU packet.

Port Types

STP assigns different ports on a switch as different types, depending on where the Root is and where the loops are in the topology. The sections that follow describe the port types and how they are selected.

Root

The Root port on a switch is the one port that has the lowest cost path to the Root switch. Path cost is calculated based on the bandwidth of the links. Table 12.1 lists the IEEE-defined values for STP path cost; note that there are old and new values. The new values were defined because of the increasingly widespread availability of multi-Gigabit link speeds; previously, a 1Gbs link had the same cost as a 10Gbps link. That made no sense and would create suboptimal STP topologies, so the costs were revised.

TABLE 12.1   STP Path Costs, Old and New

Link Speed	New Cost Value	Old Cost Value
10Gbps	2	1
1Gbps	4	1
100Mbps	19	10
10Mbps	100	100

After the switches have elected the Root for the system, each switch must then decide which port it will use to reach the Root. Some switches will have only one port that can reach the Root at all; some might have several, depending on the number and location of uplinks between the switches in the system. The exchange of BPDUs that decides the Root election also tells each switch about the path costs to reach the Root (as indicated by the value of the Root Path Cost field in the BPDU). Each switch adds its own path cost to the path cost received from the neighboring switch and chooses the port with the lowest cost as the Root Port. Figure 12.5 illustrates root port selection in a simple switched network.

Note that the Root itself does not have any Root ports: It does not need to reach the Root—it is the Root!

Designated

For each LAN segment, there must be one Designated port. This is the port that will forward traffic to the Root from the LAN segment. The Designated port is the port that has the least cost path to the Root from the LAN segment.

The Root switch has only Designated ports. Because it *is* the root, it won't have a Root port, and it can't block any of the ports that connect to other switches (because that would make the other switch's Root ports not work).

In Figure 12.6, our three switches have already elected the Root and chosen their Root ports. Switch A is the Root, so all of its ports are Designated. Switches B and C must next choose which port will block and which port will be designated on the link between them.

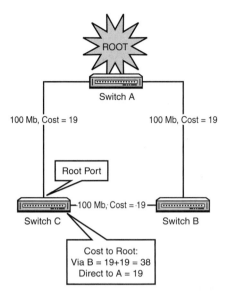

FIGURE 12.5   The Root port is the one with the lowest Root Path Cost.

The first criterion examined is which switch has the lowest root path cost. In our setup here, B and C each connect to the Root with a 100Mbps connection, with an STP cost of 19. By examining each other's BPDUs, B and C realize that they are tied for root path cost.

This is a very common scenario in modern networks where switches are directly connected over full-duplex crossover cables. One of the switches must block its port to stop the loop. The second criterion (the first tiebreaker) is the lower Bridge ID: in this case, Switch B wins and Switch C must block its port.

As we get into more complex switched systems, we get into situations where additional criteria (tiebreakers) are needed. The full list is examined in the next section, "Port Type Selection."

Port Type Selection

The order of criteria a switch goes through when deciding its Root and Designated ports is as follows:

1. The port with the lowest cumulative Root Path Cost will be the Root port/Designated port.

2. If tied between multiple ports, the port that connects to the neighboring switch with the lowest Bridge ID becomes the Root port/Designated port.

3. If there are multiple connections to that same switch, the port with the lowest assigned STP priority will be the Root port/Designated port.

4. If tied, the port with the lowest hardware number (Fa0/1 is lower than Fa0/2) will be the Root port/Designated port.

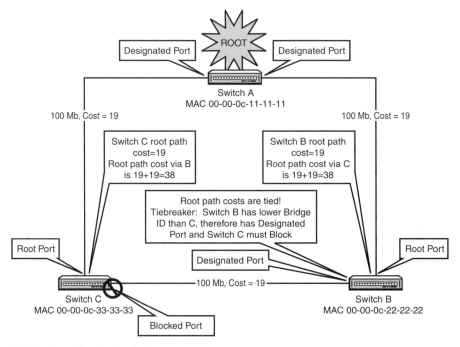

FIGURE 12.6 The Designated port selection process.

Blocked

A Blocked port is neither the Root port nor the Designated port, but is part of the redundant links between switches. In other words, it lost in the election to choose the active Root or Designated ports, but it might take over one of these roles if the active port failed. A Blocked port is the one that actually stops the loop, so it is just as important as the Root or Designated. A Blocked port does not send data; it only receives BPDUs.

Convergence

Convergence is the term used to describe the process STP goes through to achieve a stable, loop-free network. (The same term is used with reference to routing information stability as well.) When all switches have elected the Root and decided on their Root, Designated, and Blocked ports, the system is said to be converged.

Port States

With 802.1d STP, each port on each switch goes through four distinct port states in the process of convergence:

1. **Blocking**—When a switch boots up, all ports start in the blocking state. This is to prevent loops during the time that the STP topology is converging. A port that is a link between switches will stay blocked unless it becomes a Root or Designated port. Blocked ports send no data at all (not even BPDUs), but they do listen for (receive) BPDUs from other switches. All ports will also go to Blocking mode if a Topology Change Notification (TCN) BPDU is received. TCNs are issued when a new link is added or removed—the topology of the switched system is altered. When this happens, STP reacts by blocking all ports until loop-free convergence is achieved.

   If a switch dies or a link between switches fails, the other switches connected to it wait for a specific time until they begin the STP convergence process. This interval is called the Max Age Timer, and by default it is 20 seconds. Effectively, it means that a switch will wait until it has missed 10 BPDUs (which are sent every 2 seconds) from a connected switch before it kicks in the STP recalculation.

2. **Listening**—The Listening state enables a Blocked port to begin sending its own BPDUs. By default, the Listening state is 15 seconds.

3. **Learning**—The Learning state is when the switch begins populating its MAC address table. It is not yet forwarding any frames, but it is getting ready to forward by building as complete a MAC table as it can. The Listening state is also 15 seconds by default. The Listening and Learning states together are called the Forward Delay, and you might see their two 15-second timers represented as a single 30-second timer called the Forward Delay Timer.

4. **Forwarding**—The Forwarding state, as its name implies, is when the port starts forwarding frames. This is simply normal operation for a port that is not blocked.

If you take a quick look at these states and their timers, you can see that in 802.1d STP, reaching convergence can take anywhere from 30 to 50 seconds (Forward Delay [15+15]+ MaxAge[20] = 50 seconds). Understand that during this 30 to 50 seconds, no frames are being forwarded at all—no data is being sent anywhere because every port on every switch is either Blocking, Listening, or Learning. This is, of course, very detrimental to the productivity and utility of a network, especially a modern, busy one. A 50-second delay every time a topology change happens is unacceptable, so Cisco (and then the IEEE) created several enhancements to 802.1d STP to speed up the process of convergence. Some of these enhancements are discussed in the following section.

EXAM ALERT

In a converged STP system, all ports are either Blocking or Forwarding. Know the four STP port states and what exactly the port is doing in each one!

RSTP Enhancements

The Rapid Spanning Tree protocol (RSTP, IEEE 802.1w—remember, 802.1w is *Wapid Spanning Twee*) has many of its roots in Cisco-created enhancements to ordinary 802.1d STP. The primary goal of these enhancements is to speed up convergence. There are no timers in RSTP; instead, the BPDU becomes much more detailed and informative so that switches can gather more information with greater accuracy. New port states have been defined as shown in Table 12.2.

TABLE 12.2   RSTP Port States

802.1d STP	802.1w RSTP
Blocking	Discarding
Listening	Discarding
Learning	Learning
Forwarding	Forwarding

Switches wait for only three missing BPDUs before commencing the Spanning-Tree recalculation process. The process of convergence is itself much more rapid because new port types have been defined as well. In addition to the Root and Designated port types in STP, RSTP defines the Alternate and Backup port types. The Alternate port is the port that will become the Root port if the primary Root port fails. The Backup port is the port that will become the Designated port if the primary Designated port fails. The BPDUs in RSTP convey information about these port types to neighboring switches. This enhanced communication allows for quicker convergence, without relying on the 30–50 second timers in STP.

Another significant improvement in convergence speed comes from the Rapid Transition to Forwarding (RTF) features of Edge ports and link types. *Edge ports* are ports that are connected to non–STP-capable devices such as PCs, servers, or routers. These devices will not normally create STP loops, so there is no need for them to block to prevent loops. This function is enabled by Cisco's `portfast` command feature. With PortFast configured, a switch port will stop sending BPDUs (after a few have been sent as a precaution to prevent loops) and transition to the forwarding state almost immediately. This is very useful to get frames moving through the switch so hosts can get on with business—picture a database server and a PC connected to the same switch; they would not have to wait the 50 seconds for STP convergence if portfast was configured on both ports. In addition, if a port configured for portfast does receive a BPDU (perhaps because someone plugged a switch in), by default it will disable portfast and start STP on that port to prevent loops. You can also optionally configure the switch port with BPDU Guard to shut down the port if it receives a BPDU. This is more secure because it prevents the unauthorized installation of switches. BPDU Guard is covered in the Cisco CCNP curriculum.

The interface-configuration syntax to configure a Catalyst switch port with Portfast looks like this:

```
Switch(config-if)#spanning-tree portfast
```

Or, to set all ports to use portfast by default, use the global configuration command:

```
Switch(config)#spanning-tree portfast default
```

To turn PortFast off, use the `spanning-tree portfast disable` interface configuration command.

Another Cisco enhancement deals with port security; this feature set allows you (among several other options) to disable a port if more than one MAC address is detected as being connected to the port. This feature is commonly applied to ports that connect security-sensitive devices such as servers.

The following command syntax restricts access to a single MAC address and shuts the port down if another MAC connects:

```
Switch(config)#interface fa0/21
Switch(config-if)#switchport mode access
Switch(config-if)#switchport port-security
Switch(config-if)#switchport port-security maximum 1
Switch(config-if)#switchport port-security violation shutdown
```

Link Types refers to a port setting of either full duplex or half duplex. If a port is set for full duplex, RSTP assumes that it is a candidate for rapid transition because there can be only one other device at the end of such a connection. If it is set for half duplex, however, it is conceivable that there could be multiple STP-capable devices on that segment, so by default the RTF functions are disabled. It is possible to override this default.

VLAN Concepts and Applications

When you plug a bunch of PCs in to a switch and give them all IP addresses in the same network, you create a LAN. A VLAN is a Virtual LAN. The difference is that with VLANs, you still connect all the PCs to a single switch but you make the switch behave as if it were multiple, independent switches. Each VLAN is its own broadcast domain and IP subnet. In this way, you get the ability to use switches to segment broadcast domains, which up to this point was possible only with routers. Figure 12.7 illustrates a simple VLAN configuration:

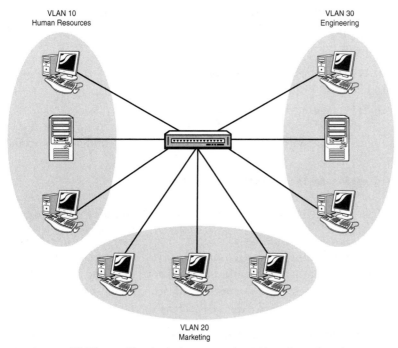

FIGURE 12.7 VLANs provide a logical segmentation of broadcast domains.

The Definition of a VLAN

A *VLAN* can be defined as a virtual broadcast domain. Instead of segmenting the broadcast domain with routers at Layer 3, you segment using switches at Layer 2. Each VLAN should be associated with its own IP subnet. (No, this is not technically a requirement, but you really want to do it this way!)

EXAM ALERT

VLANs logically divide a switch into multiple, independent switches at Layer 2.
Each VLAN is its own broadcast domain.
Each VLAN should be in its own subnet.

Benefits of VLANs

The advantages of using VLANs are as follows:

▶ VLANs increase the number of broadcast domains while reducing their size; this is the same effect that routers have, but without the need to buy a lot of routers or a big router with a lot of ports, so it's less expensive and easier to administer.

▶ VLANs provide an additional layer of security: No device in any VLAN can communicate with a device in any other VLAN until you deliberately configure a way for it to do so. An example might be a server in VLAN 10 that holds sensitive employee files for HR; no PCs from other VLANs can access VLAN 10 (or the server in it), unless you specifically configure it to do so.

▶ VLANs are flexible in terms of how they are used in network equipment: Imagine a building that has LAN cabling and a single switch installed, but four different tenants. You can create four different VLANs, one for each tenant, and no tenant will see or hear from the other tenants on the other VLANs.

▶ VLANs can span across multiple switches using trunk links. This allows you to create a logical grouping of network users by function instead of location. If you want all the marketing people to be in their own broadcast domain and IP subnet, you can create a VLAN for them on the first switch; then, you can connect another switch using a trunk link, define the same VLAN on that switch, and the marketing users on the second switch are in the same VLAN and can communicate with the marketing users on the first switch, and are isolated from other VLANs on both switches. This capability can be extended across an enterprise network campus, so that marketing users in the Whitaker Pavilion could in theory be in a VLAN with other marketing users in the Valentine Pavilion.

▶ The ability to trunk VLANs across multiple switches makes adding users, moving users, and changing users' VLAN memberships much easier.

EXAM ALERT

Know the advantages of VLANs:

▶ Increase the number of broadcast domains while reducing their size.

▶ Provide additional security.

▶ Increase the flexibility of network equipment.

▶ Allow a logical grouping of users by function, not location.

▶ Make user adds, moves, and changes easier.

Figure 12.8 illustrates a multi-switch VLAN system.

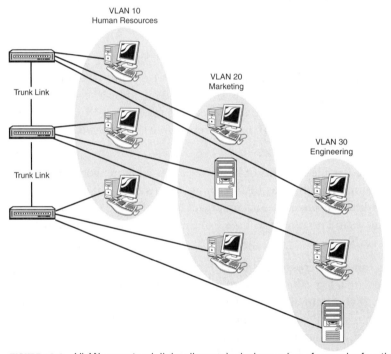

FIGURE 12.8 VLANs over trunk links allows a logical grouping of users by function.

Implementing VLANs

Implementing VLANs is done in three steps:

1. Create the VLAN.

2. Name the VLAN (this is optional but expected).

3. Assign switch ports to the VLAN.

EXAM ALERT

Know the three steps in VLAN implementation: Create it, name it, and assign ports to it.

The commands to create a VLAN vary depending on the switch model and IOS version; we stick with the Catalyst 2960 using an IOS later than 12.1(9) as our example.

The command to create a VLAN is simply **vlan** *[vlan_#]*. To name the VLAN, the equally simple command is **name** [vlan_name]. These commands are entered starting at the Global Config prompt.

To create VLAN 10 named HR, VLAN 20 named Marketing, and VLAN 30 named Engineering, the commands look like this:

```
2960#configure terminal
2960(config)#vlan 10
2960(config-vlan)#name HR
2960(config-vlan)#vlan 20
2960(config-vlan)#name Marketing
2960(config-vlan)#vlan 30
2960(config-vlan)#name Engineering
2960(config-vlan)#exit
2960(config)#exit
2960#
```

The global config prompt changes to the config-vlan prompt when you create the first VLAN; it is okay to stay in that prompt to continue creating VLANs.

With these commands, you can create all your VLANs at once, or you can go back later and add some more as needed. The VLAN configuration (names and numbers) is not stored in the Running-Config or Startup-Config file in NVRAM; rather, it is stored in Flash memory in a special file called *vlan.dat*. This means that it is possible to erase the Startup-Config file, reload the router, and be confused by the reappearance of VLANs that you thought you just deleted. To delete VLANs, you can do it one at a time using the **no vlan** [vlan_#] command, or to get rid of all of them at once, you can use the command **delete flash:vlan.dat**, which erases and resets the entire VLAN database.

CAUTION

The exact syntax for the **delete flash:vlan.dat** command is critical: no space after **flash** or the colon! If you put a space after **flash**, you could delete the entire flash directory, including your IOS. This is a very bad thing to do, and is actually quite an ordeal to fix.

> **NOTE**
>
> Cisco switches have a few default VLANs preconfigured; these are intended for the management and essential functionality of Ethernet, Token Ring, and FDDI LANs. VLAN 1, for example, is the management VLAN for Ethernet. All switch ports are in VLAN 1 by default. You cannot change or delete these default VLANs.
>
> The Cisco Catalyst 2960 will support up to 1005 VLANs defined locally.

VLANs can exist without any ports actually being in them. Adding switch ports to a VLAN is done when you want to put a host into a particular VLAN. Obviously, you need to know which physical ports your hosts are connected to so that you can add the correct port to the correct VLAN; it would be an unpopular move to put a marketing user into the Engineering VLAN; these two groups are mutually hostile.

The commands to add a switch port to a VLAN are executed at the Interface Config prompt—if you think about that, it makes sense because you are putting the port itself into the VLAN. The command is **switchport access vlan [vlan_#]**. What you are saying is "this port shall access VLAN X."

The following example puts ports Fa0/8 into VLAN 10, Fa0/13 into VLAN 20, and Fa0/14 into VLAN 30:

```
2960#config t
2960(config)#interface fa0/8
2960(config-if)#switchport access vlan 10
2960(config-if)#int fa0/13
2960(config-if)#switchport access vlan 20
2960(config-if)#int fa0/14
2960(config-if)#switchport access vlan 30
2960(config-if)#exit
2960(config)#exit
2960#
```

VLAN Membership

The commands in the previous section assign particular ports to a particular VLAN *statically*. (Static VLAN assignment is sometimes called port-based VLAN membership.) When a user changes ports (moves around the office or campus), you need to repeat the commands at the Switch(config-if)# prompt for the correct new interface. As you can imagine, if there are a lot of moves, this can become an administrative pain.

There is an alternative called *Dynamic VLAN Membership*. This feature allows you to dynamically assign VLAN membership to switch ports based on the MAC address of the host connecting to the port. You need a little service called the *VLAN Membership Policy Server (VMPS)* that holds a database of all the MAC addresses and the correct VLAN for each one; then you tell the switch ports to do dynamic VLAN assignment. When a host connects to a switch port configured to do Dynamic membership, the switch checks the MAC of the host and asks the VMPS what VLAN that MAC should be in. The switch then changes the VLAN membership of that port dynamically.

This sounds like a wonderful idea, and it can be, but it is difficult to create the VMPS database and to maintain it if your network grows quickly. Imagine having to get and maintain certain knowledge of every MAC address of every host in your network, and then keep the VMPS database updated. Dynamic VLAN membership is a good option if you have a lot of users in a lot of different VLANs moving around to many switch ports, but be ready to wrestle with some administrative issues.

Trunking

For VLANs to span across multiple switches, you obviously need to connect the switches to each other. Although it is possible to simply plug one switch into another using an Access port just as you would plug in a host or a hub, doing so kills the VLAN-spanning feature and a bunch of other useful stuff too. A switch-to-switch link must be set up as a trunk link in order for the VLAN system to work properly. A trunk link is a special connection; the key difference between an ordinary connection (an Access port) and a Trunk port is that although an Access port is only in one VLAN at a time, a Trunk port has the job of carrying traffic for *all* VLANs from one switch to another. Any time you connect a switch to another switch, you want to make it a trunk.

Some key points about trunks are as follows:

▶ A trunk can be created only on a Fast Ethernet or Gigabit Ethernet connection; 10Mb Ethernet ports are not fast enough to support the increased traffic from multiple VLANs, so the commands are not available for a regular Ethernet port.

▶ By default, traffic from all VLANs is allowed on a trunk. You can specify which VLANs are permitted (or not) to cross a particular trunk if you have that requirement, but these functions are beyond the scope of the CCNA exam.

▶ Switches (whether trunked or not) are always connected with crossover cables, not straight-through cables. In CCNA land, there is no such thing as a "smart port" that will auto-detect a crossed connection and fix it. The Catalyst 2960 has such a feature, but the exam will test your knowledge of when to use a crossover cable. For the purposes of your exams, if two switches are not connected with a crossover cable, there will be no connectivity between them, period.

EXAM ALERT

By default, all VLANs are permitted across a trunk link. Switch-to-Switch trunk links always require the use of a crossover cable, never a straight-through cable.

When creating a trunk, you must choose a trunking protocol. A trunking protocol adds a VLAN identification tag to frames coming into the switch. As those frames are forwarded across the trunk, the VLAN from which the frame originated is identifiable, and the data frame can be distributed to ports in the same VLAN on other switches—and not to different VLANs. This *frame tagging* and *multiplexing* function is what enables VLANs to span multiple switches and still keeps each VLAN as a separate broadcast domain. Figure 12.9 illustrates a simple trunk as it multiplexes frames from two separate VLANs across a single Fast Ethernet Trunk.

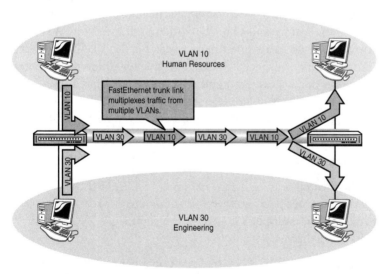

FIGURE 12.9 Trunks carry traffic from multiple VLANs across a single physical link.

Cisco supports two trunking protocols, ISL and 802.1Q, as described in the next sections.

ISL

The Inter-Switch Link (ISL) protocol is a Cisco-proprietary Layer 2 protocol. ISL operates by re-encapsulating host frames as they are received by the switch port. The ISL encapsulation adds a 26-byte header and a 4-byte trailer to the original host frame. The header includes the VLAN ID (the VLAN number) and several other fields. The trailer is a new CRC to check the integrity of the ISL frame.

There are two significant issues with ISL. The first is that it is Cisco proprietary, meaning that it will work only between two Cisco devices. In a perfect world, of course, everyone would have all Cisco gear, but the reality is a lot of non-Cisco network devices are out there. To complicate matters, Cisco has begun to phase out ISL in favor of 802.1Q; for example, the Cisco 2960 does not support ISL at all, only 802.1Q.

The second issue with ISL is frame size. If a frame is received that is already at the MTU, the addition of the 26-byte header and 4-byte trailer can create frames that are over the Ethernet MTU of 1,518 bytes (with ISL encapsulation, now at 1,548 bytes), which will be dropped as "Giant" frames by devices that do not recognize the ISL encapsulation. Figure 12.10 illustrates an ISL-encapsulated frame.

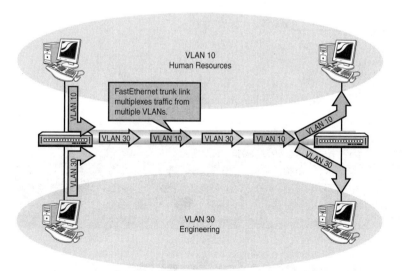

FIGURE 12.10 ISL Re-encapsulates the original host frame.

802.1Q

The IEEE-standard 802.1Q trunk encapsulation has the advantage of being an industry standard, so inter-vendor operation is much less of a problem. Often referred to as "dot1q" (because geeks like lingo), this protocol does not re-encapsulate the original frame, but instead inserts a 4-byte tag into the original header. This means that a dot1q frame will be seen as a "baby giant" of 1,522 bytes. Most modern NICs will not reject these frames if they mistakenly receive one. Figure 12.11 shows a dot1q-tagged frame.

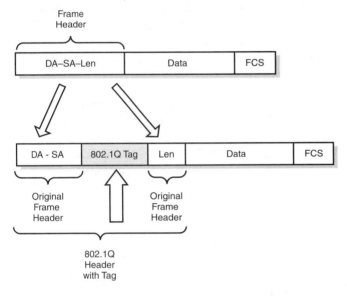

FIGURE 12.11 802.1Q inserts a 4-byte tag into the existing frame header.

> **EXAM ALERT**
>
> Cisco supports two VLAN frame tagging trunk encapsulations:
>
> ▶ ISL—Cisco proprietary, adds new 26-byte header and 4-byte trailer; Re-encapsulates original frame.
>
> ▶ 802.1Q—IEEE standard, inserts 4-byte tag into existing header.

Configuring Switches for Trunking

Configuring a switch for trunking is fairly straightforward. Once again, we focus on the Catalyst 2960 switch; other switches have slightly different capabilities and syntax, and special note of this is made when necessary.

NOTE

Cisco has implemented the Dynamic Trunking Protocol to make setting up trunks easier. DTP can send and/or receive trunk negotiation frames to dynamically establish a trunk link with a connected switch. DTP is not necessary to establish a trunk link, and like many other automatic functions, many administrators would rather not use it and instead manually configure their trunk links. The CCNA exam is not concerned with DTP, but does ask about the five port modes, so an explanation is warranted.

A switch port can be in one of five modes:

- ▶ **Off**—In Off mode, the port is an Access port and will not trunk, even if the neighbor switch wants to. This mode is intended for the connection of single hosts or hubs. DTP frames are not sent or acknowledged. The command to enable this is `switchport mode access`.

- ▶ **On**—In On mode, the port will trunk unconditionally, and trunk connectivity will happen if the neighbor switch port is set to Auto, Desirable, or NoNegotiate. DTP frames are sent but not acted upon if received. The command to enable this is `switchport mode trunk`.

- ▶ **NoNegotiate**—Sets the port to trunk unconditionally even if the neighbor switch disagrees. A trunk will form only if the neighbor switch port is set to On, Auto, or Desirable mode. DTP frames are not sent or acknowledged. The command to enable this is `switchport nonegotiate`.

- ▶ (Dynamic) **Desirable**—This mode actively solicits a trunk connection with the neighbor. DTP frames are sent and responded to if received. A trunk forms if the neighbor is set to On, Desirable, or Auto. If the neighbor is set to NoNegotiate, the trunk will not form because Desirable needs a response from the neighbor, which NoNegotiate will not send. The command to enable this is `switchport mode dynamic desirable`.

- ▶ (Dynamic) **Auto**—The port trunks only in response to a DTP request to do so. A trunk forms with a neighbor port set to on or desirable. DTP frames are not sent but are acknowledged if received. The command to enable this is `switchport mode dynamic auto`.

EXAM ALERT

Know the five switch port modes: On, Off, Desirable, Auto, and NoNegotiate.
Know the command to set permanent trunking mode:
`switchport mode trunk`

To configure a switch port to trunk, we need to set the mode and choose a trunk-ing protocol (assuming that the switch supports more than one to choose from).

The command to set the port mode is **switchport mode**, executed at the inter-face configuration prompt for the port you want to modify. Remember that to set NoNegotiate mode, the command is **switchport nonegotiate**:

```
2960(config)#int fa0/1
2960(config-if)#switchport mode    access
                                   Trunk
                                   dynamic auto
                                   dynamic desirable
2960(config-if)#switchport nonegotiate
```

To change the trunking protocol, you need to use a different type of switch because the 2960 only supports 802.1Q. We will use a 2900 for our example:

```
2900(config-if)switchport trunk encapsulation [isl ¦ dot1q]
```

> **EXAM ALERT**
>
> Know the syntax to set trunk encapsulation to 802.1Q on a 2900:
> `switchport trunk encapsulation dot1q`

VTP

Now that we have configured our trunk links and built a system of switches to carry our VLAN traffic, we can start creating and naming VLANs and assign-ing port membership to them. We can do this the hard way, by going to every switch in the system and configuring exactly the same VLAN information on each of them (and doing it again when something changes), or we can do it the easy way by using the VLAN Trunking Protocol (VTP).

VTP is a Layer 2 protocol that takes care of the steps of creating and naming VLANs on all switches in the system. We still have to set port membership to VLANs at each switch, which we can do either statically or using a VMPS.

VTP works by establishing a single switch as being in charge of the VLAN information for a *domain*. In this case, a domain is simply a group of switches that all have the same VTP domain name. This simply puts all the switches into a common administrative group.

VTP Switch Modes

In a VTP domain, there are three types of switches:

▸ **Server mode**—This is the one switch that is in charge of the VLAN information for the VTP domain. You may add, delete, and change VLAN information on this switch, and doing so affects the entire VTP domain. This way, we only have to enter our VLAN information once, and the Server mode switch propagates it to all the other switches in the domain.

▸ **Client mode**—Client mode switches get VLAN information from the Server. You cannot add, delete, or change VLAN information on a Client mode switch; in fact, the commands to do so are disabled.

▸ **Transparent mode**—A Transparent mode switch is doing its own thing; it will not accept any changes to VLAN information from the Server, but it will forward those changes to other switches in the system. You can add, delete, and change VLANs—but those changes only affect the Transparent mode switch and are not sent to other switches in the domain.

VTP Communication

In order for switches to properly communicate with VTP, four elements must be configured. First, you need to have all switches connected by working trunk links. (This, of course, implies crossover cables as well.)

Second, you need a domain name. This name can be anything you like, but make sure that it is unique in a switched system, or you can cause real problems, as you will see. The domain name must be identical on all the switches in the VTP system; this is a common misconfiguration error, and also highly tested. The domain name is case sensitive, too!

Third, you need at least one (and preferably only one) Server mode switch. Yes, you can have more than one, but you don't need or want that.

Fourth, if you want, you can configure a password so that VTP information will not be exchanged if the password does not match on the server and client switch(es). The password is optional, but it must be identical (case sensitive) on all switches in the domain. This is also highly testable!

VTP Pruning

VTP pruning is a way to conserve a little bandwidth on those trunk links. If a client switch has no ports in VLAN 10, and we enable VTP Pruning on the Server mode switch, information about VLAN 10 will not be sent down the trunk to the client mode switch. This way, switches only learn what they need to know.

VTP Configuration

Configuring VTP is done from the global config prompt. The commands are simple:

```
2960(config)#vtp mode [server ¦ client ¦ transparent}
2960(config)#vtp domain vtp_domain_name
2960(config)#vtp password vtp_password>
```

VTP Verification and Troubleshooting

The primary command used for verification and troubleshooting VTP is show vtp status. The following sample output shows what information can be drawn from this command:

```
2960#show vtp status
VTP Version                      : 2
Configuration Revision           : 0
Maximum VLANs supported locally : 1005
Number of existing VLANs         : 38
VTP Operating Mode               : Server
VTP Domain Name                  : ExamCram2
VTP Pruning Mode                 : Disabled
VTP V2 Mode                      : Disabled
VTP Traps Generation             : Disabled
MD5 digest                       : 0x57 0xCD 0x40 0x65
➥0x63 0x59 0x47 0xBD
Configuration last modified by 10.0.0.1 at 8-13-66 05:30:38
Local updater ID is 10.0.0.1
```

If you compare the output of **show vtp status** from two different switches, look for a match between them for the domain name and check that one of them is in Server mode.

EXAM ALERT

The VTP domain name and password must match on all switches for VLAN information to be propagated from the Server mode switch.

Inter-VLAN Routing

VLANs define separate broadcast domains and should be separate IP subnets. The only way to get traffic from one VLAN to another is to route between them (Inter-VLAN Routing). We have several choices for how to do this. We could have one router for every VLAN, with an Ethernet port on each connected to a switch port in each VLAN, and then interconnect all the routers; the problem here, of course, is that having so many routers and connections gets expensive and complicated, and latency can be bad.

We could get one big router with a lot of Ethernet ports and could connect one to a port in each VLAN on the switch. This is a little simpler, but still expensive and probably not as fast as it could be unless we really spend the cash.

Our last two choices are to use Router-on-a-Stick (honest, that's what it's called; we wouldn't make something like that up) or Layer 3 switching. The next section details Router-on-a-Stick.

Router-on-a-Stick

This feature takes advantage of trunk links: All VLANs can be transported across a trunk link to be distributed by the neighbor device. Suppose that we built a trunk from a switch to a router? We'd need at least a FastEthernet port on the router, and it would have to support either ISL or 802.1Q. Now all we need to do is build routable interfaces, one for each VLAN.

We do this by using sub-interfaces. A sub-interface is a virtual interface that is spawned from the physical interface, and uses the physical interface for Layer 1 connectivity. A sub-interface can be given an IP address and mask, can be shut down or enabled, can run routing protocols—in fact, there isn't much that a physical interface can do that a sub-interface can't. So if our router has a FastEthernet interface, we can configure it to run 802.1Q, build a subinterface for each VLAN, give those sub-interfaces IP addresses in the appropriate subnets for each VLAN, and let the router route between the VLANs whose traffic is coming up that trunk link. A frame destined for VLAN 30 could come up the trunk link from VLAN 10 to the Router's VLAN 10 sub-interface, get routed to VLAN 30, and leave that same port from the VLAN 30 sub-interface. The hosts in each VLAN will use the sub-interface configured for their VLAN as their default gateway.

The following example configures Router-on-a-Stick for inter-vlan routing between VLANs 10 and 30, using 802.1Q trunking on interface FastEthernet 0/1:

```
Router(config)#int fa0/1
Router(config-if)#no ip address
Router(config-if)#interface fa0/1.1
Router(config-sub-if)#encapsulation dot1q 1 native
!
! Creates sub-interface for Native VLAN 1
! (Required for dot1q functionality)
!
Router(config-sub-if)#int fa0/1.10
Router(config-sub-if)#encap dot1q 10
Router(config-sub-if)#ip address 10.10.10.1  255.255.255.0
!
! Creates sub-interface for VLAN 10 and
! applies IP address in VLAN10's subnet
!
Router(config-sub-if)#int fa0/1.30
Router(config-sub-if)#ip address 10.30.30.1  255.255.255.0
Router(config-sub-if)#encap dot1q 30
!
! Creates sub-interface for VLAN 30 and
! applies IP address in VLAN30's subnet
!
```

Figure 12.12 illustrates a typical Router-on-a-Stick application.

> **NOTE**
>
> Why is it called Router-on-a-Stick, anyway? Just because the router looks like a lollipop on the end of the trunk "stick." Geeks like to be cute.

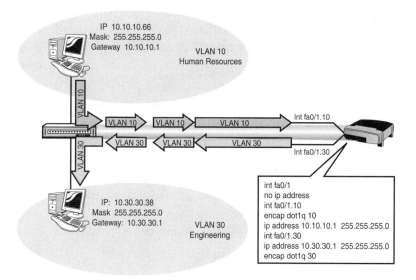

FIGURE 12.12 Router-on-a-Stick.

L3 Switching

Layer 3 switching is beyond the scope of this exam but deserves mention because it is important and cool.

A Layer 3 switch has the capability to create a virtual routed interface for each VLAN, and route between virtual interfaces for inter-vlan routing. It's similar to Router-on-a-Stick, except that there is no stick, and the router is internal to the switch and extremely fast. If you are routing a lot of inter-vlan traffic, buying and configuring a Layer 3 switch will bring you serious gains in throughput.

Not every switch is Layer 3 capable; the lowly 2960 cannot do it, but a 3550 will. Layer 3 switches are more expensive than Layer 2 switches, but are much more capable.

Exam Prep Questions

1. Which three of the following are steps in the VLAN implementation process?

   ○ **A.** Disable VTP to prevent automatic VLAN creation

   ○ **B.** Create VLANs using unique ID numbers

   ○ **C.** Apply passwords to VLANs to prevent unauthorized changes

   ○ **D.** Optionally name VLANs for easier understanding

   ○ **E.** Assign switch port VLAN membership

   ○ **F.** Convert all switch ports to trunk links to allow hosts to access VLANs

2. Which of the following are advantages of VLANs? Choose all that apply.

   ○ **A.** VLANs eliminate the need for subnets.

   ○ **B.** VLANs offer improved security.

   ○ **C.** Administrative overhead because of adds, moves, and changes is reduced.

   ○ **D.** VLANs encrypt all network traffic for improved security.

   ○ **E.** VLANs allow users to be grouped together by function or department instead of location.

   ○ **F.** VLANs eliminate broadcasts, reducing congestion.

   ○ **G.** VLANs provide virtual broadcast domain segmentation at Layer 2.

   ○ **H.** VLANs increase the number of broadcast domains while reducing their size.

3. Which two of the following are true with respect to trunk links and VLANs?

   ○ **A.** Trunk links enable VLAN traffic to span multiple switches.

   ○ **B.** Trunk links are not possible between switches from different vendors.

   ○ **C.** Trunk links should be given their own subnet to function properly.

   ○ **D.** By default, trunks enable all defined VLANs to traverse the trunk.

4. Which of the following are true with respect to the Layer 3 characteristics of VLANs? Choose all that apply.

    ○ **A.** All VLANS exist within one subnet.

    ○ **B.** Each VLAN should be associated with its own subnet.

    ○ **C.** VLANs provide Layer 3 broadcast domain segmentation at Layer 2.

    ○ **D.** VLANs provide Layer 2 collision domain separation at Layer 3.

    ○ **E.** In deploying Router-on-a-Stick, hosts should be assigned the IP address of the router sub-interface assigned to the hosts' VLAN as the hosts' default gateway address.

5. Which of the following support the multiplexing of traffic from multiple VLANs across Fast or Gigabit Ethernet links? Choose all that apply.

    ○ **A.** STP

    ○ **B.** HSRP

    ○ **C.** VTP

    ○ **D.** ISL

    ○ **E.** 802.1d

    ○ **F.** 802.11

    ○ **G.** 802.1Q

6. Which of the following are trunk port modes? Choose all that apply.

    ○ **A.** on

    ○ **B.** idle

    ○ **C.** off

    ○ **D.** blocking

    ○ **E.** auto

    ○ **F.** desirable

    ○ **G.** undesirable

7. Which two commands make a port a trunk and force it to use a multiple-vendor–compatible protocol?

   ○ **A.** `Switch(config)#`**`switchport mode trunk`**

   ○ **B.** `Switch(config-if)#`**`switchport mode trunk`**

   ○ **C.** `Switch(config-if)#`**`switchport trunk on`**

   ○ **D.** `Switch(config-if)#`**`switchport trunk compatible-mode`**

   ○ **E.** `Switch(config-if)#`**`switchport trunk encapsulation 802.1q`**

   ○ **F.** `Switch(config-if)#`**`switchport trunk encapsulation dot1q`**

8. Which of the following are VLAN Trunking Protocol switch modes? Choose all that apply.

   ○ **A.** Domain Controller

   ○ **B.** Server

   ○ **C.** Slave

   ○ **D.** Client

   ○ **e.** Independent

   ○ **F.** Transparent

9. What elements are required to create a functioning VTP system between two switches?

   ○ **A.** Matching VTP mode

   ○ **B.** Matching VTP Domain Name

   ○ **C.** Identical VTY password

   ○ **D.** Identical VTP password

   ○ **E.** A functional Access link between them

   ○ **F.** A crossover-cabled trunk link and compatible trunking protocols

   ○ **G** At least one switch set to Server, mode

   ○ **H.** Identical hold-down timers

10. What IOS feature can logically divide a switch into multiple, independent switches at Layer 2 without the use of a SawzAll?

- ○ **A.** STP
- ○ **B.** VLANs
- ○ **C.** GigaStack
- ○ **D.** VTP

11. What is the function of 802.1d STP?

- ○ **A.** Prevents routing loops in redundant topologies
- ○ **B.** Prevents Layer 2 loops in networks with redundant switched paths
- ○ **C.** Prevents frame forwarding until all IP addresses are known
- ○ **D.** Enables the use of multiple routed paths for load-sharing
- ○ **E.** Allows the propagation of VLAN information from a central source

12. What defines the root switch in an STP system? Choose 2.

- ○ **A.** The switch with the lowest Bridge ID
- ○ **B.** The switch with the highest Bridge ID
- ○ **C.** The fastest switch
- ○ **D.** The switch with the most connections to other switches
- ○ **E.** The first switch to send out a BPDU
- ○ **F.** The switch with the lowest Priority
- ○ **G.** The switch with the highest Priority

13. Which one of the following statements describes a converged STP system?

- ○ **A.** All switches are running STP.
- ○ **B.** All ports are blocking.
- ○ **C.** All ports are forwarding.
- ○ **D.** All ports that are not forwarding are blocking.

14. Which one of the following is true of the Spanning-Tree Root Path Cost?

○ **A.** It is the cost of the exit port to the Root.

○ **B.** It is the bandwidth of the exit port to the Root.

○ **C.** It is the delay in data transmission to the Root.

○ **D.** It is the cumulative cost, based on number of hops, to the Root.

○ **E.** It is the cumulative cost, based on bandwidth, of all links on the path to the Root.

Given the diagram in Figure 12.13, answer the following questions:

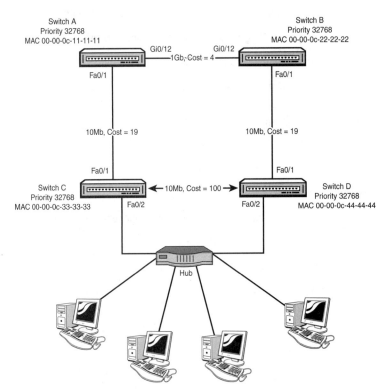

FIGURE 12.13 Network Topology for Questions 15 and 16.

15. Which switch will become the Root?

○ **A.** Switch A

○ **B.** Switch B

○ **C.** Switch C

○ **D.** Switch D

16. Which of the following will be the Designated Port for the ethernet segment between switches C and D?

- ○ **A.** Switch C, Fa0/1
- ○ **B.** Switch C, Fa0/2
- ○ **C.** Switch D, Fa0/1
- ○ **D.** Switch D, Fa0/2

Answers to Exam Prep Questions

1. Answers B, D, and E are correct. Create the VLANs, name them, and assign the ports. Answer A is incorrect; VTP does not create VLANs, it updates other switches that you have configured as part of the VTP domain with VLAN information. Answer C is incorrect; VLANs do not themselves have passwords, but the VTP system might. Answer F is incorrect; trunk links are only necessary to carry multiple-VLAN traffic between switches or routers. Access ports for hosts are assigned to a single VLAN each, which gives the host access to that VLAN.

2. Answers B, C, E, G, and H are correct; these are all stated advantages of VLANs. Answer A is incorrect; VLANs complement the use of subnets. Answer D is incorrect; VLANs have nothing whatsoever to do with encryption. Answer F is wrong. VLANs do not eliminate broadcasts; they only constrain them.

3. Answers A and D are correct; Trunking protocols label each frame with its originating VLAN number so traffic from multiple VLANs can be multiplexed across a trunk link. By default, traffic from all VLANs is permitted across a trunk. Answer B is incorrect; 802.1Q is a standardized trunking protocol that enables inter-vendor switch links. Answer C is false; trunks are a Layer 2 construct that carry traffic from multiple VLANs and their associated subnets; the trunk itself does not require a subnet of its own to function

4. Answers B, C, and E are correct. A single VLAN should be associated with a single IP subnet; each VLAN is a separate broadcast domain, segmented by the Layer 2 function of the switch, and Router-on-a-Stick configuration creates a virtual gateway (sub-interface) for each VLAN/subnet. Answer A is wrong; each VLAN should have its own subnet. Answer D is wrong; VLANs do not segment collision domains.

5. Answers D and G are correct; these are the two trunking protocols supported by Cisco. Answers A, B, C, E, and F are wrong: STP eliminates Layer 2 loops; HSRP provides redundant gateway functionality; VTP dynamically updates VLAN information; 802.1d is the IEEE specification for STP; and 802.11b is the IEEE specification for Wi-Fi.

6. Answers A, C, E, and F are correct. The on mode, off mode, auto mode, and desirable mode are trunk port modes. Answers B, D, and G are incorrect; these other modes are not associated with trunking.

7. Answers B and F are correct. These two commands make a port a trunk and force it to use multiple-vendor–compatible protocol. Answer A is incorrect; the command must be issued at the config-if prompt. Answers C, D, and E are incorrect because they are invalid commands.

8. Answers B, D, and F are correct. Server, Client, and Transparent are VLAN Trunking Protocol switch modes. Answers A, C, and E are not valid VTP modes.

9. Answers B, D, F, and G are correct. These elements are required to create a functioning VTP system between two switches. Answer A is incorrect; one switch should be the Server for the domain. Answer C is incorrect, VTY is the Telnet lines. Answer E is wrong; we need trunks between switches to make VTP work. Answer H is wrong; hold-down timers are part of a routing protocol, not VTP.

10. Answer B is correct. VLANS have the effect of totally isolating hosts in different VLANs as if they were plugged in to different switches that are not connected. A, C, and D are incorrect; STP prevents Layer 2 loops, GigaStacking uses high-speed connections to make two or more switches appear as one management unit, and VTP dynamically propagates VLAN updates to other connected switches.

11. Answer B is correct. STP prevents Layer 2 loops if redundant paths exist. Answers A, C, D, and E are incorrect; STP is not concerned with routing loops, IP addresses, routing in general, or VLAN administration.

12. Answers A and F are correct. The Bridge ID is the Priority prepended to the MAC address of the switch. The switch with the lowest Bridge ID becomes the Root; therefore, the switch with the lowest Priority will always be the Root. Answers B, C, D, E, and G are incorrect; the winning Bridge ID and Priority will be the lowest. The speed of the switch has no bearing on whether it will be the root if left to default settings. The number of connections to other switches has no impact either.

13. Answer D is correct. Convergence in STP means that all ports are either blocked to prevent loops or forwarding to allow data transmission. (However, if all ports are blocking, the system has not converged yet.) Answers A, B, and C are incorrect; all switches must run STP or run the risk of loops destabilizing the network.

14. Answer E is correct. The Root Path Cost is the accumulated cost of all the links on the path to the Root. The Cost is calculated based on the bandwidth of the links. Answers A, B, C, and D are incorrect. You must add the STP cost of all the links on the path to the Root; cost has nothing to do with delay or hop count.

15. Answer B is correct; Switch B will become the Root because it has the lowest Priority. Remember that even though A has a lower MAC, the Priority overrides this, and the switch with the lowest Priority will be the Root. Answers A, B, and C are incorrect.

16. Answer D is correct. Because D has the lower Root Path Cost (at 19) than C (at 23), D will make its port the Designated Port—even though C has a lower Bridge ID. Answers A, B, and C are incorrect; the Designated ports must be connected to the ethernet segment, and the switch with the lowest Root Path Cost will host the DP. Only if there is a tie for Root Path Cost will Bridge ID become a deciding factor.

CHAPTER THIRTEEN

IP Access Lists

Terms you'll need to understand:

✓ Standard access lists (ACL)

✓ Extended ACLs

✓ Wildcard masks

Concepts and techniques you'll need to master:

✓ Configuring and troubleshooting standard ACLs

✓ Configuring and troubleshooting extended ACLs

✓ Configuring and troubleshooting named ACLs

Introduction

Access control lists (ACLs) have a lot of uses on Cisco routers. This chapter describes their use as packet filters by which you can filter traffic coming from one network into another. However, keep in mind that an ACL can also be used for the following purposes:

▶ **Classifying and organizing traffic for quality of service**—You can use an ACL to categorize and prioritize your traffic with Quality of Service (QoS).

▶ **Filtering routing updates**—ACLs can be used with routing protocols to control what networks are advertised. Routing protocols are discussed further in Chapter 14, "Routing."

▶ **Defining interesting traffic for dial-on-demand routing (DDR)**— ACLs can be used to configure what traffic will dial a remote router when using Integrated Services Digital Network (ISDN).

▶ **Network Address Translation (NAT**—ACLs are used to identify inside local addresses when configuring NAT. NAT is discussed in greater detail in Chapter 16, "Advanced IP Concepts."

> **EXAM ALERT**
>
> Although this chapter focuses on using ACLs as packet filters, make sure you do not forget that ACLs are used for a lot more than just packet filtering. The exam will test your knowledge of the various uses of ACLs.

When used as a packet filter, ACLs can be used to filter traffic as it passes through a router. For example, suppose that Andrew, one of the authors of this book, wanted to block Mike, the other author, from being able to communicate to the web server (see Figure 13.1).

Andrew could go on his router and configure an ACL that would prevent Mike from communicating to the server while allowing all other traffic to pass through the router. ACLs then get applied on an interface in the inbound or outbound direction. When applied inbound, you are filtering as the traffic comes into the incoming interface on the router; when applied in the outbound direction, you are filtering traffic as it leaves the outgoing interface.

In Figure 13.1, the ACL can be applied inbound on Ethernet 0 or outbound on Ethernet 1. This is because Mike's traffic would come inbound on Ethernet 0 and exit on Ethernet 1. If applied inbound on interface Ethernet 1, the ACL would filter the traffic before the router could examine its routing table to determine the outgoing interface; if applied outbound on Ethernet 1, the ACL would filter Mike's traffic after the router looked in its routing table and forwarded the traffic to Ethernet 1. Later in this chapter, you learn some general rules about where you should apply ACLs.

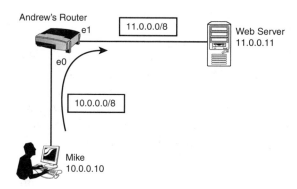

FIGURE 13.1   ACL example.

No matter where you apply the ACL, the list will process the packets and check them against your list in the order that you put the statements in. For this reason, you must be careful about the order of the statements. After you have configured your ACL, there is no way to reorder your statements. If Figure 13.1 is our example, and if you wanted to prevent Mike from accessing the web server but allow everyone else on the 10.0.0.0/8 network to access the web server, your ACL would need statements to first deny Mike's computer and then allow everyone else on the network.

Resequence Command

Okay, so a resequence command is available in IOS 12.4, but humor me and pretend that it does not exist; the CCNA test will take the stance that there is no way to reorder your statements.

If the packet is checked against each entry in the ACL and there is no match, the default action is to drop the packet. There is an implicit deny any at the end of the traffic that will drop any packet that does not match an entry in the ACL. Therefore, all traffic is denied except for what you explicitly permit. Figure 13.2 illustrates the logic of an access list that is configured to first deny Mike's computer at 10.0.0.55 and then permit all other traffic from the 10.0.0.0/8 network. (The syntax for this list will be shown later in the chapter.)

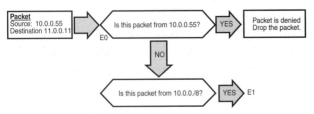

FIGURE 13.2 ACL logic.

If the order of ACL statements were reversed, and you first permitted the 10.0.0.0/8 network and then denied Mike, Mike would never be denied because the ACL would check Mike's packet and see that he belongs to the 10.0.0.0/8 network and is therefore permitted. The ACL would never get to the deny statement. Figure 13.3 illustrates the logic behind a poorly written ACL that first permitted the 10.0.0.0/8 network and then denied Mike's computer.

Likewise, if your ACL denied Mike's computer but did not permit the rest of the network, any other traffic would be denied because it was not implicitly permitted. You must have at least one permit statement in your ACL. Otherwise, you might as well just shut down the interface because all traffic is dropped.

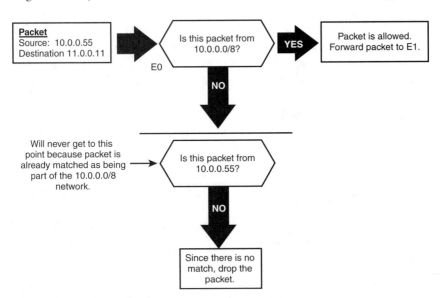

FIGURE 13.3 ACL logic of a poorly designed access list.

Types of ACLs

The previous examples illustrate the use of IP ACLs. There are many types of ACLs that you can create, including IP, AppleTalk, IPX, MAC addresses, NetBIOS, and other protocols. However, for the CCNA exam, you can breathe a sigh of relief because you only need to be familiar with configuring and troubleshooting IP ACLs.

No matter what type of ACL you use, though, you can have only one ACL per protocol, per interface, per direction. For example, you can have one IP ACL inbound on an interface and another IP ACL outbound on an interface, but you cannot have two inbound IP ACLs on the same interface.

The two types of IP ACLs that you can configure are

- Standard IP ACLs

- Extended IP ACLs

When you create an access list, you will assign it a number. There are predefined ranges for each type of access list. Table 13.1 shows the predefined ranges for IP standard and extended ACLs.

TABLE 13.1   Access List Ranges

Type	Range
IP Standard	1–99
IP Extended	100–199
IP Standard Expanded Range	1300–1999
IP Extended Expanded Range	2000–2699

Standard ACLs

A standard IP ACL is simple; it filters based on source address only. You can filter a source network or a source host, but you cannot filter based on the destination of a packet, the particular protocol being used such as the Transmission Control Protocol (TCP) or the User Datagram Protocol (UDP), or on the port number. You can permit or deny only source traffic. This is analogous to entering a new country and having customs only check your passport to verify that you (being the source) are allowed to pass through customs.

Extended ACLs

An extended ACL gives you much more power than just a standard ACL. With an extended ACL, you can filter your traffic based on any of the following criteria:

- ▶ Source address

- ▶ Destination address

- ▶ Protocol—TCP, UDP, Internet Control Messaging Protocol (ICMP), and so on

- ▶ Source port (if using TCP or UDP)

- ▶ Destination port (if protocol is TCP or UDP)

- ▶ ICMP message (if protocol is ICMP)

An IP extended access list is analogous to passing through customs, but this time the customs agent verifies not only your identity, but also asks about your destination and the purpose of your stay.

Named ACLs

One of the disadvantages of using IP standard and IP extended ACLs is that you reference them by number, which is not too descriptive of its use. With a named ACL, this is not the case because you can name your ACL with a descriptive name. The ACL named DenyMike is a lot more meaningful than an ACL simply numbered 1. There are both IP standard and IP extended named ACLs.

Another advantage to named ACLs is that they allow you to remove individual lines out of an ACL. With numbered ACLs, you cannot delete individual statements. Instead, you will need to delete your existing access list and re-create the entire list.

Configuring and Implementing

In this next section, you learn how to configure standard, extended, and named ACLs.

Configuring Standard ACLs

Because a standard access list filters only traffic based on source traffic, all you need is the IP address of the host or subnet you want to permit or deny. ACLs are created in global configuration mode and then applied on an interface. The syntax for creating a standard ACL is

```
access-list {1-99 ¦ 1300-1999} {permit ¦ deny} source-address
[wildcard mask]
```

The wildcard mask at the end of the ACL is optional with standard lists and is discussed in the upcoming section "The Wildcard Mask."

As an example, if you wanted to deny Mike's computer at 10.0.0.55 but permit all other hosts on the 10.0.0.0/8 network, you would configure the following ACL:

```
Router(config)#access-list 1 deny 10.0.0.55
Router(config)#access-list 1 permit 10.0.0.0
```

Next, you need to apply the access list on an interface. Because you have no way of specifying the destination or application of your traffic, you should apply the access list as close to the destination as possible. Given Figure 13.1 as our example, interface Ethernet 1 is closest to the destination (the web server). Traffic is leaving this interface heading for the web server, so you should apply this access list outbound on Ethernet 1. The syntax for applying your IP access list on an interface is

```
ip access-group {number ¦ name} {in ¦ out}
```

Because you want to apply this access list outbound on Ethernet 1, the syntax from global configuration would be

```
Router(config)#interface ethernet 1
Router(config-if)#ip access-group 1 out
```

The Wildcard Mask

When you configure your IP standard ACLs, you have the option of using a wildcard mask to better match the hosts and networks you want to filter. Without the use of wildcard masks, the router makes a best guess as to what the mask should be. When using IP extended ACLs, wildcard masks are not optional.

Wildcard masks define how much of an address needs to be looked at for there to be a match. For example, in the previous example, you wanted to deny Mike's computer (10.0.0.55) but allow all other hosts on that network (10.0.0.0/8). You want the router to check every bit of the source address as it passes through the router to verify that it matches the complete address 10.0.0.55, so you will need a wildcard mask that tells your router to check every bit. For matching the 10.0.0.0/8 network, however, you need only your router to check the first eight bits because you need to check only the network portion (the 10.0.0.0/8 network) and the source host address will vary.

Wildcard masks use 0s to designate what bits you want to match and 1s to designate those bits that you do not want the router to examine. If you wanted to match the 10.0.0.55 host, you would need a wildcard mask of all 0s to indicate to your router that it needs to check every bit to verify that it matches 10.0.0.55 exactly. This would be a wildcard mask of 0.0.0.0. If you wanted to match the 10.0.0.0/8 network, your wildcard mask would be all 0s in the first octet to match the 10 network and all 1s in the remaining 24 bits to tell your router not to examine the host bits. This wildcard mask, shown in Figure 13.4, would be 0.255.255.255.

If you added the wildcard mask to the syntax you learned earlier, the complete syntax would be

```
Router(config)#access-list 1 deny 10.0.0.55 0.0.0.0
Router(config)#access-list 1 permit 10.0.0.0 0.255.255.255
Router(config)#interface ethernet 1
Router(config-if)#ip access-group 1 out
```

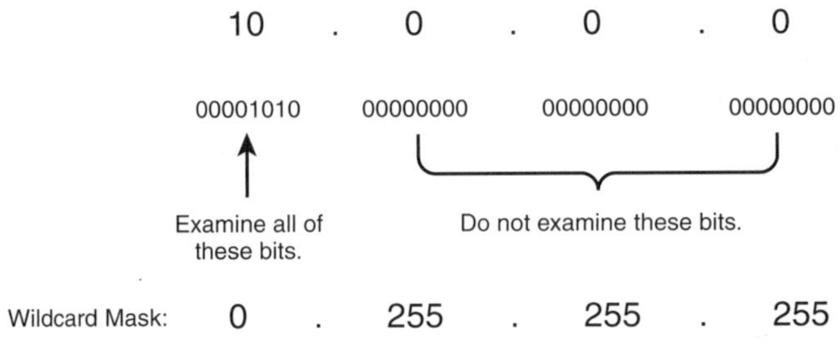

FIGURE 13.4 Wildcard mask for 10.0.0.0/8.

This example shows matching a class A network. If you wanted instead to match a class B network, the wildcard mask would be 0.0.255.255 to match the first two octets. If you wanted to match a class C network, the wildcard mask would be 0.0.0.255. Notice that the wildcard mask, when used to match a network, is the inverse of the subnet mask. For this reason, the wildcard mask is often called the *inverse mask*.

Now look at what happens when you begin subnetting your networks. Take the 192.168.12.64/28 network, for example. This is a subnetted class C network, which falls on the 16-bit boundary in the last octet. You need to match the first three octets entirely and the first four bits of the last octet because they compose the network portion of this address. By writing out the subnetwork and drawing a line at the bit boundary, you can determine how many 0s and 1s you need to make up the wildcard mask. Adding up the 1s in binary gives you the final wildcard mask of 0.0.0.15 to match the 192.168.12.64 subnetwork.

Increments	128	64	32	16	I	8	4	2	1
Subnetwork	0	1	0	0	I	0	0	0	0
Wildcard Mask	0	0	0	0	I	1	1	1	1

If you dislike working with binary and want a shortcut, you can also take the original subnet mask and subtract it from 255.255.255.255. In this example, the subnet mask would be 255.255.255.240 (/28). Subtracting this from 255.255.255.255 gives you the wildcard mask of 0.0.0.15.

Sometimes you do not want to match a network, such as when you want to match a specific host or, on the other extreme, permit or deny every host regardless of their network. There are special wildcard masks and keywords you can use to refer to these unique situations.

To match a specific host such as 10.0.0.55, you need the router to examine every bit. This can be represented with the wildcard mask of 0.0.0.0. Alternatively, you can use the keyword host before the host address and not specify any wildcard mask. Thus, the following two commands accomplish the same thing:

```
Router(config)#access-list 1 deny 10.0.0.55 0.0.0.0
Router(config)#access-list 1 deny host 10.0.0.55
```

If you wanted to match all hosts regardless of the network they are on, you can use the designation of an unspecified network (0.0.0.0) with a wildcard mask that does not examine any bits (255.255.255.255). Alternatively, you can use the keyword any. The following two commands are functionally equivalent:

```
Router(config)#access-list 1 permit 0.0.0.0 255.255.255.255
Router(config)#access-list 1 permit any
```

Wildcard Masks with Standard ACLs

Although wildcard masks are optional with standard ACLs, you should get in the habit of using them. When you are matching multiple networks with variable length subnet masks (VLSM), Cisco routers will sometimes reorder your statements if you do not specify the exact wildcard mask.

Configuring Extended ACLs

As mentioned earlier, extended ACLs allow you to filter based on the following criteria:

▸ Source address

▸ Destination address

▸ Protocol (IP, TCP, UDP, ICMP, and so on)

▸ Source port (if TCP or UDP is the protocol)

▸ Destination port (if TCP or UDP is the protocol)

▸ ICMP message (if ICMP is the protocol)

The syntax of the command varies slightly if you are filtering for general IP traffic, TCP/UDP ports, or ICMP messages. For just filtering IP traffic, the syntax is

```
access-list access-list-number {deny | permit} ip source source-
wildcard destination destination-wildcard
```

For example, if you wanted to prevent all IP traffic coming from the host 10.0.0.55 to a server with the address of 11.0.0.11 while allowing all other traffic on the 10.0.0.0/8 to access the server, the syntax would be

```
Router(config)#access-list 100 deny ip host 10.0.0.55 host 11.0.0.11
Router(config)#access-list 100 permit ip 10.0.0.0 0.255.255.255 host
11.0.0.11
```

Note the use of the keyword host before 10.0.0.55 and 11.0.0.11. This is equivalent to using a wildcard mask of 0.0.0.0.

Because you can specify both the source and destination in the extended ACL, you generally want to apply an IP extended ACL as close to the source as possible so that it is filtered as soon as possible. Using Figure 13.1 as our example, you would apply the access list inbound on interface Ethernet 0 because that is closest to the source of your traffic. The syntax for this would be

```
Router(config)#interface ethernet 0
Router(config-if)#ip access-group 100 in
```

You can also filter based on TCP or UDP port number. The syntax for filtering based on port number is the same but, instead of IP, you specify if the traffic is TCP or UDP and what the port numbers are. You have the option of specifying source port(s) and destination port(s). Remember, if you are filtering traffic going to a destination, you are going to filter based only on the destination port number and not the source port. Because source ports are typically dynamically assigned, it is not as common to specify the source port number. The syntax for an IP extended ACL that filters TCP or UDP ports is

```
access-list access-list-number {deny ¦ permit} {tcp ¦ udp} source
source-wildcard [operator [port-number(s)]] destination
destination-wildcard [operator [port-number(s)].
```

Common operator values are

▸ eq—Match any traffic that equals this port number.

▸ gt—Match any traffic that is greater than this port number.

▸ lt—Match any traffic that is less than this port number.

▸ range—Match any traffic within this range of port numbers (requires you to specify a beginning and ending port number).

For the port number, you can either enter the port number or enter the keyword for that protocol. Cisco routers provide keywords for many common protocols such as WWW, FTP, FTP-Data, Telnet, and more.

Using Figure 13.1 again as our example, you can configure an extended ACL to prevent Mike's computer at 10.0.0.55 from sending web traffic to the web server at 11.0.0.11 while allowing everyone else on the 10.0.0.0/8 network web access to the web server. Because this is an IP extended ACL, you will apply it closest to the source as possible, which would be inbound on interface Ethernet 0. The syntax for this ACL would be

```
Router(config)#access-list 100 deny tcp host 10.0.0.55 host
11.0.0.11 eq 80
Router(config)#access-list 100 permit tcp 10.0.0.0 0.255.255.255 host
11.0.0.11 eq 80
Router(config)#interface ethernet 0
Router(config-if)#ip access-group 100 in
```

For ICMP, the syntax is similar, except now you have the option of specifying an ICMP message. The two most common ICMP messages (and the ones to know for the exam) are ECHO and ECHO REPLIES. These messages are used when sending pings to a host. ECHO, sometimes called ECHO REQUESTS, is sent by the sending host, and ECHO REPLIES are sent by the recipient of the ping message to indicate that the host is up. The syntax for an IP extended ACL that filters ICMP is

```
access-list access-list-number {deny ¦ permit} icmp source
source-wildcard destination destination-wildcard [ICMP code ¦
message].
```

Because many computer attacks use ICMP (such as the Ping of Death denial of service attack and Loki ICMP tunneling), it is common for network administrators to block ICMP at their perimeter firewall. ICMP is a helpful tool for troubleshooting, however, so some administrators like to block only ICMP ECHO (ICMP type 8) messages from coming into their networks but still allow ECHO REPLIES (ICMP type 0) in. This configuration allows them to ping outbound and get an ECHO REPLY back, but prevents others from pinging into their network. As an example, if you wanted to block ICMP ECHO messages from the 10.0.0.0/8 network from going to the destination network of 11.0.0.0/8 while allowing all other IP traffic from anywhere to anywhere, the syntax would be

```
Router(config)#access-list 100 deny icmp 10.0.0.0 0.255.255.255
11.0.0.0 0.255.255.255 echo
Router(config)#access-list 100 permit ip any any
Router(config)#interface ethernet 0
Router(config-if)#ip access-group 100 in
```

This ACL blocks all ICMP type 8 echo messages from entering into the 11.0.0.0/8 network while allowing all other traffic. Note that in this example, if ICMP pings are coming from any other network to the 11.0.0.0/8 network, they would be allowed; only the 10.0.0.0/8 network is prevented from sending pings to the 11.0.0.0/8 network in this example.

Filtering Telnet and SSH Access

The ACLs shown so far help you to filter traffic as it passes through the router. In this next example, you will learn how to filter traffic to the router itself.

Routers are a critical component of any network. If a malicious hacker were to compromise one of your routers, he could reconfigure it to prevent anyone from being able to communicate across your enterprise. Therefore, it is common to use ACLs to control who is allowed Telnet or SSH access to your router.

For example, if you wanted to allow only Mike the ability to Telnet or SSH to Andrew's router (see Figure 13.1) but prevent everyone else access, you could create an ACL that allows only Mike's IP address (10.0.0.55). Remember, you do not need to add a statement to block everyone else because all traffic is denied by default unless it is explicitly permitted. Because you are controlling Telnet and SSH access to the router and not traffic passing through the router, you need to apply your ACL on the Virtual TeletYpe (VTY) lines and not on an interface. Because VTY lines are used for remote connectivity to your router and are therefore inherently Telnet (TCP port 23) and SSH (TCP port 22) traffic, you do not need an extended ACL. Instead, use an IP standard ACL to control what source host(s) are allowed Telnet and SSH access to your router. To allow Mike's computer (10.0.0.10) Telnet or SSH access but deny everyone else, the syntax would be

```
Router(config)#access-list 1 permit host 10.0.0.55
```

Applying this ACL is different from how you applied ACLs on an interface. When applying an ACL on a VTY line, the syntax is

```
Router(config-line)#access-class access-list-number {in ¦ out}
```

Because you are controlling Telnet and SSH access to the router, you should apply this ACL inbound on the VTY lines. The complete syntax to create this access list and apply it on all five VTY lines is

```
Router(config)#access-list 1 permit host 10.0.0.55
Router(config)#line vty 0 4
Router(config-line)#access-class 1 in
```

Outbound VTY Access List

ACLs on VTY lines should be applied inbound. When applied outbound, strange things begin to occur. Instead of the ACL specifying who is allowed access to Telnet to a router, the ACL specifies which hosts you are allowed to Telnet or SSH to from that router. In other words, the ACL specifies the destination, not the source address. This is a strange oddity that occurs only when applying an access list on a VTY line. For the purposes of the exam, you should remember that ACLs on VTY lines are applied inbound.

Advanced VTY Access List Options

In the previous section you learned how to permit or deny Telnet or SSH access to your router. You can specify whether you are using SSH or Telnet on your VTY line with the transport input command. For example, if you want to allow only SSH access, type the following command from the VTY line:

```
Router(config-line)#transport input ssh
```

If you want to allow both SSH and Telnet, type the following:

```
Router(config-line)#trasnport input telnet ssh
```

You can even go so far as to specify certain hosts SSH access while others are allowed Telnet access by using extended access lists. For example, if you wanted to allow the 10.0.0.5 host SSH access but allow the 10.0.0.6 Telnet access, you can use the following access list:

```
Router(config)#access-list 100 permit tcp host 10.0.0.5 any eq 22
Router(config)#access-list 100 permit tcp host 10.0.0.6 any eq 23
Router(config)#line vty 0 5
Router(config-line)#access-class 100 in
```

Notice that you do not need to specify the destination address in the access list because the router itself is the destination.

You should see now that extended access lists are very flexible. Be careful, though, because an ACL on a VTY line could leave you locked out of your own router if you mistype an IP address. If you have ever locked yourself out of your house or car, you know the feeling.

Advanced Options

There are a few additional keywords you can add to the end of an ACL to enable advanced options. These are

- `log`

- `log-input`

- `established`

The `log` keyword, when added to the end of an ACL, will log the source address every time a match is made. If you log to buffered memory (enabled with the global configuration command **logging buffered**), you can view these log entries with the command **show logging**. The logging is limited, however, because it logs only the first packet and then logs again in 5-minute intervals. The log option is available for both standard and extended ACLs.

The **log-input** keyword is similar to the `log` keyword, but it also logs the Layer 2 address of the source host being matched. In the case of ethernet networks, this would be the MAC address. In the case of Frame Relay, this would be the data-link connection identifier (DLCI) number. The **log-input** keyword can be added only to the end of extended ACLs.

The `established` keyword is another advanced feature that will allow traffic through only if it sees that a TCP session is already established. A TCP session is considered established if the three-way handshake is initiated first. This keyword is added only to the end of extended ACLs that are filtering TCP traffic.

You can use TCP established to deny all traffic into your network except for incoming traffic that was first initiated from inside your network. This is commonly used to block all originating traffic from the Internet into a company's network except for Internet traffic that was first initiated from users inside the company. The following configuration would accomplish this for all TCP-based traffic coming in to interface serial 0/0 on the router:

```
access-list 100 permit tcp any any  established
interface serial 0/0
 ip access-group 100 in
```

Although the access list is using a permit statement, all traffic is denied unless it is first established from the inside network. If the router sees that the three-way TCP handshake is successful, it will then begin to allow traffic through.

Configuring Named ACLs

Up to this point, you have learned how to configure numbered ACLs. This section teaches you how to configure named ACLs.

As mentioned earlier, named ACLs provide the benefit of using descriptive names for your ACLs and the capability to remove individual lines. If you attempt to remove an individual line from a numbered access list, it will delete the entire list; with named ACLs, this is not the case.

The syntax for named ACLs is similar to that of numbered lists. Instead of using a number, you will give it a name. Remember, though, that the number indicates what type of access list you are using (IP, IPX, and so on) and if it is standard or extended. Because you are using a named ACL, you will need to configure your router so that it knows what type of ACL you want to create and if it is to be standard or extended. The syntax for an IP named ACL is as follows:

```
ip access-list {standard | extended} name
```

After entering this global configuration command, you will be presented with the named access control list (NACL) mode where you can enter your permit or deny statements.

For example, to create an extended NACL called DenyMike that blocks the host 10.0.0.55 from sending web traffic (TCP port 80) to the web server at 11.0.0.11 but allows everyone else, the syntax would be

```
Router(config)#ip access-list extended DenyMike
Router(config-ext-nacl)#deny tcp host 10.0.0.55 host 11.0.0.11 eq 80
Router(config-ext-nacl)#permit ip any any
Router(config-ext-nacl)#interface ethernet 0
Router(config-if)#ip access-group DenyMike in
```

Treating Numbered ACLs as Named

Although it is true that you cannot delete individual lines from a numbered ACL, there is a trick around this. If you treat your numbered ACL as a named ACL, you can then delete individual lines. For example, if you had a numbered ACL named 100, you could enter the command 'ip access-list extended 100' and enter named access control list configuration mode for this ACL. Because you are in NACL mode, you can now delete individual lines (even though it is originally a numbered access list). Remember for the test, however, that only named ACLs allow you to delete individual lines in an access list. If you attempt to delete an individual line from a numbered access list, the router will delete the entire list.

Named ACLs provide clarity through descriptive names and ease of configuration because of the capability of deleting individual lines. Although named ACLs might be more attractive for real-world usage, make sure that you feel comfortable with numbered ACLs as well.

Using the SDM to Configure ACLs

Up to this point, you have learned how to configured numbered and named ACLs from the command line. You can also configure ACLs using the Cisco Security Device Manager (SDM). The SDM provides you with a graphical interface instead of your having to remember the command-line syntax (however, you'll have to know that syntax for the exam!).

To configure an ACL using the SDM, launch SDM and choose Configure. Next, select Additional Tasks and choose Access Rules under the ACL Editor folder (see Figure 13.5).

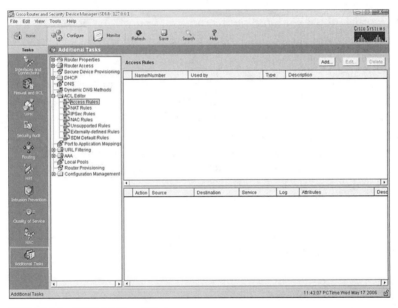

FIGURE 13.5 SDM Additional Tasks.

Next, select the Add button to bring up the Add a Rule dialog box (see Figure 13.6). On this screen you can put in a name or number for your access list, a description of the list, and the type (standard or extended).

FIGURE 13.6 Add a Rule dialog box.

After entering in an access list name or number and choosing whether it is a standard or extended list, you can click the Add button to specify your rules. The next screen that comes up will vary depending on whether you are using standard or extended. An extended access list is shown in Figure 13.7. You can do all that you can do with the command line, including specifying the source and destination, the protocol, and the ports (when applicable). You can even select to log all matches against your access list.

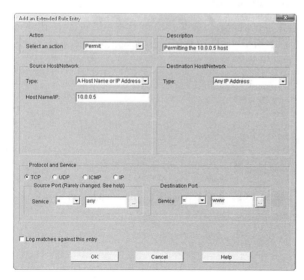

FIGURE 13.7 Add an Extended Rule Entry.

After your access list entry is created, you can click OK to go back to the Add a Rule dialog box. From here you can choose to enter additional rules, clone the rule, edit the rule, or delete the rule (shown in Figure 13.8).

FIGURE 13.8 Add a Rule dialog box with an ACL rule.

Your access list is created, but you are not done yet. Just like with the command-line syntax, you must associate the access list to an interface and specify that it is to be applied in the inbound or outbound direction. Click Associate to select your interface and direction (see Figure 13.9).

When finished configuring your access lists, click OK in the Add a Rule dialog box to exit out of the access rules editor and apply the commands to your router.

FIGURE 13.9 Associate with an Interface dialog box.

Whereas associating an ACL with an interface is pretty straightforward, removing the ACL from an interface is not. This is because you do not disassociate the access list from the ACL editor where you just applied it. Instead, you must go to the Interfaces and Connections by selecting it from the Tasks bar on the left side of the SDM. Next, click the Edit Interface/Connection tab (see Figure 13.10).

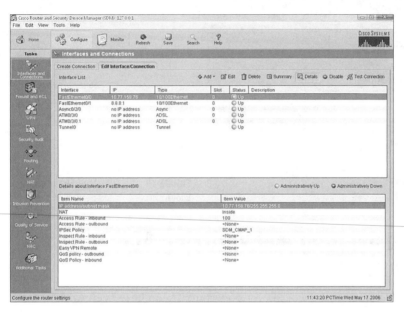

FIGURE 13.10   Edit Interface/Connection tab.

To disassociate the ACL from an interface, choose the interface you want to modify from the Interface List and click Edit. This will bring up the Interface Feature Edit Dialog box (see Figure 13.11). Next, click the Association tab. Here you can remove an ACL from an interface or add a different one. By selecting the drop-down menu, you can even choose to create a new rule, which will take you back to the access list editor.

Do make sure to notice that there is a place for both inbound and outbound access rules, so pay careful attention as to which direction you are modifying.

You now know how to successfully configure an ACL using the SDM. It certainly is a lot simpler than remembering the command-line syntax, but you should be familiar with both the command line and the SDM for the exam.

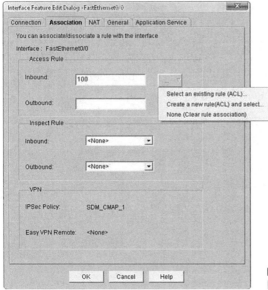

FIGURE 13.11   Interface Feature Edit
Dialog box.

Troubleshooting and Verifying ACL Configurations

In an ideal world, nothing would ever go wrong. If you have been working with computers for any length of time, you know that this is not the case. Inevitably, things do go wrong, and you will need to know how to vary and troubleshoot your configuration. There are three commands you should be familiar with when verifying and troubleshooting IP ACLs:

▶ `show ACLs`—Shows you what ACLs you have configured on your router

▶ `show ip ACLs`—Shows you only the IP ACLs you have configured on your router

▶ `show ip interface`—Shows you the direction (inbound/outbound) and placement of an ACL

The first two commands show only what ACLs you have configured on your router, but they do not show where they have been applied. The third command, `show ip interface`, shows you where the ACL has been applied and in what direction (inbound or outbound). Following is the output of the `show ip interface` command with the relevant portions highlighted:

```
Ethernet0 is up, line protocol is up
  Internet address is 10.0.0.1, subnet mask is 255.0.0.0
  Broadcast address is 255.255.255.255
  Address determined by non-volatile memory
  MTU is 1500 bytes
  Helper address is not set
  Directed broadcast forwarding is enabled
  Multicast groups joined: 224.0.0.1 224.0.0.2
  Outgoing access list is not set
  Inbound  access list is 100
  Proxy ARP is enabled
  Security level is default
  Split horizon is enabled
  ICMP redirects are always sent
  ICMP unreachables are always sent
  ICMP mask replies are never sent
  IP fast switching is enabled
  IP fast switching on the same interface is disabled
  IP SSE switching is disabled
  Router Discovery is disabled
  IP output packet accounting is disabled
  IP access violation accounting is disabled
  TCP/IP header compression is disabled
  Probe proxy name replies are disabled
```

From this output, you can see that ACL 100 is applied inbound on interface Ethernet 0.

EXAM ALERT

Anytime you configure an ACL, you should execute the `show access list` (or show ip ACLs) and `show ip interface` commands to verify the configuration.

Exam Prep Questions

1. Examine the following figure. What will the following ACL do? (Select the best answer.)

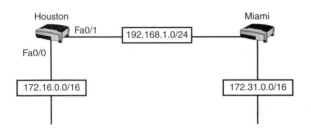

```
Houston(config)#access-list 114 deny tcp 172.16.0.0 0.0.255.255
172.31.0.0 0.0.255.255 eq 25
Houston(config)#access-list 114 deny tcp 172.16.0.0 0.0.255.255
172.31.0.0 0.0.255.255 eq 80
Houston(config)#access-list 114 permit tcp 172.16.0.0 0.0.255.255
172.31.0.0 0.0.255.255 eq 25
Houston(config)#access-list 114 permit tcp 172.16.0.0 0.0.255.255
172.31.0.0 0.0.255.255 eq 80
Houston(config)#interface fastethernet0/0
Houston(config-if)#ip access-group 114 in
```

- ○ **A.** Deny SMTP and WWW traffic sourced from Houston's ethernet network and destined for Miami's ethernet network.

- ○ **B.** Permit SMTP and WWW traffic sourced from Houston's ethernet network and destined for Miami's ethernet network.

- ○ **C.** Nothing. This is an invalid ACL.

- ○ **D.** Deny all traffic.

2. What is true about named ACLs? Select all that apply.

- ○ **A.** Named ACLs allow you to remove individual lines; numbered ACLs do not.

- ○ **B.** The name of the access list must be limited to eight characters or fewer.

- ○ **C.** You must specify whether the access list is standard or extended.

- ○ **D.** Named ACLs cannot be used with NAT.

- ○ **E.** You do not need to specify the protocol if you are using a named access list to filter IP traffic.

3. Examine the following figure. Which of the following configurations would allow Telnet access to the Tokyo router for the user named Ross but deny all other Telnet access? Select all that apply.

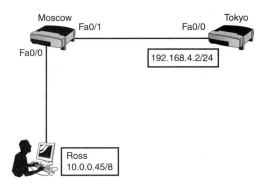

- ○ **A.** Moscow(config)# `access-list 100 deny ip any any`

  Moscow(config)#`access-list 100 permit tcp host 10.0.0.45 host 192.168.4.2 eq 23`

  Moscow(config)#`interface fastethernet 0/0`

  Moscow(config-if)#`ip access-group 100 in`

- ○ **B.** Moscow(config)#`access-list 199 permit tcp host 10.0.0.45 192.168.4.2 0.0.0.0 eq 23`

  Moscow(config)#`interface fastethernet 0/0`

  Moscow(config-if)#`ip access-group 199 in`

- ○ **C.** Moscow(config)#`access-list 125 permit tcp 10.0.0.45 0.0.0.0 host 192.168.4.2 eq Telnet`

  Moscow(config)#`interface fastethernet0/1`

  Moscow(config-if)#`ip access-group 125 out`

- ○ **D.** Tokyo(config)#`access-list 173 permit tcp host 10.0.0.45 host 192.168.4.2 eq 23`

  Tokyo(config)#`interface fastethernet0/0`

  Tokyo(config-if)#`ip access-group 173 in`

- ○ **E.** Tokyo(config)#`access-list 40 permit host 10.0.0.45`

  Tokyo(config)#`line vty 0 4`

  Tokyo(config-line)#`access-class 40 in`

- ○ **F.** Tokyo(config)#`access-list 87 permit host 10.0.0.45`

  Tokyo(config)#`line vty 0 4`

  Tokyo(config-line)#`access-class 1 in`

4. Examine the following figure. Based on the figure, you want to configure an access list that prevents users on the 172.16.32.0/21 and 172.17.32.0/21 networks from sending pings to the 172.18.32.0/21 network. You still, however, want to send pings out from the 172.18.32.0/21 network. What commands would you enter on the Blue router to make this work?

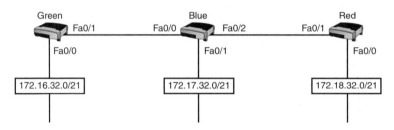

○ **A.** Blue(config)#**access-list 100 deny icmp 172.16.32.0 0.0.7.255 172.18.32.0.0 0.0.7.255 echo**

   Blue(config)#**access-list 100 deny icmp 172.17.32.0 0.0.7.255 172.18.32.0 0.0.7.255 echo**

   Blue(config)#**access-list 100 permit ip any any**

   Blue(config)#**interface fastethernet 0/2**

   Blue(config-if)#**ip access-group 100 out**

○ **B.** Blue(config)#**access-list 100 deny icmp 172.16.32.0 0.0.15.255. 172.18.32.0 0.0.15.255 echo**

   Blue(config)#**access-list 100 deny icmp 172.17.32.0 0.0.15.255 172.18.32.0 0.0.15.255 echo**

   Blue(config)#**access-list 100 permit ip any any**

   Blue(config)#**interface fastethernet 0/2**

   Blue(config-if)#**ip access-group 100 out**

○ **C.** Blue(config)#**access-list 100 deny icmp 172.16.32.0 0.0.7.255 172.18.32.0.0 0.0.7.255 echo**

   Blue(config)#**access-list 100 deny icmp 172.17.32.0 0.0.7.255 172.18.32.0 0.0.7.255 echo**

   Blue(config)#**access-list 100 permit ip any any**

   Blue(config)#**interface fastethernet 0/1**

   Blue(config-if)#**ip access-group 100 in**

○ **D.** Blue(config)#**access-list 100 deny icmp 172.16.32.0 0.0.15.255. 172.18.32.0 0.0.15.255 echo**

Blue(config)#**access-list 100 deny icmp 172.17.32.0 0.0.15.255 172.18.32.0 0.0.15.255 echo**

Blue(config)#**access-list 100 permit ip any any**

Blue(config)#**interface fastethernet 0/1**

Blue(config-if)#**ip access-group 100 in**

5. You want to filter FTP access sourced from the 192.168.99.192/27 network yet allow all other traffic to pass. You do not care about the destination. You enter the following command on your router, yet FTP traffic coming from the 192.168.99.192/27 network is still allowed. Why?

```
Router(config)#access-list 100 deny tcp any 192.168.99.192
    0.0.0.31 eq 20
Router(config)#access-list 100 deny tcp any 192.168.99.192
    0.0.0.31 eq 21
Router(config)#access-list 100 permit ip any any
Router(config)#interface serial 0/0
Router(config-if)#ip access-group 100 in
```

○ **A.** The port numbers are wrong.

○ **B.** FTP uses UDP, not TCP.

○ **C.** The source and destination are backward.

○ **D.** The permit statement should be first.

6. What would be the proper wildcard mask to permit all odd numbered hosts on the 10.48.0.0/12 network?

○ **A.** access-list 1 permit 10.48.0.0 0.0.15.255

○ **B.** access-list 1 permit 10.48.0.1 0.0.15.254

○ **C.** access-list 1 permit 10.48.0.0 0.0.15.1

○ **D.** access-list 1 permit 10.48.0.0 0.0.0.254

○ **E.** access-list 1 permit 10.48.0.0 0.0.0.255

7. What types of ACLs are processed after the router examines the routing table and sends the packet to the outgoing interface? Select all that apply.

   ○ **A.** IP standard inbound

   ○ **B.** IP extended inbound

   ○ **C.** IP standard outbound

   ○ **D.** IP extended outbound

8. What command can you enter to verify that an access list has been applied on your interface?

   ○ **A.** `show ip interface brief`

   ○ **B.** `show ACLs`

   ○ **C.** `show ip ACLs`

   ○ **D.** `show ip interface`

9. Where should you apply your ACLs? Select all that apply.

   ○ **A.** Standard ACLs should generally be applied closest to the source.

   ○ **B.** Standard ACLs should generally be applied closest to the destination.

   ○ **C.** Extended ACLs should generally be applied closest to the source.

   ○ **D.** Extended ACLs should generally be applied closest to the destination.

10. What does the following named access list do?

```
Router(config)#ip access-list extended QueACL
Router(config-ext-nacl)#permit tcp any 192.168.15.8 0.0.0.3 eq 119
Router(config-ext-nacl)#interface fastethernet1/3
Router(config-if)#ip access-group QueACL in
```

   ○ **A.** Allows NNTP traffic coming into the Fa1/3 interface to the 192.168.15.8 255.255.255.252 network, but denies everything else.

   ○ **B.** Allows SMTP traffic coming into the Fa1/3 interface to the 192.168.15.8 host, but denies everything else.

   ○ **C.** Allows NNTP traffic coming into the Fa1/3 interface to the 192.168.15.8 host, but denies everything else.

   ○ **D.** Allows SMTP traffic coming into the Fa1/3 interface to the 192.168.15.8/30 network, but denies everything else.

   ○ **E.** Allows all traffic to pass because no deny statement is given.

Answers to Exam Prep Questions

1. Answer D is correct. ACLs are top-down, meaning that they check the packet against your statements in the order that you enter them. In this example, the access list would first deny SMTP and WWW traffic sourced from Houston's ethernet network and destined for Miami's ethernet network. Following this, the access list permits SMTP and WWW traffic. However, because this traffic was first denied, the packet will never get permitted. Additionally, because all traffic is denied by default unless explicitly permitted, all other traffic will be denied. Thus, this access list denies all traffic. Answer A, although technically correct, is not the best answer because all traffic is being denied, not just SMTP and WWW traffic. Answer B is incorrect because SMTP and WWW traffic is being denied first. Answer C is incorrect because this is a perfectly acceptable, albeit poorly written, access list.

2. Answers A and C are correct. Answer B is wrong because named ACLs can be longer than eight characters. Answer D is wrong because you can use named ACLs with NAT. Answer E is wrong because you do always need to specify the protocol when using a named access list.

3. Answers B, C, and E are correct. Answer B configures the access list using the host keyword for the 10.0.0.45 host; answer C configures the access list using the host keyword for the 192.168.4.2 host; answer E configures the access list using the host keyword for both the 192.168.4.2 and the 10.0.0.45 host. Answer A is incorrect because the first deny statement would block all traffic, including the Telnet traffic. Answer D is incorrect because this would block Telnet traffic going through the Tokyo router and not traffic going to the Tokyo router. (ACLs applied to an interface are for traffic passing through the router and never for traffic destined to the router.) Answer F is incorrect because the wrong access list is applied on the VTY lines.

4. Answer A is correct. The correct wildcard mask is 0.0.7.255 for all networks. You can apply this access list inbound on Fa0/1 and Fa0/0 or outbound on Fa0/2. Although the general rule is to apply extended ACLs inbound closest to the source, none of the answers did this correctly (making this a tricky question). Answer B is incorrect because the wildcard masks are wrong. Answers C and D are incorrect because they are applied inbound on Fa0/1. The 172.16.32.0/21 network would still have been allowed through. Answer D is additionally wrong because the wrong wildcard mask is used.

5. Answer C is correct. Answer A is wrong because the port numbers are correct. Answer B is wrong because FTP does use TCP. Answer D is wrong because if the permit statement is first, all traffic would be allowed through (ACLs are top-down.)

6. Answer B is correct. All odd numbered hosts would have the one bit turned on in the last octet. Therefore, you need to check all hosts that have the one bit turned on (set to 1). You do not care about the other host bits. The default wildcard mask for a /12 network is 0.0.15.255, but because you want to match only those hosts that have the one bit turned on, you will need a wildcard mask of 0.0.15.254. Answer A is incorrect because this would match both even- and odd-numbered hosts. Answer C is incorrect because this would match all hosts from 10.48.0.0 through 10.48.255.0. Answers D and E are incorrect because they have the wrong wildcard mask.

7. Answers C and D are correct. Outbound ACLs are processed after the routing table is checked and the outbound interface is chosen. Answers A and B are incorrect because they are both inbound.

8. Answer D is correct. The command `show ip` interface will verify the direction and placement of an access list on an interface. Answer A is incorrect because this shows only brief output that does not include access list information. Answers B and C are incorrect because they do not show where the ACL is applied.

9. Answers B and C are correct. Standard ACLs should generally be applied outbound closest to the destination of the traffic because you have no other way of referencing the destination. Extended ACLs should generally be applied inbound closest to the source because you can specify the destination and you want to filter the traffic as early as possible. Answers A and D are incorrect because the directions are the opposite from what they should be.

10. Answer A is correct. TCP port 119 is used by NNTP, and the wildcard mask 0.0.0.3 matches the 192.168.15.8 255.255.255.252 (/30) subnet. Answers B and D are wrong because this access list permits NNTP, not SMTP. Answer C is wrong because this access list permits traffic to the 192.168.15.8/30 network, not a specific host. Answer E is wrong because no deny statement is necessary; all traffic is implicitly denied, except for what is explicitly permitted.

CHAPTER FOURTEEN

Routing

Terms you'll need to understand:

✓ Distance Vector

✓ Link State

✓ Administrative Distance

✓ Enhanced Interior Gateway Routing Protocol (EIGRP)

✓ Open Shortest Path First (OSPF)

Concepts and techniques you'll need to master:

✓ Configuring EIGRP

✓ Configuring OSPF

Introduction

In Chapter 10, "Basic Routing," you learned about static, default, and RIP routing. These are good solutions for small networks but do not scale well. Static routing becomes prone to errors and is cumbersome to do on a large scale, default routing does not help in getting to various networks within an enterprise, and RIP routing has a maximum hop count limitation of fifteen hops. For larger networks you need a scalable solution. Two good solutions are the Enhanced Interior Gateway Protocol (EIGRP) and the Open Shortest Path First (OSPF) routing protocols.

EIGRP

EIGRP is a hybrid routing protocol developed by Cisco to replace IGRP. It uses the Diffusing Update Algorithm (DUAL) developed by Dr. J. J. Garcia-Luna-Aceves. Similar to RIP, it has a maximum hop count, but its maximum is 224. Unlike RIP, however, it does not send out periodic updates. Instead, EIGRP sends updates only when there is a change in the network.

Characteristics of EIGRP

EIGRP uses the bandwidth and delay of an interface by default, with the option of factoring Reliability, Load, and MTU. EIGRP maintains three tables, as shown in Figure 14.1:

▶ Neighbor table

▶ Topology table

▶ Routing table

EIGRP begins by sending HELLO packets out all active interfaces. The router listens for HELLO packets from other routers. From the HELLO packets, the router learns of neighboring routers, which get listed in the neighbor table. After the router knows of its neighbors, it begins exchanging routes with its neighbors. These routes go into the topology table, which is similar to a routing table, but no decision has been made yet as to the best route. Instead, the topology table is used to build a map of the network with different speed limits (bandwidth) on the different roads (links). The DUAL algorithm is run against the topology table, and two routes are determined as a result:

▶ **Successor Route**—This is the best route as determined by the DUAL algorithm. This route gets injected into the routing table and is the one used when packets are routed.

▶ **Feasible Successor Route**—This is the next best route and is kept in the topology table. It is used only in the event that the primary successor route goes down.

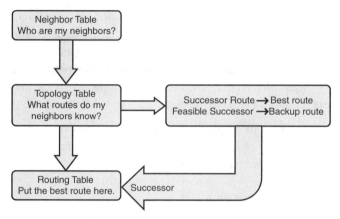

Neighbor Table
Who are my neighbors?

Topology Table
What routes do my
neighbors know?

Successor Route → Best route
Feasible Successor → Backup route

Routing Table
Put the best route here. Successor

FIGURE 14.1 EIGRP tables.

By having a feasible successor route, the router is ready to instantly inject another route into the routing table should the successor ever go down. This makes convergence very rapid with EIGRP.

In addition to being a rapidly converging protocol, EIGRP is the only routing protocol that supports multiple Layer 3 protocols, namely IP, AppleTalk, and IPX. All the other routing protocols mentioned in this chapter support only IP. EIGRP maintains separate tables for each of the three protocols it supports.

Another distinction of EIGRP is its use of two administrative distance values. EIGRP uses administrative distance 90 for routes learned through EIGRP. Routes can also be redistributed into EIGRP from another routing protocol. When this occurs, redistributed routes get an administrative distance of 170. Internal routes are best described as those that are direct testimony, or trusted the most, whereas external routes are like hearsay and are therefore trusted less.

EXAM ALERT

Remember the main characteristics of EIGRP:
▶ Hybrid protocol
▶ Supports IP, AppleTalk, and IPX
▶ Has two administrative distance values, one for internal and one for external (redistributed routes)
▶ Uses Bandwidth and Delay by default in calculating its metric, but can also factor Reliability, Load, and MTU

Implementing EIGRP

Basic EIGRP configuration is not that different from configuring RIP. The primary difference for basic configuration is that you must specify an autonomous system number that defines your routing domain. The autonomous system number is assigned globally for the routing process and can be any number you want, but that same number must be used on all routers. Routing updates will not be exchanged between routers with different autonomous numbers. Because the exam focuses heavily on troubleshooting, make sure you always check that the autonomous numbers match in the exam scenarios.

The following example shows how to configure EIGRP for a router connected to networks 192.168.10.0/24 and 192.168.20.0/24. The autonomous system number is 1 and is specified when entering the routing process.

```
Router(config)#router eigrp 1
Router(config-router)#network 192.168.10.0
Router(config-router)#network 192.168.20.0
```

Similar to RIP version 2 and OSPF, EIGRP can be a classless routing protocol. By default, it is classful. To enable classless routing, type the following command under the routing process:

```
Router(config-router)#no auto-summary
```

Verifying and Troubleshooting EIGRP

A good engineer does not just configure routing but knows to verify the configuration with show commands. The most common **show** command when verifying your routing configuration is **show ip route**. This command was discussed in Chapter 10, so it is not discussed here. Keep in mind, though, that this is best command to use to see whether your routing table is being populated.

You can use other commands besides **show ip route** to verify your EIGRP configuration. These include **show ip protocols** and **show ip eigrp topology**.

The first command, **show ip protocols**, is helpful to see your autonomous system number and the networks you are advertising.

```
Router# show ip protocols
Routing Protocol is "eigrp 1"
  Outgoing update filter list for all interfaces is not set
  Incoming update filter list for all interfaces is not set
  Redistributing: eigrp 1
  Automatic network summarization is in effect
  Routing for Networks:
```

```
    192.168.0.0
Routing Information Sources:
  Gateway          Distance      Last Update
    192.168.1.0         90       0:02:36
    192.168.2.0         90       0:03:04
    192.168.3.0         90       0:03:04
Distance: internal 90 external 170
```

Table 14.1 summarizes the important lines of this command.

TABLE 14.1 Summary of Show IP Protocols Output

Output	Description
Outgoing/incoming filters	Used to filter routing updates between routers.
Redistributing	Covered in the Cisco Certified Network Professional (CCNP) exam. This pertains to redistributing information between routing protocols and is outside the scope of this exam.
Automatic network In summarization is in effect	Whether the **no auto-summary** command has been applied. this example, the command has not been applied, and EIGRP is doing classful routing.
Routing for networks	Which networks your router is advertising to other routers.
Routing information sources	This defines which routers are sending your EIGRP routes, the administrative distance for those routes, and the last time your router received an update from other routers.
Distance	The administrative distance for internal and external routes.

The second command is show ip eigrp topology. As the command suggests, this outputs your topology table. Your topology table contains all the routes your router knows about. Here is where you will also see your successor (best routes) and your feasible successor (backup routes):

```
Router# show ip eigrp topology

IP-EIGRP Topology Table for process 77

Codes: P - Passive, A - Active, U - Update, Q - Query, R - Reply,
       r - Reply status

P 172.16.0.0 255.255.0.0, 2 successors, FD is 36251776
        via 172.16.17.1 (36251776/36226176), Ethernet0
        via 172.16.18.1 (36251776/36226176), Ethernet1
P 172.20.0.0 255.255.0.0, 1 successors, FD is 307200
        via 172.16.81.28 (307200/281600), Ethernet1
        via 172.16.19.5 (702311/295210), Ethernet2
```

From this output you can begin to get an idea of the topology of your network. Notice that for the 172.16.0.0/16 network you have two successors. This is because the metric is the same for both networks and, subsequently, you will load balance across two networks. The metric that is put in the routing table is the first number in parenthesis (36251776 in this example) and is called the feasible distance (FD).

The 172.20.0.0 network has only one successor route out Ethernet1 that is learned from a router with the IP address 172.16.81.28. You also have a backup route (feasible successor) out Ethernet2 that is learned from a router at 172.16.19.5.

For the exam, make sure you are comfortable analyzing the output of these show commands.

Active Versus Passive Routes

You will notice in the output of the `show ip eigrp topology` command that the routes begin with a P for passive. According to the legend at the beginning of this output, a route can also be A for active. A passive route is when your routing table has fully converged. An active route is when a route has changed and your routers are querying other routers to discover the change in the topology. Ideally, your routes should be in passive mode.

OSPF

Another scalable routing protocol is the Open Shortest Path First (OSPF) protocol. OSPF was developed by the Internet Engineering Task Force (IETF) in 1988 as a more scalable solution than RIP. Unlike EIGRP, OSPF is an open standard and is not Cisco proprietary. It uses the Shortest Path First (SPF) algorithm developed by Edgar Dijkstra. It is a link-state routing protocol, which means that it sends updates only when there is a change in the network, and instead of sending routing updates, it sends link state advertisements (LSAs) instead.

Characteristics

OSPF is a polite protocol. Unlike chatty RIP, which broadcasts out its entire routing table every 30 seconds regardless of whether other routers want to hear it, OSPF takes a more gentlemanlike approach to routing. First, OSPF sends out hello messages to neighboring routers to announce itself as an OSPF router and discover who its neighbor routers are. Routers have to agree on certain parameters (such as timers and being on a common subnet) before they can become neighbors. After its neighbor routers are discovered, they begin to exchange information about networks (links) it knows about, using messages called link state advertisements (LSAs). After exchanging all routes, the routers send out updates only when there is a change, and they send information only for that affected route, not the entire routing table. Routers take the link state advertisements heard from other routers and place those routes in its link state database (similar to the topology database in EIGRP). Routers then run the SPF algorithm to determine the best route to a destination and place that route in the routing table.

To determine the best path, OSPF uses a metric called cost, which Cisco defines as 10^8/bandwidth. If you had a 100Mbps link, the cost would be 1 because 100,000,000/100,000,000. Here are some other common costs:

▶ 10Mbps: 10

▶ 1.544Mbps (T1): 64

▶ 64Kbps: 1562

EXAM ALERT

These examples are not included just to impress you with the authors' math abilities. You should know the formula to determine the cost of a link. Given the bandwidth of an interface, know how to calculate the OSPF cost.

The bandwidth costs are based on a bandwidth reference of 100Mb. If you have faster links in your enterprise, such as gigabit ethernet, you can change what OSPF bases its cost on by using the auto-cost reference bandwidth command. For example, to change your OSPF to use 109/bandwidth (1,000,000 or GB), type the following command under the router process configuration mode:

```
Router(config-router)#auto-cost reference-bandwidth 1000000
```

To maintain consistency throughout your network, you should set the same bandwidth reference across on all your routers.

The SPF algorithm places each router as the "root" of a tree and calculates the shortest path from itself to each destination. The shortest path then gets put into the routing table and is used to route packets to their destination.

Hierarchical Routing

An important concept to grasp with OSPF is that it is a hierarchical protocol. Hierarchical routing protocols break up your autonomous system into multiple areas and summarize routes between areas. If summarized wisely, you can cut down a significant portion of routing updates by advertising only the summarized route.

As the number of networks increases in your domain, the amount of processing required on each router increases. To lower the amount of processing required, you can use route summarization. Route summarization looks for the same sequence of bits used in subnetworks and creates a less-explicit summary route. For example, Figure 14.2 shows four networks in area 2:

▶ 172.16.0.0/24

▶ 172.17.0.0/24

▶ 172.18.0.0/24

▶ 172.19.0.0/24

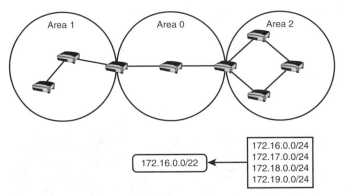

FIGURE 14.2   OSPF summarization.

The first octet, 172, is the same for all four routes, but the second octet differs. By looking for similar bits, we can create a single summary route:

	128	64	32	16	8	4	2	1
16	0	0	0	1	0	0	0	0
17	0	0	0	1	0	0	0	1
18	0	0	0	1	0	0	1	0
19	0	0	0	1	0	0	1	1

The bits are the same up to the 4-bit position. Only the 16-bit position is set to 1, so by ignoring the last two bits (because they change), we are left with 172.16.0.0. The subnet mask has changed, however, because we are no longer working with a /24. Instead, our subnet mask has moved two places to the left because the last two bit positions vary for the four networks. Our resulting summarized route is 172.16.0.0/22 (255.255.252.0). This will be the route that gets injected into area 0 from area 2.

The routers in area 0 and area 1 have to process only the one summarized route instead of four individual routes. Being able to summarize your routes between areas provides several benefits:

- **Less processing on routers**—This is not only because of the single network statement (in contrast to four), but also because of the lack of recalculation should a more specific network (that is, a /24) go down.

- **Instability hidden from other routers**—If a single network goes down in area 2, it will not affect the routers in area 0 and area 1.

- **Fast convergence**—Because fewer routes are sent to area 0, the routers in areas 0 and 1 can converge faster.

- **Less bandwidth overhead**—There is less bandwidth because only one route is sent, so the advertisement is smaller.

- **Greater control over routing updates**—Because you gain control over routing updates, you can control what routes get sent from one area to another.

You might have noticed that both area 2 and area 1 are connected via area 0. Area 0 is the "backbone" area in OSPF, and all other areas must be connected to it. Routes are then summarized into your backbone area.

Designated and Backup Designated Routers

Summarizing is an excellent way to conserve on your precious bandwidth. On networks that contain more than two routers, OSPF can also conserve bandwidth by electing a designated router for that network that all routers communicate with. Routers exchange information with a designated router instead of each other. This cuts down significantly on the number of advertisements.

The process of using a designated router is somewhat complex, so let's go through it one step at a time. First, the designated router (DR) is elected on only two types of networks:

- **Broadcast multi-access**—Ethernet, token ring
- **Nonbroadcast multi-access**—Frame Relay, ATM, X.25

On a point-to-point network with only two routers, there is no need for this type of election. Remember that on a point-to-point network, there is no point (of having a DR).

Second, the DR is not the only type of router elected on these types of networks. A backup designated router (BDR) is used in the event that a DR should fail.

The DR and BDR election is as follows:

1. The router with the highest priority becomes the DR. The router with the second-highest priority becomes the BDR. Priority is a number between 0 and 255 and is configured on an interface with the command `ip ospf_priority` *priority_number*. The default priority is 1, and if the router is set to priority 0, it will never become a DR or BDR.

2. In the case of a tie, such as when every router's priority is left to the default of 1, the tie breaker is the router with the highest router ID.

Every router has an identifier called a router ID (RID) that is used to identify itself in its messages. The router ID is an IP address and is assigned as follows:

1. The router ID can be configured with the `router-id` command under the OSPF routing process. You can choose a valid IP address that you are using on the router or make up a new one.

2. If the `router-id` command is not used, the numerically highest IP address on any loopback interface is chosen as the router ID. A loopback interface is a virtual, software-only interface that never goes down.

3. If you do not have any loopback interfaces configured, the highest IP address on any active physical interface is chosen as the router ID.

See if you can spot the router ID given the following IP addresses on a router:

Serial 0/0: 192.168.100.19

FastEthernet 0/0: 10.0.0.1

Loopback 0: 172.16.201.200

Although the highest IP address is the one configured on the serial interface, a loopback interface takes precedence over any physical interfaces. Therefore, the router ID would be 172.16.201.200.

EXAM ALERT

The `router-id` command is common in the real world, but for the test, make sure that you know the process the router uses to select a router ID if the `router-id` command is not used. It first looks at the highest IP address on any logical (loopback) interface, and if no loopback interfaces exist, it looks at the highest IP address on any active physical interface.

Let's review. On broadcast and nonbroadcast multi-access networks, a designated router and backup designated router are elected. The election is done by first choosing the routers with the highest priority value or, if the priorities are same, choosing the routers with the highest router ID. The router ID is chosen by the highest IP address on any loopback interface or, if no loopback interfaces are configured, the highest IP address on any active physical interface. Whew! That's a lot of work, but in the end it will conserve a significant amount of bandwidth by minimizing the number of link-state messages.

Now that we have elected a DR and BDR, the next phase is ready to begin. In Figure 14.3, you see five routers. The Mocha router is the DR, and the Latte router is the BDR. Instead of all routers sending link-state advertisements to each other, they send out messages only to the DR and BDR. Messages are sent to the multicast address of 224.0.0.6; both the DR and BDR belong to this multicast group address.

Next, the Mocha router, which is the DR, takes the information it learned from the other routers and sends it back out to all routers, as shown in Figure 14.4. Messages are sent to the AllSPFRouter multicast address of 224.0.0.5; all routers running OSPF are members of this multicast group address.

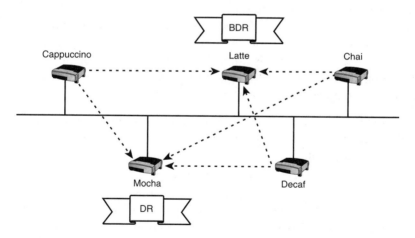

FIGURE 14.3 OSPF DR/BDR operation.

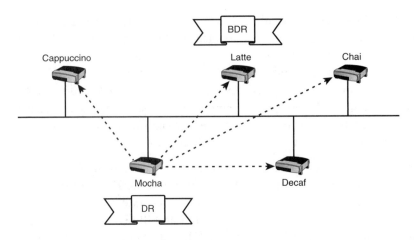

FIGURE 14.4 DR sends to 224.0.0.6.

Implementing OSPF

Understanding the complexities involved in OSPF is the difficult part; configuring it is fairly straightforward. The process is the same as with the other protocols. First, we enable the routing protocol. This is done with the command `router ospf <process-id>`. The process ID can be any number you prefer between 1 and 65,535. Note that this is not the same as the autonomous system number found in IGRP and EIGRP. Here, the process ID is local to the router and does not need to match other routers.

The next step is to activate OSPF on your interfaces and advertise your networks. This is done with the network command as before, but the syntax is a little different. Here, the syntax is

`network` *network address wild card mask* `area` *area-id*

Note that you specify a wildcard mask in the configuration. Wildcard masks are covered in Chapter 13, "IP Access Lists." Here, wildcard masks are used to match the IP address that is being used on an interface.

Take a look at Figure 14.5, where we come across our three friends again: Moe, Larry, and Curly. Given this example, the configuration for Moe would be

```
Moe(config)#router ospf 1
Moe(config-router)#network 192.168.10.0 0.0.0.255 area 0
Moe(config-router)#network 192.168.20.0 0.0.0.255 area 0
```

Larry's configuration would be

```
Larry(config)#router ospf 1
Larry(config-router)#network 192.168.20.0 0.0.0.255 area 0
Larry(config-router)#network 192.168.40.0 0.0.0.255 area 1
```

Finally, Curly's configuration would be

```
Curly(config)#router ospf 1
Curly(config-router)#network 192.168.40.0 0.0.0.255 area 1
Curly(config-router)#network 192.168.50.0 0.0.0.255 area 1
```

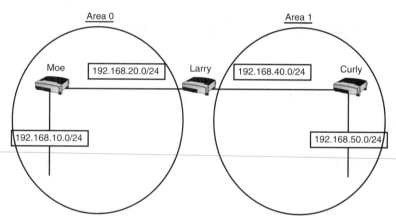

FIGURE 14.5 OSPF scenario.

The wildcard mask used in these statements is matching the IP address on the interface. Here, we are matching the entire network, of which the IP address is a part. For example, on Curly's router, the command network 192.168.40.0 0.0.0.255 area 1 tells the router to match all addresses that begin with 192.168.40. The last octet, which has 255 in the wildcard mask, is ignored. The router examines the IP addresses of its directly connected interfaces and activates OSPF on those interfaces that match the statement.

Because you are using wildcard masks to match the IP address on your directly connected interfaces, you could also use the wildcard mask of 0.0.0.0 to match the exact address. Just as with IP access lists in Chapter 13, a wildcard mask of 0.0.0.0 would match a specific address. For example, if Curly had the IP address of 192.168.40.1 on one interface and 192.168.50.1 on another interface, you could configure Curly's router using a wildcard mask of 0.0.0.0:

```
Curly(config)router ospf 1
Curly(config-router)#network 192.168.40.1 0.0.0.0 area 1
Curly(config-router)#network 192.168.50.1 0.0.0.0 area 1
```

Using a wildcard mask that matches the IP address of the interface is equivalent to using a wildcard mask that matches the network where the IP address resides. For the exam, focus on matching the entire network (0.0.0.255 wildcard mask in the previous example); the reasons behind which one you should choose are outside the scope of this book and, for that matter, the exam.

> **EXAM ALERT**
>
> The syntax for OSPF is slightly different from other routing protocols. Make sure that you feel comfortable configuring OSPF. Remember, it uses a process ID, not an autonomous system. Also, OSPF uses wildcard masks and not subnet masks in its configuration.

There are two optional commands that you should be familiar with for the CCNA exam. These commands, configured under the interface, are

- `ip ospf priority` *priority_number*—This is used to change the priority of an interface for the DR/BDR election.

- `ip ospf cost` *cost*—This is used to manually change the cost of an interface.

Verifying and Troubleshooting OSPF

For verification, you can use the `show ip protocols` and `show ip route` as before. Other commands you can use to verify your configuration are

- `show ip ospf interface`—This command displays area ID and DR/BDR information.

- `show ip ospf neighbor`—This command displays neighbor information.

You can use the `debug ip ospf events` command to troubleshoot OSPF. This command is helpful to troubleshoot why routers are not forming a neighbor relationship with each other. Similar to EIGRP, OSPF routers form neighbor relationships before exchanging any routing information. Several items must line up, however, for a neighbor adjacency to be established:

- Timers must be the same on both routers. OSPF uses hello timers that define how often they send out hello messages and dead timers that define how long after a router stops hearing a Hello message does it declare its neighbor as down.

- ▶ Interfaces connecting the two routers must be in the same area.

- ▶ Password authentication, if being used, must be the same.

- ▶ Type of area must be the same. (This last item is outside the scope of the CCNA test, but it is covered on the CCNP BSCI exam.)

Neighbors are formed automatically or can be established through the use of the neighbor command done under the routing process. Sometimes the neighbor adjacency does not form, and the **debug ip ospf events** command can help you to troubleshoot what is going wrong. The following debug output shows an example of an adjacency not forming because of two routers having different timers configured:

```
Router#debug ip ospf events
OSPF: hello with invalid timers on interface FastEthernet0/0
hello interval received 10 configured 10
netmask received 255.255.0.0 configured 255.255.0.0
dead interval received 40 configured 60
```

Exam Prep Questions

1. You are working in an environment that is running IP, IPX, and AppleTalk. What routing protocol inherently supports all three of these protocols?

   ○ **A.** RIP version 1

   ○ **B.** RIP version 2

   ○ **C.** OSPF

   ○ **D.** IGRP

   ○ **E.** EIGRP

2. How is the router ID chosen in OSPF? Select all that apply.

   ○ **A.** Highest loopback IP address

   ○ **B.** Highest physical IP address if no loopback exists

   ○ **C.** Lowest loopback IP address

   ○ **D.** Lowest physical IP address if no loopback exists

3. Examine the following figure. What routing protocol can you use to accommodate the given addressing scheme? Select all that apply.

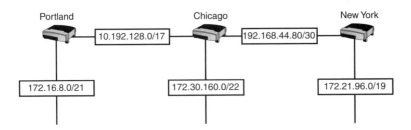

   ○ **A.** RIP version 1

   ○ **B.** RIP version 2

   ○ **C.** EIGRP

   ○ **D.** OSPF

   ○ **E.** IGRP

4. OSPF supports hierarchical routing. What benefits do you gain from using a routing protocol that supports hierarchical routing? Select all that apply.

   ○ **A.** Hierarchical routing speeds up the time for all routers to converge.

   ○ **B.** Hierarchical routing requires less configuration.

   ○ **C.** Hierarchical routing reduces the amount of routing overhead.

   ○ **D.** Hierarchical routing hides network instability from routers in other areas.

   ○ **E.** Hierarchical routing requires less design considerations.

5. What is the cost of a 128K link in OSPF?

   ○ **A.** 1562

   ○ **B.** 64

   ○ **C.** 781

   ○ **D.** 10

6. You have a serial interface with the IP address of 192.168.22.33/30. How would you add this link to area 0 in the OSPF process?

   ○ **A.** `Router(config-router)#network 192.168.22.32 0.0.0.3 area 0`

   ○ **B.** `Router(config-router)#network 192.168.22.32 255.255.255.252`

   ○ **C.** `Router(config-router)#network 192.168.22.33 0.0.0.3 area 0`

   ○ **D.** `Router(config-router)#network 192.168.22.33 255.255.255.252 area 0`

7. Which of the following protocols maintains a topology table?

   ○ **A.** RIP version 1

   ○ **B.** RIP version 2

   ○ **C.** Static routing

   ○ **D.** EIGRP

For questions 8–10 refer to the following figure and configuration.

Router	Fa0/0	Fa0/1
Botswana	10.7.18.5/30	10.0.23.33/27
Ukraine	10.0.23.34/27	10.202.114.129/28
Tanzania	10.202.114.130/28	10.5.5.0/24

```
Botswana
router ospf 1
 network 10.7.18.4 0.0.0.30 area 1
 network 10.0.23.32 0.0.0.63 area 0

Ukraine
router ospf 1
 network 10.0.23.32 0.0.0.63 area 0
 network 10.202.114.128 0.0.0.15 area 0

Tanzania
router ospf 11
 network 10.202.114.128 0.0.0.15 area 2
 network 10.5.5.0 0.0.0.255 area 3
```

8. What is wrong with the Botswana configuration?

   ○ **A.** The wildcard mask for the network on the Fastethernet0/0 interface is incorrect.

   ○ **B.** The wildcard mask for the network on the Fastethernet0/1 interface is incorrect.

   ○ **C.** The OSPF process ID is incorrect.

   ○ **D.** Area 1 is not directly connected to area 0.

   ○ **E.** The network on fastethernet0/1 is in the wrong area.

9. What is wrong with the Ukraine configuration?

   ○ **A.** The wildcard mask for the network on the Fastethernet0/0 interface is incorrect.

   ○ **B.** The wildcard mask for the network on the Fastethernet0/1 interface is incorrect.

   ○ **C.** The OSPF process ID is incorrect.

   ○ **D.** The network on fastethernet0/0 is in the wrong area.

   ○ **E.** The network on fastethernet0/1 is in the wrong area.

10. What is wrong with the Tanzania configuration?

- ○ **A.** The wildcard mask for the network on the Fastethernet0/0 interface is incorrect.
- ○ **B.** The wildcard mask for the network on the Fastethernet0/1 interface is incorrect.
- ○ **C.** The OSPF process ID is incorrect.
- ○ **D.** Area 3 is not directly connected to area 0.
- ○ **E.** The network on fastethernet0/1 is in the wrong area.

Answers to Exam Prep Questions

1. Answer E is correct. EIGRP is the only routing protocol that supports IP, IPX, and AppleTalk. RIP, OSPF, and IGRP are routing protocols that support only IP, so therefore answers A, B, C, and D are incorrect.

2. Answers A and B are correct. OSPF chooses the highest IP address of any logical loopback interfaces or, if no loopback interfaces are configured, the highest IP address on any physical interface that is active at the moment the OSPF process begins. Answers C and D are incorrect because they imply that the lowest IP address is used, which is not the case with OSPF's router ID.

3. Answers B, C, and D are correct. The addressing scheme is using noncontiguous subnets and therefore requires a routing protocol that supports variable length subnet masks (VLSM). Routing protocols that support VLSM are called classless routing protocols, and RIP version 2, EIGRP, and OSPF are all classless. RIP version 1 and IGRP are classful and support only full length subnet masks.

4. Answers A, C, and D are correct. When you hear the term *hierarchical routing*, think areas and route summarization. OSPF, which supports hierarchical routing, allows you to summarize networks from one area into another. Instead of routers needing to know about all the individual networks in another area, they need to know only about the summary route. The fewer routes result in faster convergence and less routing overhead and, should a network in an area go down, it will not affect routers in other areas. Answer B is incorrect because OSPF will cause additional configuration to be performed. Answer E is incorrect because OSPF typically requires more design than nonhierarchical routing protocols such as RIP to ensure an addressing scheme that allows for summarization between areas.

5. Answer C is correct. Cost is defined as 10^8/bandwidth. Thus, 100,000,000 / 128,000 equals 781. Answer A is incorrect because this is the cost to a 64K link. Answer B is incorrect because this is the cost of a 1.544 T1 link. Answer D is incorrect because this is the cost of a 10MB link.

6. Answer A is correct. The IP address of the interface is 192.168.22.33/30, which is on network 192.168.22.32. Although you could have entered 192.168.22.33 0.0.0.0 area 0, this was not a valid option. Only answer A has the correct network and wildcard mask. This is tricky because it requires you to determine both the network address and the correct OSPF syntax. Answer B uses a subnet mask and not a wildcard mask, so it is incorrect. Answer C is incorrect because it does not list the correct network address. Answer D is also incorrect because it does not list the correct address and because it uses a subnet mask in which a wildcard mask is required.

7. Answer D is correct. EIGRP maintains a neighbor, topology, and routing table. Answers A, B, and C are incorrect; RIP versions 1 and 2 and IGRP do not have topology tables. Instead, they run their algorithm and place the best route directly in the routing table.

8. Answer A is correct. When matching a subnet, the wildcard mask is the inverse of the subnet mask. Fastethernet0/0 is a /30 network that in dotted notation is 255.255.255.252. The inverse of this is 0.0.0.3, not 0.0.0.30. There is nothing wrong with the rest of the configuration, so answers B, C, D, and E are all incorrect.

9. Answer E is correct. This is a tricky one that requires a process of elimination. Answers A and B are incorrect because the wildcard masks are correct for the networks on those interfaces. Answer C is incorrect because a router's process ID is unique to that router and can be different from other routers. Answer D is incorrect because it is in area 0 and it is connected to another router (Botswana) that also has an attached interface (Fa0/1) in area 0. For answer E, you have to compare the Tanzania configuration, which has its Fastethernet0/0 in area 2. You must be in the same area as the interface that you are attaching to and these areas do not match. Either Tanzania or Ukraine has the incorrect area, but nothing in the diagram or output will tell you which router is improperly configured. However, by using process of elimination you can eliminate the other wrong answers and are left with only E as the correct answer. Ruling out the wrong answers is a great technique to use on the exam if you get stuck.

10. Answer D is correct. The rules of OSPF state that all areas must have a connection to the backbone area 0. In this configuration, Tanzania has its Fastethernet0/1 interface in area 3 and its Fastethernet0/0 interface in area 2. Area 2 is connected to the Ukraine, which has a connection to area 0. However, area 3 does not have a connection to area 0. There is nothing wrong with the remaining configuration, so answers A, B, C, and E are all incorrect.

CHAPTER FIFTEEN

Wide-Area Networks

Terms you'll need to understand:

✓ Challenge Handshake Authentication Protocol (CHAP)

✓ Password Authentication Protocol (PAP)

✓ Permanent Virtual Circuit (PVC)

✓ Committed Information Rate (CIR)

✓ Local Management Interface (LMI)

✓ Backward Explicit Congestion Notification (BECN)

✓ Forward Explicit Congestion Notification (FECN)

✓ High-Level Data Link Control (HDLC)

✓ Point-to-Point Protocol (PPP)

✓ Virtual Private Networks (VPNs)

Concepts and techniques you'll need to master:

✓ Configuring PPP (point-to-point)

✓ Configuring Frame Relay

✓ Components of IPsec VPNs

✓ Use of SSL VPNs

Introduction

There are two major types of networking: local-area network (LAN) and wide-area network (WAN). This chapter discusses WANs.

A WAN is a network that spans a broad geographical area and includes such technologies as ATM, Frame Relay, leased lines, and ISDN. These wide-area networking services are leased from providers.

In its simplest definition, wide-area networking can be broken into three categories:

▸ Leased line

▸ Circuit switched

▸ Packet switched

Leased-line WAN solutions use synchronous serial interfaces to connect two sites. This is the easiest to configure and provides the best reliability. However, this is also the most expensive over long distances.

The second option is circuit-switched technologies. These technologies include both modems connected to asynchronous interfaces and ISDN technologies. With circuit-switched solutions, you establish a circuit between two sites using a telephone company.

The final option is packet-switched technologies, which also use synchronous serial interfaces similar to leased-line solutions, but with these, a virtual circuit is established between two or more sites, and your data packets are switched across a service provider's network. The service provider's network is transparent to the customer; you will not be able to see any of your provider's equipment. Packet-switched technologies include Frame Relay, ATM, and X.25. They are commonly used when leased-line solutions become cost prohibitive.

Encapsulation Types

With each WAN solution, there is an encapsulation type. Encapsulations wrap an information envelope around your data that is used to transport your data traffic. If you use leased line as your wide-area networking choice, you can encapsulate your data inside a High-Level Data-Link Control (HDLC) frame,

PPP frame, or Serial Line IP (SLIP) frame. For packet-switched networks, you can encapsulate or package your data in X.25 frames, Frame Relay, or Asynchronous Transfer Mode (ATM) frames. (ATM and Frame Relay have multiple encapsulation envelope format choices that you can use.) Finally, in circuit-switched environments, you have HDLC, PPP, or SLIP as you do with leased line, but with circuit-switched solutions, it is more common to use PPP as your choice. This is because of the options available with PPP that are catered to using telephone-based circuit-switched networks. These options include such things as authentication and compression. Table 15.1 illustrates the different encapsulations as they are used by various WAN technologies.

TABLE 15.1 WAN Encapsulations

	Leased Lines	Circuit-Switched	Packet-Switched
HDLC	X	X	
PPP*	X	X	
SLIP	X	X	
Frame Relay**			X
ATM***			X
X.25			X

* Technically, it is possible to have PPP run over ATM and Frame Relay, but it is not necessary to know this for the CCNA exam.

** Frame Relay actually has two types of encapsulations: IETF and Cisco.

***ATM has several types of encapsulations, but it is not necessary to know these for the CCNA exam.

Cisco HDLC

The default encapsulation on a serial interface is HDLC. The original HDLC encapsulation was defined by the International Organization for Standards (ISO), those same folks who developed the OSI model. The ISO version of HDLC had one shortcoming, however; it had no options to support multiple Layer 3 routed protocols. As a result, most vendors have created their own form of HDLC. Cisco is no exception because it has its own proprietary form of HDLC to support various Layer 3 protocols such as IPX, IP, and AppleTalk. Figure 15.1 illustrates the difference between the ISO and Cisco HDLC frame formats.

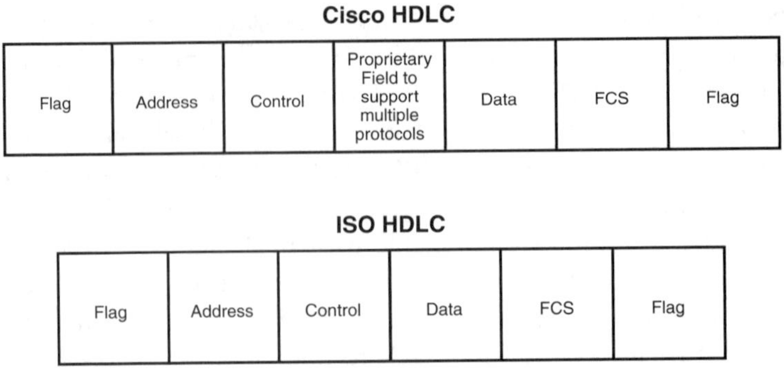

Cisco HDLC

Flag	Address	Control	Proprietary Field to support multiple protocols	Data	FCS	Flag

ISO HDLC

Flag	Address	Control	Data	FCS	Flag

FIGURE 15.1 Cisco and ISO HDLC formats.

EXAM ALERT

Vendors love to test your knowledge of the default settings for their products. Make sure you know that HDLC is the default encapsulation on a serial interface.

PPP

Point-to-Point Protocol (PPP), defined in RFC 1661, is used to encapsulate network layer protocols over point-to-point links. PPP can be used over asynchronous, synchronous, or ISDN links.

Components

PPP has two sublayers called network control protocol (NCP) and link control protocol (LCP).

NCP is responsible for supporting multiple Layer 3 protocols. Each protocol has its own NCP, such as the IPCP for IP communication and IPXCP for IPX communication. Think of NCP as the "packager"; it is responsible for packaging, or encapsulating, your packets into a control protocol that is readable by PPP.

The link control protocol is used for establishing the link and negotiating optional settings. These options include

> ▶ **Compression**—You can compress your data to conserve bandwidth across your WAN. Options for compression are Stacker and Predictor.

> ▶ **Callback**—With callback, you dial into a router using a modem or ISDN and then disconnect. The other router then calls you back at a predefined number. This option is used for centralized billing and security reasons.

▶ **Multilink**—Multilink allows you to bundle together more than one link to create more bandwidth. (Traffic will load balance across the links.) For example, you can bundle two 64K channels together to get a combined 128K.

▶ **Authentication**—You can use authentication to verify a router's identity when it is connecting into your router. Options for authentication include CHAP and PAP.

You can think of LCP as the "negotiator" because it is responsible for negotiating these options between two routers.

> **EXAM ALERT**
>
> Know the various options of PPP. Remember CCMA (it sounds similar to CCNA), which stands for compression, callback, multilink, and authentication.

Authentication with PAP and CHAP

There are two types of authentications you can use with PPP:

▶ Password Authentication Protocol (PAP)

▶ Challenge Handshake Authentication Protocol (CHAP)

PAP uses a two-way authentication process where the username and password is sent followed by a response message indicating successful or failed authentication. CHAP, however, is much more paranoid about its authentication. It performs a three-way authentication process as shown in Figure 15.2, which takes place not only at the beginning of a connection, but also every two minutes. As if that wasn't paranoid enough, CHAP never sends the password across the link. Instead, an MD5 hash is used to mask the password.

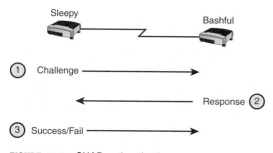

FIGURE 15.2 CHAP authentication.

Configuration

Configuring authentication is a four-step process:

1. Configure your hostname.

2. Configure the username and password list for other routers to authenticate to your router.

3. Enable PPP encapsulation.

4. Enable PAP or CHAP authentication.

The hostname takes on a special significance with PPP because it is used as the username to authenticate to another router. For example, suppose that you had two routers named Sleepy and Bashful, as shown in Figure 15.3. For Sleepy, its hostname is used as the username to authenticate to Bashful. For Bashful, its hostname is used as the username to authenticate to Sleepy. Use the hostname command to configure the hostname on each router:

Sleepy:

```
Router(config)#hostname Sleepy
```

Bashful:

```
Router(config)#hostname Bashful
```

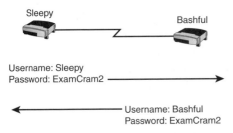

FIGURE 15.3 PPP configuration example.

Next, configure the username and password for other routers to authenticate to you. For the Sleepy router, you will need to configure a username and password for the Bashful router to authenticate to it. Likewise, you will need to configure a username and password for the Sleepy router to authenticate to the Bashful router. Both routers must use the same password. Use the global configuration username command to configure your username and password. The syntax for this command is

username *name* **password** *password*

For example,

Sleepy:

```
Sleepy(config)#username Bashful password ExamCram2
```

Bashful:

```
Bashful(config)#username Sleepy password ExamCram2
```

> **TIP**
>
> The hostnames and passwords are case sensitive. The hostname `sleepy` is different from the hostname `sleepy`. Make sure that you check the case of your letters when configuring PPP authentication.

The third step in configuring PPP is to enable PPP encapsulation on the interface using the encapsulation command. For example, to configure PPP encapsulation on the ISDN BRI 0 interface, type the following:

```
Sleepy(config)#interface bri 0
Sleepy(config-if)#encapsulation ppp
```

Finally, you will need to configure your authentication. The interface level command to do this is

```
ppp authentication [chap ¦ chap pap ¦ pap]
```

If you choose the chap pap option, it will try CHAP authentication first, and if that fails, it will try PAP. Newer IOS versions (12.3 and 12.4) will also support EAP, MS-Chap, and MS-Chap version 2. Following is the final configuration for the two routers using CHAP authentication:

Sleepy:

```
Router(config)#hostname Sleepy
Sleepy(config)#username Bashful password ExamCram2
Sleepy(config)#interface bri0
Sleepy(config-if)#encapsulation ppp
Sleepy(config-if)#ppp authentication chap
```

Bashful:

```
Router(config)#hostname Bashful
Bashful(config)#username Sleepy password ExamCram2
Bashful(config)#interface bri0
Bashful(config-if)#encapsulation ppp
Bashful(config-if)#ppp authentication chap
```

Verification and Troubleshooting

Verifying and troubleshooting PPP can be done with two commands:

- ► `show interfaces`

- ► `debug ppp authentication`

The `show interfaces` command will show you if the line protocol is up or down and the state of LCP. LCP will report in the closed state if it was unable to establish a connection to another router. Following is a sample output from the Sleepy router:

```
Sleepy(config)#show interfaces bri0
BRI0 is up, line protocol is up
Hardware is BRI
  MTU 1500 bytes, BW 64 Kbit, DLY 20000 usec, rely 255/255, load 1/255
  Encapsulation PPP, loopback not set, keepalive not set
 LCP Open
Closed: IPXCP
Listen: CCP
Open: IPCP, CDPCP
<...output omitted...>
```

The `debug ppp authentication` command will show you your authentication as it happens. Following is the output of this command on a router using CHAP authentication:

```
Sleepy#debug ppp authentication
PPP bri0: Send CHAP challenge id=34 to remote
PPP bri0: CHAP challenge from Bashful
PPP bri0: CHAP response received from Bashful
PPP bri0: CHAP response id=34 received from Bashful
PPP bri0: send CHAP success id=34 to remote
```

Frame Relay

Frame Relay is a scalable WAN solution that is often used as an alternative to leased lines when leased lines prove to be cost prohibitive. With Frame Relay, you can have a single serial interface on a router connecting into multiple remote sites through virtual circuits.

Concepts and Terminology

You should be familiar with many terms when working with Frame Relay. The following sections introduce you to these terms and their definitions.

Virtual Circuits and Network Design

Your virtual circuits can be either permanent or switched. A permanent virtual circuit (PVC) is always connected and, once up, operates very much like a leased line. A switched virtual circuit (SVC) is more like DDR with ISDN; the circuit is established only when it is needed. Of these two, PVCs are much more common.

DLCI

Circuits are identified by data-link connection identifiers (DLCI). DLCIs are assigned by your provider and are used between your router and the Frame Relay provider. In other words, DLCIs are locally significant.

For example, in Figure 15.4, there are three routers named Sleepy, Grumpy, and Bashful. The Sleepy router is connected to a Frame Relay provider that provides permanent virtual circuits to both the Bashful and Grumpy routers. DLCI 100 defines the PVC to Bashful, and DLCI 200 defines the PVC to Grumpy. Although it is not shown in the figure, Bashful and Grumpy will likewise have DLCIs to define their PVCs back to Sleepy.

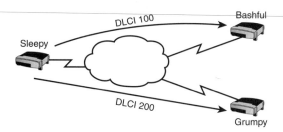

FIGURE 15.4 Frame Relay PVCs.

As an analogy, DLCIs are like shipping docks. If you work for a shipping company, you might have several ships attached to docks that are each going to a different destination. When you have a package to ship, you just need to take it to the ship headed for the destination. It is the captain's job to know how to reach the destination.

DLCIs are like these docks. They are significant only on your side. You send your packet out the relevant DLCI, and the provider's job is to figure out how to get that frame to its destination.

LMI

Behind the scenes is a little helper called the local management interface (LMI) that works as a status inquiry and reporting message. LMI messages are sent between your router and the Frame Relay provider's equipment to verify and report on the status of your PVC. The three possible states that your PVC can be in are

▸ **Active**—Active is good. Active means that everything is up and operational.

▸ **Inactive**—Inactive is bad. Inactive means that you are connected to your Frame Relay provider, but there is a problem with the far-end connection. The problem is most likely between the far-end router and its connection to the Frame Relay provider. You should contact your provider to troubleshoot the issue.

▸ **Deleted**—Deleted is also bad. Deleted means that there is a problem between your router and the Frame Relay provider's equipment. You should contact your provider to troubleshoot this issue.

Because of the frequency of LMI messages sent between your router and the Frame Relay provider, LMI is also used as a keepalive mechanism. Should your router stop hearing LMI messages, it will know that there is a problem with your PVC.

There are three types of LMI. These can be manually configured (discussed later in the configuration section) or, with IOS 11.2 and higher, can be autodetected. The three types of LMI are

▸ Cisco

▸ Ansi

▸ Q933A

CIR

The committed information rate (CIR) is the guaranteed rate at which you are allowed to pass data for a particular PVC. When ordering a PVC, you will request a local access rate (the bandwidth of the physical connection) and the CIR for a PVC. For example, you may order a T1, which has a local access rate of 1.544Mb, for the Sleepy router, a CIR of 128K for the PVC to Bashful, and a CIR of 512K for Grumpy.

BECN and FECN

Frame Relay is generous with its bandwidth. If there is no congestion on your link, you are allowed to burst above the CIR rate. Any traffic sent above your CIR is marked as being Discard Eligible (DE) and, in the event of congestion, will be dropped.

When congestion does occur, congestion notification messages are sent out to notify both the sending and the receiving routers that congestion has occurred and that they should slow down their transmission rates. A Backward Explicit Congestion Notification (BECN) is sent back to the sender and a Forward Explicit Congestion Notification (FECN) is sent forward to the destination to notify them of congestion.

A BECN message is sent back to the source only when the destination sends a frame back. Because the provider must wait for a message to return to set the BECN bit in the frame header, the FECN bit is sent to the destination to request some traffic to be sent back in the reverse direction. Without this, the source might never know that congestion has occurred.

In Figure 15.5, traffic is congested going from the Sleepy router to the Bashful router. A FECN is sent to the Bashful router, and a BECN is sent back to the Sleepy router.

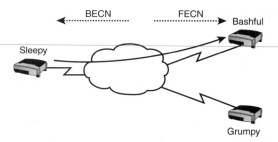

FIGURE 15.5   Congestion on a Frame Relay network.

Inverse-Arp

Frame Relay needs a mechanism to map Layer 3 addresses withLayer 2 Frame Relay DLCIs. This can be done through a static map command (shown later in the configuration section) or through inverse-arp. Just like Ethernet ARP, inverse-arp is used to map a Layer 3 address to a Layer 2 address. However, Ethernet ARP maps an IP address to a MAC address and inverse-arp works to map an IP address (or other protocol) to a DLCI.

In Figure 15.6 Sleepy will need a Layer 3 to Layer 2 map to connect to Bashful, which has IP address 10.0.0.2. Using inverse-arp, Sleepy will automatically create a map telling it to use DLCI 100 to get to IP address 10.0.0.2.

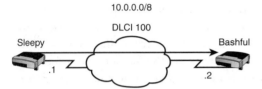

FIGURE 15.6   Inverse-arp example.

NBMA

Frame Relay is a nonbroadcast multi-access (NBMA) medium, which means that broadcast traffic is not allowed to traverse Frame Relay traffic. There are ways, however, to circumvent the NBMA nature of Frame Relay to allow broadcasts to cross the Frame Relay cloud. These are discussed in the configuration section.

The Split-Horizon Problem

The split-horizon rule (described in Chapter 10, "Basic Routing") states that a route learned on an interface should not be advertised back out that same interface. This poses a problem in NBMA networks where multiple circuits can connect to a single interface in a hub-and-spoke topology.

Hub-and-spoke topologies are commonly used to connect multiple branch offices to a headquarters office. For example, in Figure 15.7, the Bashful and Grumpy routers have circuits to the Sleepy router but not to each other. In this example, Sleepy is operating as the headquarters office. When Grumpy advertises its 13.0.0.0/8 network to the Sleepy router, it is sent into serial 0/0, but the Sleepy router is not allowed to send it back out serial0/0. This causes a problem because serial0/0 is also connected to the Bashful router. As a result, the Bashful router will never know about the 13.0.0.0/8 network.

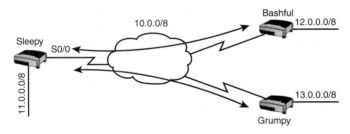

FIGURE 15.7   Split-horizon problem.

You have four options to get around the split-horizon problem:

- ▶ Disable split horizon with the `no ip split-horizon` command. If you are not careful, this could create a loop.

- ▶ Have a fully meshed topology where every router has a PVC to every other router. This can get expensive.

- ▶ Use static routes instead of dynamic routing protocols. This is not a scalable solution.

- ▶ Use subinterfaces. This is your best option.

Subinterfaces

A *subinterface* is a subset of an existing physical interface. As far as the router is concerned, the subinterface is a separate interface. By creating subinterfaces, each circuit can be on its own subnet.

There are two types of subinterfaces:

- ▶ Point-to-point—This maps a single IP subnet to a single subinterface and DLCI.

- ▶ Multipoint—This maps a single IP subnet to multiple DLCIs on a subinterface.

Of these two, only point-to-point subinterfaces address the issue of split horizon. In Figure 15.8, subinterfaces are used on the Sleepy router. Subinterface serial0/0.1 is connected to the Bashful router and subinterface serial0/0.2 is connected to the Grumpy router. Now when Grumpy advertises the 13.0.0.0/8 network to Sleepy, it is sent to the subinterface. Sleepy can forward that information on to the Bashful router because the Bashful router is connected to a logically (but not physically) different interface.

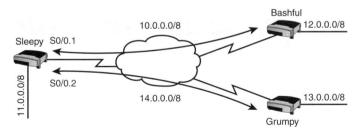

FIGURE 15.8   Split horizon with subinterfaces.

Configuration

Configuring Frame Relay involves the following steps:

- ▶ Changing the encapsulation for Frame Relay

- ▶ Configuring the LMI type (optional for IOS 11.2 or higher)

- ▶ Configuring the Frame Relay map (optional unless you are using subinterfaces)

- ▶ Configuring subinterfaces (optional)

- ▶ If using a point-to-point subinterface, configuring your DLCI

To begin, select the Frame Relay encapsulation on the interface. There are two types of Frame Relay encapsulations: Cisco and IETF. Cisco is the default. The syntax to set your encapsulation is

```
encapsulation frame-relay [ietf]
```

Next, you can configure the LMI type. The three LMI types are Cisco, Ansi, and Q933a. For IOS 11.2 and higher, the LMI type is automatically detected. For earlier IOS versions, enter the following command under the interface:

```
frame-relay lmi-type [cisco ¦ ansi ¦ q933a]
```

The third option, configuring a static Frame Relay map, is optional unless you are using subinterfaces. The Frame Relay map will map a Layer 3 address to a local DLCI. This step is optional because inverse-arp will automatically perform this map for you. The syntax for a Frame Relay map is as follows:

```
frame-relay map protocol address dlci [broadcast] [cisco ¦ ietf]
```

Table 15.2 describes each of these parameters.

TABLE 15.2 `frame-relay map` Command

Parameter	Description
protocol	Layer 3 protocol such as IP or IPX.
address	The Layer 3 address of the remote router (such as an IP address or IPX address).
Dlci	Your local DLCI defining your PVC to the remote router.
broadcast	Optional, this allows for broadcasts and multicasts to traverse your NBMA Frame Relay network.
Cisco | ietf	Optional, this allows you to change your Frame Relay encapsulation per DLCI.

For example, if you were connected to another router using DLCI 100 and the router had the IP address of 10.0.0.2, your `frame-relay map` statement would be

```
Router(config-if)#frame-relay map ip 10.0.0.2 100
```

If you want to use a routing protocol across your Frame Relay network, you will need to add the keyword `broadcast` to the end of this command. Routing protocols use broadcasts and multicasts by default, and Frame Relay does not enable broadcasts and multicasts without the use of the `broadcast` keyword. If you are using inverse-arp to create your maps for you, `inverse-arp` assumes that you want to use routing protocols and adds the broadcast feature for you.

If you are using a routing protocol in a hub-and-spoke topology, you will probably want to use subinterfaces to avoid the split-horizon problem. To configure a subinterface, remove the IP address off the main interface and put it under the subinterface. Configuring a subinterface involves assigning it a number and specifying the type. The following command creates point-to-point subinterface serial0/0.1:

```
Router(config)#interface serial0/0.1 point-to-point
```

To create a multipoint subinterface, enter multipoint instead:

```
Router(config)#interface  serial0/0.1 multipoint
```

After entering one of these commands you will be taken to the subinterface configuration mode where you can enter your IP address:

```
Router(config-subif)#ip address 10.0.0.2 255.0.0.0
```

If you are using a multipoint subinterface, you will need to configure frame-relay maps and you cannot rely on inverse-arp.

If you are using a point-to-point subinterface, you will need to assign a DLCI to the subinterface. This is only for point-to-point subinterfaces; this is not needed on the main interface or on multipoint subinterfaces. To assign a DLCI to a point-to-point subinterface, enter the following command under the subinterface:

```
frame-relay interface-dlci dlci
```

Now let's put the entire configuration together. The following configuration will configure Frame Relay for the Sleepy router using a point-to-point subinterface to connect to the Bashful router and a multipoint subinterface to connect to the Grumpy router. (A point-to-point could also have been used, but we'll use multipoint so you can see both methods.) Figure 15.9 shows the topology for the configuration.

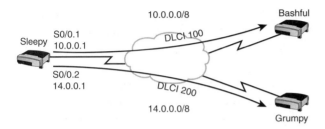

FIGURE 15.9 Frame Relay configuration.

```
interface serial 0/0
encapsulation frame-relay
!
! Take the IP address off the main interface:
no ip address
!
! Configure the connection to the Bashful router
interface serial 0/0.1 point-to-point
ip address 10.0.0.1 255.0.0.0
frame-relay interface-dlci 100
!
! Configure the connection to the Grumpy router
interface serial 0/0.2 multipoint
ip address 14.0.0.1 255.0.0.0
frame-relay map ip 14.0.0.3 200 broadcast
```

> **TIP**
>
> Many engineers like to configure their subinterface number to be the same as the DLCI. For example, if you had a subinterface connected to DLCI 100, your subinterface may be serial 0/0.100.

Verification and Troubleshooting

There are three verification commands and one troubleshooting command you should be familiar with for the exam.

The three commands you can use to verify your configuration are

▶ `show frame-relay lmi`

▶ `show frame-relay pvc`

▶ `show frame-relay map`

The **show frame-relay lmi** command (displayed in the following) will show LMI statistics, including the number of status inquiries sent and received. Because the status inquiries and responses are used as continuous keepalives, these should be incrementing.

```
LMI Statistics for interface Serial1 (Frame Relay DTE) LMI TYPE = ANSI
   Invalid Unnumbered info 0        Invalid Prot Disc 0
   Invalid dummy Call Ref 0         Invalid Msg Type 0
   Invalid Status Message 0         Invalid Lock Shift 0
   Invalid Information ID 0          Invalid Report IE Len 0
   Invalid Report Request 0         Invalid Keep IE Len 0
   Num Status Enq. Sent 140         Num Status msgs Rcvd 139
   Num Update Status Rcvd 0         Num Status Timeouts 0
```

The **show frame-relay pvc** command (displayed in the following) will inform you of the status of your PVC. The status should read ACTIVE. This is also where you will see if your router is receiving BECN and FECN messages.

```
DLCI = 100, DLCI USAGE = LOCAL, PVC STATUS = ACTIVE, INTERFACE = Serial0/0

   input pkts 120          output pkts 70          in bytes 5122
   out bytes 3366          dropped pkts 0          in FECN pkts 0
   in BECN pkts 0          out FECN pkts 0         out BECN pkts 0
   in DE pkts 0            out DE pkts 0
   out bcast pkts 7        out bcast bytes 1366
   pvc create time 1d04h, last time pvc status changed 00:30:32
```

The **show frame-relay map** command (displayed in the following) will show you any static maps configured and maps created by inverse-arp. This command will also show you the status of your PVC.

```
Serial0/0 (up): ip 10.0.0.1 dlci 100(0x64,0x1840), dynamic,
           broadcast,, status defined, active
```

EXAM ALERT

Remember, the three show frame-relay commands and what they do. Show frame-relay lmi shows your LMI statistics, whereas show frame-relay pvc and show frame-relay map will show your PVC status.

For troubleshooting, you can execute the **debug frame-relay lmi** command. This command shows you LMI messages in real-time:

```
Serial 0/0 (out) : StEnq, clock 202121241, myseq 120, mineseen,
119, yourseen 140, DTE up
PVC IE 0x64, length 0x6, dlci 100, status 0, bandwidth 64000
```

VPNs

Although Frame Relay and leased lines are the ideal WAN solutions for most organizations, you may opt for an IPsec or Secure Socket Layer (SSL) virtual private network (VPN). There are several reasons why you may want to use a secure VPN:

- **Cost savings**—Packet-switched and dedicated leased lines may be too expensive for your organization. With IPSec and SSL VPNs, you can use your existing connection to the Internet for your WAN.

- **Backup**—If your organization requires high availability, IPSec and SSL VPNs can be used as a backup connection should your primary connection go down.

- **Security**—If you want an additional layer of security in your organization, you may want to use IPsec or SSL VPNs.

- **Telecommuters**—For the mobile and home user, IPSec and SSL VPNs are the only practical and secure solution for them to connect into your organization's network.

IPSec VPNs use a suite of IP security protocols to provide a means of securing TCP/IP communication. SSL VPNs use secure HTTP but work only with HTTP traffic. Of course, if that's all you knew about the two types, the exam would be too easy and we wouldn't want that, so let's take a look at these topics more in depth.

> **EXAM ALERT**
>
> You do not need to know how to configure IPSec or SSL VPNs for the CCENT or CCNA exam, but you do need to be familiar with how they work—including the reasons why you would use a VPN and their major components.

IPsec VPNs

IPsec provides the following security benefits:

- Authentication of every IP packet
- Verification of the data integrity for each packet
- Confidentiality of your packet payload
- Anti-replay protection to verify that each packet is unique

To accomplish these benefits, IPsec uses several components, including security protocols, key management exchanges, and security algorithms as described in Table 15.3.

TABLE 15.3 IPSec Components

IPSec Component	Description	Examples
Security Protocols	Methods that use security algorithms to secure communications	Authentication Header (AH) Encapsulating Security Payload (ESP)
Key Management	Responsible for exchanging secret keys that are used in the algorithms to secure IPSec VPNs	Internet Security Association and Key Management Protocol (ISAKMP) Internet Key Exchange (IKE) Secure Key Exchange Mechanism (SKEME) Oakley
Security Algorithms	The mathematical algorithms used to secure communications	Data Encryption Standard (DES) Triple DES (3DES) Advanced Encryption Standard (AES) Message Digest (MD5) Secure Hashing Algorithm (SHA-1)

The security protocols include encapsulating security payload (ESP) and authentication header (AH). Both define the headers (and, in the case of ESP, the trailers) involved when securing your communications. ESP provides confidentiality, integrity, origin authentication, and anti-replay (for more on these terms, see Chapter 9, "Basic Network Security"). AH does not provide confidentiality but does provide integrity, origin authentication, and optional partial sequence integrity for anti-replay.

NOTE

ESP uses IP protocol 50 and AH uses IP protocol 51. Make sure you have these protocols allowed through your firewall. Remember, these are IP protocols and not port numbers.

The headers and trailers used with ESP and AH depend on whether you are using your VPN in tunnel mode or transport mode. If you want to create a VPN between two networks, you will use tunnel mode. Tunnel mode is usually configured between a VPN appliance such as a router with VPN capabilities, Adaptive Security Appliance (ASA), or VPN Concentrator. If you are looking to protect two hosts, such as the communication between two servers on a network, you will use transport mode.

Figure 15.10 shows how your IP packet will have new headers and trailers when using AH and ESP in transport mode. AH adds a header between the original IP header and the Layer 4 (TCP or UDP) header. AH uses a mathematical process called *hashing* that is used for authentication. The process is similar to how police use fingerprints. A fingerprint is a small representation of who you are that can be used to verify your identity. In the same way, AH takes a fingerprint of your entire packet that is verified on the receiving side. The same mathematical process is run on both sides, and if the result is the same on both the sending and receiving sides, the message is considered authenticated.

In comparison, ESP adds a new ESP header and ESP trailer. These are used to encrypt your packet. Notice that the original IP header is not changed with transport mode. The ESP authentication trailer is added to the end, which works the same way as the AH header by authenticating the packet.

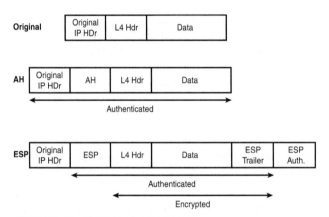

FIGURE 15.10 IPsec in transport mode.

Figure 15.11 shows how your IP packet will have new headers and trailers when using AH and ESP in tunnel mode. Recall that tunnel mode is used when protecting communication between two gateways. The big difference between transport mode and tunnel mode from a technical standpoint is that with tunnel mode the IP packet is encapsulated into another packet by adding a new IP header that is removed on arrival at the VPN gateway endpoint. This is a lot like transporting your car on a ferry boat. The original payload in your car does not change, but now you have a new means of transport. When you get to the destination, your car will get off the ferry boat and resume driving. In the same way, when your packet gets to the far end destination, it strips off the new tunnel header and resumes communication as the original IP packet.

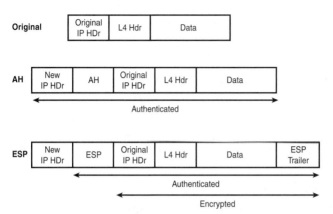

FIGURE 15.11 IPsec in tunnel mode.

The headers used with ESP and AH rely on mathematical algorithms to secure your communication. If every implementation used the same variables in its formula, you would get the same mathematical result every time you sent the same data packet. This obviously would not be very secure, so to ensure uniqueness with your IPSec implementation, a secret key can be used that acts as a unique variable during the mathematical process so that the results are different with each implementation of IPSec. This key is called a *shared key* because both VPN endpoints will use the same key. Keeping this key secret is important, just as it is to keep the key to your house protected. It doesn't matter how many locks you have on your house, if people have access to your key, they can get into your home.

IPSec uses the Internet Key Exchange (IKE) to periodically exchange your secret keys. IKE uses UDP 500, so make sure you have that port unfiltered on your external firewalls to allow IKE to communicate. IKE encompasses three components:

- **Oakley**—Uses Diffie-Helman (DH) algorithm to generate and exchange secret keys.

- **ISAKMP**—Protocol framework that forms the basis of key exchange by defining the message formats and types.

- **SKEME**—Uses public key encryption to authenticate keying material.

The details of how each of these works is outside the scope of the exam. Do know, however, that Diffie-Helman (DH) is the algorithm used within IKE to generate and exchange secret keys. The Diffie-Helman algorithm uses its own set of keys to secure the exchange of keys used for secure IPSec communication. Think of it as storing a key within a locked box. You need to unlock the box with a different key to the get to the key inside the box.

Unlike IPSec shared keys, Diffie-Helman uses public key cryptography where each VPN tunnel endpoint will have its own public and private key. You do not need to be familiar with the inner workings of public key cryptography for the CCNA exam; that is covered in the professional certification tracks such as Cisco Certified Network Professional (CCNP) and Cisco Certified Security Professional (CCSP).

The last components of IPSec VPNs are the security algorithms used. There are two types of security algorithms that you need to be aware of:

> **Encryption algorithms**—These provide confidentiality of your data. Encryption algorithms include Advanced Encryption Standard (AES), Data Encryption Standard (DES), and Triple DES (3DES)

> **Message integrity algorithms**—These provide you with authentication and integrity. Message integrity algorithms include Message Digest 5 (MD5) and Secure Hashing Algorithm (SHA-1)

These security algorithms do have a trade-off in that although they secure your communication, they also require processing power and their encryption over-head can reduce the amount of actual throughput you get on your network. Still, the cost savings, security, and flexibility you get with IPSec VPNs are attractive to many network managers.

SSL VPNs

All the components of IPSec can make VPNs very complicated. A simpler alter-native is to use Secure Socket Layer (SSL) VPNs. SSL is used frequently to secure Hypertext Transfer Protocol (HTTP) traffic, such as when you are accessing a secure e-commerce site. Many organizations use HTTP for internal intranets and for thin client communication. With Cisco's Web VPN solution, users can authenticate first to a Cisco Adaptive Security Appliance (ASA) via a secure web interface before being allowed access to web applications. These are easy for end users and administrators but have the disadvantage of working only with web-based applications.

Exam Prep Questions

1. Frame Relay NBMA networks present problems with split horizon if the topology is not a full mesh. What could you do to get around issues of split horizon in Frame Relay networks? Select the best answer.

   ○ **A.** Enable the command `split-horizon frame-relay` on each serial interface.

   ○ **B.** Create subinterfaces and put each DLCI on its own subinterface.

   ○ **C.** Disable routing protocols on Frame Relay interfaces.

   ○ **D.** Create static routes on your spoke routers.

2. Which of the following are components of the LCP phase of PPP? Select all that apply.

   ○ **A.** Compression

   ○ **B.** Authentication

   ○ **C.** QoS

   ○ **D.** Multilink

3. What are the three Frame-Relay LMI types? Select three.

   ○ **A.** HDLC

   ○ **B.** Cisco

   ○ **C.** Q933A

   ○ **D.** IETF

   ○ **E.** ANSI

4. Given the following configurations, why is the router not routing traffic?

```
router rip
 network 10.0.0.0
 network 11.0.0.0
!
interface fastethernet0/0
 ip address 10.0.0.1 255.0.0.0
!
interface serial0/0
 ip address 11.0.0.1 255.0.0.0
 encapsulation frame-relay
 frame-relay map ip 11.0.0.2 255.0.0.0
```

    ○ **A.** RIP configuration is incorrect.

    ○ **B.** IP addresses are incorrect.

    ○ **C.** The `frame-relay map` statement is incorrect.

    ○ **D.** Router is missing a `static route` statement.

5. You have a Cisco router set to the default encapsulation. You connect it to a Juniper router running HDLC encapsulation. Why are the two routers unable to communicate?

    ○ **A.** The default encapsulation on the Cisco router is PPP. You must change it to HDLC.

    ○ **B.** The default encapsulation on the Cisco router is IETF. You must change it to HDLC.

    ○ **C.** The Cisco HDLC implementation is proprietary and is therefore incompatible with other vendor's HDLC implementations.

    ○ **D.** Cisco routers can only connect to other Cisco routers. You must replace the Juniper router with a Cisco router.

6. What commands can you enter to check the state of your Frame-Relay PVC? Select all that apply.

    ○ **A.** `show frame-relay lmi`

    ○ **B.** `show frame-relay pvc`

    ○ **C.** `show frame-relay map`

    ○ **D.** `show frame-relay status`

    ○ **E.** `show frame-relay`

7. Which of the following algorithms is responsible for secure key exchange?

    ○ **A.** 3DES

    ○ **B.** SHA-1

    ○ **C.** Diffie-Helman

    ○ **D.** AES

8. Which of the following are reasons why you may want to implement a VPN? (Select all that apply.)

    ○ **A.** To save on costs

    ○ **B.** To simplify your WAN configuration

    ○ **C.** As a backup solution to your primary WAN

    ○ **D.** To provide an additional layer of security

9. Which of the following is not provided by AH? Select all that apply.

    ○ **A.** Data integrity

    ○ **B.** Data confidentiality

    ○ **C.** Origin authentication

    ○ **D.** Username authentication

Answers to Exam Prep Questions

1. Answer B is correct. You should create a subinterface for each DLCI. This will require a different subnet on each subinterface, but you resolve split-horizon issues. Answer A is incorrect because there is not a `split-horizon frame-relay` command. Answers C and D would technically resolve your problem, but they would limit the functionality of your routers. Therefore, answers C and D are not the best answers.

2. Answers A, B, and D are all correct. The LCP phase is responsible for the initial link-setup and negotiating options such as compression, callback, multilink, and authentication. Answer C is incorrect because this not a component of LCP.

3. Answers B, C, and E are correct. Answer A is incorrect because HDLC is a WAN Layer 2 encapsulation, not a Frame-Relay LMI type. Answer D is incorrect because IETF is a Frame-Relay encapsulation type, not a Frame-Relay LMI type.

4. Answer C is correct. If you were not using routing protocols, the `frame-relay map` statement would be correct. However, because you are using a routing protocol, you must have the broadcast keyword at the end for routing protocols to work. Answer A is incorrect because RIP is configured correctly. Answer B is incorrect because the IP addresses are correct. Answer D is incorrect because the router is running RIP and does not need a static route.

5. Answer C is correct. Cisco's HDLC contains a proprietary data field that makes it incompatible with other vendors' implementations of HDLC. Answer A and B are incorrect because the default encapsulation is HDLC, not PPP or IETF. Although answer D would make some Cisco salespeople happy, answer D is not the correct answer either. Cisco can communicate with other vendors but not with the default encapsulation.

6. Answers B and C are correct. Answer A is incorrect because `show frame-relay lmi` shows your LMI statistics and not your PVC status. Answers D and E are incorrect because these are invalid commands.

7. Answer C is correct. Diffie-Helman is part of the Internet Key Exchange (IKE) and is the algorithm used to securely and dynamically exchange keys. Answers A and D are wrong because these are encryption algorithms used to provide data confidentiality. Answer B is incorrect because this is a message integrity algorithm used to provide authentication and integrity.

8. Answers A, C, and D are correct. Answer A is correct because you will save costs by using your existing Internet connection. Answer B is incorrect because it will add to the complexity of your configurations and not reduce it. Answer C is correct because companies can use a VPN as a backup connection to their primary WAN by failing over to their Internet connection. Finally, answer D is correct because VPNs can encrypt and/or hash your packets.

9. Answers B and D are correct. Answer B is correct because Authentication Header (AH) does not provide confidentiality through encryption algorithms; this is accomplished by using ESP. Answer D is correct because AH works with the data packets themselves and there is no username authentication (this would occur at a higher layer in the OSI model). Answers A and C are incorrect because AH does provide data integrity and origin authentication.

CHAPTER SIXTEEN

Advanced IP Concepts

Terms you'll need to understand:

✓ VLSM
✓ Classful and Classless
✓ Route Summarization
✓ Contiguous
✓ Longest Match
✓ NAT, PAT, and Overload
✓ IPv6

Techniques you'll need to master:

✓ Advanced Subnetting
✓ IP Route Table Interpretation
✓ Predicting the Routing Decision
✓ Route Summarization
✓ Configuring NAT and PAT
✓ Recognizing and Compressing IPv6 Addresses

Introduction

This chapter looks at the relationship between the IP address and subnet mask in more detail, as well as how it can be manipulated for more efficient network functionality. The Network Address Translation/Port Address Translation service is also explained and sample configurations are demonstrated. Finally, IP Version 6 is introduced and some of its features are explained.

VLSM

Variable Length Subnet Masking or VLSM (RFC 1812) can be defined as the capability to apply more than one subnet mask to a given class of addresses throughout a routed system. Although this is common practice in modern networks, there was a time when this was impossible because the routing protocols in use could not support it. Classful protocols such as RIPv1 do not include the subnet mask of advertised networks in their routing updates; therefore, they cannot possibly learn the existence of more than one mask length. Only classless routing protocols—EIGRP, OSPF, RIPv2, IS-IS, and BGP—include the subnet mask for the networks they advertise in their routing updates and thus publish a level of detail that makes VLSM possible.

The main push for VLSM came from the need to make networks the right size.

Subnetting logically creates the appropriately-sized networks, but without the capability for routing protocols to advertise the existence (for example) of both a /26 and a /30 network within the same system. Prior to VLSM-capable routing protocols, the network in our example would have been confined to using only /26 masks throughout the system. The use of VLSM has two main advantages that are closely linked:

▶ It makes network addressing more efficient.

▶ Provides the capability to perform route summarization (discussed in the next section).

EXAM ALERT

Know the definition of VLSM and its two main advantages.

An illustration of the need for VLSM is shown in Figure 16.1.

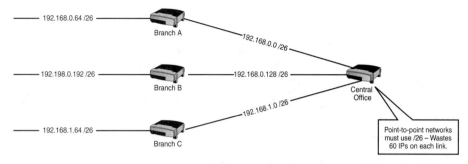

FIGURE 16.1   Inefficient addressing without VLSM.

The diagram shows several branch offices using subnetted Class C (/26) addresses that provide each branch with 62 possible host IPs. The branches are connected to the central office via point-to-point WAN links. The ideal mask to use for such a link is /30 because it provides only 2 hosts, one for each end of the link. The problem arises when the routing protocols are configured: Prior to VLSM, the /30 networks could not be used because the /26 networks existed in the same system and the classful routing protocols could only advertise one mask per class of address. All networks, including the little /30 links, had to use the same mask of /26. This wastes 60 IP addresses on each WAN link.

With the implementation of VLSM-capable routing protocols, we can deploy a /30 mask on the point-to-point links, and the routing protocols can advertise them as /30s along with the /26s in the branches because the subnet mask for each network is included in the routing updates. Figure 16.2 illustrates the preferred, optimized addressing scheme that takes advantage of VLSM.

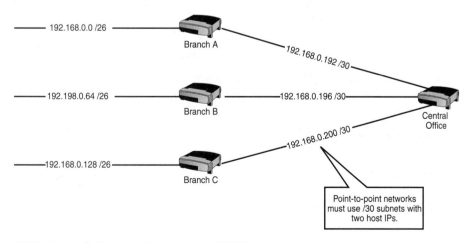

FIGURE 16.2   Optimized addressing using VLSM.

Note that using VLSM has allowed us to make the point-to-point link networks the ideal size (two hosts on each) using /30 masks. This has allowed us to use a single subnetted Class C network for all the addressing requirements in this scenario—and as you'll see, it makes a perfect opportunity to summarize these routes. This is what is meant by "more efficient addressing"—in other words, making networks the right size without depleting the limited address space or limiting future growth.

Route Summarization

If subnetting is the process of lengthening the mask to create multiple smaller subnets from a single larger network, route summarization can be described as shortening the mask to include several smaller networks into one larger network address. As the network grows large, the number of individual networks listed in the IP route table becomes too big for routers to handle effectively. They get slower, drop packets, and even crash. This, of course, is an undesirable state of affairs. With more than 160,000 routes (at the time of this writing, anyway) known to major Internet routers, some way to reduce the number of entries is not only desirable, but also critical.

In the previous VLSM example, all the subnets for the branches and the WAN links were created from the 192.168.0.0 /24 Class C network. If we take that diagram and put it into context, we can see how route summarization can reduce the number of entries in the route table, as shown in Figure 16.3.

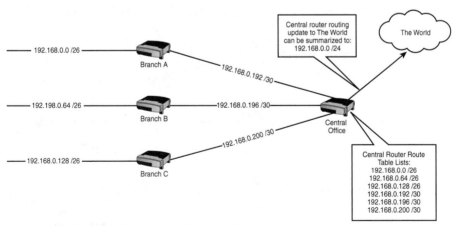

FIGURE 16.3 Simple route summarization example.

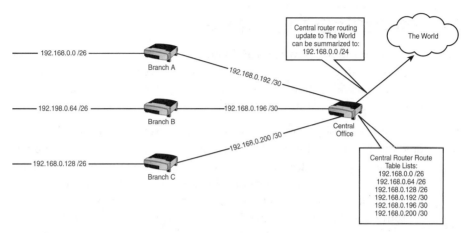

The Central Office router can either send a routing update with all the subnets it knows about listed individually, or it can send a single line in the update that essentially says, "Send anything that starts with 192.168.0 to me." Both methods work; the issue is one of scalability. No router will ever collapse under the load of advertising six subnets, but make it six thousand subnets and it makes a huge difference in performance if you summarize as much as possible.

Route summarization takes a set of contiguous networks or subnets and groups them together using a shorter subnet mask. The advantages of summarization are that it reduces the number of entries in the route table, which reduces load on the router and network overhead, and hides instability in the system behind the summary, which remains valid even if summarized networks are unavailable.

NOTE

The word "contiguous" sometimes confuses people. It is not a typo of "continuous"; the word means "adjacent or adjoining." For example, when we make subnets using a 16 increment, the first four NetIDs are .0, .16, .32, and .48. Those four subnets are contiguous because they are adjacent to each other. If we take the last four subnets from that same increment, .192, .208, .224, and .240, they are contiguous with each other, but not with the first four—there are a bunch of subnets between the two sets.

EXAM ALERT

Know the definition and advantages of route summarization.

Summarization Guidelines

It is important to follow a few rules and guidelines when summarizing. Serious routing problems will happen otherwise—such as routers advertising networks inaccurately and possibly duplicating other routers' advertisements, sub-optimal or even totally incorrect routing, and severe data loss.

The first rule is to design your networks with summarization in mind, even if you don't need it yet. This means that you will group contiguous subnets together behind the router that will summarize them—you do not want to have some subnets from a summarized group behind some other router. The summary is essentially saying, "I can reach the networks represented by this summary; send any traffic for them through me." If one (or more) of the networks behind the summarizing router is unavailable, traffic will be dropped—but not by the summarizing router, because the summary is still valid. The packet will get routed to the router that connects to the dead network, and dropped there. Advance planning, including making plenty of room for future growth, will give you a solid, scalable network design that readily lends itself to summarizing. Figure 16.4 shows a badly designed network that will be almost impossible to summarize because the subnets are discontiguous, with individual subnets scattered all over the system.

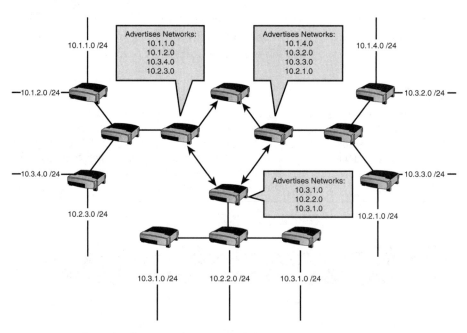

FIGURE 16.4   Poor planning prevents proper performance.

The second rule is to summarize into the core of your network. The core is where the bigger, faster, busier routers are—like the Central Office router in the previous example. These routers have the job of dealing with high volumes of traffic headed for all different areas of the network, so we do not want to burden them with big, highly detailed route tables. The further you get from the core, the more detail the routers need to get traffic to the correct destination network. It's much like using a map to drive to a friend's house; you don't need a great deal of detail when you are on the highway, but when you get into the residential areas, you need to know very precise information if you have a hope of finding the place.

Figure 16.5 illustrates the same network after your friendly neighborhood Cisco Certified Internetwork Expert has spent the afternoon readdressing the network and configuring summarization. This network will scale beautifully and have minimal performance issues (at least because of route table and routing update overhead).

Following these rules will give you one of the additional benefits of summarization as well: hiding instability in the summarized networks. Let's say that one of the branches is having serious spanning-tree problems because an MCP was allowed to configure a Cisco switch. (This is actually a felony in some states.) That route could be "flapping"—up, down, up, down—as spanning-tree wreaks havoc with your network. The router will be doing its job, sending out updates every time the route flaps. If we were not summarizing, those flapping messages would propagate through the entire corporate system, putting a totally unnecessary and performance-robbing load on the routers. Once you summarize, the summary is stable: It can't flap because it is not a real network. It's just like a spokesperson at a press conference: "The rumors of a fire at the Springfield plant have had no impact on production whatsoever." Meanwhile, the Springfield plant could be a charred hulk. The summary is still valid, and traffic will still be sent to the router connected to the flapping network. This keeps people from asking any more questions about the Springfield fire...however, if someone were to send a shipment to Springfield, it would be hastily redirected to another site (or dropped). All we have done is hide the problem from the rest of the world, so we don't flood the Net with rapid-fire routing updates.

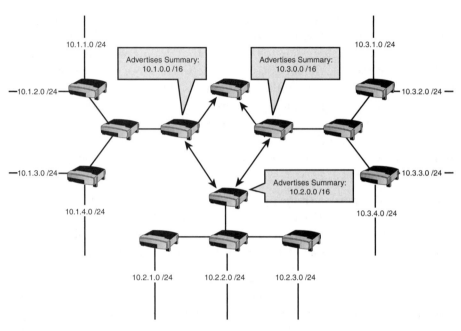

FIGURE 16.5   Proper planning prevents poor performance.

Determining Summary Addresses

When using classless routing protocols, creating summary addresses is a totally manual process. Classful routing protocols perform automatic summarization, but that is not as fancy as it sounds. They simply treat any subnet as the classful address from which it was created, which works if your networks are built with this in mind; however, in reality that is too simplistic and real networks need more customized summarization. The upshot of all this is that you need to understand how to determine the summary address given a set of networks to be summarized, and you also need to be able to figure out if a particular network is included in a given summary.

Remember that summarization is exactly the opposite of subnetting; in fact, another term for summarization is supernetting. (You might also see it called aggregation.) When we subnet, we lengthen the mask, doubling the number of networks each time we add an extra bit to the mask. Supernetting does the opposite: For each bit we retract or shorten the mask, we combine networks into groups that follow the binary increment numbers.

To illustrate this, let's look at the private Class B address space. These networks are listed as follows:

172.16.0.0 /16

172.17.0.0 /16

172.18.0.0 /16

172.19.0.0 /16

172.20.0.0 /16

172.21.0.0 /16

172.22.0.0 /16

172.23.0.0 /16

172.24.0.0 /16

172.25.0.0 /16

172.26.0.0 /16

172.27.0.0 /16

172.28.0.0 /16

172.29.0.0 /16

172.30.0.0 /16

172.31.0.0 /16

If you look carefully, you will notice that the range of networks is identified in the second octet. The octet where the range is happening is referred to as the interesting octet. This is your first clue where to begin your summarization.

The next step is to figure out what the binary values of the network's range are. The binary values for the interesting octet are shown in Figure 16.6.

```
16 = 0 0 0 1 0  0 0 0
17 = 0 0 0 1 0  0 0 1
18 = 0 0 0 1 0  0 1 0
19 = 0 0 0 1 0  0 1 1
20 = 0 0 0 1 0  1 0 0
21 = 0 0 0 1 0  1 0 1
22 = 0 0 0 1 0  1 1 0
23 = 0 0 0 1 0  1 1 1
24 = 0 0 0 1 1  0 0 0
25 = 0 0 0 1 1  0 0 1
26 = 0 0 0 1 1  0 1 0
27 = 0 0 0 1 1  0 1 1
28 = 0 0 0 1 1  1 0 0
29 = 0 0 0 1 1  1 0 1
30 = 0 0 0 1 1  1 1 0
31 = 0 0 0 1 1  1 1 1
```
FIGURE 16.6 Binary values for Class B private range second octet.

You should see a pattern in the binary values: The first four bits are all the same. The range is actually happening in the last four bits in the second octet; those four bits range from 0000 through 1111; the first four bits are common for all 16 networks in the range.

The next step is to identify those common bits. While you are learning how to do this, it's a good idea to write out the binary for the range and draw a line that represents the boundary between the common bits and the variable bits in the range. Remember, be absolutely sure that your boundary line is in the right place: For all the networks in the range, everything to the left of the line must be identical, and everything to the right will be the ranging values.

The next step is easy. We are about to summarize: All we need to do is to build a subnet mask that puts a 1 under all of the common bits in the range, and a 0 under everything else—Ones to the left of the boundary, and zeroes to the right, as shown in Figure 16.7.

The last step is to actually create the summary statement. A summary is always an IP address plus a mask; the IP is usually a Net ID, and it should be the first network in the range. In our example, the first NetID is 172.16.0.0 so that is the IP we will use. For the mask, the first octet is the same in the whole range, and we have figured out that the first four bits in the second octet are always the same. Remembering that a mask is always a string of 1s followed by a string of 0s, this means that we should mask all eight bits in the first octet and the first four in the second octet, so our mask looks like this:

11111111.11110000.00000000.00000000

That can also be expressed as

255.240.0.0 or /12

So, our summary statement becomes:

172.16.0.0 255.240.0.0

or

172.16.0.0 /12

Reverse engineering this is the same process. You are given a summary statement and asked what networks it includes. The octet in which the mask changes from 1s to 0s is the interesting one, where the range will be defined. Jot down the address and mask in that octet in binary and see what possible values are in the range. Then check the networks to see if those are in the range. Figure 16.8 gives an example.

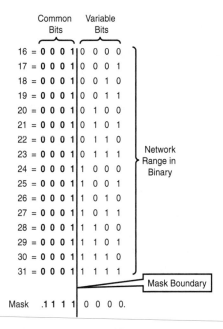

FIGURE 16.7   Identifying and masking the common bits in a summary.

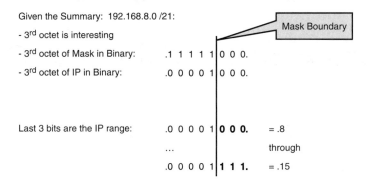

Given the Summary: 192.168.8.0 /21:

- 3rd octet is interesting

- 3rd octet of Mask in Binary:

- 3rd octet of IP in Binary:

Last 3 bits are the IP range:

Therefore, the range of networks is 192.168.8.0 through 192.168.15.0

- Network 192.168.12.0 /24 would be in this range.

- Network 192.168.16.0 /24 would not be in this range.

- Network 192.168.0.0 /24 would not be in this range.

FIGURE 16.8   Summary address analysis.

The Routing Decision

Routers perform the basic function of switching packets inbound on one interface to another interface outbound. The decision as to which outbound interface to use is based on information stored in the Route Table. The Route Table always stores the best known route to a particular destination network. There are several criteria the router uses to choose which routes are the best, and we now examine four of them.

Administrative Distance

If a router learns of two routes to a given network, say one from RIP and one from OSPF, the routing information source with the lowest administrative distance (AD) will be chosen and used. RIP has an AD of 120, and OSPF has an AD of 110. OSPF, therefore, is more trusted as a source of routing information, and the route learned from OSPF will be installed in the route table.

> **EXAM ALERT**
>
> You should know the ADs of all the routing protocols listed in Table 16.1.

TABLE 16.1   Administrative Distances

Protocol	Default Administrative Distance
Connected Interface	0
Static Route	1
EIGRP	90
IGRP	100
OSPF	110
IS-IS	115
RIP	120

Valid Next-Hop Address

In all but a few exceptional cases (notably with some static route implementations), the router cannot install a route in the route table unless the next-hop address specified by that route is valid. In other words, if the device to which traffic destined for a particular network must be sent is not available, the route is invalid and will be dropped from the route table.

Best Metric

Given that we might learn more than one route to a given network from any one protocol, the router distinguishes between these routes by comparing the metrics. A *metric* is a measurement of how good a particular route is, expressed as a number. Each routing protocol uses different metrics and different algorithms to calculate them as you saw in Chapter 10, "Basic Routing." The simple rule is: The lower the metric, the better the route. If two routes have equal metrics, more than one route can be used at a time. (The router will load balance using all routes equally.)

Longest Match

The Longest Match rule is the criterion that a router will use to determine the best route given a choice between two or more that are very similar. The longest match refers to the longest prefix length, or the longest matching string of bits in the route as compared to the destination address of the packet being routed.

The concept behind this rule is very simple: The longer the match in the prefix, the more detailed the route is. Let us look at an example to clarify; Figure 16.9 shows a simplified output of the IP Route Table:

Simplified IP Route Table:

172.16.8.0 /24 via 192.168.0.1, Ethernet 0
172.16.10.0 /30 via 192.168.0.1, Ethernet 0
172.16.10.64 /26 via 192.168.1.1, Ethernet 1
172.16.10.0 /24 via 192.168.2.1, Ethernet 2
0.0.0.0 /0 via 24.16.5.65, Serial 0

FIGURE 16.9 The longest prefix match is the best route.

Assume that a packet has arrived at the router with a destination IP of 172.16.10.131. The router examines its IP route table and discovers that there are five entries in the route table. The entries are sorted per network according to the length of the mask for that network.

The first entry (172.16.0.0 /24) is compared to the destination IP of the packet. The /24 in the route table entry specifies that the first 24 bits of the prefix should be compared for the longest match. Because the destination IP of the packet is 172.16.10.131, the first 24 bits do not match, and this entry is not a possible route for this packet.

The router repeats the process for the remaining four entries. The second, third, and fourth entries all match for their respective prefix lengths of /28, /26, and /24. The fifth entry is a default route, which by definition matches any address, but with a /0 prefix length.

So now the router must decide which entry is the best route to use for the packet in question. All of the entries are valid, but the one with the longest prefix length match—172.16.10.128 /28—is chosen as the best. The default route is a poor match in this case because there are other, more precise routes with longer prefix matches.

Having made its routing decision, the router switches the packet out the Ethernet 0 interface and begins processing the next packet.

EXAM ALERT

Interpretation of the IP route table is a fundamental and highly testable skill. Make sure that you are fully able to make the correct routing decision given a destination IP and a sample output of `show ip route`.

IPv6

Up to this point, when we talked about IP or an IP address, we were referring to IP Version 4. IPv4 was created to build a defense department network in the early 1970s. At the time, no one foresaw that the Internet as we know it today was going to happen. The designers of the TCP/IP suite of protocols did not plan for their little project to balloon into the largest network in the world and revolutionize the commercial, cultural, and communications behavior of the whole planet.

But it did, and a couple problems came to light rather quickly when the Internet started to really catch on. One really tricky one was that the address "space" was originally handed out without quite enough thought and planning as to who got what size chunks, and what routers would be responsible for those chunks. At the time it didn't matter; there were plenty of addresses to go around. But as the routers started to get really large route tables, with all these networks being added, they had trouble dealing with it. Routers at the time were relatively small and slow, and when the route tables became so large, they were overloaded, slow to do their jobs, and generally poor performers. Solutions were urgently needed because the Internet was growing very fast and the problem was only getting worse.

The solutions came in things like VLSM-capable protocols, route summarization, a reassignment and redistribution of addresses, and the NAT service. These solutions have allowed the IPv4 address space to continue to function and serve as the address system for the Internet, but the second problem is one we can't get around: The mathematical reality is that there are not enough IP addresses available to meet the demand (especially in Europe and Asia). More people want Internet addresses than there are addresses to hand out.

This is where IPv6 comes in. Whereas an IPv4 address is a 32-bit string, theoretically providing more than 4 billion IP addresses (for the sake of clarity I'll ignore the fact that a large number of theses addresses are not really usable). An IPv6 address is 128 bits long, providing about $3.4[ts]10^{38}$ possible addresses, or as the story goes, 500,000,000,000,000,000,000,000,000,000 addresses for each of the 6.5 billion people on the planet. Running out of IPv6 addresses is not expected to be a problem.

Along with the sheer number of addresses available, IPv6 also cleans up a few of the issues with IPv4, making the operation and management of large internetworks easier and more efficient, and adds some useful new functionality as well. So now we can easily envision a world where anything we want can have an Internet IP address (including silly things such as the fridge), where an Internet-enabled mobile phone can keep its IP address as it moves across the globe, and all the difficulty and headache caused by using VPNs through NAT disappears.

IPv6 Address Allocation

An organization called the Internet Corporation for Assigned Network Numbers (ICANN) has the overall responsibility for dividing up the IPv6 address space. They do so with the benefit of a better understanding of the global demand for Internet IP addresses and the luxury of a huge number of addresses to hand out.

The system works like this: First , remember that for the Internet to work well, we need to use route summarization so that the route tables don't get huge and slow the routers down. Route summarization works best if every router is responsible only for its "branch of the tree," with smaller branches feeding into larger and larger ones as we get closer to the core or trunk of the tree. This allows the possibility for a single router to advertise a summary that in effect says, "I can reach all North American routes." That big router connects to other routers that summarize routes for four major Internet service providers (ISPs). Each ISP router connects to smaller ISPs or large enterprise customers, who advertise the summaries that represent the addresses assigned to them. Figure 16.10 gives some idea of how this system works.

The beauty of the system is that it is organized, planned, and executed in advance, with efficient routing in mind. The large number of addresses available also means that changes at or below the ISP level, for example, because of mergers or large customers changing Internet providers, do not affect the global routing information at the core.

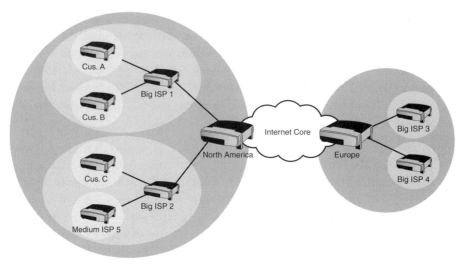

FIGURE 16.10 Global IPv6 Address Design.

IPv6 Address Notation

IPv6 addresses are different in appearance from IPv4. Of course, they are 128 bits long, so even in binary they would be four times longer than a 32-bit IPv4 address, but in notation that humans read and write the format is still different. Instead of using dotted decimal in four octets, we use hexadecimal in eight sets of four characters separated by colons, like this:

2201:0FA0:080B:2112:0000:0000:0000:0001

The use of hex makes it a little easier to represent all those 128 bits in a shorter format because each character represents 4 bits. But it's still a long thing to type out, and remember that network people are generally lazy—so we have a couple of truncation methods to make the long addresses even shorter. The first method is that we are allowed to drop leading zeros—zeros that appear at the beginning of each set, like so:

2201:FA0:80B:2112:0:0:0:1

That makes for a little less typing and a little more clarity. Pay attention to the fact that dropping zeros at the end of each set is *not* allowed! Dropping leading zeros does not change the value of the set; dropping zeros at the end does (like removing a zero from the end of your paycheck amount—not good!)

The second truncation method we can use is to condense contiguous groups of all-zero sets. In our example, there are three sets that are all zeros. We can represent these by a double colon, like this:

2201:FA0:80B:2112::1

This is as short as it gets. We are only allowed to do the double-colon trick once in any address, so if you see an address with two double-colons in it, it is *not* valid. Here's an example:

2201::BCBG::1

One last piece of the addressing notation: the mask. We do not represent the mask as another set of hex characters; instead, we identify the *Prefix Length* with slash notation. This is not as confusing at it seems: the slash notation simply identifies how many bits identify the network part, with the remainder being the host part.

As an example, the North American registry ARIN (American Registry for Internet Numbers) was given the block of 2620:0000::/23 in September 2006. This indicates that the first 23 bits of 2620:0000:: identify the block of addresses that the North American routers will advertise to the rest of the world. From this point, ARIN will assign chunks of that space to the Big ISPs; Big ISP1 might get 2620:0100::/24, and Big ISP2 might get 2620:0200::/24. Those ISPs then hand out pieces of their chunk to smaller ISP or big customers, and the prefix length will get bigger as the chunks gets smaller—this should feel familiar because what we are doing here is subnetting. Don't worry, you won't be expected to subnet in IPv6. Not yet at least...

Types of IPv6 Addresses

An IPv6 address will be one of the following three types. Some will be familiar, but there is one brand-new one, too.

- ▸ **Unicast**—An IPv6 unicast address is the same as an IPv4 unicast address; it is an IP that is assigned to an interface on a host. It can be the source of an IP packet or the destination for one. A packet sent to a unicast address goes to the one host with that address.

- ▸ **Multicast**—Just like in IPv4, a single IPv6 multicast address is assigned to multiple hosts so that a packet sent to the address may be delivered to multiple hosts more or less at the same time. IPv6 Multicast addresses always start with the prefix FF00::/8.

▸ **Anycast**—An anycast address is a single address that is assigned to multiple hosts. This is similar to a multicast, except that a packet for the anycast address will be delivered to the *one* host that is nearest according to the routing protocol's idea of distance. There is no special prefix for anycast addresses.

There is no such thing as a broadcast in IPv6. Ever. Any requirement for broadcasting is performed by a multicast instead.

> **EXAM ALERT**
>
> Know the three IPv6 address types. Remember that IPv6 cannot broadcast, ever! Any answers with the word "broadcast" in them are invalid.

IPv6 Address Configuration

For hosts to use IPv6 addresses, an IPv6 protocol stack must be installed. This likely means that you will need to upgrade your router IOS to provide IPv6 support. Then you can choose one of four options for address assignment.

To understand the address assignment choices better, we need to examine the concepts of stateful versus stateless configuration and the EUI-64 address format.

In IPv6, we can use DHCP to assign IP addresses just like in IPv4. The admin must set up the server with a scope of IPv6 addresses to hand out. The mechanisms used to discover and assign addresses are a little different, but the net result is the same. This is called stateful addressing, where the DHCP server keeps track of what hosts have been assigned what IPv6 address—in other words, the state of the host DHCP-wise.

There is another option for dynamic addressing in IPv6 called *stateless autoconfiguration*. This feature allows a host to choose and configure an address for itself. The host that wants an address learns what the /64 network prefix is on the local link, then appends its MAC address (in a special 64-bit format called EUI-64), thus generating a 128-bit IPv6 address that is unique to that host because it incorporates the unique MAC of the host.

The EUI-64 format is not so difficult to understand. We simply take the 48-bit MAC address and put a special pattern, FFFE, after the first 24 bits (the six OUI characters), followed by the rest of the six hex characters in the host MAC. The only trick is that according to IPv6 rules, the seventh bit in an EUI-64 address must be 1, which identifies that the burned-in MAC address has been modified.

This is a little confusing, to be sure, but you can relax because the host determines and configures its EUI-64 address all by itself, if you tell it to. Here's what an EUI-64 address conversion looks like:

Original MAC:

00-15-C5-CB-42-2B

Original MAC in binary:

00000000-00010101-11000101-11001011-01000010-00101011

7th bit = 0

Change 7th bit to 1:

00000010-00010101-11000101-11001011-01000010-00101011

EUI-64 MAC now:

02-15-C5-CB-42-2B

EUI-64 Address = </64 net_ID_variable>:0215:C5FF:FECB:422B

So, back to the four choices. The following really simplifies the options:

▶ **Static Configuration**—The administrator chooses and assigns a static IPv6 address to the host NIC. It is the admin's responsibility to choose an address that will function and be valid in the network to which the host is connected.

▶ **Static configuration using EUI-64**—The administrator manually configures the address with the local /64 network prefix followed by the host's MAC in EUI-64 format.

▶ **Dynamic Configuration using DHCP to assign 128-bit address**— The host is set to obtain its address from DHCP, and the DHCP server is set up to hand out IPv6 addresses from a scope.

▶ **Dynamic Configuration using stateless autoconfiguration with EUI-64**—The host is set to obtain its address automatically, but the DHCP server either does not exist (which works fine by the way), or if it does, it only informs the host of the /64 local network prefix.

IPv6 Router Configuration

Assuming your IOS provides IPv6 support, giving it an IPv6 address is really easy. The command is carried out at the interface configuration prompt:

```
interface fastethernet 1/0
ipv6 address 2001:AB00:00FF:1::/64 eui-64
```

Notice the eui-64 switch; this tells the router to figure out its own EUI-64 address to follow the /64 prefix provided. Without that, you must provide a full 128-bit address in the command.

To verify your configuration, use the `show ipv6 interface` command at the interface configuration prompt. The following is a sample output (with different addresses applied). You can see multiple addresses in use by the interface for global unicast, link-local, and multiple multicast groups:

```
Router#show ipv6 interface
  Serial1/0 is up, line protocol is up
    IPv6 is enabled, link-local address is FE80::A8BB:CCFF:FE00:D200
    Global unicast address(es):
      2001:1:33::3, subnet is 2001:1:33::/64 [TENTATIVE]
    Joined group address(es):
      FF02::1
      FF02::1:FF00:3
      FF02::1:FF00:D200
    MTU is 1500 bytes
    ICMP error messages limited to one every 100 milliseconds
    ICMP redirects are enabled
    ND DAD is enabled, number of DAD attempts: 1
    ND reachable time is 30000 milliseconds
  Router#
```

IPv6 Features

IPv6 has a couple features that you should keep in mind:

▶ **IPSec**—Support for IPsec is built in and mandatory for IPv6; this means that every packet can be protected by IPSec transport on every IPv6 host if so configured.

▶ **Mobility**—IP mobility is built in, but obviously not mandatory because some hosts are not mobile.

▶ **Fixed header size**—The IPv6 header is fixed at 40 bytes or 320 bits. Figure 16.11 shows the IPv6 header.

▶ **ICMP for IPv6 has changed, adding new functionality**—One example of the new tricks it has learned is Path MTU (PMTU) Discovery: Before transmitting a packet, a host can send an ICMP message to learn what the smallest MTU on any link is between the sender and the destination. Then, the host sends packets that are no larger than that value. This clever trick relieves routers of having to fragment and reassemble packets over a small-MTU link, which can be a real performance hog.

According to RFC 1981, hosts not using PMTU will transmit packets at the minimum IPv6 link MTU, which is actually quite small and likely to be inefficient.

▶ **IPv6 makes extensive use of Router Solicitation (RS) and Router Advertisement (RA) messages**—These are multicast messages to the addresses FF02::1 and FF00::2, respectively. The RS is sent from a host to all routers on the link as a multicast, and the RA message is sent from a router to all hosts on the link, also as a multicast. This is one way that the hosts learn whether DHCP is supported on the link, and possibly the DHCP server address.

The IPv6 Header

As mentioned in the preceding section, the IPv6 header is fixed at 40 bytes (320 bits) in length. Figure 16.11 shows the header fields and their sizes, and this section identifies what the fields are for.

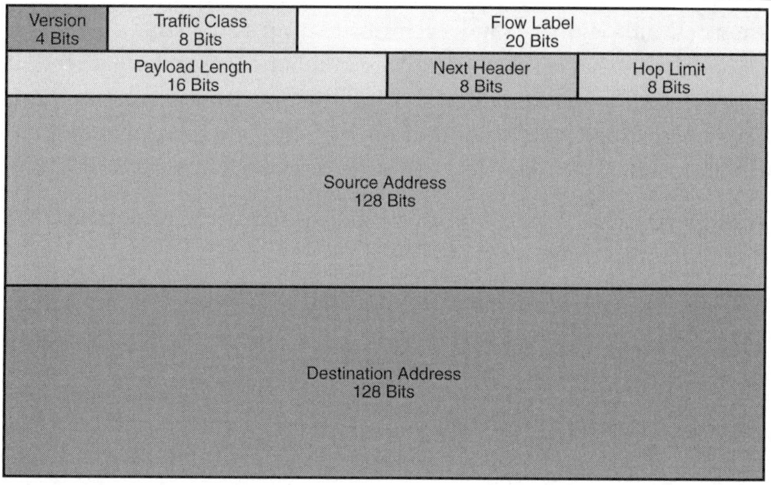

FIGURE 16.11 The IPv6 Header.

The Version field identifies the IP version of this packet; for IPv6, obviously the version will be 6.

The Traffic Class field is where QoS marking for Layer 3 can be identified. In a nutshell, the higher the value of this field, the more important the packet. Your Cisco routers (and some switches) can be configured to read this value and send a high-priority packet sooner than other lower ones during times of congestion. This is very important for some applications, especially VoIP.

The Flow Label is a number that identifies this packet as one of a flow of packets in a stream from sender to receiver; a good example is a VoIP call. It's best for VoIP if all the packets in a given call get sent along exactly the same path to the receiving phone, so that they arrive in the same order they were sent. The flow label is one mechanism that IPv6 routers can use to keep track of different application flows and try to make sure that all the packets within a flow get treated the same way.

The Payload Length field indicates how big the payload of this packet is; it can be variable, so the router needs to know where the packet is supposed to end. That way it knows if anything went missing. This is especially important because there is no header checksum, as there used to be in IPv4.

The Next Header field identifies what Layer 4 protocol is in the payload of this packet (same function as the Protocol field in IPv4).

The Hop Limit field is a cool one: Whereas in IPv4 there was a TTL field that limited the life of a packet to 255 hops (the IPv4 TTL value starts at 255 and is decremented by at least 1 as a packet is processed by a router; if it reaches 0, the packet is dropped. This prevents the packet from being endlessly misrouted around the Internet, although it could be misrouted up to 255 hops), IPv6 is smarter: the Hop Limit value is set to the actual number of hops the packet will go through to reach its destination. This hop information comes from the IPv6 routing protocols. The Hop Limit is still decremented by 1 at each router, but the more accurate value means that the packet can't be misrouted even by one hop.

The Source and Destination Address fields are self-explanatory; remember that the full 128-bit address for each is listed.

IPv6 Transition Strategies

Clearly, things are moving toward IPv6. The U.S. government has specified that all federal agencies must deploy IPv6 by 2008. The Peoples Republic of China has a five-year plan for deployment of IPv6 called the *China Next Generation Internet*. The process, though, is not going to affect every single host in these large networks overnight. Cisco wants you to be aware of their strategies for the transition to using IPv6 while still maintaining IPv4 functionality.

> **TIP**
>
> Putting CCNA Exam studying aside for a moment, we strongly recommend that you start learning how to use IPv6 in your labs now. It is your big chance to be ready when the boss walks in and says "We need to deploy IPv6 connectivity because of blah blah blah. Can you do it?" When you say "Sure, no problem" and gain massive respect, that's when you can send us an email and thank us.

The easiest IPv6 transition choice is called Dual Stack. Dual stacking means that the host (router, PC, printer, and so on) runs both the IPv4 and IPv6 protocol stacks and can send and receive both types of packets, probably (but not necessarily) on the same interface. The drawback here is the additional load on the host and whether an IPv6 stack for that device is available (your old router might not be able to run IPv6).t

Tunneling mode creates a tunnel for one protocol through another. You can picture taking an IPv6 packet from the head office, encapsulating it inside an IPv4 packet to transition across the provider network, then decapsulating it on the other side and forwarding the IPv6 packet into the remote branch office. This is known as a 6-to-4 tunnel. These tunnels have a special address range of 2002::/16.

Translation means taking an IPv6 packet, removing the IP header, and replacing it with an IPv4 header that approximates the original IPv6 information as much as possible.

Tunneling is often associated with a NAT router, and sometimes is known as NAT-PT (for Protocol Translation). What happens here is that the IPv6 packet header is removed and replaced with an IPv4 header (or vice versa), effectively changing from one protocol to the other. The big issues with NAT-PT are latency, performance loading, and the loss of header information in the translation process.

You won't need to actually *do* any IPv6 configuration for your test, but they might ask you *how* to do it, or if the config they show you is valid. t

Exam Prep Questions

1. Which routing protocols support VLSM? Choose all that apply.

   ○ **A.** RIPv1

   ○ **B.** RIPv2

   ○ **C.** IGRP

   ○ **D.** HSRP

   ○ **E.** EIGRP

   ○ **F.** OSPF

   ○ **G.** BGP

2. What characteristic of VLSM-capable routing protocols enables the use of different subnet masks against a single address class within a system?

   ○ **A.** The capability to configure the protocol on a subnetted interface

   ○ **B.** Compliance with RFC 1918 addressing

   ○ **C.** The use of areas and autonomous systems

   ○ **D.** The inclusion of the subnet mask for each network advertised in routing updates

   ○ **E.** The capability to perform automatic route summarization

3. Which of the following is the best summary statement for the following range of networks?

   192.168.1.0 /24–192.168.15.0 /24

   ○ **A.** 192.168.1.0

   ○ **B.** 192.168.1.0 255.255.240.0

   ○ **C.** 192.168.1.0 0.0.15.0

   ○ **D.** 192.168.1.0 255.255.248.0

   192.168.0.0 255.255.240.0

4. Which of the following is the best summary statement for the following range of networks?

192.168.24.0 /24–192.168.31.0 /24

   ○ **A.** 192.168.24.0 255.255.240.0

   ○ **B.** 192.168.24.0 /28

   ○ **C.** 192.168.24.0 /21

   ○ **D.** 192.168.0.0 /27

5. Which of the following networks are included in the summary 172.16.0.0 /13? Choose all that apply.

   ○ **A.** 172.0.0.0 /16

   ○ **B.** 172.16.0.0 /16

   ○ **C.** 172.24.0.0 /16

   ○ **D.** 172.21.0.0 /16

   ○ **E.** 172.18.0.0 /16

6. What are the advantages of route summarization? Choose three.

   ○ **A.** Ensures job security for network admins because of difficulty of configuration

   ○ **B.** Reduces routing update traffic overhead

   ○ **C.** Reduces the impact of discontiguous subnets

   ○ **D.** Reduces CPU and memory load on routers

   ○ **E.** Identifies flapping interfaces

   ○ **F.** Hides network instability

7. True or false: Route summarization is mandatory.

   ○ **A.** True

   ○ **B.** False

8. Examine the following partial output of show ip route. Which next hop will the router use to send packets to the 172.16.32.0 network?

```
Gateway of last resort is 10.1.1.3
C 192.168.3.0/24 is directly connected, Ethernet1
C 172.16.2.0/24 is directly connected, Serial0
172.16.0.0.0/16 is variably subnetted, 2 subnets, 2 masks
D 172.16.32.0/20 [90/10545152] via 10.1.1.1
D 172.16.32.0/24 [90/314368] via 10.1.1.2
S* 0.0.0.0/0 [1/0] via 10.1.1.3
```

- ○ **A.** The default route
- ○ **B.** 10.1.1.3
- ○ **C.** 10.1.1.1
- ○ **D.** 10.1.1.2

9. Which of the following is a valid IPv6 address format?

- ○ **A.** G412:AFFA:2001:0000:0000:0000:0000:0001
- ○ **B.** 2001:8888:EEEE:1010:0000:0000:0000:0001
- ○ **C.** 2001::8888::1
- ○ **D.** 2010:2112:5440:1812:1867

12. Which of the following is a valid IPv6 unicast address format?

- ○ **A.** 2001:8888:EEEE:1010:0000:0000:0000:0001
- ○ **B.** FF00:0000:0000:0002:00C0:00A8:0001:0042
- ○ **C.** 2001:8888::2FFE::00A8
- ○ **D.** FFFF:FFFF:FFFF:FFFF:FFFF:FFFF:FFFF

10. Which of the following are valid IPv6 address formats for the same address? Choose 3.

- ○ **A.** 2001:0000:0000:0200:0222:0000:0000:0001
- ○ **B.** 2001:0000:0000:02:0222:0000:0000:0001
- ○ **C.** 2001:0:0:200:222:0:0:1
- ○ **D.** 2001::200:222::1
- ○ **E.** 2001:0:0:200:222::1

11. Which of the following is a valid IPv6 unicast address?

⭘ **A.** FF00:2112:1812:5440::1

⭘ **B.** 1812:2112:5440:1

⭘ **C.** 255:255:255:255:255:255:255:255:255

⭘ **D.** None of the above.

Answers to Exam Prep Questions

1. Answers B,E, F, and G are correct. Answers A and C are wrong; RIPv1 and IGRP do not support VLSM because they do not include the net mask in their updates. Answer D is wrong because HSRP is not a routing protocol.

2. Answer D is correct. Answer A is incorrect because any routing protocol can be configured on a subnetted interface. Answer B is wrong because the RFC 1918 addresses have nothing to do with routing protocol support for VLSM. Answer C refers to the scalability of OSPF—again nothing to do with VLSM. Answer E is characteristic of non-VLSM capable protocols, which automatically summarize to the classful boundary.

3. Answer E is correct. Answers A and C use incorrect syntax; Answer D uses the wrong mask. Answer B looks correct, but it does not use the correct network ID; the range must always start at a binary increment, in this case 0, not 1. Note that the correct summary does include the 192.168.0.0/24 network as well (not just 192.168.1-15.0/24). This is intended to confuse and distract you!

4. Answer C is correct. Answer A uses the wrong mask and supernets more than the specified networks. Answer B subnets instead of summarizes. Answer D uses the wrong address and mask.

5. Answers B, D, and E are correct. The networks in answers A and C are out of the range, which is 16 through 23.

6. Answers B, D, and F are correct. Answer A might have an element of truth, but Cisco does not have much of a sense of humor. Answer C is incorrect because discontiguous subnets are a real problem if you intend to summarize. Answer E is incorrect; route summarization does not identify but rather hides the effects of flapping interfaces.

7. False. Although it might be a good idea in many cases, route summarization is never mandatory (not counting routing protocols that automatically summarize).

8. Answer D is correct; the longest match rule stipulates that the route with the longest string of bits that match the destination IP prefix of the packet being routed will be the route used. In this case, we have two candidate routes to 172.16.32.0, one with a /20 prefix and the other with a /24 prefix. /24 wins, and the packets will be sent to the next hop of 10.1.1.2 specified by that route.

9. Answer B is correct. IPv6 addresses must have eight sets of four valid hex characters. A is wrong because "G" is not a valid hex character. C is wrong because it uses the :: notation twice, which is invalid. D is wrong because it uses only five sets.

10. Answer A is correct; IPv6 addresses must have eight sets of four valid hex characters. B is wrong because it starts with FF, which indicates a multicast address, not a unicast. C is wrong because it uses :: twice, which is invalid. Answer D is wrong because there are only seven sets, and it's unlikely that a unicast would ever use the all 1s address if there were eight sets.

11. Answers A, C, and E are correct. These are the same address, represented in three valid notations: A is not truncated, C has dropped leading zeroes, and E has compressed the contiguous all-zero groups with the ::. B is wrong because it drops trailing zeros, not leading ones. D is wrong because it uses the :: twice, which is invalid.

12. Answer D is correct; none of these is a valid unicast format. Answer A is an IPv6 multicast (starts with FF00/8); Answer B has only four sets instead of eight. Note that if there had been a double colon before the last 1, it could have been correct. Answer C uses the decimal 255 to confuse you; it could have been correct except that there are nine sets.

CHAPTER SEVENTEEN

Blueprint for Connecting and Securing a Branch Office

Terms you'll need to understand:

- ✓ VLAN
- ✓ VTP
- ✓ Trunk
- ✓ Port Security
- ✓ Default Route
- ✓ NAT

Concepts and techniques you'll need to master:

- ✓ VLAN creation and naming
- ✓ Assigning switch ports to a VLAN
- ✓ Setting VTP parameters
- ✓ Building trunk links
- ✓ Port Security
- ✓ Subnetting
- ✓ Assigning IP addresses to a switch and to router interfaces
- ✓ Establishing PPP WAN connections
- ✓ Creating and applying IP access control lists to manage Telnet, ICMP and inbound Internet connections
- ✓ Configuring and troubleshooting a static default route
- ✓ Configuring and troubleshooting OSPF dynamic routing
- ✓ Configuring Static NAT and PAT using a pool of addresses

Introduction

This chapter presents several configuration requirements for installing and connecting a new switch and router in a branch office. Your job is to assess the scenario and determine what configurations need to be applied to meet the given requirements. All the skills you practice here are testable; your goal is to finish all the labs in fewer than 30 minutes.

> **CAUTION**
>
> Do *not* perform any of these lab exercises on equipment that is connected to a live/
> production network. If in doubt, ask your network administrator if what you are about
> to do is approved.

Switch Configuration Requirements

Some of the switch configuration concepts for this scenario are included in the list that follows. As you review them, you should start to visualize and plan what they are asking you to do. Imagine the commands to perform these actions, and especially the order in which you will execute them. Drawing a network diagram for yourself is never a bad idea. Ideally, you should be able to fully visualize your design and the configurations needed to implement it. With practice, you can "be the packet" in your mind.

- Creating and naming a VLAN
- Assigning switch ports to a VLAN
- Setting Port Security
- Setting VTP parameters
- Building trunk links
- Assigning IP address and default gateway

You have been given a new 2960 switch that your company recently purchased for the new Vancouver branch office. Two additional switches will be installed at a later date as well, and we will make preparations for that. Your tasks will be as follows:

1. On the switch, assign a host name of VAN-SW-A.

2. Create and name the following VLANs without entering the VLAN database:

   ▸ VLAN 10, name Resources

   ▸ VLAN 20, name Staff

   ▸ VLAN 30, name Voice (this VLAN is for future use).

3. Assign the following port settings:

   ▸ Port fa0/1 through 10 in VLAN 10

   ▸ Port fa0/11 through 22 in VLAN 20

   ▸ Port Gi0/1 is a trunk port to the Router (Remember that the 2960 does not support ISL trunks). You are instructed to configure the trunks as 100Mbps, Full Duplex.

   ▸ Port fa0/23 is a trunk port to VAN-SW-B (to be added later)

   ▸ Port fa0/24 is a trunk port to VAN-SW-C (to be added later)

4. Verify your VLAN and trunk settings.

5. Configure VTP: VAN-SW-A is the Server for the VTP domain Exam Cram, with the password of `cisco`.

6. Verify your VTP settings.

7. Assign the switch the IP address of 172.16.0.2 /26.

8. Set the switch's default gateway to 172.16.0.1.

9. Set port fa0/1 through fa0/10 to allow connection from only one MAC address, and make that port shut down if more than one MAC connects. These ports will connect to servers in the Resources VLAN.

10. Set the privileged EXEC password to `cisco`. This password should be encrypted.

11. Secure Telnet access to the switch by applying the password `cisco23` to the first five VTY lines.

12. Secure local console access with the password of `ciscocon`.

VAN-SW-A Solution

The following configuration is a good solution to the scenario requirements. There are other switch configurations that would achieve the same goals; we have tried to include as many testable commands as possible. Remark lines (indicated by "!") after the commands indicate which task the lines above it solve.

```
Switch>
Switch#configure terminal
Switch(config)#hostname VAN-SW-A
! Task 1: Assigns host name
VAN-SW-A(config)#vlan 10
VAN-SW-A(config-vlan)#name Resources
VAN-SW-A(config-vlan)#vlan 20
VAN-SW-A(config-vlan)#name Staff
VAN-SW-A(config-vlan)#vlan 30
VAN-SW-A(config-vlan)#name Voice
VAN-SW-A(config-vlan)#exit
! Task 2: Creates and names VLANs
VAN-SW-A(config)#interface range fa0/1 - 10
VAN-SW-A(config-if-range)#switchport access vlan 10
! Task 3: Assigns ports 1-10 to VLAN 10
VAN-SW-A(config-if-range)#interface range fa0/11 - 22
VAN-SW-A(config-if-range)#switchport access vlan 20
! Task 3: Assigns ports 11-22 to VLAN 20
VAN-SW-A(config-if-range)#interface fa0/23 - 24
VAN-SW-A(config-if-range)#switchport mode trunk
VAN-SW-A(config-if-range)#speed 100
VAN-SW-A(config-if-range)#duplex full
! Task 3: Sets fa0/23 and fa0/24 to
! permanent trunk mode, 100Mbps, Full Duplex
VAN-SW-A(config-if-range)interface gi0/1
VAN-SW-A(config-if)#switchport mode trunk
VAN-SW-A(config-if)#speed 100
VAN-SW-A(config-if)#duplex full
! Task 3:Sets gi0/1 to permanent trunk mode, 100Mbps, Full Duplex
VAN-SW-A(config-if)#<ctrl-z>
VAN-SW-A#
VAN-SW-A#show vlan
VLAN Name                      Status      Ports
---- --------------------      ---------   -------------------------
1    default                   active      Gi0/1, Gi0/2

10   Resources       active          Fa0/1, Fa0/2, Fa0/3, Fa0/4,
                                             fa0/5, Fa0/6, Fa0/7,
                                     Fa0/8,
                                             Fa0/9, Fa0/10
```

```
20    Staff                        active           Fa0/11, Fa0/12, Fa0/13,
Fa0/14, Fa0/15, Fa0/16,
Fa0/17, Fa0/18, Fa0/19,
Fa0/20Fa0/21

30    Voice                        active
<output truncated>
!
```

!Task 4: Verifies VLANs and ports assignments
```
 VAN-SW-A#show interface fa0/23 trunk
Port           Mode          Encapsulation  Status        Native vlan
fa0/23         on            802.1q         not-trunking  1


Port           Vlans allowed on trunk
fa0/23         1-4094


Port           Vlans allowed and active in management domain
Fa0/23         1-4094
Port           Vlans in spanning tree forwarding state and not pruned
Fa0/23         1-4094
!
VAN-SW-A#show interface fa0/24 trunk
Port           Mode          Encapsulation  Status        Native vlan
Fa0/24         on            802.1q         not-trunking  1


Port           Vlans allowed on trunk
Fa0/24         1-4094


Port           Vlans allowed and active in management domain
Fa0/24         1-4094
Port           Vlans in spanning tree forwarding state and not pruned
Fa0/24         1-4094

VAN-SW-A#show interface gi0/1 trunk
Port           Mode          Encapsulation  Status        Native vlan
Gi0/1          on            802.1q         trunking      1


Port           Vlans allowed on trunk
Gi0/1          1-4094


Port           Vlans allowed and active in management domain
Gi0/1          1-4094
Port           Vlans in spanning tree forwarding state and not pruned
Gi0/1          1-4094
```
!Task 4: Verifies Trunking on Fa0/23-24, Gi0/1
```
VAN-SW-A#config t
VAN-SW-A(config)#vtp domain ExamCram
VAN-SW-A(config)#vtp password cisco
VAN-SW-A(config)#vtp server
VAN-SW-A(config)#exit
```

```
! Task 5: Assigns VTP parameters
VAN-SW-A#sh vtp status
VTP Version                     : 2
Configuration Revision          : 0
Maximum VLANs supported locally : 1005
Number of existing VLANs        : 8
VTP Operating Mode              : Server
VTP Domain Name                 : ExamCram
VTP Pruning Mode                : Disabled
VTP V2 Mode                     : Disabled
VTP Traps Generation            : Enabled
MD5 digest                      : 0x3A 0x29 0x86 0x39 0xB4 0x5D 0x58 0xD7
!
! Task 6:Verifies VTP settings
VAN-SW-A#config t
VAN-SW-A(config-if)#interface vlan 1
VAN-SW-A(config-if)#ip address 172.16.0.2  255.255.255.192
! Task 7: Assigns switch IP address
VAN-SW-A(config-if)#exit
VAN-SW-A(config)#ip default-gateway 172.16.0.1
! Task 8: Sets switch default gateway
VAN-SW-A(config)#int fa0/1 - 10
VAN-SW-A(config-if-range)#switchport port-security
VAN-SW-A(config-if-range)#switchport port-security maximum 1
VAN-SW-A(config-if-range)#switchport port-security violation shutdown
! Task 9: Assigns port-security parameters
VAN-SW-A(config-if-range)#exit
VAN-SW-A(config)#enable secret cisco
! Task 10: Sets encrypted Privileged Exec password
VAN-SW-A(config)#line vty 0 4
VAN-SW-A(config-line)#login
VAN-SW-A(config-line)#password cisco23
! Task 11: Sets VTY access password
VAN-SW-A(config-line)#line con 0
VAN-SW-A(config-line)#login
VAN-SW-A(config-line)#password ciscocon
! Task 12: Sets Console access password
<ctrl+z>
VAN-SW-A#copy run start
VAN-SW-A#exit
```

Router Configuration Requirements

The router configurations tasks will touch on the following areas. Remember to think about what these need for configuration and start to plan your approach.

- IP Addressing

- Subnetting

- Inter-VLAN Routing

- PPP WAN Connection

- NAT Overload to a Pool

- IP ACLs

- OSPF and Default routing

The branch office uses a new 2821 series router, with two Gigabit-Ethernet interfaces and a serial interface for the PPP WAN connection. The router will perform Inter-VLAN routing using Router-on-a-Stick on Gi0/0 and provide NAT services for connection to the Internet. The ISP will exchange dynamic routing information with this router using OSPF in Area 0. The Voice VLAN should not be included in the OSPF routing. Your tasks are as follows:

1. Assign the router a host name of VAN-Gateway.

2. Configure Inter-VLAN Routing by assigning IP addresses to the physical and virtual interfaces. The IP addressing for each interface is as follows:

   - Gi0/0: 172.16.0.1 /26

   - S0/0: 192.168.66.65 /28

   - VLAN 10: 172.16.0.65 /26

   - VLAN 20: 172.16.0.129 /26

   - VLAN 30: 172.16.0.193 /26

3. Set the Serial0/0 encapsulation to PPP.

4. Configure NAT as follows:

   ▶ Allow VLANs 1, 10, and 20 to be translated. Do not allow VLAN 30 to be translated.

   ▶ The ISP has assigned the range of 192.168.66.66 through 192.168.66.77 as the pool of addresses to translate to. Name the pool **IntPool**. Ensure all VLAN 1, 10, and 20 hosts can use addresses from this range.

5. Prevent all outside networks from pinging any inside network. Until the security team comes in to configure the advanced security settings, allow only IP traffic from established outbound connections inbound on s0/0.

6. Configure OSPF routing for VLANs 1, 10, and 20 to the ISP network, using Area 0 for all interfaces. Do not advertise the Voice VLAN network.

7. Configure a Static Default route to the ISP gateway IP of 192.168.66.78.

Router Solution

The following configuration is a good solution to the problems posed by the scenario. There may be other configs that also work, but again we are emphasizing those that we think you need to know for the test. The remark lines describing the solution to the task are included after the task configuration.

```
Router#configure terminal
Router(config)#hostname VAN-Gateway
! Task 1: Assigns hostname
VAN-Gateway(config)#interface gi0/0
VAN-Gateway(config-if)#ip address 172.16.0.1 255.255.255.192
VAN-Gateway(config-if)#no shut
VAN-Gateway(config-if)#interface gi0/0.10
VAN-Gateway(config-if)#encapsulation dot1q 10
VAN-Gateway(config-if)#ip address 172.16.0.65 255.255.255.192
VAN-Gateway(config-if)#interface gi0/0.20
VAN-Gateway(config-if)#encapsulation dot1q 20
VAN-Gateway(config-if)#ip address 172.16.0.129 255.255.255.192
VAN-Gateway(config-if)#interface gi0/0.30
VAN-Gateway(config-if)#encapsulation dot1q 30
VAN-Gateway(config-if)#ip address 172.16.0.193 255.255.255.192
! Configures inter-VLAN routing: Physical interface is native vlan
(defaults to VLAN 1);
! Other sub-interfaces are virtual interfaces for their respective VLANs.
```

```
VAN-Gateway(config-if)#interface s0/0
VAN-Gateway(config-if)#encapsulation ppp
VAN-Gateway(config-if)#ip address 192.168.66.65 255.255.255.240
VAN-Gateway(config-if)#no shut
VAN-Gateway(config-if)#exit
! Task 3: Configures S0/0 with PPP and correct IP address
VAN-Gateway(config)#access-list 1 permit 172.16.0.0 0.0.0.63
VAN-Gateway(config)#access-list 1 permit 172.16.0.64 0.0.0.63
VAN-Gateway(config)#access-list 1 permit 172.16.0.128 0.0.0.63
VAN-Gateway(config)#ip nat pool IntPool 192.168.66.66 192.168.66.77 net-
mask 255.255.255.240
VAN-Gateway(config)#ip nat inside source list 1 pool IntPool overload
VAN-Gateway(config)#interface gi0/0
VAN-Gateway(config-if)#ip nat inside
VAN-Gateway(config-if)#interface gi0/0.10
VAN-Gateway(config-if)#ip nat inside
VAN-Gateway(config-if)#interface gi0/0.20
VAN-Gateway(config-if)#ip nat inside
VAN-Gateway(config-if)#interface s0/0
VAN-Gateway(config-if)#ip nat outside
VAN-Gateway(config-if)#exit
! Task 4: Configures NAT with ACL permitting specified networks,
! a NAT pool with valid addresses and mask,
! a NAT statement identifying source and destination for translation,
! and "inside" and "outside" interfaces.
VAN-Gateway(config)#access-list 101 deny icmp any any
VAN-Gateway(config)#access-list 101 permit ip any any established
VAN-Gateway(config)#interface s0/0
VAN-Gateway(config-if)#ip access-group 101 in
VAN-Gateway(config-if)#exit
! Task 5: Applies specified security with ACL on the outside interface
VAN-Gateway(config)#router ospf 99
VAN-Gateway(config-router)#network 172.16.0.0   0.0.0.63 area 0
VAN-Gateway(config-router)#network 172.16.0.64   0.0.0.63 area 0
VAN-Gateway(config-router)#network 172.16.0.128 0.0.0.63 area 0
VAN-Gateway(config-router)#network 192.168.66.64  0.0.0.15 area 0
VAN-Gateway(config-router)#exit
! Task 6 : Configures OSPF routing
VAN-Gateway(config)#ip route 0.0.0.0  0.0.0.0  192.168.66.78
VAN-Gateway(config)#exit
! Task 7: Sets default route to ISP
VAN-Gateway#copy run start
```

Exam Prep Questions

1. Why was no encapsulation specified for the trunk links on the switch in the preceding scenario?

   - ○ **A.** Because the Cisco switch supports only Cisco's Inter-Switch Link trunk protocol.

   - ○ **B.** Because best practices recommend that trunk protocols be auto-negotiated.

   - ○ **C.** Because using a standards-based protocol such as 802.1q helps ensure intervendor operability.

   - ○ **D.** Because the 2960 supports only 802.1q, so the router must be configured to match.

2. ACL 101 in the preceding Router solution uses the keyword `established`. What is the effect of this configuration?

   - ○ **A.** Restricts inbound traffic only to established office applications; custom, gaming or "hacker" traffic is implicitly denied.

   - ○ **B.** Allows traffic inbound only in response to outbound requests from an inside host.

   - ○ **C.** Requires that an established tunnel exist before traffic will be permitted.

   - ○ **D.** It has no effect without a "permit" statement.

3. Andy, Stewart, and Gordon have replaced the NICs in some of the servers in the Resource VLAN. When they are restarted, none of them can establish a network connection. What is the most likely problem?

   - ○ **A.** Defective NICs.

   - ○ **B.** The switch is behaving as configured.

   - ○ **C.** Defective switch.

   - ○ **D.** No route to the network exists.

4. Examine the following partial configuration from the router. What NAT configuration line is missing?

```
VAN-Gateway(config)#access-list 1 permit 172.16.0.0 0.0.0.63
VAN-Gateway(config)#access-list 1 permit 172.16.0.64 0.0.0.63
VAN-Gateway(config)#access-list 1 permit 172.16.0.128 0.0.0.63
VAN-Gateway(config)#ip nat pool IntPool 192.168.66.66 192.168.66.77
netmask 255.255.255.240
VAN-Gateway(config)#interface gi0/0
VAN-Gateway(config-if)#ip nat inside
```

```
VAN-Gateway(config-if)#interface gi0/0.10
VAN-Gateway(config-if)#ip nat inside
VAN-Gateway(config-if)#interface gi0/0.20
VAN-Gateway(config-if)#ip nat inside
VAN-Gateway(config-if)#interface s0/0
VAN-Gateway(config-if)#ip nat outside
```

- ○ **A.** VAN-Gateway(config)#**ip nat inside source list 1 pool IntPool overload**

- ○ **B.** VAN-Gateway(config)#**ip nat source list 1 inside pool IntPool overload**

- ○ **C.** `VAN-Gateway(config)#ip nat inside source list 101 pool IntPool`
  `overload`

- ○ **D.** `VAN-Gateway(config)#ip nat inside source list 1 overload pool`
  `IntPool`

- ○ **E.** None of the above.

5. True or false: The Spanning Tree Protocol is running on VAN-SW-A?

- ○ **A.** True

- ○ **B.** False

6. How many valid host IPs are available in the VLAN 30 subnet (including those already assigned)?

- ○ **A.** 30

- ○ **B.** 126

- ○ **C.** 14

- ○ **D.** 62

7. The ISP has informed you that it is changing the subnet mask of the connection to its router to /29. Your router's IP is not changing, but the ISP address is now 192.168.66. All remaining IPs in the subnet are available for the NAT pool. What will the new NAT pool statement look like?

- ○ **A.** ip nat pool IntPool 192.168.66.67 192.168.66.70 mask 255.255.255.248

- ○ **B.** ip nat pool IntPool 192.168.66.67 192.168.66.70 netmask 0.0.0.248

- ○ **C.** ip nat pool IntPool 192.168.66.67 192.168.66.70 netmask
  255.255.255.248

- ○ **D.** ip nat pool IntPool 192.168.66.66 192.168.66.70 netmask
  255.255.255.248

8. Duncan suggests the following configuration for the VAN-Gateway router. What is the problem with this partial config?

```
!
VAN-Gateway(config)#interface gi0/0
VAN-Gateway(config-if)#no ip address
VAN-Gateway(config-if)#no shut
VAN-Gateway(config-if)#interface gi0/0.1
VAN-Gateway(config-if)#encapsulation isl 1
VAN-Gateway(config-if)#ip address 172.16.0.1 255.255.255.192
VAN-Gateway(config-if)#interface gi0/0.10
VAN-Gateway(config-if)#encapsulation isl 10
VAN-Gateway(config-if)#ip address 172.16.0.65 255.255.255.192
VAN-Gateway(config-if)#interface gi0/0.20
VAN-Gateway(config-if)#encapsulation isl 20
VAN-Gateway(config-if)#ip address 172.16.0.129 255.255.255.192
VAN-Gateway(config-if)#interface gi0/0.30
VAN-Gateway(config-if)#encapsulation isl 30
VAN-Gateway(config-if)#ip address 172.16.0.193 255.255.255.192
!
```

   ○ **A.** There is no problem with this configuration.

   ○ **B.** The IP addresses are invalid with the masks shown.

   ○ **C.** ISL trunking is not supported on VAN-Gateway.

   ○ **D.** ISL trunking is not supported on VAN-SW-A.

9. Examine the partial configuration that follows. Why is this configuration invalid?

```
!
VAN-SW-A(config)#router ospf 99
VAN-SW-A(config-router)#network 172.16.0.0   0.0.0.63 area 0
VAN-SW-A(config-router)#network 172.16.0.64   0.0.0.63 area 0
VAN-SW-A(config-router)#network 172.16.0.128 0.0.0.63 area 0
VAN-SW-A(config-router)#network 192.168.66.64  0.0.0.15 area 0
VAN-SW-A(config-router)#exit
!
```

   ○ **A.** All wildcard masks must be changed to decimal masks.

   ○ **B.** Network configuration statements must use the <host_ip> <0.0.0.0> address/mask format.

   ○ **C.** There is nothing wrong with the configuration.

   ○ **D.** The configuration given will not work on this device.

10. Examine the partial configuration that follows. Why is this configuration invalid?

```
!
VAN-SW-A(config)#router ospf 0
VAN-SW-A(config-router)#network 172.16.0.0   0.0.0.63 area 0
VAN-SW-A(config-router)#network 172.16.0.64  0.0.0.63 area 0
VAN-SW-A(config-router)#network 172.16.0.128 0.0.0.63 area 0
VAN-SW-A(config-router)#network 192.168.66.64  0.0.0.15 area 0
VAN-SW-A(config-router)#exit
!
```

- ◯ **A.** The Area ID is invalid.
- ◯ **B.** There is nothing wrong with this configuration.
- ◯ **C.** The Process ID is invalid.
- ◯ **D.** The wildcard masks are invalid.

Answers to Exam Prep Questions

1. Answer D is correct. The 2960 does not support ISL, so the router must be configured for 802.1q. Answer A is incorrect; the switch supports only 802.1q. Answer B is wrong; trunk encapsulation cannot be negotiated between a router and a switch, only between two switches. Even then, best practices recommend hard-coding trunk encapsulation. Answer C is wrong because it is not relevant to this scenario, however true it may be.

2. Answer B is correct; the `established` keyword lets traffic back in in response to traffic that was sent out. Answer A is wrong; this sounds more like Network-Based Application Recognition (NBAR), but has nothing to do with the `established` keyword. Answer C is wrong; there is no requirement for tunnels. Answer D is wrong; it is already part of a permit statement.

3. Answer B is correct; the switch is configured for port-security, so when the MAC addresses of the new NICs attempt to connect to the switch, the ports shut down. Answer A is wrong; it's unlikely that all the new NICs are defective. Answer C is wrong; given what we know of the config, it is not the most likely problem. Answer D is wrong; hosts do not need a route to their own LAN; our problem here is at Layer 1 and 2, not Layer 3.

4. Answer A is correct. Answers B and D use invalid syntax; Answer C names the wrong ACL.

5. Answer A (true) is correct. Spanning Tree is running by default, and we see no evidence of it being disabled (which would be a bad idea anyway).

6. Answer D is correct. A /26 provides 62 valid hosts. All other answers are incorrect.

7. Answer C is correct. The remaining available addresses are .67 through .70, and the new mask ends with .248. Answer A is incorrect; the keyword is `netmask`, not `mask`. Answer B is wrong; the mask is invalid. Answer D is wrong; the IP range includes the ISP router.

8. Answer D is correct; if the router uses this config, the switch will not be able to trunk with it. Answer A is therefore incorrect. Answer B is wrong; there is no problem with the IPs and masks. Answer C is wrong; the router will support ISL trunking, but the switch will not.

9. Answer D is correct. This is a nasty trick question; the command prompt indicates that this config was written for the switch. Even though it would be impossible to get this configuration (the switch would return errors), you can expect some exam questions to be unrealistic in this way. Answer A is wrong; OSPF needs wildcards. Answer B is wrong; there are many valid address/mask formats in OSPF configuration. Answer C is wrong because the configuration was entered on a switch that does not support OSPF (or any routing for that matter).

10. Answer C is correct; the valid range for the Process ID is 1–65535. Answer B is therefore incorrect. Answer A is not correct; the area ID can be anything from 0 through 65535. Answer D is wrong; the wildcards masks are perfectly valid.

Practice Exam #1

Hints and Pointers

If you are reading this, you likely feel ready to tackle the CCNA exam and need to assess your skills to see if you can spot any weaknesses. As you take this practice exam, the authors recommend the following test taking tips:

▶ **Read each question twice**—There is a big difference between reading a question that you think reads, "Which of the following are true," but really reads, "Which of the following are not true." Be sure to read each question carefully so that you can fully understand the question.

▶ **Read the answers starting from the bottom**—When you read the answers from the bottom, you force yourself to carefully read each answer. If you read the answers from the top, you might find yourself quickly selecting an answer that looks vaguely right and skipping over the other answers that might have been a better answer.

▶ **Time yourself**—The CCNA exam is a 90 minute exam. Time yourself during this practice exam to make sure that you stay within this time limit.

▶ **If you do not know the answer to a question, make a note of it**—Go back and review any trouble areas later. You should be interested not only in finding the answer to the question, but also in mastering that particular topic in its entirety. If you are unsure about one aspect of a topic, chances are you might be unsure about other areas related to that same topic.

▶ **Mentally get yourself in the frame of mind to take a test**—To properly assess yourself, take this practice exam as you would take the real exam. This means that you should find yourself a quiet place without any distractions so that you can focus on each question. (Yes, that includes turning off the television.) You can have some scratch paper to write on, but calculators are not allowed on the real exam, so do not use them on the practice exam.

▶ **If you cannot determine the correct answers, begin eliminating the incorrect answers**—If there are four options and you know that three are absolutely wrong, the fourth option has to be the correct one.

▶ **Continue taking this practice exam until you get a perfect score**—When you can consistently score high on these practice exams, you are ready to take the real exam.

▶ **Don't despair**—Should you not do so well on the practice exam, do not worry. It only means that you need to continue studying. Be glad that you are able to spot your weak areas now and not after taking the real exam. Go back through and review your problem areas.

We wish you the best of luck in your pursuit of the coveted CCNA certification.

Practice Exam #1

1. You need to assign an IP address on a router for a new Ethernet network. You need to assign the router to the first IP address on the second useable subnet taken from the major Class C network of 192.168.25.0/24. The subnet must support at least 13 hosts on each subnet, but you must allow for as many subnets as possible. In addition, the router has been configured with the `ip subnet-zero` command. Given these requirements, what address would you assign on the router?

   - ○ **A.** 192.168.25.14
   - ○ **B.** 192.168.25.17
   - ○ **C.** 192.168.25.33
   - ○ **D.** 192.168.25.49
   - ○ **E.** 192.168.25.1

2. You have been asked to troubleshoot a NAT configuration for the network shown in the figure. Another engineer has entered the following configuration into the router:

```
access-list 4 permit 172.21.248.0 0.0.1.255
ip nat pool NATPOOL 192.168.191.66 192.168.191.70 netmask
     255.255.255.248
ip nat inside source list 4 pool NATPOOL
!
interface serial 1/0
 ip address 192.168.191.65 255.255.255.248
 ip nat oustide
!
interface fastethernet 0/3
 ip address 172.21.254.1 255.255.254.0
 ip nat inside
!
```

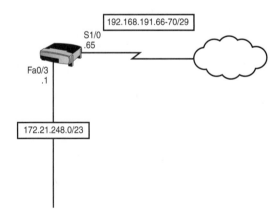

There is a problem with this configuration: Not all users are able to access the Internet. What is wrong with the configuration that causes this problem?

○ **A.** The pool configuration is incorrect.

○ **B.** The **ip nat inside** and **ip nat outside** commands are on the wrong interfaces.

○ **C.** The keyword '**overload**' is missing.

○ **D.** The access list is incorrect.

○ **E.** The IP addresses are incorrect.

3. What type of attack involves a flooding of SYN packets to open TCP sessions to a server?

○ **A.** Worm

○ **B.** Social engineering

○ **C.** Reconnaissance

○ **D.** Denial of service

4. Which of the following is used to identify a wireless network?

○ **A.** SSID

○ **B.** WEP Key

○ **C.** 802.11g

○ **D.** ESS

5. Examine the following output. Which line below is most responsible for a trunk not forming on FastEthernet0/1?

```
Switch#show interfaces fastethernet0/1 switchport
Name: Fa0/1
Switchport:Enabled
Administrative Mode: static access
Operational Mode: static access
Administrative Trunking Encapsulation: dot1q
Operational Trunking Encapsulation: native
Negotiation of Trunking: Off
Access Mode VLAN: 1 (default)
Voice VLAN: none
Administrative private-vlan host-association: none
Administrative private-vlan mapping: none
Operational private-vlan: none
Trunking VLANs Enabled: ALL
Pruning VLANs Enabled: 2-1001
Capture Mode Disabled
Capture VLANs Allowed: ALL

Protected: false
```

```
Voice VLAN: none (inactive)
Appliance trust: none
Switch#show running-config
<<output omitted>>
interface FastEthernet0/1
no ip address
duplex full
speed auto
```

- ○ **A. no ip address**
- ○ **B. Negotiation of Trunking: Off**
- ○ **C. Pruning VLANs: 2-1001**
- ○ **D. Access Mode VLAN: 1 (default)**

6. Which of the following routed protocols does EIGRP support?

- ○ **A.** Appletalk
- ○ **B.** Banyan Vines
- ○ **C.** IPX
- ○ **D.** IP
- ○ **E.** LAT

7. Your boss has asked you to secure your Telnet sessions on your routers. What is the correct configuration to allow only two Telnet sessions to run at a time with an encrypted password of 'Que'?

- ○ **A.** Configuration #1

    line vty 0 4

     login

    password Que

- ○ **B.** Configuration #2

    line vty 0 2

    password Que

    enable secret Que

- ○ **C.** Configuration #3

    line vty 0 1

     login

     password Que

    service password-encryption

○ **D.** Configuration #4

   line vty 0 1

     login

   enable secret Que

○ **E.** Configuration #5

   line vty 0 4

     login

     password Que

   service password-encryption

8. Examine the figure shown. OSPF is running on RouterA, RouterB, RouterC, and
   RouterD. RIP is running on RouterD and RouterE. Based on the figure, which path will
   RouterA take to get to RouterD?

   ○ **A.** RouterA will take the path through RouterE.

   ○ **B.** RouterA will take the path through RouterB.

   ○ **C.** RouterA will load balance across RouterE and RouterB.

   ○ **D.** Not enough information is given to answer this question.

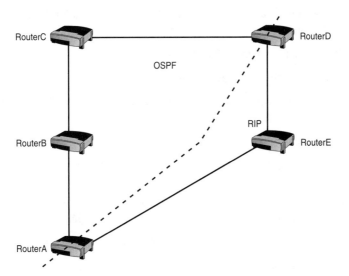

9. Which of the following is a valid host IP address? Select all that apply.

- ○ **A.** 172.16.17.0/20
- ○ **B.** 192.168.4.64/28
- ○ **C.** 10.0.145.144/30
- ○ **D.** 172.30.15.18/29

10. What would be the correct syntax to create and apply an access list inbound on fastethernet 0/0 that would allow all hosts on the 172.19.40.0/21 network Telnet access to a server with the IP address 10.0.0.55?

- ○ **A.** Router(config)#**access-list 100 permit udp 172.19.40.0 0.0.7.255 host 10.0.0.55 eq 23**

  Router(config)#**interface fastethernet0/0**

  Router(config-if)#**ip access-group 100 in**

- ○ **B.** Router(config)#**access-list 100 permit tcp 172.19.40.0 0.0.15.255 host 10.0.0.55 eq 23**

  Router(config)#**interface fastethernet0/0**

  Router(config-if)#**ip access-group 100 in**

- ○ **C.** Router(config)#**access-list 100 permit udp 172.19.40.0 0.0.15.255 host 10.0.0.55 eq 23**

  Router(config)#**interface fastethernet0/0**

  Router(config-if)#**ip access-group 100 in**

- ○ **D.** Router(config)#**access-list 100 permit tcp 172.19.40.0 0.0.7.255 host 10.0.0.55 eq 23**

  Router(config)#**interface fastethernet0/0**

  Router(config-if)#**ip access-group 100 in**

11. You are working on a router that does not have any loopback interfaces. Without the presence of a loopback interface, how do you choose the Router ID in OSPF?

- ○ **A.** You must create a loopback interface. Without it, OSPF is not activated.
- ○ **B.** It is the highest IP address among all physical interfaces that are active when OSPF is started.
- ○ **C.** It is the highest IP address among all physical interfaces regardless if they are active when OSPF first starts.
- ○ **D.** It is the lowest IP address among all physical interfaces.

12. Examine the figure that follows. You want to reduce the size of your routing table on R2. Which of the following is an example of a route summary that represents the local area networks on R4?

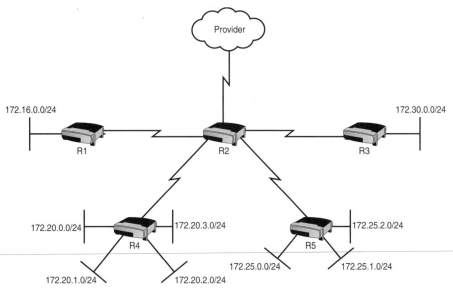

  ○ **A.** `172.20.0.0/22 is subnetted, 1 subnet`

   `D 172.20.0.0 [90/31255610] via 172.17.0.3, 2w1d,`
   `S0/0/0`

  ○ **B.** `172.20.0.0/20 is subnetted, 1 subnet`

   `D 172.20.0.0 [90/31255610] via 172.17.0.3, 2w1d,`
   `S0/0/0`

  ○ **C.** `172.21.0.0/23 is subnetted, 1 subnet`

   `D 172.20.0.0 [90/31255610] via 172.17.0.3, 2w1d,`
   `S0/0/0`

  ○ **D.** `172.21.0.0/22 is subnetted, 1 subnet`

   `D 172.20.0.0 [90/31255610] via 172.17.0.3, 2w1d,`
   `S0/0/0`

13. Which of the following information is included with the **show cdp neighbors detail** command? Select all that apply.

  ○ **A.** Device name

  ○ **B.** Platform

  ○ **C.** Capabilities

  ○ **D.** IOS version

  ○ **E.** IP address

14. You try to create a VLAN that is automatically propagated out to all other switches. The switch allows you to create the VLAN, but it is not propagated to other switches. You execute the `show vtp status` command (shown below). What is wrong?

```
Switch> show vtp status
VTP Version                    : 2
Configuration Revision         : 0
Maximum VLANs supported locally: 250
Number of existing VLANs       : 15
VTP Operating Mode             : Transparent
VTP Domain Name                :
VTP Pruning Mode               : Disabled
VTP V2 Mode                    : Disabled
VTP Traps Generation           : Disabled
MD5 digest                     : 0xBF 0x84 0x94 0x33 0xFC 0xAF 0xB5
0x70
Configuration last modified by 0.0.0.0 at 0-0-00 00:00:00
```

- ○ **A.** No domain name is assigned. You must first assign a domain name before any VLAN information is sent out to other switches.

- ○ **B.** The VTP version number is wrong.

- ○ **C.** You must first enable VTP pruning.

- ○ **D.** You must change the VTP mode to Server before any VLAN information is sent out to other switches.

15. How many broadcast domains are there in the figure shown?

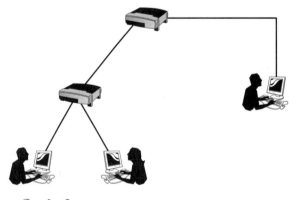

- ○ **A.** One
- ○ **B.** Two
- ○ **C.** Three
- ○ **D.** Four
- ○ **E.** Five

16. Examine the figure shown. Your computer has the IP address 172.16.64.201/22, and you try to access a website on the web server with the IP address 172.16.129.48/22. Unfortunately, you are unable to access the site. Below are the partial configurations on RouterA and RouterB:

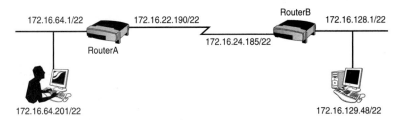

```
RouterA
interface fastethernet3/1
 ip address 172.16.64.1 255.255.252.0
interface serial0/0
 ip address 172.16.22.190 255.255.255.252.0
ip route 172.16.128.0 255.255.252.0 172.16.24.185
RouterB
interface fastethernet0/0
 ip address 172.16.128.1 255.255.252.0
interface serial0/0
 ip address 172.16.24.185 255.255.252.0
ip route 172.16.64.0 255.255.252.0 172.16.22.190
```

Why are you unable to access the website?

- ○ **A.** The static route is incorrect on RouterA.
- ○ **B.** The serial0/0 on RouterA is on a network different from bri0/0 on RouterB.
- ○ **C.** The server is on a network different from fastethernet0/0 on RouterB.
- ○ **D.** The static route on RouterB is incorrect.
- ○ **E.** Your computer uses an invalid IP address.

17. Examine the figure that follows. There is a significant amount of traffic between the workstations and the server on VLAN200. Which switch would be the best choice as the root switch for VLAN 200?

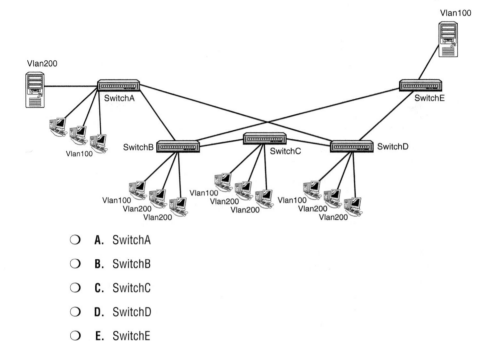

- O **A.** SwitchA
- O **B.** SwitchB
- O **C.** SwitchC
- O **D.** SwitchD
- O **E.** SwitchE

18. Examine the figure. You are running EIGRP on all routers, but you are unable to route to all networks in the diagram. You have narrowed the problem down to RouterB. Below is the EIGRP configuration for RouterB:

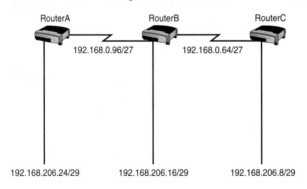

```
RouterB(config)#router eigrp 1
RouterB(config-router)#network 192.168.206.16
RouterB(config-router)#network 192.168.0.96
RouterB(config-router)#network 192.168.0.64
```

What is wrong with this configuration that causes this problem?

- ○ **A.** It is missing the **no auto-summary** command.
- ○ **B.** The **network** statements are wrong.
- ○ **C.** The mask is missing.
- ○ **D.** It is missing the **auto-summary** command.
- ○ **E.** The **maximum-paths** command is missing.

19. Examine the following output. What does the highlighted portion refer to?

```
Router#show ip protocols
Routing Protocol is "eigrp 1"
  Outgoing update filter list for all interfaces is not set
  Incoming update filter list for all interfaces is not set
  Default networks flagged in outgoing updates
  Default networks accepted from incoming updates
  EIGRP metric weight K1=1, K2=0, K3=1, K4=0, K5=0
  EIGRP maximum hopcount 100
  EIGRP maximum metric variance 2
  Redistributing: eigrp 1
  EIGRP NSF-aware route hold timer is 240s
  Automatic network summarization is not in effect
  Maximum path: 3
  Routing for Networks:
          10.0.0.0/8
          172.16.0.0/16
          172.17.0.0/16
  Routing Information Sources:
          Gateway Distance        Last Update
          172.16.1.1      90      00:15:12
          172.17.0.1      90      00:15:10
  Distance: internal 90 external 170
```

- ○ **A.** EIGRP will load balance across 3 equal cost paths.
- ○ **B.** There can be up to 4 different EIGRP networks in the routing table.
- ○ **C.** EIGRP will load balance across 3 unequal cost paths.
- ○ **D.** EIGRP knows of 3 different networks.

20. You have the public range of 2.2.2.0/25 from your ISP. You want to subnet this further to create a public address pool of six addresses that you are going to use to NAT your inside local addresses. Which of the following configurations allow you to NAT your inside local addresses of 192.168.14.0/24 to a pool of six addresses taken from the 2.2.2.0/25 subnet?

○ **A.** interface ethernet0

   ip nat inside

   interface serial0

   ip nat outside

   access-list 1 permit 192.168.14.0 0.0.0.255

   ip nat pool NATPOOL 2.2.2.9 2.2.2.14 netmask 255.255.255.248

   ip nat inside source list 1 pool NATPOOL overload

○ **B.** interface ethernet 0

   ip nat inside

   interface serial 0

   ip nat outside

   access-list 1 permit 2.2.2.8 0.0.0.7

   ip nat pool NATPOOL 192.168.14.0 192.168.14.255 netmask
   255.255.255.0

   ip nat inside source list 1 pool NATPOOL overload

○ **C.** interface ethernet 0

   ip nat inside

   interface serial 0

   ip nat outside

   access-list 1 permit 192.168.14.0 0.0.0.255

   ip nat pool NATPOOL 2.2.2.9 2.2.2.15 netmask 255.255.255.240

   ip nat inside source list 1 pool NATPOOL overload

○ **D.** interface ethernet 0

   ip nat inside

   interface serial 0

   ip nat outside

   access-list 1 permit 2.2.2.0 0.0.0.255

   ip nat pool NATPOOL 192.168.14.1 192.168.14.254 netmask
   255.255.255.0

   ip nat inside source list 1 pool NATPOOL overload

21. Examine the figure. You are running frame-relay between two routers. When you check the status of the interface on RouterA, it shows that the interface is up, but the line protocol is down. What is wrong?

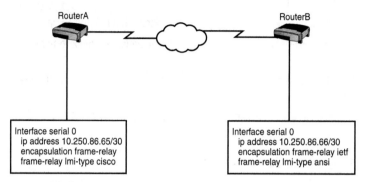

RouterA

RouterB

Interface serial 0
ip address 10.250.86.65/30
encapsulation frame-relay
frame-relay lmi-type cisco

Interface serial 0
ip address 10.250.86.66/30
encapsulation frame-relay ietf
frame-relay lmi-type ansi

- ○ **A.** The LMI types do not match.
- ○ **B.** The encapsulation types do not match.
- ○ **C.** The configuration is incomplete.
- ○ **D.** The routers are on different subnets.

22. Ping and Traceroute operate at what layer of the OSI model?

- ○ **A.** Network
- ○ **B.** Transport
- ○ **C.** Application
- ○ **D.** Session
- ○ **E.** Data-link

23. The output of the **show ip route** command is shown below. A packet is sent destined for the 192.168.5.0/24 network. What happens? Select all that apply.

```
Router#show ip route
CODES: C - CONNECTED, S - STATIC, I - IGRP, R - RIP, M - MOBILE, B -
BGP
        D - EIGRP, EX - EIGRP EXTERNAL, O - OSPF, IA - OSPF INTER AREA
        N1 - OSPF NSSA EXTERNAL TYPE 1, N2 - OSPF NSSA EXTERNAL TYPE 2
        E1 - OSPF EXTERNAL TYPE 1, E2 - OSPF EXTERNAL TYPE 2, E - EGP
        I - IS-IS, L1 - IS-IS LEVEL-1, L2 - IS-IS LEVEL-2, * - CANDIDATE
          DEFAULT
        U - PER-USER STATIC ROUTE, o - ODR
GATEWAY OF LAST RESORT IS NOT SET
D       172.16.0.0 [90/2195456] VIA 10.16.10.1,  00:09:45, SERIAL0
D       172.31.1.0 [90/2681856] VIA 192.168.10.5 00:01:55, SERIAL1
C       10.0.0.0 IS DIRECTLY CONNECTED, SERIAL0
C       192.168.10.0 IS DIRECTLY CONNECTED, SERIAL1
```

○ **A.** The packet is sent out interface Serial 1.

○ **B.** The packet is sent out interface Serial 0.

○ **C.** The packet is dropped.

○ **D.** The packet load balances across interfaces Serial 0 and Serial 1.

○ **E.** An ICMP Destination Unreachable message is sent back to the source.

24. Which of the following are true statements about the following command? (Select all that apply)

    `ip route 192.168.1.0 255.255.255.0 10.1.24.1`

    ○ **A.** The command creates a default route.

    ○ **B.** The command creates a static route.

    ○ **C.** Traffic for the 10.1.24.0 network is forwarded to the 192.168.1.0 network.

    ○ **D.** Traffic for the 192.168.1.0 network is forwarded to 10.1.24.1.

    ○ **E.** The command is used when configuring distance vector routing protocols.

25. In OSPF, what is the cost of a T1?

    ○ **A.** 1,544

    ○ **B.** 10

    ○ **C.** 100

    ○ **D.** 64

26. What is a common subnet mask on point-to-point wide area network links that would allow only two valid IP addresses?

    ○ **A.** 255.255.255.224

    ○ **B.** 255.255.255.240

    ○ **C.** 255.255.255.248

    ○ **D.** 255.255.255.252

    ○ **E.** 255.255.255.255

27. Which of the following commands configures a default gateway address on a switch?

    ○ **A.** Switch#ip default-gateway 10.0.0.1 255.0.0.0

    ○ **B.** Switch(config)#ip default-gateway 10.0.0.1 255.0.0.0

    ○ **C.** Switch(config)#ip default-gateway 10.0.0.1

    ○ **D.** Switch(config-router)#ip default-gateway 10.0.0.1

28. What is the maximum hop count for EIGRP?

    ○ **A.** 255

    ○ **B.** 224

    ○ **C.** 15

    ○ **D.** 1

    ○ **E.** Unlimited

29. What is happening in the spanning-tree learning state?

    ○ **A.** Port is transitioning to forward state.

    ○ **B.** Port is preventing loops.

    ○ **C.** Port is forwarding data.

    ○ **D.** Port is populating the MAC table.

30. What type of cable would you use between a router and a switch?

    ○ **A.** Rollover cable

    ○ **B.** Null modem cable

    ○ **C.** Crossover cable

    ○ **D.** Straight-through cable

31. You type the following configuration into a router. When you execute the **show ip route** command, however, you do not notice any new routes. What is wrong with the configuration that causes this problem?

```
router rip
 network 10.0.0.0
 network 172.19.0.0
 version 2
interface serial 0/0
 ip address 10.0.0.1 255.0.0.0
 frame-relay map ip 10.0.0.2 100
 frame-relay interface-dlci 100
 no frame-relay inverse-arp
interface ethernet 0/0
 ip address 172.19.0.1 255.255.0.0
```

    ○ **A.** The **frame-relay map** command is missing the broadcast keyword.

    ○ **B.** RIP should be running version 1, not version 2.

    ○ **C.** Inverse-arp should be enabled.

    ○ **D.** RIP is not activated on the interfaces.

32. What is used in factoring the routing metric used by EIGRP? Select all that apply.

- ○ **A.** Bandwidth
- ○ **B.** Hop count
- ○ **C.** Delay
- ○ **D.** Cost

33. CHAP can be described as what type of authentication?

- ○ **A.** One-way handshake
- ○ **B.** Two-way handshake
- ○ **C.** Three-way handshake
- ○ **D.** Four-way handshake

34. What does the following access control list do?

```
Router(config)#ip access-list extended QueACL
Router(config-ext-nacl)#permit tcp 172.30.31.192 0.0.0.15 10.0.4.0
        0.0.3.255 eq 110
Router(config-ext-nacl)#permit tcp 172.30.31.192 0.0.0.15 10.0.4.0
        0.0.3.255 eq 25
Router(config-ext-nacl)#interface fastethernet0/0
Router(config-if)#ip access-group QueACL in
```

- ○ **A.** Allows NTP and SNMP from the 172.30.31.192/28 network to the 10.0.4.0/22 network
- ○ **B.** Allows SMTP and POP from the 172.30.31.192/29 network to the 10.0.4.0/21 network
- ○ **C.** Allows SMTP and POP from the 172.30.31.192/28 network to the 10.0.4.0/22 network
- ○ **D.** Allows SNMP and POP from the 172.30.31.192/28 network to the 10.0.4.0/21 network

35. What type of cable should you use between two switches?

- ○ **A.** Straight-through cable
- ○ **B.** Crossover cable
- ○ **C.** Rollover cable
- ○ **D.** V.35 cable

36. Routing occurs at what layer of the TCP/IP model?

○ **A.** Internet

○ **B.** Network

○ **C.** Application

○ **D.** Transport

37. Where is the feasible successor route stored in EIGRP?

○ **A.** Neighbor table

○ **B.** Route table

○ **C.** Adjacency table

○ **D.** Topology table

○ **E.** Link state database

38. Which of the following addresses are on the same network as the host with an IP address of 192.168.6.81/29? Select all that apply.

○ **A.** 192.168.6.79

○ **B.** 192.168.6.89

○ **C.** 192.168.6.85

○ **D.** 192.168.6.82

39. On what type of networks would you elect a DR? Select all that apply.

○ **A.** Broadcast multi-access

○ **B.** NBMA

○ **C.** Point-to-point

○ **D.** Point-to-multipoint

○ **E.** Point-to-multipoint nonbroadcast

40. What type of cable would you plug into a T1 interface with a built-in CSU/DSU?

○ **A.** Serial

○ **B.** Rollover

○ **C.** UTP

○ **D.** Coax

○ **E.** Fiber

41. Which of the following is used to identify traffic from different VLANs?

- ○ **A.** 802.11g
- ○ **B.** 802.1d
- ○ **C.** 802.11b
- ○ **D.** 802.1q

42. In the following configuration, what does the number 2 represent?

```
Router eigrp 2
 network 192.168.100.0
 network 172.16.0.0
```

- ○ **A.** Process ID
- ○ **B.** Autonomous system number
- ○ **C.** The number of networks
- ○ **D.** The router ID

43. Which of the following commands would correctly configure Telnet access for three VTY lines and encrypt both the enable and Telnet passwords?

- ○ **A.** enable password que

     service password-encryption

     line vty 0 2

       login

       password que

- ○ **B.** enable secret que

     service password-encryption

     line vty 0 3

       login

       password que

○ **C.** enable secret que

    service password-encryption

    line vty 0 2

      login

      password que

○ **D.** enable secret que

    service password-encryption

    line vty 0 4

      login

      password que

44. Which of the following are mechanisms that distance vector routing protocols use to prevent loops? Select all that apply.

○ **A.** Split horizon

○ **B.** Poison reverse

○ **C.** Spanning-tree

○ **D.** Dijkstra algorithm

○ **E.** Hold-down timers

45. You have a class B network that you want to subnet to create at least 1,000 networks with as many hosts as possible on each subnet. What subnet mask should you use?

○ **A.** 255.255.255.224

○ **B.** 255.255.252.0

○ **C.** 255.255.255.192

○ **D.** 255.255.254

○ **E.** 255.255.255.128

46. Examine the figure. You want to configure an access list that would permit everyone on the 172.16.0.0/16 network to access resources on the 172.18.0.0/16 network but deny everyone else. You configure the following access-list:

`access-list 1 permit 172.16.0.0 0.0.255.255`

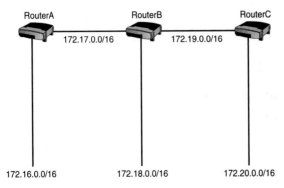

On what router and in what direction should you apply this access list?

- ○ **A.** Apply it inbound on RouterA's Ethernet 0 interface
- ○ **B.** Apply it outbound on RouterA's Ethernet 1 interface
- ○ **C.** Apply it inbound on RouterB's Ethernet 1 interface
- ○ **D.** Apply it inbound on RouterC's Ethernet 1 interface
- ○ **E.** Apply it outbound on RouterC's Ethernet 0 interface

47. What is the broadcast address for the 172.19.48.0/21 network?

- ○ **A.** 172.19.55.255
- ○ **B.** 172.19.48.255
- ○ **C.** 172.19.63.255
- ○ **D.** 172.19.51.255
- ○ **E.** 172.19.64.255

48. What is the benefit to having a hierarchical design with OSPF? Select all that apply.

- ○ **A.** Smaller routing tables mean less overhead.
- ○ **B.** If a network in an area goes down, it will not affect the summarized route in other areas.
- ○ **C.** Convergence is faster.
- ○ **D.** Less configuration on the area border routers.
- ○ **E.** Feasible successors are chosen faster.

49. In spanning-tree, how long does it take a port to go from the blocking state to the forwarding state?

○ **A.** 10 seconds

○ **B.** 20 seconds

○ **C.** 30 seconds

○ **D.** 40 seconds

○ **E.** 50 seconds

50. What device would you use to create more collision domains on your network?

○ **A.** Router

○ **B.** Hub

○ **C.** Switch

○ **D.** Repeater

51. Which command shows you the current IOS that is in use on a router?

○ **A.** `show version`

○ **B.** `show flash`

○ **C.** `show IOS`

○ **D.** `show running-config`

52. Examine the figure. RIP is configured between RouterA, RouterB, and RouterC; however, you are unable to ping the 172.20.0.0/16 network from RouterA. The configurations of the routers are as follows:

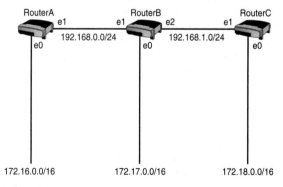

RouterA
```
router rip
 network 172.16.0.0
 network 172.17.0.0
```
RouterB
```
router rip
 network 172.18.0.0
```

```
network 172.19.0.0
RouterC
router rip
network 172.19.0.0
network 172.20.0.0
```

What is wrong with the configuration that causes this problem?

    ◯ **A.** The command 'version 2' is missing on all three routers.

    ◯ **B.** A default route is missing.

    ◯ **C.** The configuration on RouterB is incomplete.

    ◯ **D.** There is not enough information to answer this question.

    ◯ **E.** The interface connected to the 172.18.0.0/16 is shut down.

53. Below is the output of the **show interface serial 0** command that has been executed on two routers. Both routers are connected to each other on the serial interfaces through a leased line; however, you are unable to ping across the serial interface. What is wrong?

```
RouterA
Serial 0 is up, line protocol is down
Hardware is MCI Serial
Internet address is 192.168.15.170, subnet mask is 255.255.255.0
MTU 1500 bytes, BW 1544 Kbit, DLY 20000 usec, rely 255/255, load 1/255
Encapsulation HDLC, loopback not set, keepalive set (10 sec)
Last in   put 0:00:08, output 0:00:00, output hang never
Output queue 0/40, 0 drops; input queue 0/75, 0 drops
Five minute input rate 0 bits/sec, 0 packets/sec
Five minute output rate 0 bits/sec, 0 packets/sec
8192 packets input, 141256 bytes, 0 no buffer
Received 5125 broadcasts, 0 runts, 0 giants
4 input errors, 0 CRC, 0 frame, 0 overrun, 0 ignored, 3 abort
1 carrier transitions 21351 packets output, 1531572 bytes,
0 underruns 0 output errors, 0 collisions, 2 interface resets, 0 restarts
RouterB
Serial0/0 is up, line protocol is down
Hardware is PowerQUICC Serial
Internet address is 192.168.15.170/24
MTU 1500 bytes, BW 1544 Kbit, DLY 20000 usec,
reliability 255/255, txload 1/255, rxload 1/255
Encapsulation PPP, loopback not set
Keepalive set (10 sec)
LCP Closed
Closed: IPXCP
Listen: CCP
Open: IPCP, CDPCP
Last input 00:00:00, output 00:00:00, output hang never
Output queue 0/40, 0 drops; input queue 0/75, 0 drops
```

```
Five minute input rate 0 bits/sec, 0 packets/sec
Five minute output rate 0 bits/sec, 0 packets/sec
2251 packets input, 13515 bytes, 0 no buffer
Received 61367 broadcasts, 0 runts, 0 giants
8 input errors, 0 CRC, 0 frame, 0 overrun, 0 ignored, 2 abort
2 carrier transitions 23515 packets output, 89234 bytes,
0 underruns 0 output errors, 0 collisions, 2 interface resets, 0
  restarts
```

- ○ **A.** The encapsulations do not match.
- ○ **B.** There is a problem with the cable on RouterA.
- ○ **C.** The provider's router is misconfigured.
- ○ **D.** There is a problem with the cable on RouterB.
- ○ **E.** There is a clocking problem on RouterA.

54. What is wrong with the following OSPF configuration that causes this problem?

```
Router ospf 65535
 network 192.168.0.4 255.255.255.252 area 0
 network 192.168.0.8 255.255.255.248 area 1
interface fastethernet 0/0
 ip address 192.168.0.9 255.255.255.248
interface serial 0/0
ip address 192.168.0.5 255.255.255.252
```

- ○ **A.** The IP addresses and the network statements under the router configuration do not match.
- ○ **B.** The process ID number is too high.
- ○ **C.** The wrong masks are used under the OSPF process.
- ○ **D.** The areas are not the same for the two networks.

55. Given the following output, how were the hosts learned on the router?

```
Router# show hosts
Default domain is Que
Name/address lookup uses domain service
Name servers are 255.255.255.255
Host              Flag            Age   Type
Address(es)
RouterA      (perm, OK)  0        IP    192.168.100.1
RouterB      (perm, OK)  0        IP    192.168.200.1
```

○ **A.** Through a DNS server

○ **B.** Through the IP host command

○ **C.** Through the DNS dynamic-discovery command

○ **D.** Through a routing protocol

○ **E.** Through ARP

56. On what type of device would you typically configure the clock rate?

○ **A.** Router.

○ **B.** Switch.

○ **C.** CSU/DSU.

○ **D.** This is configured on the provider's router.

57. CDP is found at what layer of the OSI model?

○ **A.** Datalink

○ **B.** Network

○ **C.** Transport

○ **D.** Session

○ **E.** Application

58. Which of the following are methods to secure your Telnet access on a router? Select all that apply.

○ **A.** Secure your passwords with the enable password command.

○ **B.** Use SSH instead of Telnet.

○ **C.** Configure an access list on an interface blocking Telnet access.

○ **D.** Configure an access list on the VTY lines that allows only hosts that need access.

59. What would cause an OSPF adjacency not to form between two routers? Select all that apply.

○ **A.** Routers are using incompatible IOS versions.

○ **B.** The interfaces connecting the two routers are on different subnets.

○ **C.** Routers are using different OSPF passwords.

○ **D.** The interfaces connecting the two routers are in different areas.

○ **E.** The process ID numbers do not match between the two routers.

Answer Key to Practice Test #1

Answers at a Glance to Practice Exam I

1. B	21. B	41. D
2. E	22. A	42. B
3. D	23. C, E	43. C
4. A	24. B, D	44. A, B, E
5. B	25. D	45. C
6. A, C, D	26. D	46. E
7. C	27. C	47. A
8. B	28. B	48. A, B, C
9. A, D	29. D	49. E
10. D	30. D	50. C
11. B	31. A	51. A
12. A	32. A, C	52. C
13. A, B, C, D, E	33. C	53. A
14. D	34. C	54. C
15. B	35. B	55. B
16. B	36. A	56. C
17. A	37. D	57. A
18. A	38. C, D	58. B, D
19. C	39. A, B	59. B, C, D
20. A	40. C	

Answers with Explanations

Question 1

Answer B is the correct answer. A /28 network would give you 14 hosts on each network. The network increment of a /28 network is 16. Because the `ip subnet-zero` command is on the router, you can use the zero subnet, making the second subnet 192.168.25.16 and the first useable IP address 192.168.25.17. Answers A, C, D, and E are incorrect because each of these addresses is on a different subnet.

Question 2

Answer E is the correct answer. According to the diagram, the network attached to the FastEthernet0/3 interface is 172.21.248.0/23, although the configuration shows that FastEthernet 0/3 is configured for 172.21.254.1/23, which is on a different subnet. Answer A is incorrect because there is nothing incorrect with the pool configuration. Answer B is incorrect because the `ip nat outside` and `ip nat inside` commands are on the correct interfaces. Answer C is incorrect because the scenario does not ask you to overload your pool of addresses. Answer D is incorrect because there is nothing incorrect with the access list configuration.

Question 3

Answer D is the correct answer. A denial of service is an attack where a malicious hacker will attempt to disable access to a host, network, or application. A common type of denial of service attack is a SYN flood, where an attacker will send thousands of packets with the SYN bit set, but will not respond with an ACK when the system sends back a SYN-ACK message. This results in filling up the maximum number of allowable half-open TCP sessions on a host, which could potentially prevent some systems from accepting legitimate TCP requests. Answers A, B, and C are incorrect because these attacks do not involve sending SYN floods.

Question 4

Answer A is correct. A Service Set Identifier (SSID) is used to identify a wireless network. Answer B is incorrect because WEP keys are used for securing wireless networks but do not identify wireless networks. Answer C is incorrect because 802.11g is a type of wireless network, but does not identify wireless networks. Answer D is incorrect because Extended Service Set (ESS) is a method of grouping multiple basic service set (BSS) networks and is identified by a single SSID.

Question 5

Answer B is correct. Switches use the Dynamic Trunking Protocol to dynamically negotiate a trunk. If DTP is turned off (as it is in the output), the interface will not negotiate to be a trunk link. With the interface being set to static access, it is manually configured to be an access link. Answer A is incorrect because you do not put an IP address on a Layer 2 switched port and it is irrelevant to bringing up a trunk link. Answer C is incorrect because VTP pruning does not impact trunk negotiation. Answer D is incorrect because having an interface configured for a VLAN does not impact trunk negotiation.

Question 6

Answers A, C, and D are the correct answers. EIGRP supports AppleTalk, IP, and IPX. Answers B and E are incorrect because EIGRP does not support Banyan Vines or LAT.

Question 7

Answer C is the correct answer. You want to configure two Telnet sessions. Because Cisco begins its numbering with 0, you would configure lines 0 through 1. The commands to configure Telnet authentication are login and password. The service password-encryption global configuration command is used to encrypt all unencrypted passwords on your router. Only answer C has the correct configuration. Answer A is incorrect because it configures all five Telnet lines and not just the first two. Answer A is also incorrect because it is not encrypting your passwords. Answer B is incorrect because it configures the first three Telnet lines and not just the first two. Answer D is incorrect because it does not have the proper configuration for Telnet authentication. Finally, answer E is incorrect because it configures all five configuration lines and not just the first two.

Question 8

Answer B is the correct answer. RouterA is learning of the networks attached to RouterD via OSPF and RIP. When a router is learning of networks through more than one routing source, it chooses the best path based on whichever source has the lowest administrative distance. RouterA is learning the path through OSPF from RouterB and through RIP from RouterE. OSPF has an administrative distance of 110, and RIP has an administrative distance of 120. Because RIP's administrative distance is higher than OSPF's administrative distance, the path through RouterB is preferred. Answer A is incorrect because OSPF has a lower administrative distance than RIP. Answer C is incorrect because RouterA will choose RouterB based on administrative distance. Answer D is incorrect because enough information is given to answer this question.

Question 9

Answers A and D are the correct answers. Answers B and C are incorrect because these are network addresses and therefore cannot be configured on hosts.

Question 10

Answer D is the correct answer. Answers A and C are incorrect because Telnet uses TCP and not UDP. Answer B is incorrect because the wildcard mask for the 172.19.40.0/21 network is incorrect.

Question 11

Answer B is the correct answer. OSPF will first choose the highest IP address on any loopback interface for its router ID. If no loopback interfaces are configured, the highest IP address on any active physical interface is chosen. Answer A is incorrect because you do not loopback interfaces to run OSPF. Answer C is incorrect because the interfaces must be active (up) when OSPF is initialized in order for OSPF to consider using them as the router ID. Answer D is incorrect because the highest IP address is chosen, not the lowest.

Question 12

Answer A is the correct answer. The summary address for 172.20.0.0/24–172.20.4.0/24 is 172.20.0.0/22. To determine a summary address for a range of networks, work out the bits that are the same for each network and ignore the rest. Answer B is incorrect because it is the wrong mask. Answer C is incorrect because it is the wrong mask and summarized network. Answer D is incorrect because it is the wrong summarized network.

Question 13

Answers A, B, C, D, and E are the correct answers. You can view all of these with the show cdp neighbors detail command. Note that the show cdp entry * command is equivalent.

Question 14

Answer D is the correct answer. Only VTP Server mode allows you to make VLAN changes that propagate out to other switches. Currently, the switch operates in VTP Transparent mode, so any changes are local to the switch. Answers A, B, and C are incorrect because domain name, version numbers, and VTP pruning are irrelevant to passing VLAN information between switches.

Question 15

Answer B is the correct answer. Routers break up your broadcast domains. There is one router in this diagram with two interfaces. Each interface is in its own broadcast domain, so there are two broadcast domains in this diagram.

Question 16

Answer B is the correct answer. Interface Serial0/0 on RouterA is on the 172.16.20.0/22 network, but interface Serial0/0 on RouterB is on the 172.16.24.0/22 network. Answers A and D are incorrect because there is nothing incorrect with the static routes. Answer C is incorrect because the server and the router's interface are on the 172.16.128.0/22 network. Finally, answer E is incorrect because the IP address 172.16.64.201/22 is a completely valid IP address.

Question 17

Answer A is the correct answer. The root bridge should be the central point in your topology because all its ports will be forwarding, allowing for optimal data transfer. Because VLAN 200 has the majority of communication going to SwitchA, SwitchA should be the root bridge. Answers B, C, D, and E are incorrect because that might place some ports on SwitchA into blocking mode, which would allow suboptimal paths in your switched network.

Question 18

Answer A is the correct answer. EIGRP is classful by default, which means that it automatically summarizes your subnetworks at the /8, /16, and /24 bit boundaries. The no auto-summary command, entered within the EIGRP configuration mode, causes EIGRP to become classless and sends out the subnet mask in updates. Answer B is incorrect because there is nothing incorrect with the network statements. Answer C is incorrect because the mask is not necessary. (As a side note, EIGRP can use wildcard masks like OSPF, but they are not required.) Answer D is incorrect because you want to disable auto-summary, not turn it on. Finally, answer E is incorrect because the maximum-paths command modifies load-balancing parameters, which is irrelevant to the problem.

Question 19

Answer C is correct. Unlike OSPF and RIP, EIGRP can load balance across unequal cost paths. In this scenario, your router can load balance across three unequal cost paths. Answer A is incorrect because EIGRP will load balance across unequal and equal cost paths. Answer B is incorrect because there can be many EIGRP networks in the routing table and maximum path does not refer to the maximum number of entries in a routing table. Answer D is incorrect because maximum path does not refer to the networks EIGRP know about (this is found under "Routing for Networks").

Question 20

Answer A is the correct answer. Only answer A has the correct configuration that allows for a pool of six addresses. Answers B and D are incorrect because the access-lists are referencing the inside global addresses instead of the inside local addresses and the pools are referencing inside local addresses instead of inside global addresses. Answer C is incorrect because the pool allows for seven addresses and not six.

Question 21

Answer B is the correct answer. Although the LMI types do not have to match, the encapsulation types do. One router uses IETF encapsulation, and the other uses the default (Cisco). Answer A is incorrect because the routers can run different LMI types. (LMI runs only from the router to the frame-relay provider and can therefore be different on both sides of the frame-relay virtual circuit.) Answer C is incorrect because the configuration is complete. Answer D is incorrect because the routers are both on the same 10.250.86.64/30 subnet.

Question 22

Answer A is the correct answer. Ping and Traceroute use ICMP, which operates at the network layer.

Question 23

Answers C and E are the correct answers. The 192.168.5.0/24 network is not in the routing table, and a default route was not set up (as evidenced by the statement GATEWAY OF LAST RESORT IS NOT SET). Therefore, you can say goodbye to any packet destined for the 192.168.5.0/24 network. The router drops the packet and sends back an ICMP type 3 Destination Unreachable (DU) message to the source of the packet. Because the routing table does not have this entry, answers A, B, and D are incorrect.

Question 24

Answers B and D are correct. This command creates a static route that will forward all traffic destined for the 192.168.1.0/24 network to the router with the

IP address of 10.1.24.1. Answer A is incorrect because this is not a default route. An example of a default route would be ip route 0.0.0.0 0.0.0.0 10.1.24.1. Answer C is incorrect because it describes the opposite of what the static route is doing. Answer E is incorrect because this command is used for a static route and not for routing protocols.

Question 25

Answer D is the correct answer. Cisco defines OSPF cost as 10^8/bandwidth. If you take 100,000,000 (10^8) and divide it by the 1,544,000 (a T1), you get 64.766. Because remainders are not factored into the metric, you are left with 64. For the test, you should know the common metrics such as 1 for a 100Mb connection, 10 for a 10Mb connection, 64 for a T1 connection, and 1,562 for a 64Kbs connection. Answer A is incorrect because this is the bandwidth of a T1 and not the cost. Answer B is incorrect because this is the cost for a 10Mb link. Answer C is incorrect because this would be the cost for a 1Mb link.

Question 26

Answer D is the correct answer. A /30, or 255.255.255.252, mask is common on point-to-point wide area network links because this mask allows for two addresses. Because you need only two addresses on point-to-point links, this mask is ideal because it gives you just enough addresses to assign IP addresses to both routers while saving on your overall IP address space.

Question 27

Answer C is the correct answer. Only answer C has the correct configuration to assign a default gateway. Answers A and D are incorrect because the command should be entered from global configuration mode. Answer B is incorrect because you do not enter the subnet mask with this command.

Question 28

Answer B is the correct answer. Although the default maximum is 100, the absolute maximum hop count for EIGRP is 224. Answer A is incorrect because 255 is the absolute maximum hop count for IGRP, not EIGRP. Answer C is incorrect because this is the maximum hop count for RIP. Answer D is incorrect because this is the TTL used for routing updates, not the maximum hop count. (Having a TTL of 1 means that the routing updates will be sent only to the next router; the next router will then have to generate a new routing update and send it out to pass it on.) Answer E is incorrect because EIGRP does have a maximum hop count; OSPF is the routing protocol with an unlimited hop count.

Question 29

Answer D is the correct answer. The spanning-tree states are blocking, listening, learning, and forwarding. In the learning state, the port is populating the MAC table so that when it moves to forwarding state, it is capable of making intelligent decisions as to where it should send frames. Otherwise, without the learning state, when the port becomes active, it would flood frames out all ports until it learns MAC addresses. Answer A is incorrect because this describes the listening state and not the learning state. Answer B is incorrect because this describes the blocking state. Finally, answer C is incorrect because this describes the forwarding state.

Question 30

Answer D is the correct answer. You would use a straight-through cable between a router and switch. The switch is then responsible for crossing over the transmit and receive communication path. Answer A is incorrect because a rollover cable is used to connect to a console port. Answer B is incorrect because a null modem cable is used between two asynchronous serial ports. Answer C is incorrect because a crossover cable would be used between two switches or between two routers, but not between a router and a switch.

Question 31

Answer A is the correct answer. Without the broadcast keyword, broadcast and multicast-based routing updates are not sent across the link. Answer B is incorrect because the RIP version is irrelevant to get RIP to work across frame-relay. Answer C is incorrect because inverse-arp has nothing to do with getting your routing updates across a frame-relay network. Finally, answer D is incorrect because RIP is activated on the interfaces. When you enter the network statements under the RIP configuration mode, it automatically enables RIP on the interfaces where those networks reside.

Question 32

Answers A and C are the correct answers. IGRP and EIGRP can also factor in reliability, load, and MTU. Answer B is incorrect because this is the metric used by RIP. Answer D is incorrect because this is the metric used by OSPF and IS-IS.

Question 33

Answer C is the correct answer. CHAP is a three-way handshake authentication protocol. One router sends a challenge, the second router sends an MD5 hash of the password, and the first router sends a success or fail response (therefore, three messages).

Question 34

Answer C is the correct answer. The access list is permitting TCP port 110 and 25, which POP and SMTP use. Answer A is incorrect because NTP (UDP 123) or SNMP (UDP ports 160 and 161) do not use these ports. Answer B is incorrect because the masks are incorrect. Answer D is incorrect because SNMP traffic is not referenced in the access list; only POP and SMTP are.

Question 35

Answer B is correct. You should use a crossover cable to connect two switches together. Answer A is incorrect because this is used to connect a switch to an end device, not two switches. Answer C is incorrect because a rollover cable is used to connect a PC to a network device via a console connection. Answer D is incorrect because V.35 cables are used for wide area networks.

Question 36

Answer A is the correct answer. Routing occurs at the Internet layer of the TCP/IP model. Answer B is incorrect because the Network layer is on the OSI model, not the TCP/IP model. Answers C and D are incorrect because these are different layers.

Question 37

Answer D is the correct answer. The feasible successor is stored in the topology table. Should the successor route go down in the routing table, the feasible successor would take over and the DUAL algorithm would work to elect a new feasible successor. Answer A is incorrect because this is where you would find neighbor information and not the feasible successor. Answer B is incorrect because this is where you would find the successor. Answers C and E are incorrect because these tables are used with OSPF, not EIGRP.

Question 38

Answers C and D are the correct answers. The IP address is on the 192.168.6.80/29 network. A /29 network uses an increment of 8, so the next network is 192.168.6.88. Therefore, your range is 192.168.6.80–192.168.6.87 but, because you cannot use the first or last address of each subnet (they are the network and broadcast addresses), your range of valid host addresses are 192.168.6.81– 192.168.6.86. Only answers C and D have IP addresses in this range.

Question 39

Answers A and B are the correct answers. DR elections are used with OSPF routing. These elections occur only on broadcast multi-access and nonbroadcast multi-access (NBMA) networks.

Question 40

Answer C is the correct answer. If the router has a built-in CSU/DSU, you use a standard straight-through RJ-45 UTP connector coming from the wall jack to the router. While you may also use a RJ-48 STP connector, this was not one of the answers. If the CSU/DSU were external, you would have a straight-through cable from the wall jack to the CSU/DSU and then a serial cable from the CSU/DSU to the router. Because the question mentions a built-in CSU/DSU, you use a UTP cable.

Question 41

Answer D is the correct answer. 802.1q is the IEEE standard for trunks. 802.1q trunking works by tagging frames with their associated VLAN ID. Answers A and C are incorrect because these are wireless standards. Answer B is incorrect because 802.1d is the standard for spanning tree.

Question 42

Answer B is the correct answer. EIGRP and IGRP both require autonomous system numbers. This can be any number you want between 1 and 65,535, but all routers must share this same number for routing updates to pass between them. Answer A is incorrect because process IDs are used in OSPF, not EIGRP. Answer C is incorrect because the number is the AS number, not the number of networks. Answer D is incorrect because the router ID is chosen automatically and is not specified with the `router eigrp` command. Answer D is also incorrect because, although there are router IDs with EIGRP, at the CCNA level the router IDs take on only significance with OSPF.

Question 43

Answer C is the correct answer. You need the **enable secret** and **service password-encryption** commands to encrypt your passwords. Because the question asks to configure only three Telnet lines, you configure lines 0–2. Therefore, answer C is correct. Answer A is incorrect because the enable password is not encrypted. Answer B is incorrect because the command line vty 0 3 encrypts four Telnet sessions and not two (which the question asks). Finally, answer D is incorrect because it configures all five Telnet sessions.

Question 44

Answers A, B, and E are the correct answers. Reverse poisoning and triggered updates are other options used to prevent loops in switched networks. Answer C is incorrect because spanning-tree is used to prevent loops in switched networks, not routed networks. Answer D is incorrect because the Dijkstra algorithm is used with OSPF, which is a link-state routing protocol, not distance-vector.

Question 45

Answer C is the correct answer. The subnet mask 255.255.255.192 is borrowing 10 bits from a class B network. The formula to determine your networks (assuming that you cannot use subnet-zero) is 2^n-2. Borrowing 10 bits gives you 1,022 networks ($2^{10}-2=1022$). Answer A is incorrect because the 255.255.255.224 mask gives you 2,046 networks and 30 hosts. Although this meets the requirement of providing at least 1,000 networks, it does not provide as many host addresses as the 255.255.255.192 mask. (It provides 62 host addresses on each network.) Answer B is incorrect because it only gives you 62 networks. Answer D is incorrect because it only gives you 126 networks. Finally, answer E is incorrect because it only gives you 510 networks.

Question 46

Answer E is the correct answer. A standard access list has been configured, and the general rule is that standard access lists should be applied as close to the destination as possible. The Ethernet 0 interface on RouterC is the interface closest to the destination. Therefore, answer E is correct, and the other answers, which apply it on other routers or on the wrong interface, are incorrect.

Question 47

Answer A is the correct answer. A /21 subnet has a network increment of 8 in the third octet. The next network, then, is 172.19.56.0. One less than the next network is 172.19.55.255 (answer A). Answer B is incorrect because this is a valid host address on the same network. Answer C is incorrect because this is a broadcast address on the 172.19.56.0 network. Answer D is incorrect because this a valid host address on the same network. Finally, answer E is incorrect because this is a valid host address on the 172.19.64.0 network.

Question 48

Answers A, B, and C are the correct answers. Having a hierarchical design makes it easy to supernet (summarize your networks). This question really tests to see if you understand the benefit of summarizing your networks. Summarizing your networks results in less overhead, which, subsequently, equate to smaller routing tables (answer A). If a particular subnet goes down, it does not affect the summarized route in other areas (answer B). Also, having fewer routes means that the routers have less to process, which results in faster convergence (answer C). Answer D is incorrect because summarization actually involves more configuration on a router, not less. Answer E is incorrect because feasible successors are used with EIGRP, not OSPF.

Question 49

Answer E is the correct answer. The blocking state takes 20 seconds, and the listening and learning states take 15 seconds each for a total of 50 seconds.

Question 50

Answer C is the correct answer. Switches (and bridges) are used to create more collision domains because each segment on a switch or bridge is its own collision domain. Answer A is incorrect because a router is used to create more broadcast domains, not collision domains. Answer B is incorrect because a hub actually creates more congestion on a network and not fewer collision domains. Answer D is incorrect because a repeater amplifies only a signal and does not create more collision domains.

Question 51

Answer A is the correct answer. Show version displays the name of the current IOS version in use on a router. Answer B is incorrect because this shows you the name of all IOS images on a router but not the one currently in use. Answer C is incorrect because this is an invalid command. Finally, answer D is incorrect because this command shows you the current configuration in NVRAM and not the current IOS version.

Question 52

Answer C is the correct answer. RouterB is missing the 172.17.0.0/16 network. Answer A is incorrect because the RIP version 2 is not necessary to make this scenario work. Answer B is incorrect because a default route is unnecessary.

Answer D is incorrect because you do have enough information to answer this problem. Finally, although the interface connected to 172.18.0.0/16 does need to be up for you to communicate across the network, nothing in the scenario indicates that the interface is down. In addition, the better answer is C because, even if the interface is not shut down, it cannot work unless the 172.17.0.0/16 network is added under the RIP process on RouterB.

Question 53

Answer A is the correct answer. RouterA uses HDLC encapsulation, and RouterB is using PPP encapsulation. Answers B and D are incorrect because nothing in the output indicates that there is a problem with the cabling. Answer C is incorrect because nothing in the output reveals information about how the provider is configured. Finally, answer E is incorrect because the problem is with the encapsulations, not clocking. However, clocking problems can cause the line protocol to not function, although the output indicates that the problem is with encapsulations and not clocking.

Question 54

Answer C is the correct answer. OSPF uses wildcard masks and not subnet masks. The correct OSPF configuration is

```
Router OSPF 65545
  network 192.168.0.4 0.0.0.3 area 0
  network 192.168.0.8 0.0.0.7 area 1
```

Answer A is incorrect because the IP addresses on the interfaces are on the same networks referenced under the OSPF routing process configuration. Answer B is incorrect because the number of the process ID is irrelevant. Answer D is incorrect because the areas do not have to be the same number.

Question 55

Answer B is the correct answer. The output shows the flag perm, which means that they were permanently learned through the IP host global configuration command. Answer A is incorrect because the flag temp would show if they were learned through a DNS server. Answer C is incorrect because there is no such thing as a DNS dynamic-discovery command. Answer D is incorrect because routing protocols have nothing to do with learning hostname to IP address mappings. Answer E is incorrect because DNS or static mappings are used to map IP address to hostnames, not ARP. ARP is used to map IP addresses to MAC addresses.

Question 56

Answer C is the correct answer. The clock rate is typically configured on the CSU/DSU in production networks. Often, the CSU/DSU comes built into the router, but even if it is built into the router, the CSU/DSU still provides the clocking and not the router. Although it is true that you can configure clocking on a router with the clock rate interface command, this is done on lab environments and not on production networks. The question asks for the typical configuration, not for unique lab environments. Therefore, answer C is correct and answer A is incorrect. Answers B and D are incorrect because clocking is not configured on switching or on the provider's network. Although it is possible to provide clocking from the provider, this is not the typical configuration. For the CCNA exam, remember that clocking is done at the CSU/DSU.

Question 57

Answer A is the correct answer. CDP uses multicasts frames at the Datalink layer of the OSI model. All other answers reference other OSI layers and are therefore incorrect.

Question 58

Answers B and D are correct. You can secure your remote access to a router by using SSH instead of Telnet because SSH encrypts traffic between your computer and the router. You can also configure an access list that allows only certain hosts access to the VTY lines. Answer A is incorrect because the enable password is not a method of providing added security to your router. Answer C is incorrect because configuring an access list on an interface to block Telnet access would only block Telnet traffic as it passes through a router and not Telnet attempts to a router.

Question 59

Answers B, C, and D are the correct answers. In addition to these answers, the interfaces connecting the two routers must be configured to use the same timers and stub configuration (stub areas are covered more heavily on the CCNP exams and not at the CCNA level). Answer A is incorrect because the two routers can run different IOS versions. Answer E is incorrect because the process ID is locally significant to each router and does not have to match the process ID on other routers.

Practice Exam #2

1. Which of the following are valid host addresses on the same subnet as the 192.168.14.69/28 host? [Select all that apply.]

   ○ **A.** 192.168.14.63

   ○ **B.** 192.168.14.65

   ○ **C.** 192.168.14.81

   ○ **D.** 192.168.14.64

   ○ **E.** 192.168.14.78

2. Your coworker calls you and informs you that VTP is not working between two switches. What advice can you give your coworker to troubleshoot VTP? [Select all that apply.]

   ○ **A.** Make sure that a trunk is configured between the two switches.

   ○ **B.** Make sure that both switches are in the same VTP domain.

   ○ **C.** Make sure that both switches are operating in the same VTP mode.

   ○ **D.** Make sure that both switches are using the same VTP password.

   ○ **E.** Make sure that both switches are using the same hostname.

3. When configuring frame-relay subinterfaces, what configuration steps should you take for the main interface? [Select all that apply.]

   ○ **A.** Configure the DLCI on the main interface.

   ○ **B.** Configure the IP address on the main interface.

   ○ **C.** Take the IP address off the main interface.

   ○ **D.** Configure the frame-relay encapsulation on the main interface.

   ○ **E.** Take the frame-relay encapsulation off the main interface.

4. What statement is true for a named access list that is not true for a numbered access list?

   ○ **A.** You can only do a standard named access list; you cannot do an extended named access list.

   ○ **B.** You can delete individual lines in a named access list; you cannot delete individual lines in a numbered access list.

   ○ **C.** You can only apply named access lists on VTY lines; you cannot apply them on an interface.

   ○ **D.** You can only do IP named access lists; you cannot do IPX named access lists.

5. Which of the following are true statements about access ports? Select all that apply.

   ○ **A.** Carries traffic for one VLAN

   ○ **B.** Performs interVLAN connectivity when connected to a router port that is divided into subinterfaces

   ○ **C.** Carries traffic for many VLANs

   ○ **D.** Uses straight-through cables to connect into end devices

6. Examine the figure that follows. Which of the following switches would be the root bridge in this scenario?

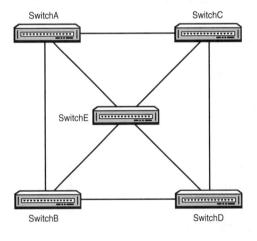

SwitchA
Priority: 32768
MAC: 03-0C-2F-9B-44-B8

SwitchB
Priority: 16384
MAC: 04-0C-2F-9B-44-B8

SwitchC
Priority: 16384
MAC: 04-0C-F2-9B-44-B8

SwitchD
Priority: 32768
MAC: 03-0C-2F-B9-44-B8

   ○ **A.** SwitchA

   ○ **B.** SwitchB

   ○ **C.** SwitchC

   ○ **D.** SwitchD

7. Examine the output below. Based on this output, which of the following are true statements?

```
RIP: received update from 10.0.0.1 on Serial 0
      172.16.0.0 in 1 hops
      172.17.0.0 in 2 hops
      172.18.0.0 in 3 hops
RIP: Sending update to 255.255.255.255 via Serial 0 (10.0.0.2)
      subnet 192.168.0.0, metric 1
RIP: Sending update to 255.255.255.255 via Ethernet 0 (192.168.0.1)
      subnet 10.0.0.0, metric 1
      subnet 172.16.0.0, metric 2
      subnet 172.17.0.0, metric 3
      subnet 172.18.0.0, metric 4
```

    ○ **A.** Split-horizon is not working.

    ○ **B.** The router is running RIP version 2.

    ○ **C.** The router is on the 172.16.0.0 network.

    ○ **D.** Split-horizon is working.

    ○ **E.** You will not be able to ping a host with the address of 172.18.15.9.

8. You have just created a configuration in your favorite text editor with some basic commands that you want to put on a new router (see configuration below). You copy your template and paste it into the new router. When you go to telnet into the router, you get a message saying that your computer could not open a connection to the host. What is wrong?

```
! Configuration for new router
hostname NewRouter
enable password letmein
service password-encryption
interface Ethernet 0
 ip address 192.168.125.97 255.255.255.240
interface serial 0
 description ***WAN Link to Cincinati***
 encapsulation frame-relay
 ip address 192.168.125.113 255.255.255.252
line vty 0 4
 login
 password letmein
 logging synchronous
```

    ○ **A.** The encapsulation is wrong on the serial interface.

    ○ **B.** The telnet configuration is incomplete.

    ○ **C.** The Ethernet interface is missing the `no shut` command.

    ○ **D.** The `login` and `password` commands are entered in the wrong order.

    ○ **E.** The router is missing a console password.

9. Which of the following commands shows you if a router is acting as the designated router for one of its interfaces?

   ○ **A.** `show ip ospf database`

   ○ **B.** `show ip ospf interface`

   ○ **C.** `show ip ospf`

   ○ **D.** `show ip ospf summary-address`

10. Which of the following correctly matches the names of the protocol data units (PDUs) with their respective layers?

    7. Application   A. Data

    6. Presentation   B. Bits

    5. Session   C. Frames

    4. Transport   D. Segments

    3. Network   E. Packets

    2. Data-Link

    1. Physical

    ○ **A.** 7-A, 6-A, 5-A, 4-D, 3-E, 2-C, 1-B

    ○ **B.** 7-A, 6-A, 5-A, 4-E, 3-D, 2-C, 1-B

    ○ **C.** 7-A, 6-A, 5-A, 4-C, 3-E, 2-D, 1-B

    ○ **D.** 7-A, 6-A, 5-A, 4-D, 3-C, 2-E, 1-B

11. Which of the following commands will display IP to MAC address mappings on a Windows PC?

    ○ **A.** `ipconfig /all`

    ○ **B.** `ping 127.0.0.1`

    ○ **C.** `tracert`

    ○ **D.** `arp -a`

12. What happens when you turn on a new router?

    ○ **A.** You are sent to the `Router#` prompt.

    ○ **B.** You are sent to the `Router>` prompt.

    ○ **C.** You are asked to enter the initial default password of `ciscorouter`.

    ○ **D.** You are given the option to enter initial system configuration information.

13. What commands would you use to see the layer 3 information of a neighboring Cisco device? [Select all that apply.]

   ○ **A.** `show cdp neighbors`

   ○ **B.** `show cdp neighbors detail`

   ○ **C.** `show cdp entry *`

   ○ **D.** `show cdp traffic`

14. You just connected three switches together via trunk links. Based on the following output, which switch will be the root bridge?

```
Floor1#show spanning-tree
Spanning tree 1 is executing the IEEE compatible Spanning Tree protocol
 Bridge Identifier has priority 32768, address 0002.fd29.c602
 Configured hello time 2, max age 20, forward delay 15
Floor2#show spanning-tree
Spanning tree 1 is executing the IEEE compatible Spanning Tree protocol
 Bridge Identifier has priority 16384, address 0002.fd29.c604
 Configured hello time 2, max age 20, forward delay 15
Floor3#show spanning-tree
Spanning tree 1 is executing the IEEE compatible Spanning Tree protocol
 Bridge Identifier has priority 32768, address 0002.fd29.c601
    Configured hello time 2, max age 20, forward delay 15
```

   ○ **A.** The Floor1 switch.

   ○ **B.** The Floor2 switch.

   ○ **C.** The Floor3 switch.

   ○ **D.** There is not enough information to answer this question.

15. Which of the following are valid frame-relay encapsulations? [Select all that apply.]

   ○ **A.** Cisco

   ○ **B.** Ansi

   ○ **C.** Q933A

   ○ **D.** IETF

16. You need to subnet a class C network to allow for at least eight subnets with as many hosts as possible on each subnet. The command `ip subnet-zero` is applied on your router. What subnet mask would meet this requirement?

   ○ **A.** 255.255.255.128

   ○ **B.** 255.255.255.192

   ○ **C.** 255.255.255.224

   ○ **D.** 255.255.255.240

   ○ **E.** 255.255.255.248

17. What is the maximum hop count for OSPF?

   ○ **A.** 15

   ○ **B.** 224

   ○ **C.** 255

   ○ **D.** Unlimited

18. What is true about the User Datagram Protocol (UDP)? [Select all that apply.]

   ○ **A.** UDP performs a three-way handshake before transferring data.

   ○ **B.** UDP uses less bandwidth than TCP.

   ○ **C.** UDP provides reliable delivery.

   ○ **D.** UDP is a connectionless protocol.

19. Examine the figure. What type of cable would you use in this scenario?

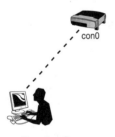

   ○ **A.** Crossover

   ○ **B.** Rollover

   ○ **C.** Straight-through

   ○ **D.** Serial

20. Which of the following is not a step you would take when configuring VLANs on a switch?

   ○ **A.** Create the VLAN

   ○ **B.** Name the VLAN

   ○ **C.** Assign a password to the VLAN

   ○ **D.** Associate the VLAN with an interface

21. Examine the figure below. A user sitting at HostA is sending a packet of data to HostB. When the packet returns, what will be the destination MAC address when the packet is coming from HostB and going to RouterB?

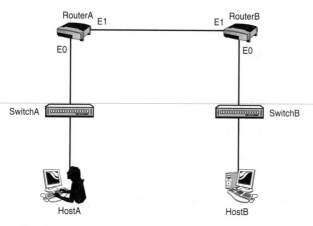

   ○ **A.** RouterA's E0 MAC address

   ○ **B.** HostA's MAC address

   ○ **C.** RouterB's E0 MAC address

   ○ **D.** SwitchB's MAC address

22. Which of the following are examples of private IP addresses? [Select all that apply.]

   ○ **A.** 172.31.14.0

   ○ **B.** 172.33.0.10

   ○ **C.** 192.186.0.8

   ○ **D.** 10.5.0.0

23. Which of the following describes the difference between a switch and a bridge?

   ○ **A.** A bridge is typically faster than a switch.

   ○ **B.** A switch is faster than a bridge.

   ○ **C.** A bridge is a layer 1 device, and a switch is a Layer 2 device.

   ○ **D.** A switch is a layer 1 device, and a bridge is a Layer 2 device.

24. Which of the following is the correct configuration that would allow telnet access from the 10.0.0.5 host to your router?

   ○ **A.** **access-list 100 permit tcp host 10.0.0.5 any eq telnet**

         line vty 0 4

         access-class 100 in

   ○ **B.** **access-list 1 permit host 10.0.0.5**

         line vty 0 4

         ip access-group 1 in

   ○ **C.** **access-list 1 permit host 10.0.0.5**

         line vty 0 4

         access-class 1 in

   ○ **D.** **access-list 100 permit tcp host 10.0.0.5 any eq telnet**

         line vty 0 4

         access-class 100 out

25. You want your router to be a DR on its Ethernet segment. All the other routers on the segment are set to the default priority value. Which of the following commands would configure your router to win the DR election?

   ○ **A.** `router ospf` *process-id*

         `ip ospf priority 255`

   ○ **B.** `router ospf` *process-id*

         `ospf priority 255`

   ○ **C.** `interface Ethernet 0`

         `ip ospf priority 255`

   ○ **D.** `interface Ethernet 0`

         `ospf priority 255`

26. You execute the **show ip interface brief** command on a router and see that an interface is administratively down. What could you do to bring the interface to the up state?

   ○ **A.** Execute the **no shutdown** command on the interface

   ○ **B.** Reset the cable on the interface

   ○ **C.** Execute the **interface up** command on the interface

   ○ **D.** Enter the **clock rate** command on the interface

27. Examine the figure. HostA is unable to communicate with HostB. What is wrong?

Router E1
192.168.16.29/28

Router E0
192.168.16.45/28

HostB
192.168.16.16/28

HostA
192.168.16.34/28

   ○ **A.** HostA has an invalid IP address.

   ○ **B.** HostB has an invalid IP address.

   ○ **C.** The router's E0 interface has an invalid IP address.

   ○ **D.** The router's E1 interface has an invalid IP address.

28. What type of technology would you use to prevent unauthorized hosts from accessing the LAN?

   ○ **A.** Switchport access lists

   ○ **B.** Port security

   ○ **C.** Encrypted enable secret passwords

   ○ **D.** WEP username and password

29. Which of the following commands would you use to display an administrative message when a person connects to a router?

   ○ **A. banner message**

   ○ **B. banner motd**

   ○ **C. banner**

   ○ **D. banner display**

30. What command would you use to see if clocking is stopped on an interface?

- ○ **A.** show controllers
- ○ **B.** show ip interface
- ○ **C.** show interface
- ○ **D.** show running-config

31. At what layer of the OSI model would you find windowing and sequence numbers?

- ○ **A.** Application
- ○ **B.** Data-Link
- ○ **C.** Network
- ○ **D.** Physical
- ○ **E.** Transport

32. Examine the output that follows. Why is this switch not the root bridge for the VLAN shown?

```
switch#show spanning-tree vlan 10
VLAN0010
  Spanning tree enabled protocol rstp
  Root IDPriority      4106
         Address0003.C832.9885
         Cost        19
         Port        1 (FastEthernet0/1)
         Hello Time 2 sec Max Age 20 sec Forward Delay 15
sec

Bridge IDPriority 32778 (priority 32768 sys-id-ext 1)
         Address0003.2201.830D.E774
         Hello Time 2 sec Max Age 20 sec Forward Delay 14
sec
         Aging Time 300
Interface     Role    Sts     Cost     Prio.Nbr   Type
-----------   ----    ----    ------   ---------  -----
Fa0/10        Root    FWD     19       128.1      P2p
Fa0/11        Altn    BLK     38       128.1      P2p
Fa0/12        Desg    FWD     38       128.1      P2p
```

- ○ **A.** It has a lower bridge ID than the root bridge.
- ○ **B.** It has a higher bridge ID than the root bridge.
- ○ **C.** All of its ports are not in the root state.
- ○ **D.** It has a higher cost than the root bridge.

33. Examine the figure. How many collision domains are there in this network?

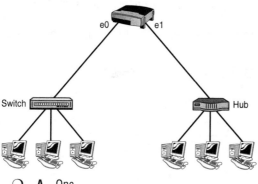

- ○ **A.** One
- ○ **B.** Three
- ○ **C.** Five
- ○ **D.** Seven
- ○ **E.** Nine

34. What is a rogue AP?

- ○ **A.** An AP that has a faulty component, causing it to "jam" other APs by transmitting collision frames at maximum power.
- ○ **B.** An AP that can be easily moved to any location in the building.
- ○ **C.** An unauthorized AP that is installed to facilitate the capture of information.
- ○ **D.** An AP that does not follow the accepted WLAN standards, but uses proprietary protocols instead.

35. Examine the figure. This network is small with only 15 hosts on an Ethernet segment and a single connection out to the Internet. What routing protocol would you recommend between RouterA and the ISP router?

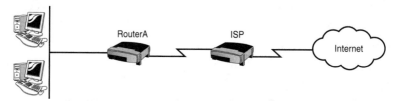

- ○ **A.** A default route on RouterA and a static route on the ISP router
- ○ **B.** BGP on RouterA and a static route on the ISP router
- ○ **C.** RIP on both RouterA and the ISP router
- ○ **D.** A static route on both RouterA and the ISP router
- ○ **E.** A default route on both RouterA and the ISP router

36. Examine the figure. You are a consultant for this network. The network is running RIPv1 and, despite your best efforts, the company refuses to convert to RIPv2. The company has been given a class C address, which it wants to subnet to allow for one useable subnet on each network segment. Assuming RIPv1, how many host addresses can it get on each subnet?

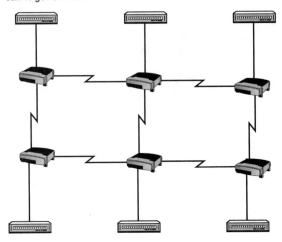

- ○ **A.** You cannot subnet with RIPv1
- ○ **B.** 6
- ○ **C.** 30
- ○ **D.** 14
- ○ **E.** 2

37. The following access-list would permit which of the following host addresses? [Select all that apply.]

```
access-list 19 permit 172.17.80.0 0.0.15.255
```

- ○ **A.** 172.17.95.12
- ○ **B.** 172.17.96.100
- ○ **C.** 172.17.84.0
- ○ **D.** 172.17.99.2
- ○ **E.** 172.17.97.4

38. Which of the following are examples of wide area network encapsulations? [Select all that apply.]

- ○ **A.** CHAP
- ○ **B.** PPP
- ○ **C.** HDLC
- ○ **D.** Frame Relay

39. Examine the figure. The company in the diagram has just implemented EIGRP, but routing does not appear to be working. What could be missing from the configuration to prevent EIGRP from working?

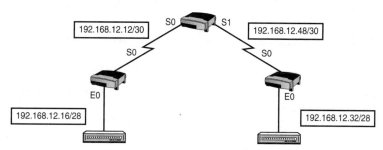

- ○ **A.** Nothing is missing; EIGRP supports full-length subnet masks (FLSM) only.
- ○ **B.** The `no auto-summary` command is missing on all routers.
- ○ **C.** The subnet masks are missing from the configuration.
- ○ **D.** The `auto-summary` command is missing on all routers.
- ○ **E.** The `version 2` command is missing on all routers.

40. You are running RIP on a router but you are unable to receive any routing updates across your frame-relay network. Given the configuration output below, what is wrong?

```
interface fastethernet0/0
 ip address 10.16.0.1 255.240.0.0
interface serial0/0
 ip address 192.168.44.133 255.255.255.252
 encapsulation frame-relay
 no frame-relay inverse-arp
 frame-relay map ip 192.168.44.134 100
 frame-relay interface-dlci 100
router rip
 version 2
 network 10.0.0.0
 network 192.168.44.0
```

- ○ **A.** The `frame-relay map` command is incomplete.
- ○ **B.** The RIP configuration does not specify the correct networks.
- ○ **C.** Inverse-arp needs to be enabled.
- ○ **D.** RIP will not work across frame-relay as it is a nonbroadcast multi-access medium, and RIP requires broadcast communication.
- ○ **E.** The serial interface is on a different subnet than the IP address specified in the `frame-relay map` command.

41. Which of the following frequency bands is used by 802.11a?

   ○ **A.** 2.4MHz

   ○ **B.** 2.4GHz

   ○ **C.** 5KHz

   ○ **D.** 5GHz

42. Examine the figure below. Assuming you are running both EIGRP and RIP, what path would RtrA take to get to RtrE?

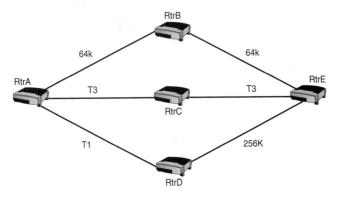

   ○ **A.** It will take the path through RtrB.

   ○ **B.** It will take the path through RtrC.

   ○ **C.** It will take the path through RtrD.

   ○ **D.** It will load balance across all three routers.

43. Examine the figure below. Given the diagram and the following configuration, why is NAT not working?

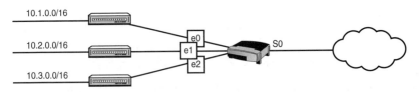

```
Interface serial 0
  ip address 200.100.50.25 255.255.255.252
Interface ethernet 0
  ip address 10.1.0.1 255.255.0.0
Interface ethernet 1
  ip address 10.2.0.1 255.255.0.0
Interface ethernet 2
```

```
  ip address 10.3.0.1 255.255.0.0
Access-list 1 permit 10.1.0.0 0.0.255.255
Access-list 1 permit 10.2.0.0 0.0.255.255
Access-list 1 permit 10.3.0.0 0.0.255.255
Ip nat inside source list 1 interface serial 0
  overload
```

- ○ **A.** It is using the wrong access-list.

- ○ **B.** The ip nat inside and ip nat outside commands are missing.

- ○ **C.** The IP addresses are incorrect.

- ○ **D.** The ip nat pool command is missing.

44. Given the following output of two switches, why is VLAN information not being sent between them?

```
Switch1#show vtp status
VTP version                       2
Configuration revision            10
Maximum VLANs supported locally   68
Number of existing VLANs          8
VTP Operational Mode              Server
VTP Domain Name                   TTC1532
VTP Pruning Mode                  Disabled
<output omitted>
Switch2#show vtp status
VTP version                       2
Configuration revision            10
Maximum VLANs supported locally   68
Number of existing VLANs          8
VTP Operational Mode              Server
VTP Domain Name                   TTC1523
VTP Pruning Mode                  Disabled
<output omitted>
```

- ○ **A.** The VTP operational mode is incorrect.

- ○ **B.** The switches are running the wrong VTP version for Ethernet LANs.

- ○ **C.** VTP pruning is disabled.

- ○ **D.** The VTP domain names are incorrect.

45. Examine the figure below. All ports are running FastEthernet. The default STP priority is being used. Which port would go into blocking mode?

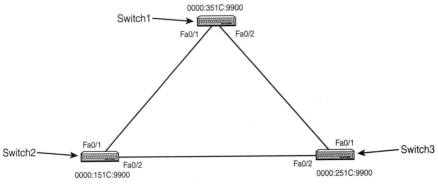

Switch1 → 0000:351C:9900

Fa0/1   Fa0/2

Fa0/1 (Switch2)   Fa0/1 → Switch3
Switch2 →
Fa0/2   Fa0/2
0000:151C:9900   0000:251C:9900

- ○ **A.** Fa1/0 on Switch2
- ○ **B.** Fa0/1 on Switch3
- ○ **C.** Fa0/2 on Switch1
- ○ **D.** Fa0/1 on Switch1

46. Examine the figure. Based on this diagram, which ports are access ports? [Select all that apply.]

- ○ **A.** Switch1:Fa0/2
- ○ **B.** Switch2:Fa0/1
- ○ **C.** Switch1:Fa0/12
- ○ **D.** Switch2:Fa0/10
- ○ **E.** Router1:Fa0/0
- ○ **F.** Switch3:Fa0/20

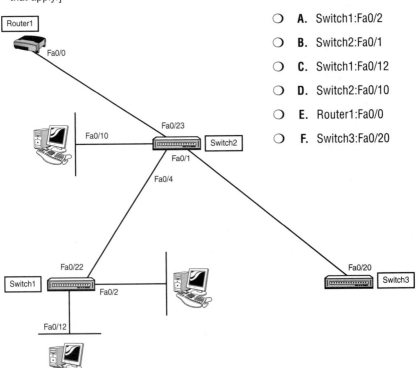

47. What is `inverse arp` used for?

    ◯ **A.** `Inverse arp` maps a MAC address to an IP address.

    ◯ **B.** `Inverse arp` maps a DLCI address to an IP address.

    ◯ **C.** `Inverse arp` maps a dialer string to an IP address.

    ◯ **D.** `Inverse arp` maps a Router address to an IP address.

48. Entering the `show ip route` command on a router shows the following output:

```
O      172.16.0.0/16 [110/1562] via 192.168.1.1, 00:41:09,
Serial0
```

What is true about this output? [Select all that apply.]

    ◯ **A.** The router is running EIGRP.

    ◯ **B.** The router is running OSPF.

    ◯ **C.** The cost is 1562.

    ◯ **D.** The hop count is 1562.

49. You have a single network connected to your ISP. What type of routing would allow the internal clients to reach the Internet?

    ◯ **A.** RIP

    ◯ **B.** Static route

    ◯ **C.** Default route

    ◯ **D.** OSPF

    ◯ **E.** EIGRP

50. You attempt to telnet to a router but you cannot. However, you can successfully ping the router. What could be wrong? [Select all that apply.]

    ◯ **A.** The routing protocol is not set up properly.

    ◯ **B.** A telnet password has not been configured.

    ◯ **C.** An access-list is configured on the VTY lines.

    ◯ **D.** An interface is shut down.

51. Which of the following are valid unicast addresses? [Select all that apply.]

○ **A.** 192.168.14.5/30

○ **B.** 192.168.14.40/30

○ **C.** 192.168.14.123/30

○ **D.** 192.168.14.13/30

52. If you send a packet to a network that a router does not have in its routing table and no default route is established, what will the router do with your packet? [Select all that apply.]

○ **A.** It will send an ICMP destination unreachable message back to the source of the packet.

○ **B.** It will drop the packet.

○ **C.** It will send the packet back to the source.

○ **D.** It will send an ICMP administratively prohibited message back to the source.

53. What are the components that make up a Bridge ID? [Select all that apply.]

○ **A.** IP address

○ **B.** MAC address

○ **C.** Priority number

○ **D.** Platform number

54. In EIGRP, where would you find the feasible successor route?

○ **A.** Neighbor table

○ **B.** Topology table

○ **C.** Route table

○ **D.** Adjacency table

55. When is a packet processed by an inbound access list?

○ **A.** After being sent to the outbound interface

○ **B.** Before it is sent to an outbound interface

○ **C.** While being processed by the routing table

○ **D.** By the packet security engine

Answer Key to Practice Test #2

Answers at a Glance to Practice Exam 2

1. B, E	20. C	39. B
2. A, B, D	21. C	40. A
3. C, D	22. A, D	41. D
4. B	23. B	42. B
5. A, D	24. C	43. B
6. B	25. C	44. D
7. D	26. A	45. C
8. C	27. B	46. A, C, D
9. B	28. B	47. B
10. A	29. B	48. B, C
11. D	30. A	49. C
12. D	31. E	50. B, C
13. B, C	32. B	51. A, D
14. B	33. C	52. A, B
15. A, D	34. C	53. B, C
16. C	35. A	54. B
17. D	36. D	55. B
18. B, D	37. A, C	
19. B	38. B, C, D	

Answers with Explanations

Question 1

Answers B and E are the correct answers. The 192.168.14.69 host is on the 192.168.14.64/28 network with an increment of 16 with 14 valid host addresses on each subnet. The range of valid host addresses for this network is 192.168.14.65 through 192.168.14.78. Answers B and E both fall within this range. Answer A is incorrect because this is a broadcast address. Answer C is incorrect because this address is on a different network. Answer D is incorrect because this is a network address.

Question 2

Answers A, B, and D are the correct answers. You need a trunk configured between the two switches for VTP to work. Both switches need to be in the same VTP domain and have the same VTP password. Answer C is incorrect because the modes can differ. Answer E is incorrect because the hostname is irrelevant.

Question 3

Answers C and D are the correct answers. When configuring subinterfaces, you should configure the encapsulation on the main interface but take the IP address off of it and place it under the subinterface. Answer A is incorrect because the DLCI should go under the subinterface and not on the main interface. Answer B is incorrect because the IP address should go under the subinterface. Answer E is incorrect because the frame-relay encapsulation goes on the main interface and not the subinterface.

Question 4

Answer B is the correct answer. Named access lists allow you to delete individual lines; numbered do not. If you attempt to delete an individual line out of a numbered access list, the entire list will be removed. Answer A is incorrect because you can do both an IP extended and an IP standard named access list. Answer C is incorrect because named access lists can be used for more than just VTY line access control. Answer D is incorrect because you can do named access lists for other protocols—such as IPX—as well.

Question 5

Answers A and D are correct. An access port is one that is connected directly to an end device, such as a PC, using a straight-through cable. The port carries traffic for a single VLAN. Answers B and C are incorrect because these describe trunk links.

Question 6

Answer B is the correct answer. The switch with the lowest Bridge ID is the root bridge. A Bridge ID consists of a configurable priority value followed by the base MAC address. In this example, SwitchB has the numerically lowest Bridge ID. The other answers are incorrect because they have numerically higher Bridge IDs.

Question 7

Answer D is the correct answer. Split-horizon is working (which makes answer A incorrect) because the routes received on Serial 0 are not sent back out Serial 0. Answer B is incorrect because version 1 is being used, not version 2. Answer C is incorrect because the router is on the 10.0.0.0 and 192.168.0.0 network and not the 172.16.0.0 network. Finally, answer E is incorrect because you can ping the host 172.18.15.9 because it is only three hops away.

Question 8

Answer C is the correct answer. The default state of an interface is shut down. Unless the `no shut` command is entered, the interface remains down and you are unable to ping it. Answer A is incorrect because nothing in the scenario or configuration indicates that there is a problem with the encapsulation. Answer B is incorrect because the telnet configuration is complete. Answer D is incorrect because the order of the commands under the VTY lines does not matter. Finally, answer E is incorrect because a console password is not necessary to telnet into a router.

Question 9

Answer B is the correct answer. `show ip ospf interface` shows you if you are a DR, BDR, or DROTHER (not a DR or BDR). Answer A is incorrect because the `show ip ospf database` command shows you the OSPF LSA database, but not if you are the DR. Answer C is incorrect because the `show ip ospf` command shows you general information about the OSPF process, but not about the DR decisions. Answer D is incorrect because the `show ip ospf summary-address` shows you networks that have been summarized, but not the DR or BDR routers.

Question 10

Answer A is the correct answer. Application, Presentation, and Session layers all relate to Data. The Transport layer relates to segments. The Network layer relates to packets (also called datagrams). The Data-Link layer relates to frames. Finally, the Physical layer relates to bits. The other answers are wrong because the orders of the PDUs are incorrect.

Question 11

Answer D is the correct answer. Your ARP table contains the IP address to MAC address mappings and can be viewed on a Windows PC with the arp -a command. Answer A is incorrect because that command will display your PC network configuration. Answer B is incorrect because that command will test your TCP/IP protocol stack. Finally, answer C is wrong because tracert displays the list of routers on a path to a network destination.

Question 12

Answer D is the correct answer. When a new router boots up it will take you to the system configuration dialog, which will ask a series of questions that lead you through the initial system configuration. Answers A and B are incorrect because you will first be prompted with the initial system configuration dialog. Answer C is incorrect because there is no default password of ciscorouter. (There are some routers that do ship with a default password, but the password is not ciscorouter, and the exam does not test on this.)

Question 13

Answers B and C are the correct answers. Both commands will show you the IP address (layer 3 information) of neighboring devices. Below is sample output of these commands with the layer three (network layer) information highlighted.

```
- - - - - - - - - - - - - - - - - - - - - - - - - -
Device ID: Router
Entry address(es):
   IP address: 192.168.100.254
Platform: cisco 1604,  Capabilities: Router
Interface: Serial0,  Port ID (outgoing port): Serial0
Holdtime : 128 sec
<...output omitted for brevity...>
```

Answer A is incorrect because this command is limited and does not give you the IP address. Answer D is incorrect because this command shows only CDP statistics, not IP addresses.

Question 14

Answer B is the correct answer. The Floor2 switch has the lowest priority (16384) so is therefore the root bridge. The Floor1 and Floor3 switch (answers A and C) have higher priorities, so therefore they are not the root bridge. Answer D is incorrect because enough information is included in the question to answer it.

Question 15

Answers A and D are the correct answers. This question depends on your ability to memorize facts; you either know this, or you don't. Answers B and C are incorrect because these are LMI types and not frame-relay encapsulations.

Question 16

Answer C is the correct answer. The subnet mask 255.255.255.224 with the `ip subnet-zero` command allows for 8 subnets and 30 hosts on each subnet. Answer A is incorrect because it allows only for 2 subnets. Answer B is incorrect because this allows only for 4 subnets. Answers D and E are incorrect because you can get more subnets out of a mask of 255.255.255.224 than you can with masks of 255.255.255.240 (/28) or 255.255.255.248 (/29).

Question 17

Answer D is the correct answer. OSPF has an unlimited hop count. Answer A is incorrect because this is the hop count for RIP. Answer B is incorrect because this is the maximum hop count for EIGRP. Answer C is incorrect because this is the maximum hop count for IGRP.

Question 18

Answers B and D are the correct answers. UDP uses less bandwidth and is a connection-less protocol. Answers A and C are incorrect because these describe TCP.

Question 19

Answer B is correct. You use a rollover cable to connect a PC to a console port (Con0) on a router. A crossover cable (answer A) is used between two end devices or between two routers. A straight-through cable (answer C) is used between a switch and an end device. A serial cable (answer D) is used for wide area network (WAN) connections.

Question 20

Answer C is the correct answer. There is no way to assign a password to a VLAN. Answers A, B, and D are all incorrect because these are steps you would take to create a VLAN.

Question 21

Answer C is the correct answer. When the packet is returning on the remote segment, it will have the source MAC address of HostB and the destination MAC address of RouterB. Answers A, B, and D are incorrect because they do not return on any of these choices.

Question 22

Answers A and D are the correct answers. Answer A is a private Class B address, whereas answer D is a private Class A address. Answers B and C are incorrect because they are public addresses.

Question 23

Answer B is the correct answer. A switch uses ASIC chips and is therefore faster than a bridge (making answer A incorrect). Answers C and D are incorrect because bridges and switches are both layer 2 devices.

Question 24

Answer C is the correct answer. This is the only answer with the correct configuration. Answers A and D are incorrect because these are extended access lists, which is not necessary on VTY lines. Answer B is incorrect because the wrong command is used to apply the access list on the VTY lines.

Question 25

Answer C is the correct answer. OSPF priority is changed on an interface with the `ip ospf priority` command. Answers A and B are incorrect because the commands are done on an interface and not under the OSPF router configuration mode. Answer D is incorrect because the wrong command is used under the interface.

Question 26

Answer A is the correct answer. To enable an interface from the administratively down state, you must execute the `no shutdown` command. Answer B is incorrect because nothing is wrong with the cable. Answer C is incorrect because there is no such thing as the `interface up` command. Answer D is incorrect because the `clock rate` command is not necessary to take an interface out of the administratively down state.

Question 27

Answer B is the correct answer. HostB has a network address and not a valid host address. Answers A, C, and D are incorrect because these are all valid IP addresses.

Question 28

Answer B is correct. You can use port security to allow only certain hosts access to a network. Answer A is incorrect because access lists are typically put on Layer 3 routed ports, not Layer 2 switched ports. Answer C is incorrect because encrypted enable secret passwords are used to secure a network device, such as a switch, but have no bearing on preventing unauthorized hosts on a network. Finally, answer D is incorrect because WEP uses a key, not a username and password (and even if it did, this would prevent only a user and not a host).

Question 29

Answer B is the correct answer. `banner motd` is used to create a banner. Answers A, C, and D are incorrect because these are all bogus commands.

Question 30

Answer A is correct. `show controllers` is the only command listed that will inform you if clocking is stopped on an interface. Answers B and C will show you information about the interface but not about clocking. Answer D will not show you whether clocking is working correctly.

Question 31

Answer E is the correct answer. Windowing and sequence numbers are components of TCP, which is found at the transport layer. TCP is not found at the other layers, so answers A, B, C, and D are incorrect.

Question 32

Answer B is correct. The switch with the lowest Bridge ID is the root bridge. In this scenario, the switch has a Bridge ID of 32768.0003.2201.830D.E774, whereas the root bridge has a lower Bridge ID of 4106.0003.C832.9885. (Note that the switch is using Per-VLAN Spanning Tree + (PVST+), which extends the bridge ID by adding the VLAN number to the base priority.) Answer A is incorrect because if the switch had a lower Bridge ID, it would be the root. Answer C is incorrect because a root bridge would have all its ports in the designated state, not root state. Answer D is incorrect because the cost is not the initial factor in determining the root bridge.

Question 33

Answer C is the correct answer. There are four collision domains on the left out of the router's ethernet 0 interface (one collision domain for each segment coming out of the switch), and there is one collision domain on the right out of the router's ethernet 1 interface. Because there are only five collision domains in all, answers A, B, D, and E are all incorrect.

Question 34

Answer C is correct. A rogue AP is usually put in place by a malicious attacker or an inside facilitator to capture information from clients that associate to it unknowingly. Answers A, B, and D have nothing to do with rogue access points.

Question 35

Answer A is the correct answer. You need a default router on RouterA to allow the users to access the Internet. The ISP, however, would suffice with a simple static route because there is only one network attached to RouterA. Answers B, C, D, and E are incorrect because these solutions would not meet the objective.

Question 36

Answer D is the correct answer. You have 13 subnets, so you need a /28 subnet mask, which would allow for 13 hosts. Because the company is running RIPv1, you must use the same subnet mask on all links.

Question 37

Answers A and C are the correct answer. This access list permits all hosts on the 172.17.80.0/20 network. The range of valid IP addresses would be 172.17.80.1 through 172.17.95.254. Only answer A and C fall within this range.

Question 38

Answers B, C, and D are the correct answers. Answer A is incorrect because it is not a valid wide area network encapsulation.

Question 39

Answer B is the correct answer. The `no auto-summary` command is needed because you are using variable length subnet masks. Without the **no auto-summary** command, VLSM is not allowed. Answer A is incorrect because EIGRP does support VLSM. Answer C is incorrect because the subnet masks are not necessary to make this work. Answer D is incorrect because you need the no **auto-summary** command. (The **auto-summary** command is already there.) Answer E is incorrect because this is a RIP command, not an EIGRP command.

Question 40

Answer A is the correct answer. The **frame-relay map** command is missing the keyword broadcast at the end, which is necessary to support the use of broadcast and multicast based routing protocols. Answer B is incorrect because the RIP configuration does specify the correct networks. Answer C is incorrect because **inverse-arp** is irrelevant to making this work. Answer D is incorrect because RIP will work across NBMA networks when you have the broadcast keyword added to the end of the `frame-relay map` command. Answer E is incorrect because the IP addresses are correct.

Question 41

Answer D is correct. 802.11a uses the 5GHz range, not 2.4GHz, and certainly not anything in the MHz or KHz range.

Question 42

Answer B is the correct answer. Assuming that you are running both EIGRP and RIP, the router will take the path that EIGRP chooses (lower administrative distance). Because EIGRP looks at bandwidth as one component of its composite metric, EIGRP would take the path through RtrC. This is the only path it would take; therefore, answers A, C, and D are incorrect.

Question 43

Answer B is the correct answer. The `ip nat inside` and `ip nat outside` commands are missing from the interfaces. Answer A is incorrect because the access list configuration is correct. Answer C is incorrect because the IP addresses are correct. Answer D is incorrect because the configuration is performing NAT overload and does not need a pool.

Question 44

Answer D is the correct answer. The two switches are using different VTP domain names. Answer A is incorrect because the modes are fine. Answer B is incorrect because nothing is wrong with the VTP version. Answer C is incorrect because VTP pruning does not need to be enabled to make VTP operational.

Question 45

Answer C is the correct answer. The root bridge would be the Switch2. Interface Fa0/1 on Switch1 and Fa0/2 on Switch3 would both be root ports and go into forwarding mode. For Fa0/2 on Switch1 and Fa0/1 on Switch3, the tie breaker would be the bridge ID. Since Switch1 has a higher MAC address and the default priority is being used, Switch1 would place Fa0/2 in blocking mode and Fa0/1 on Switch3 would go into forwarding mode. Only Fa0/2 on Switch1 would be in blocking mode, so answers A, B, and D are incorrect.

Question 46

Answers A, C, and D are the correct answers. Access ports are those ports connected to access devices such as computers. Answers B, E, and F are incorrect because these are trunk ports that are connecting switches and routers together.

Question 47

Answer B is the correct answer. Inverse arp maps a frame-relay data link connection identifier (DLCI) to the next hop IP address. Answers A, C, and D are incorrect because these are not the correct definition of inverse arp.

Question 48

Answers B and C are the correct answers. The 'O' in the output, along with the administrative distance of 110, indicates that this entry was learned via OSPF. The cost is included next to the administrative distance (1562). Answer A is incorrect because the router is running OSPF and not EIGRP. Answer D is incorrect because OSPF uses cost as its metric and not hop count.

Question 49

Answer C is the correct answer. If you only have a single network, a default route would be sufficient. Answers A, D, and E are incorrect because they are not necessary if you only have a single network.

Question 50

Answers B and C are the correct answers. If telnet has not been properly configured or an access list is blocking you, telnet will not work. Answers A and D are incorrect because the question states that you are able to ping the router (which you would not be able to do if answers A and D were correct).

Question 51

Answers A and D are the correct answers. Answer B is incorrect because this is a network address, and answer C is incorrect because this is a broadcast address.

Question 52

Answers A and B are the correct answers. The router will drop the packet back and send an ICMP destination unreachable message back to the source. Answer C is incorrect because the router will drop the packet, not send it back. Answer D is incorrect because administratively prohibited messages are only sent if the packet was denied because of a filter such as an access list.

Question 53

Answers B and C are the correct answers. The bridge ID is composed of a configurable priority plus the base MAC address. Answers A and D are incorrect because these are not used in calculating the bridge ID.

Question 54

Answer B is the correct answer. The feasible successor is the backup route and is found in the topology table. Answers A and C are incorrect because the feasible successor route is not found in the neighbor or route table. Answer D is also incorrect because the feasible successor is not found in the adjacency table and because the adjacency table is used with OSPF and not EIGRP.

Question 55

Answer B is correct. A packet will be processed before it is forwarded to an outbound interface when an inbound access list is applied. Answer A is incorrect because that describes an outbound access list. Answer C is incorrect because access lists used for packet filtering are processed when entering interface queues and not when performing a route lookup. Answer D is incorrect because there is no such thing as a "packet security engine." That answer is there simply to distract and mislead you.

What's on the CD-ROM

The CD-ROM features an innovative practice test engine powered by MeasureUp, giving you yet another effective tool to assess your readiness for the exam.

Multiple Test Modes

MeasureUp practice tests can be used in Study, Certification, or Custom modes.

Study Mode

Tests administered in Study mode allow you to request the correct answer(s) and explanation to each question during the test. These tests are not timed. You can modify the testing environment during the test by selecting the Options button.

You can also specify the objectives or missed questions you want to include in your test, the timer length, and other test properties. You can also modify the testing environment during the test by selecting the Options button.

In Study mode, you receive automatic feedback on all correct and incorrect answers. The detailed answer explanations are a superb learning tool in their own right.

Certification Mode

Tests administered in Certification mode closely simulate the actual testing environment you will encounter when taking a licensure exam and are timed. These tests do not allow you to request the answer(s) and/or explanation to each question until after the exam.

Custom Mode

Custom mode allows you to specify your preferred testing environment. Use this mode to specify the categories you want to include in your test, the timer length, number of questions, and other test properties. You can modify the testing environment during the test by selecting the Options button.

Attention to Exam Objectives

MeasureUp practice tests are designed to appropriately balance the questions over each technical area covered by a specific exam. All concepts from the actual exam are covered thoroughly to ensure that you're prepared for the exam.

Installing the CD

System Requirements:

- ▶ Windows 95, 98, ME, NT4, 2000, or XP
- ▶ 7MB disk space for testing engine
- ▶ An average of 1MB disk space for each individual test
- ▶ Control Panel Regional Settings must be set to English (United States)
- ▶ PC only

To install the CD-ROM, follow these instructions:

1. Close all applications before beginning this installation.
2. Insert the CD into your CD-ROM drive. If the setup starts automatically, go to step 6. If the setup does not start automatically, continue with step 3.
3. From the Start menu, select Run.
4. Click Browse to locate the MeasureUp CD. In the Browse dialog box, from the Look In drop-down list, select the CD-ROM drive.
5. In the Browse dialog box, double-click Setup.exe. In the Run dialog box, click OK to begin the installation.
6. On the Welcome screen, click MeasureUp Practice Questions to begin installation.
7. Follow the Certification Prep Wizard by clicking Next.
8. To agree to the Software License Agreement, click Yes.

9. On the Choose Destination Location screen, click Next to install the software to `C:\Program Files\Certification Preparation`. If you cannot locate MeasureUp Practice Tests on the Start menu, see the section titled "Creating a Shortcut to the MeasureUp Practice Tests," later in this appendix.

10. On the Setup Type screen, select Typical Setup. Click Next to continue.

11. In the Select Program Folder screen, you can name the program folder where your tests will be located. To select the default, click Next and the installation continues.

12. After the installation is complete, verify that Yes, I Want to Restart My Computer Now is selected. If you select No, I Will Restart My Computer Later, you cannot use the program until you restart your computer.

13. Click Finish.

14. After restarting your computer, choose Start, Programs, Certification Preparation, Certification Preparation, MeasureUp Practice Tests.

15. On the MeasureUp Welcome Screen, click Create User Profile.

16. In the User Profile dialog box, complete the mandatory fields and click Create Profile.

17. Select the practice test you want to access and click Start Test.

Creating a Shortcut to the MeasureUp Practice Tests

To create a shortcut to the MeasureUp Practice Tests, follow these steps:

1. Right-click your desktop.

2. From the Shortcut menu, select New, Shortcut.

3. Browse to `C:\Program Files\MeasureUp Practice Tests` and select the `MeasureUpCertification.exe` or `Localware.exe` file.

4. Click OK.

5. Click Next.

6. Rename the shortcut MeasureUp.

7. Click Finish.

After you complete step 7, use the MeasureUp shortcut on your desktop to access the MeasureUp products you ordered.

Technical Support

If you encounter problems with the MeasureUp test engine on the CD-ROM, please contact MeasureUp at (800) 649-1687 or email support@measureup.com. Support hours of operation are 7:30 a.m. to 4:30 p.m. EST. In addition, you can find Frequently Asked Questions (FAQ) in the Support area at www.measure-up.com. If you would like to purchase additional MeasureUp products, call (678) 356-5050 or (800) 649-1687 or visit www.measureup.com.

APPENDIX B

Need to Know More?

Introduction

This appendix provides a list of references that we think are useful either for CCENT/CCNA exam preparation or for general networking knowledge.

CCENT and Basic Networking

▶ The Cisco CCNA Prep Center is a mine of useful resources, with reference articles, videos, forums, mock tests, and links to other material, as well. Sign up and visit often; you'll see the two of us online every once in a while, too:

www.cisco.com/go/prepcenter

▶ *CCNA Exam Prep 2* (Exam 640-801); ISBN: 0-7897-3519-9

Our good friend and mentor Dave Minutella, along with his coauthors Heather Stevenson and Jeremy Cioara, wrote the companion volume to this book. *CCNA Exam Prep 2* covers all the CCNA material in much greater detail and in a superbly accessible writing style. If you like our book, you'll like theirs, too.

▶ *CCNA Portable Command Guide*, 2nd ed.; ISBN-10: 1-58720-193-3

All the CCNA 640-802 commands in one compact, portable resource.

▶ *CCENT/CCNA ICND1 Official Exam Certification Guide* (CCENT Exam 640-822 and CCNA Exam 640-802), 2nd ed.; ISBN-10: 1-58720-182-8

The Grand Master of CCNA authors, Mike's colleague Wendell Odom has just finished an updated set of texts for the new exams.

▶ *CCNA Video Mentor* (Exam 640-802); ISBN-10: 1-58720-168-2

Wendell Odom shows his face and delivers a great series of tutorials on CCNA configuration skills. Great for a Friday night.

▶ *CCNA Flash Cards and Exam Practice Pack* (CCENT Exam 640-822 and CCNA Exams 640-816 and 640-802), 3rd ed.; ISBN-10: 1-58720-190-9

Some people love to use flash cards as a convenient way to put themselves on the spot. Mike was the technical editor for this book, so it gets the stamp of approval.

▶ The IEEE is the standards authority for networking. For information on any 802.x standard, they are the original source:

www.ieee.org

▶ For the definitive—and exhaustive—list of port numbers, visit this website:

www.iana.org/assignments/port-numbers

▶ Cisco has created a simple and effective Flash presentation on the Spanning-Tree Protocol. It's a bit dated in that it uses bridges instead of switches, but the theory is well presented:

www.cisco.com/warp/public/473/spanning_tree1.swf

▶ This page on Cisco's public documentation site links to many ethernet-related topics:

www.cisco.com/en/US/tech/tk389/tk214/tsd_technology_support_protocol_home.html

▶ The following is the home page for the Catalyst 2960 Series LAN switches. You will find links to command references, configuration guides, and other interesting information:

www.cisco.com/en/US/products/ps6406/tsd_products_support_series_home.html

▶ The following page links to several documents discussing WAN technologies, including Frame Relay, PPP, and HDLC. There is much more detail in these documents than a CCNA needs, so just look for the relevant sections.

www.cisco.com/en/US/tech/tk713/tsd_technology_support_category_home.html

CCNA/ICND2 and Other Advanced Topics

- *CCNA ICND2 Official Exam Certification Guide* (CCNA Exams 640-816 and 640-802), 2nd ed.; ISBN-10: 1-58720-181-X

  The second half of Wendell Odom's revised CCNA library. You might want to consider buying the set; it is sometimes less expensive that way.

- Cisco's documentation page for routing protocols. All of them are included; remember that you need to learn only about RIPv2, EIGRP, and OSPF for the CCNA exam.

  www.cisco.com/en/US/tech/tk365/tsd_technology_support_protocol_home.html

- *Cisco IOS Access Lists*; ISBN 1-56592-385-5

  O'Reilly has published Jeff Sedayao's work on Cisco Access Lists for years now. If your job involves using ACLs, you want this book on your shelf. It's the one with the donkey on it. Caution: there are a few errors that can be scary for beginners.

- For security-related topics, visit the following sites regularly:

  www.securityfocus.com

  www.zone-h.org

  www.isc.sans.org

- All the following sites are excellent sources of info and links regarding IPv6.

  www.ipv6.org

  www.icann.org

  www.cisco.com/en/US/tech/tk872/tsd_technology_support_protocol_home.html

- Cisco's support page for wireless LANs, including security:

  www.cisco.com/en/US/tech/tk722/tk809/tsd_technology_support_protocol_home.html

- Cisco's Documentation home page; it's all here:

  www.cisco.com/univercd/home/home.htm

Glossary

A

access list   Rules applied to a router that will determine traffic patterns for data.

administrative distance   A value that ranges from 0 through 255, which determines the priority of a source's routing information.

advanced distance vector protocol   A routing protocol that combines the strengths of the distance vector and link state routing protocols. Cisco Enhanced Interior Gateway Routing Protocol (EIGRP) is considered an advanced distance vector protocol.

application layer   The highest layer of the OSI model (Layer 7). It is closest to the end user and selects appropriate network services to support end-user applications such as email and FTP.

ARP (Address Resolution Protocol)   A protocol used to map a known logical address to an unknown physical address. A device performs an ARP broadcast to identify the physical address of a destination device. This physical address is then stored in cache memory for later transmissions.

AS (autonomous system)   A group of networks under common administration that share a routing strategy.

ATM (Asynchronous Transfer Mode)
A dedicated-connection switching technology that organizes digital data into units and transmits them over a physical medium using digital signal technology.

attenuation   A term that refers to the reduction in strength of a signal. Attenuation occurs with any type of signal, whether digital or analog. Sometimes referred to as *signal loss*.

Authentication Header (AH)   A header used with IPSec that provides integrity and authentication.

B

bandwidth   The available capacity of a network link over a physical medium.

BECN (Backward Explicit Congestion Notification)   A Frame Relay message that notifies the sending device that there is congestion in the network. A BECN bit is sent back in the direction from where the frame was sent (the source).

BGP (Border Gateway Protocol)   An exterior routing protocol that exchanges route information between autonomous systems.

boot field   The lowest four binary digits of a configuration register. The value of the boot field determines the order in which a router searches for Cisco IOS software.

BPDU (Bridge Protocol Data Unit)
Data messages that are exchanged across the switches within an extended LAN that uses a spanning-tree protocol topology.

bridge   A device used to segment a LAN into multiple physical segments. A bridge uses a forwarding table to determine which frames need to be forwarded to specific segments. Bridges isolate local traffic to the originating physical segment, but forward all nonlocal and broadcast traffic.

broadcast   A data frame that's sent to every node on a local segment.

C

carrier detect signal   A signal received on a router interface that indicates whether the physical layer connectivity is operating properly.

CDP (Cisco Discovery Protocol)   A Cisco proprietary protocol that operates at the data link layer. CDP enables network administrators to view a summary protocol and address information about other directly connected Cisco routers (and some Cisco switches).

channel   A single communications path on a system. In some situations, channels can be multiplexed over a single connection.

CHAP (Challenge Handshake Authentication Protocol) An authentication protocol for the Point-to-Point Protocol (PPP) that uses a three-way, encrypted handshake to force a remote host to identify itself to a local host.

checksum A field that performs calculations to ensure the integrity of data.

CIDR (Classless Interdomain Routing) Implemented to resolve the rapid depletion of IP address space on the Internet and to minimize the number of routes on the Internet. CIDR provides a more efficient method of allocating IP address space by removing the concept of classes in IP addressing. CIDR enables routes to be summarized on powers-of-two boundaries; therefore, it reduces multiple routes into a single prefix.

CIR (Committed Information Rate) The rate at which a Frame Relay link transmits data, averaged over time. CIR is measured in bits per second. This is the committed rate that the service provider guarantees for a Frame Relay connection.

classful addressing Categorizes IP addresses into ranges that are used to create a hierarchy in the IP addressing scheme. The most common classes are A, B, and C, which can be identified by looking at the first three binary digits of an IP address.

classless addressing Classless addressing does not categorize addresses into classes and is designed to deal with wasted address space.

CO (central office) The local telephone company office where all local loops in an area connect.

configuration register A numeric value (typically displayed in hexadecimal form) used to specify certain actions on a router.

congestion A situation that occurs during data transfer if one or more computers generate network traffic faster than it can be transmitted through the network.

console A terminal attached directly to the router for configuring and monitoring the router.

convergence The process by which all routers within an internetwork route information and eventually agree on optimal routes through the internetwork.

counting to infinity A routing problem in which the distance metric for a destination network is continually increased because the internetwork has not fully converged.

CPE (customer premise equipment) Terminating equipment such as telephones and modems supplied by the service provider, installed at the customer site, and connected to the network.

CRC (cyclic redundancy check) An error-checking mechanism by which the receiving node calculates a value based on the data it receives and compares it with the value stored within the frame from the sending node.

CSMA/CA (Carrier Sense Multiple Access/Collision Avoidance) A physical specification used in wireless networks to provide contention-based frame transmission. A sending device first listens to detect if there is any activity and, if it is clear, sends the frame. The sending device will send a signal telling other devices not to transmit.

CSMA/CD (Carrier Sense Multiple Access/Collision Detection) A physical specification used by ethernet to provide contention-based frame transmission. CSMA/CD specifies that a sending device must share physical transmission media and listen to determine whether a collision occurs after transmitting. In simple terms, this means that an ethernet card has a built-in capability to detect a potential packet collision on the internetwork.

cut-through switching A method of forwarding frames based on the first six bytes contained in the frame. Cut-through switching provides higher throughput than store-and-forward switching because it requires only six bytes of data to make the forwarding decision. Cut-through switching does not provide error checking like its counterpart store-and-forward switching.

D

DCE (data communications equipment) The device at the network end of a user-to-network connection that provides a physical connection to the network, forwards traffic, and provides a clocking signal used to synchronize data transmission between the DCE and DTE devices.

de-encapsulation The process by which a destination peer layer removes and reads the control information sent by the source peer layer in another network host.

default mask A binary or decimal representation of the number of bits used to identify an IP network. The class of the IP address defines the default mask. A default mask is represented by four octets of binary digits. The mask can also be presented in dotted decimal notation.

default route A network route (that usually points to another router) established to receive and attempt to process all packets for which no route appears in the route table.

delay The amount of time necessary to move a packet through the internetwork from source to destination.

demarc The point of demarcation is between the carrier's equipment and the customer premise equipment (CPE).

Diffie-Helman The algorithm used to securely exchange secret shared keys used in IPSec.

discard eligibility bit A bit that can be set to indicate that a frame can be dropped if congestion occurs within the Frame Relay network.

distance vector protocol An interior routing protocol that relies on distance and vector or direction to choose optimal paths. A distance vector protocol requires each router to send all or a large part of its route table to its neighboring routers periodically.

DLCI (data link connection identifier) A value that specifies a permanent virtual circuit (PVC) or switched virtual circuit (SVC) in a Frame Relay network.

DNS (domain name system) A system used to translate fully qualified hostnames or computer names into IP addresses, and vice versa.

dotted decimal notation A method of representing binary IP addresses in a decimal format. Dotted decimal notation represents the four octets of an IP address in four decimal values separated by decimal points.

DTE (data terminal equipment) The device at the user end of the user-to-network connection that connects to a data network through a data communications equipment (DCE) device.

dynamic route A network route that adjusts automatically to changes within the internetwork.

E

EGP (Exterior Gateway Protocol) A routing protocol that conveys information between autonomous systems; it is widely used within the Internet. The Border Gateway Protocol (BGP) is an example of an exterior routing protocol.

EIGRP (Enhanced Interior Gateway Routing Protocol) A Cisco proprietary routing protocol that includes features of both distance vector and link state routing protocols. EIGRP is considered an advanced distance vector protocol.

Encapsulating Security Payload (ESP) An IPSec header that provides confidentiality, authentication, and integrity.

encapsulation Generally speaking, encapsulation is the process of wrapping data in a particular protocol header. In the context of the OSI model, encapsulation is the process by which a source peer layer includes header and trailer control information with a Protocol Data Unit (PDU) destined for its peer layer in another network host. The information encapsulated instructs the destination peer layer how to process the information.

EXEC The user interface for executing Cisco router commands.

F

FCS (frame check sequence)   Extra characters added to a frame for error control purposes. FCS is the result of a cyclic redundancy check (CRC).

FECN (Forward Explicit Congestion Notification)   A Frame Relay message that notifies the receiving device that there is congestion in the network. An FECN bit is sent in the same direction in which the frame was traveling, toward its destination.

Flash   Router memory that stores the Cisco IOS image and associated microcode. Flash is erasable, reprogrammable ROM that retains its content when the router is powered down or restarted.

flow control   A mechanism that throttles back data transmission to ensure that a sending system does not overwhelm the receiving system with data.

Frame Relay   A switched data link layer protocol that supports multiple virtual circuits using High-Level Data Link Control (HDLC) encapsulation between connected devices.

frame tagging   A method of tagging a frame with a unique user-defined virtual local area network (VLAN). The process of tagging frames allows VLANs to span multiple switches.

FTP (File Transfer Protocol)   A protocol used to copy a file from one host to another host, regardless of the physical hardware or operating system of each device. FTP identifies a client and server during the file-transfer process. In addition, it provides a guaranteed transfer by using the services of the Transmission Control Protocol (TCP).

full duplex   The physical transmission process on a network device by which one pair of wires transmits data while another pair of wires receives data. Full-duplex transmission is achieved by eliminating the possibility of collisions on an ethernet segment, thereby eliminating the need for a device to sense collisions.

G

global configuration mode   A router mode that enables simple router configuration commands—such as router names, banners, and passwords—to be executed. Global configuration commands affect the whole router rather than a single interface or component.

H

half duplex   The physical transmission process whereby one pair of wires is used to transmit information and the other pair of wires is used to receive information or to sense collisions on the physical media. Half-duplex transmission is required on ethernet segments with multiple devices.

handshake   The process of one system making a request to another system before a connection is established. Handshakes occur during the establishment of a connection between two systems, and they address matters such as synchronization and connection parameters.

HDLC (High-Level Data Link Control) A bit-oriented, synchronous data link layer protocol that specifies data encapsulation methods on serial links.

header Control information placed before the data during the encapsulation process.

hierarchical routing protocol A routing environment that relies on several routers to compose a backbone. Most traffic from nonbackbone routers traverses the backbone routers (or at least travels to the backbone) to reach another nonbackbone router. This is accomplished by breaking a network into a hierarchy of networks, where each level is responsible for its own routing.

hold-down The state into which a route is placed so that routers will not advertise or accept updates for that route until a timer expires.

hop count The number of routers a packet passes through on its way to the destination network.

hostname A logical name given to a router.

HSSI (High-Speed Serial Interface) A physical standard designed for serial connections that require high data transmission rates. The HSSI standard allows for high-speed communication that runs at speeds up to 52Mbps.

I

ICMP (Internet Control Message Protocol) A protocol that communicates error messages and controls messages between devices. Thirteen types of ICMP messages are defined. ICMP enables devices to check the status of other devices, to query the current time, and to perform other functions such as ping and traceroute.

IEEE (Institute of Electrical and Electronics Engineers) An organization whose primary function is to define standards for networks LANs.

initial configuration dialog The dialog used to configure a router the first time it is booted or when no configuration file exists. The initial configuration dialog is an optional tool used to simplify the configuration process.

inside global The term to describe your inside addresses after they have been translated with network address translation (NAT). Inside global addresses are registered addresses that represent your inside hosts to your outside networks.

inside local The addresses on the inside of your network before they are translated with network address translation (NAT).

interfaces   Router components that provide the network connections in which data packets move in and out of the router. Depending on the model of router, interfaces exist either on the motherboard or on separate, modular interface cards.

interior routing protocol   A routing protocol that exchanges information within an autonomous system. Routing Information Protocol (RIP) and Open Shortest Path First (OSPF) are examples of interior routing protocols.

Internet Key Exchange   A component of IPSec that is used to dynamically and securely exchange secret keys. IKE uses Diffie-Helman to exchange keys.

IP (Internet Protocol)   One of the many protocols maintained in the TCP/IP suite of protocols. IP is the transport mechanism for Transmission Control Protocol (TCP), User Datagram Protocol (UDP), and Internet Control Message Protocol (ICMP) data. It also provides the logical addressing necessary for complex routing activity.

IP extended access list   An access list that provides a way of filtering IP traffic based on the source IP address, destination IP address, TCP port, UDP port, IP precedence field, TOS field, ICMP-type, ICMP-code, ICMP-message, IGMP-type, and TCP-established connections.

IP standard access list   An access list that provides a way of filtering IP traffic on a router interface based on the source IP address or address range.

IPsec   A suite of security protocols that is used to provide a secure VPN. IPsec can operate in tunnel mode, where a new IP header is added, or transport mode, where the original IP header is used.

ISL (interswitch link)   A protocol used to enable virtual local area networks (VLANs) to span multiple switches. ISL is used between switches to communicate common VLANs between devices.

K

keepalive frames   Protocol Data Units (PDUs) transmitted at the data link layer that indicate whether the proper frame type is configured.

L

LAN protocols   Protocols that identify Layer 2 protocols used for the transmission of data within a local area network (LAN). The three most popular LAN protocols used today are ethernet, token ring, and Fiber Distributed Data Interface (FDDI).

LCP (Link Control Protocol)   A protocol that configures, tests, maintains, and terminates Point-to-Point Protocol (PPP) connections. LCP is a sublayer of the Point-to-Point Protocol (PPP).

link state advertisement   A packet that contains the status of a router's links or network interfaces.

link state protocol   An interior routing protocol in which each router sends only the state of its own network links across the network, but sends this information to every router within its autonomous system or area. This process enables routers to learn and maintain full knowledge of the network's exact topology and how it is interconnected. Link state protocols use a "shortest path first" algorithm.

LLC (Logical Link Control) sublayer   A sublayer of the data link layer. The LLC sublayer provides the software functions of the data link layer.

LMI (Local Management Interface)   A set of enhancements to the Frame Relay protocol specifications used to manage complex networks. Some key Frame Relay LMI extensions include global addressing, virtual circuit status messages, and multicasting.

load   An indication of how busy a network resource is. CPU utilization and packets processed per second are two indicators of load.

local loop   The line from the customer's premises to the telephone company's central office (CO).

logical addressing   Network layer addressing is most commonly referred to as *logical addressing* (versus the physical addressing of the data link layer). A logical address consists of two parts: the network and the node. Routers use the network part of the logical address to determine the best path to the network of a remote device. The node part of the logical address is used to identify the specific host to forward the packet on the destination network.

logical ANDing   A process of comparing two sets of binary numbers to result in one value representing an IP address network. Logical ANDing is used to compare an IP address against its subnet mask to yield the IP subnet on which the IP address resides. ANDing is also used to determine whether a packet has a local or remote destination.

M

MAC (Media Access Control) address   A physical address used to define a device uniquely.

MAC (Media Access Control) layer   A sublayer of the data link layer that provides the hardware functions of the data link layer.

metric   The relative cost of sending packets to a destination network over a specific network route. Examples of metrics include bandwidth, delay, and reliability.

MIB (management information database)   A database that maintains statistics on certain data items. The Simple Network Management Protocol (SNMP) uses MIBs to query information about devices.

multicasting   A process of using one IP address to represent a group of IP addresses. Multicasting is used to send messages to a subset of IP addresses in a network or networks.

multipath routing protocol   A routing protocol that load balances over multiple optimal paths to a destination network when the costs of the paths are equal.

multiplexing   A method of flow control used by the transport layer in which application conversations are combined over a single channel by interleaving packets from different segments and transmitting them.

N

NAT (Network Address Translation)   The process of translating your multiple, internal IP addresses to a single registered IP address on the outside of your network.

NBMA (nonbroadcast multiaccess)   A multiaccess network that either does not support broadcasts or for which sending broadcasts is not feasible.

NCP (network control protocol)   A collection of protocols that establishes and configures different network layer protocols for use over a Point-to-Point Protocol (PPP) connection. NCP is a sublayer of PPP.

NetBIOS (Network Basic Input/Output System)   A common session layer interface specification from IBM and Microsoft that enables applications to request lower-level network services.

NIC (network interface card)   A board that provides network communication capabilities to and from a network host.

NVRAM (nonvolatile random access memory)   A memory area of the router that stores permanent information, such as the router's backup configuration file. The contents of NVRAM are retained when the router is powered down or restarted.

O

OSI (Open Systems Interconnection) model   A layered networking framework developed by the International Organization for Standardization. The OSI model describes seven layers that correspond to specific networking functions.

OSPF (Open Shortest Path First)   A hierarchical link state routing protocol that was developed as a successor to the Routing Information Protocol (RIP).

P

packet switching   A process by which a router moves a packet from one interface to another.

PAP (Password Authentication Protocol)   An authentication protocol for the Point-to-Point Protocol (PPP) that uses a two-way, unencrypted handshake to enable a remote host to identify itself to a local host.

PDU (Protocol Data Unit)   A unit of measure that refers to data that is transmitted between two peer layers within different network devices. Segments, packets, and frames are examples of PDUs.

peer-to-peer communication   A form of communication that occurs between the same layers of two different network hosts.

ping   A tool for testing IP connectivity between two devices. Ping is used to send multiple IP packets between a sending and a receiving device. The destination device responds with an Internet Control Message Protocol (ICMP) packet to notify the source device of its existence.

POP (point of presence)   A physical location where a carrier has installed equipment to interconnect with a local exchange carrier.

PPP (Point-to-Point Protocol)   A standard protocol that enables router-to-router and host-to-network connectivity over synchronous and asynchronous circuits such as telephone lines.

presentation layer   Layer 6 of the OSI model. The presentation layer is concerned with how data is represented to the application layer.

privileged mode   An extensive administrative and management mode on a Cisco router. This router mode permits testing, debugging, and commands to modify the router's configuration.

protocol   A formal description of a set of rules and conventions that defines how devices on a network must exchange information.

PSTN (public switched telephone network)   The circuit-switching facilities maintained for voice analog communication.

PVC (permanent virtual circuit)   A virtual circuit that is permanently established and ready for use.

R

RAM (random access memory)   A memory area of a router that serves as a working storage area. RAM contains data such as route tables, various types of caches and buffers, as well as input and output queues and the router's active configuration file. The contents of RAM are lost when the router is powered down or restarted.

RARP (Reverse Address Resolution Protocol)   This protocol provides mapping that is exactly opposite to the Address Resolution Protocol (ARP). RARP maps a known physical address to a logical address. Diskless machines that do not have a configured IP address when started typically use RARP. RARP requires the existence of a server that maintains physical-to-logical address mappings.

reliability   A metric that allows the network administrator to assign arbitrarily a numeric value to indicate a reliability factor for a link.

The reliability metric is a method used to capture an administrator's experience with a given network link.

RIP (Routing Information Protocol)
A widely used distance vector routing protocol that uses hop count as its metric.

ROM (read-only memory)
An area of router memory that contains a version of the Cisco IOS image—usually an older version with minimal functionality. ROM also stores the bootstrap program and power-on diagnostic programs.

ROM monitor mode
A mode on a Cisco router that allows basic functions such as changing the configuration register value or uploading an IOS via xmodem.

route aggregation
The process of combining multiple IP address networks into one superset of IP address networks. Route aggregation is implemented to reduce the number of route table entries required to forward IP packets accurately in an internetwork.

route poisoning
A routing technique by which a router immediately marks a network as unreachable as soon as it detects that the network is down. The router broadcasts the update throughout the network and maintains this poisoned route in its route table for a specified period of time.

route table
An area of a router's memory that stores the network topology information used to determine optimal routes. Route tables contain information such as destination network, next hop, and associated metrics.

routed protocol
A protocol that provides the information required for the routing protocol to determine the topology of the internetwork and the best path to a destination. The routed protocol provides this information in the form of a logical address and other fields within a packet. The information contained in the packet enables the router to direct user traffic. The most common routed protocols include Internet Protocol (IP) and Internetwork Packet Exchange (IPX).

router ID
The router identifier used with OSPF. The router ID is selected as the highest IP address among all loopback interfaces. If loopback interfaces are not configured, the router ID is the highest IP address of any active physical interface at the moment that OSPF is initialized.

router modes
Modes that enable the execution of specific router commands and functions. User, privileged, and setup are examples of router modes that allow you to perform certain tasks.

routing algorithms   Well-defined rules that aid routers in the collection of route information and the determination of the optimal path.

routing loop   An event in which two or more routers have not yet converged and are propagating their inaccurate route tables. In addition, they are probably still switching packets based on their inaccurate route tables.

routing protocols   Routing protocols use algorithms to generate a list of paths to a particular destination and the cost associated with each path. Routers use routing protocols to communicate among each other the best route to use to reach a particular destination.

RS-232   A physical standard used to identify cabling types for serial data transmission for speeds of 19.2Kbps or less. RS-232 connects two devices communicating over a serial link with either a 25-pin (DB-25) or 9-pin (DB-9) serial interface. RS-232 is now known as *EIA/TIA-232*.

running configuration file   The current configuration file that is active on a router.

RXBoot   A router-maintenance mode that enables router recovery functions when the IOS file in Flash has been erased or is corrupt.

S

Secure Shell (SSH)   A protocol that allows for secure communication between a client and a router. It is a secure alternative to Telnet.

Secure Socket Layer (SSL)   A common method of securing HTTP communication. It is also used for web-based VPNs where users are first authenticated via a web GUI before gaining access to secure web applications.

Service Set Identifier (SSID)   A 32-bit unique identifier that is used to name a wireless network.

session layer   As Layer 5 of the OSI model, the session layer establishes, manages, and terminates sessions between applications on different network devices.

setup mode   The router mode triggered on startup if no configuration file resides in nonvolatile random access memory (NVRAM).

shortest path first   See link state protocol.

sliding windows   A method by which TCP dynamically sets the window size during a connection, enabling the receiving device involved in the communication to slow down the sending data rate.

SMTP (Simple Mail Transfer Protocol)
A protocol used to pass mail messages between devices, SMTP uses Transmission Control Protocol (TCP) connections to pass the email between hosts.

socket   The combination of the sending and destination Transmission Control Protocol (TCP) port numbers and the sending and destination Internet Protocol (IP) addresses defines a socket. Therefore, a socket can be used to define any User Datagram Protocol (UDP) or TCP connection uniquely.

Spanning Tree Protocol   A protocol used to eliminate all circular routes in a bridged or switched environment while maintaining redundancy. Circular routes are not desirable in Layer 2 networks because of the forwarding mechanism employed at this layer.

split horizon   A routing mechanism that prevents a router from sending information that it received about a network back to its neighbor that originally sent the information. This mechanism is useful in preventing routing loops.

startup configuration file   The backup configuration file on a router.

static route   A network route that is manually entered into the route table. Static routes function well in simple and predictable network environments.

store-and-forward switching   A method of forwarding frames by copying an entire frame into the buffer of a switch and making a forwarding decision. Store-and-forward switching does not achieve the same throughput as its counterpart, cut-through switching, because it copies the entire frame into the buffer instead of copying only the first six bytes. Store-and-forward switching, however, provides error checking that is not provided by cut-through switching.

subinterface   One of possibly many virtual interfaces on a single physical interface.

subnetting   A process of splitting a classful range of IP addresses into multiple IP networks to allow more flexibility in IP addressing schemes. Subnetting overcomes the limitation of address classes and allows network administrators the flexibility to assign multiple networks with one class of IP addresses.

switch   Provides increased port density and forwarding capabilities as compared to bridges. The increased port densities of switches enable LANs to be microsegmented, thereby increasing the amount of bandwidth delivered to each device.

T

TCP (Transmission Control Protocol)

One of the many protocols maintained in the TCP/IP suite of protocols. TCP provides a connection-oriented and reliable service to the applications that use it.

TCP three-way handshake   A three-step process whereby a TCP session is established. In the first step, the sending device sends the initial sequence number with the SYN bit set in the TCP header. The receiver sends back a packet with the SYN and ACK bits set. In the third and final step, the sender sends a packet with the ACK bit set.

TCP windowing   A method of increasing or reducing the number of acknowledgments required between data transmissions. This enables devices to throttle the rate at which data is transmitted.

Telnet   A standard protocol that provides a virtual terminal. Telnet enables a network administrator to connect to a router remotely.

TFTP (Trivial File Transfer Protocol)

A protocol used to copy files from one device to another. TFTP is a stripped-down version of FTP.

traceroute   An IP service that allows a user to utilize the services of the User Datagram Protocol (UDP) and the Internet Control Message Protocol (ICMP) to identify the number of hops between sending and receiving devices and the paths taken from the sending to

the receiving device. Traceroute also provides the IP address and DNS name of each hop. Typically, traceroute is used to troubleshoot IP connectivity between two devices.

trailer   Control information placed after the data during the encapsulation process. See *encapsulation* for more detail.

transport layer   As Layer 4 of the OSI model, it is concerned with segmenting upper-layer applications, establishing end-to-end connectivity through the network, sending segments from one host to another, and ensuring the reliable transport of data.

trunk   A switch port that connects to another switch to enable virtual local area networks (VLANs) to span multiple switches.

tunnel   A tunnel takes packets or frames from one protocol and places them inside frames from another network system. See *encapsulation*.

U

UDP (User Datagram Protocol)   One of the many protocols maintained in the TCP/IP suite of protocols, UDP is a Layer 4, best-effort delivery protocol and, therefore, maintains connectionless network services.

user mode   A display-only mode on a Cisco router. Only limited information about the router can be viewed within this router mode; no configuration changes are permitted.

V

V.35 A physical standard used to identify cabling types for serial data transmission for speeds up to 4Mbps. The V.35 standard was created by the International Telecommunication Union-Telecommunication (ITU-T) standardization sector.

VLAN (virtual local-area network) A technique of assigning devices to specific LANs based on the port to which they attach on a switch rather than the physical location. VLANs extend the flexibility of LANs by allowing devices to be assigned to specific LANs on a port-by-port basis versus a device basis.

VLSM (variable-length subnet masking) VLSM provides more flexibility in assigning IP address space. (A common problem with routing protocols is the necessity of all devices in a given routing protocol domain to use the same subnet mask.) Routing protocols that support VLSM allow administrators to assign IP networks with different subnet masks. This increased flexibility saves IP address space because administrators can assign IP networks based on the number of hosts on each network.

VTP (VLAN Trunking Protocol) A protocol for configuring and administering VLANS on Cisco network devices. With VTP, an administrator can make configuration changes centrally on a single Catalyst series switch and have those changes automatically communicated to all the other switches in the network.

W

WANs (wide-area networks) WANs use data communications equipment (DCE) to connect multiple LANs. Examples of WAN protocols include Frame Relay, Point-to-Point Protocol (PPP), and High-Level Data Link Control (HDLC).

well-known ports A set of ports between 1 and 1,023 that are reserved for specific TCP/IP protocols and services.

Wired Equivalent Protocol (WEP) A security protocol used in Wi-Fi networks that encrypts packets over radio waves. It offers 40-bit and 104-bit encryption (often referred to 64- and 128-bit encryption because of the added initialization vector in the algorithm).

Wi-Fi Protected Access (WPA)/Wi-Fi Protected Access 2 (WPA) Security protocols for Wi-Fi networks that provide greater security than WEP.

Index

C

O

P

Q–R

X–Y–Z

THIS BOOK IS SAFARI ENABLED

INCLUDES FREE 45-DAY ACCESS TO THE ONLINE EDITION

The Safari® Enabled icon on the cover of your favorite technology book means the book is available through Safari Bookshelf. When you buy this book, you get free access to the online edition for 45 days.

Safari Bookshelf is an electronic reference library that lets you easily search thousands of technical books, find code samples, download chapters, and access technical information whenever and wherever you need it.

TO GAIN 45-DAY SAFARI ENABLED ACCESS TO THIS BOOK:

- Go to **www.examcram.com/safarienabled**
- Complete the brief registration form
- Enter the coupon code found in the front of this book on the "Copyright" page

If you have difficulty registering on Safari Bookshelf or accessing the online edition, please e-mail customer-service@safaribooksonline.com.